RODIN AND DANCE

The Essence of Movement

THE COURTAULD Gallery

MUSÉE RODIN

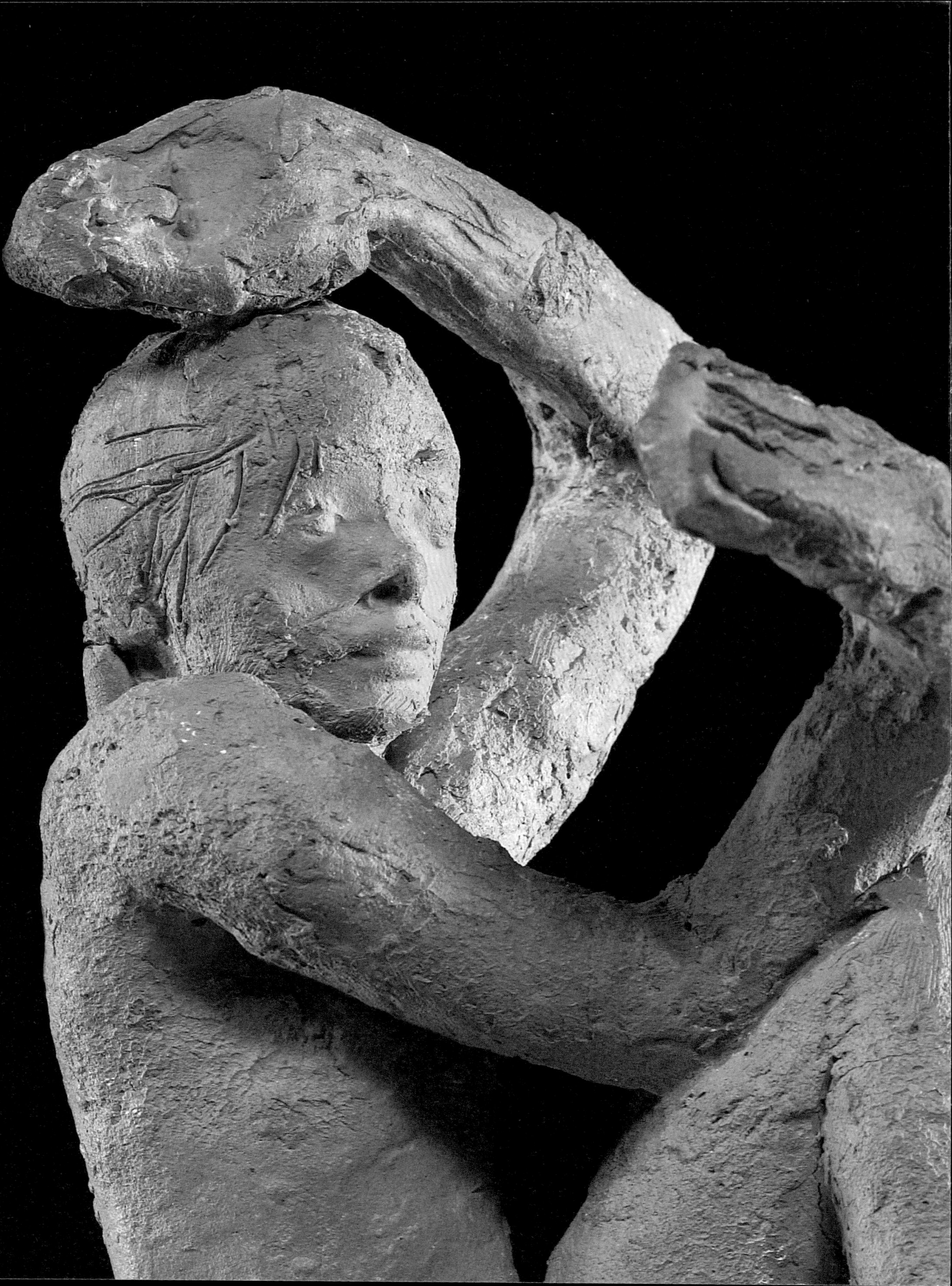

RODIN AND DANCE

The Essence of Movement

EDITED BY
Alexandra Gerstein

CONTIBUTORS
Juliet Bellow
Sophie Biass-Fabiani
François Blanchetière
Agnès Cascio
Kate Edmondson
Alexandra Gerstein
Antoinette Le Normand-Romain
Juliette Lévy

THE COURTAULD GALLERY
AND THE MUSÉE RODIN
IN ASSOCIATION WITH
PAUL HOLBERTON PUBLISHING

This catalogue is published on the occasion of the exhibition

RODIN AND DANCE

The Essence of Movement

The Courtauld Gallery, London
20 October 2016 – 22 January 2017

The Courtauld is supported by the Higher Education Funding Council for England (HEFCE)

HIGHER EDUCATION FUNDING COUNCIL FOR ENGLAND hefce

ISBN 978 1 907372 99 5

British Library Catalogue in Publishing Data
A CIP record of this publication is available from the British Library

Produced by Paul Holberton publishing, London
89 Borough High St, London SE1 1NL
WWW.PAUL-HOLBERTON.NET

Designed and typeset by Laura Parker
Origination and printing by e-Graphic, Verona

CONTENTS

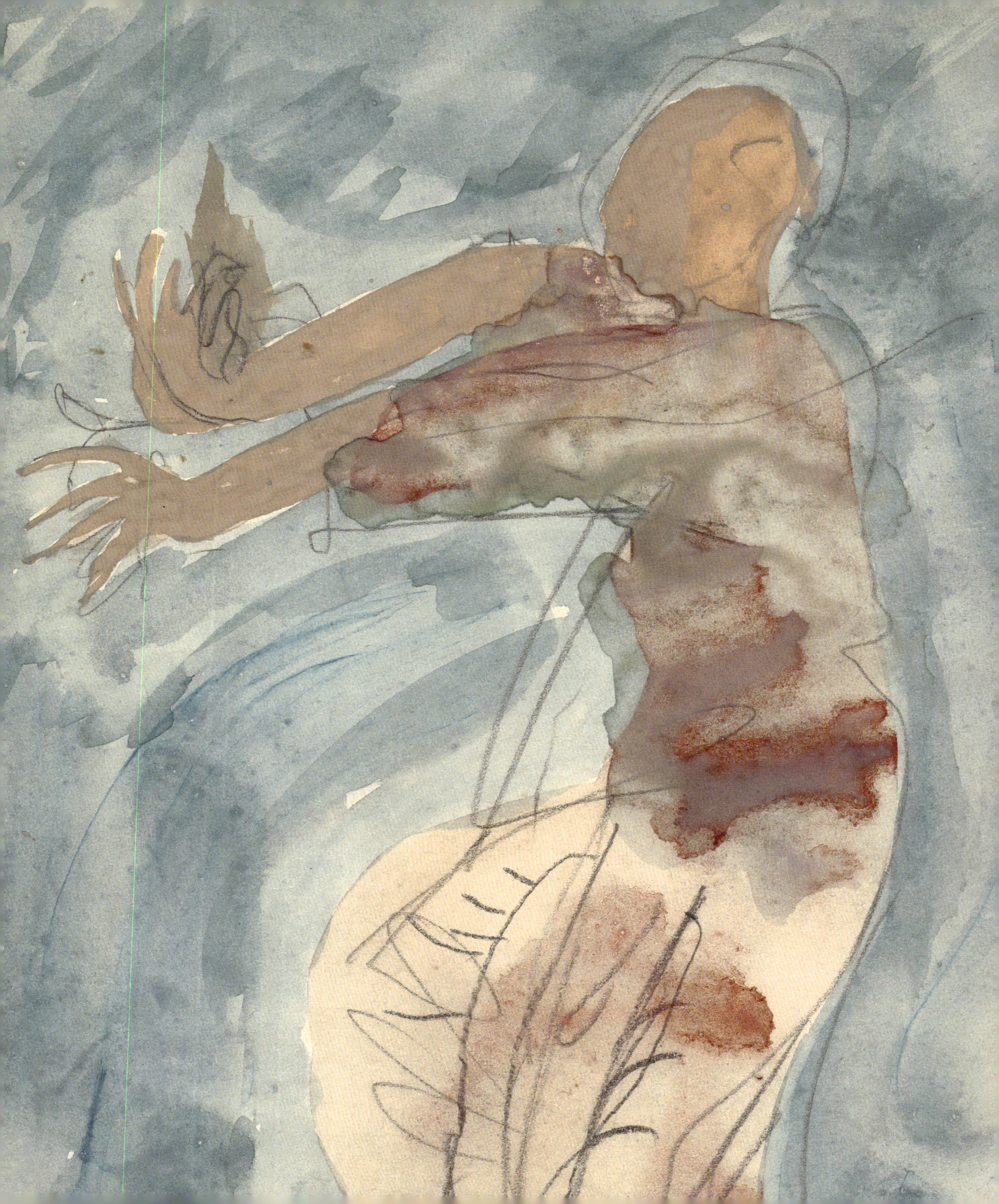

DIRECTORS' FOREWORD

The reopening in late 2015 of the magnificently restored Hôtel Biron, home since 1919 of the Musée Rodin, has given a powerful new impulse to public enjoyment and understanding of Rodin's work. Here, amongst the sweep of beautifully conceived displays charting the artist's creative development is an arrangement of small plaster and terracotta figures, startling in their originality. Presented as a group, the figures leap, twist and stretch in a series of extraordinary, gravity-defying acrobatic poses. Known as the *Mouvements de danse*, these sculptural studies are the focus of the present exhibition.

Produced in Rodin's final decade and never exhibited during his lifetime, the *Mouvements de danse* have remained largely unexamined. This exhibition and publication provide the first detailed account of all the sculptures in the group. The exhibition considers the series in the context of Rodin's fascination with new dance forms which appeared on the Paris stage around 1900 and which were closely allied to his own deep interest in expressive movement. It includes a particularly rich selection of drawings and watercolours, underlining how integrally connected sculpture and drawing were in Rodin's highly creative late period.

The exhibition has been developed by The Courtauld Gallery in full partnership with the Musée Rodin, which has lent from its unparallelled collection with outstanding generosity. The Courtauld is immensely grateful to the Musée Rodin for agreeing to the display of these works in London and for its strong research collaboration. The Musée Rodin likewise thanks the Courtauld for this opportunity to study in a very in-depth way the series of *Mouvements de danse* and thus to advance our knowledge of Rodin's creative process. We are grateful to Alexandra Gerstein, the exhibition's curator, for her exceptional personal commitment to the project. She benefitted from support across the Musée Rodin. In particular, we acknowledge the essential and expert contributions of Sophie Biass-Fabiani and François Blanchetière. Colleagues in the archives of the Musée Rodin were unfailingly generous with their time, and we also thank the conservators who led the important study of the casts and moulds. At The Courtauld, Kate Edmondson was an invaluable member of the team. In Paris, Aline Magnien was an enthusiastic early supporter of our collaboration, and we are also grateful to Antoinette Le Normand-Romain for her encouragement. Colleagues from the Royal Central School of Speech and Drama in London provided a stimulating and novel practitioners' perspective.

The exhibition has received generous support from many loyal friends and benefactors. We thank them most warmly. A grant from the wonderful Friends of The Courtauld gave us the early confidence to proceed with the project. The International Music and Art Foundation generously contributed to the drawings element of the exhibition and we are similarly indebted to an anonymous benefactor whose gift is in memory of Melvin R. Seiden. The support received from the Henry Moore Foundation was very meaningful and resonant for the project. We further extend our warm thanks to the Daniel Katz Gallery, Stuart and Bianca Roden, Stuart Lochhead and Sophie Richard, Mark and Cathy Corbett, and Benjamin Proust Fine Art. Finally, we wish to thank H.E. Madame Sylvie Bermann, French Ambassador to the United Kingdom of Great Britain and Northern Ireland, and François Croquette, Cultural Counsellor and Director, Institut français du Royaume-Uni, for their warm support and encouragement of this collaboration between our two institutions.

ERNST VEGELIN VAN CLAERBERGEN
Head of The Courtauld Gallery

CATHERINE CHEVILLOT
Directrice du Musée Rodin

ACKNOWLEDGEMENTS

The exhibition would not have been possible without the support and assistance provided by a number of key individuals and institutions. Above all, I would like to thank the director and curators of the Musée Rodin in Paris for agreeing to lend so generously from their collections and for their truly collegial approach to the project. I am especially indebted to Sophie Biass-Fabiani and François Blanchetière for welcoming me on so many return visits to consult the sculpture and drawings, and for their steady encouragement and expert contributions to the catalogue. I would also like to thank colleagues at the Musée Rodin for their unstinting support in all other areas of the research and planning of the exhibition: Dominique Brisset, Sandra Boujot, Julie Davodet, Cyrielle Durox, Bénédicte Garnier, Audrey d'Hendecourt, Jérome Manoukian, Véronique Mattiussi, Hélène Pinet and Diane Tytgat. I am grateful to Agnès Cascio and Juliette Lévy for their detailed investigation into the making of the *Mouvements de danse*.

I would like to thank Juliet Bellow and Antoinette Le Normand-Romain for the excellent essays they have contributed to the catalogue. This exhibition also benefitted from the scholarly contributions of staff and graduates of the Royal Central School of Speech and Drama in London, and I would like to thank in particular Ayse Tashkiran, Vanessa Ewan, Ana Marambio and Rachel Nouchy for applying aspects of the discipline of Movement Direction to the understanding of Rodin's late movement studies.

Many colleagues associated with The Courtauld were instrumental in bringing this exhibition and its catalogue to fruition. My particular thanks are due to Kate Edmondson, who provided insightful analyses of the drawings on loan to the exhibition, and Sophie Harrison, Chris Hopkins, Chloe Le Tissier, Karin Kyburz, George Mogg and Ernst Vegelin for their professionalism and support throughout the preparation of the exhibition; to Laura Parker and Paul Holberton for style and patience in the design and editing of the catalogue; to Belinda Moore and Adam Follett for the technical diagram; and to Alan Farley for his simple and effective exhibition design.

The following colleagues and friends offered valuable assistance: Graeme Barraclough, Julia Blanks, Alixe Bovey, Wilkie Branson, Claire Bray, Viola Bruni, Emily Butcher, Jean Michel Buck, Stephanie Buck, Martin Caiger-Smith, Stephanie Christodoulou, Philippe Comar, Charlotte De Mille, Justine Dilien, Jessica Feather, Stéphane Ferrand, Hannah Foster, Jonathan Freund, Olivia Geraghty, Emma Gladstone, Ketty Gottardo, Antony Hopkins, Henrietta Hine, Lisa Hodermarsky, Nancy Ireson, Shobana Jeyasingh, Claudette Joannis, Gérard Jouhet, Vicky Kontou, Catherine Lampert, Colin Lindley, Nicola London, Aline Magnien, Caireen McGinn, Joseph Mercier, Barbara Musetti, Patricia Nebenzahl, Eliane Orléans-Gerstein, Camilla Pietrabissa, Kim Schenck, Trista Selous, Karen Serres, Adrien Sina, Rachel Sloan, Emmanuel Schwartz, Anne Wagner, Philip Ward-Jackson, Sophie Weygand and Sarah Wilson.

EXHIBITION SUPPORTERS

The Courtauld Gallery wishes to thank the following donors for their generous support of the exhibition:

Friends of The Courtauld

International Music and Art Foundation

Anonymous in memory of Melvin R. Seiden

The Daniel Katz Gallery, London

The Henry Moore Foundation

Stuart and Bianca Roden

We would also like to thank the following individuals and organisations for their kind support:

Stuart Lochhead and Sophie Richard

Mark and Cathy Corbett

Benjamin Proust Fine Art Ltd – London

We would also like to thank the Embassy of France in London and the Institut français du Royaume-Uni for their support of the exhibition.

This exhibition has been made possible by the provision of insurance through the Government Indemnity Scheme. The Courtauld Gallery would like to thank HM Government for providing indemnity and extends its thanks to the Department for Culture, Media and Sport and to the Arts Council England for administering the scheme.

IMAF INTERNATIONAL MUSIC & ART FOUNDATION

HENRY MOORE FOUNDATION

SAMUEL COURTAULD SOCIETY

DIRECTOR'S CIRCLE

Anonymous
Andrew and Maya Adcock
Farah Asemi and Hassan Alaghband
I C Carr
Christie's
Michael Cohen and Erin Bell
Nicholas and Jane Ferguson
Mr Sam Fogg
Nicholas and Judith Goodison
Dr Martin Halusa
Morten and Dana Høegh
Nick Hoffman
James Hughes-Hallett
Eugenia and Thomas Korossy
Mr Wah Kheong and Ms Tina Leong
Christopher and Janey McLaren
Scott and Suling Mead
Phillips International Auctioneers and Valuers
Maurice and Elizabeth Pinto
Marie-Christine Poulain and Read Gomm
Derek and Inks Raphael
Charles Rose
Sir Paul and Lady Ruddock
Sotheby's
Nicolai and Katja Tangen
Elke and Michael von Brentano
Erik and Kimie Vynckier
John Watson and Betsy Blackwell
Niklas and Catherine Zennström

PATRONS' CIRCLE

Anonymous
Mrs Kate Agius
Geoffrey and Julian Agnew Trust
Lord and Lady Aldington
Giancarla and Michael Alen-Buckley
Mr Sandy Arbuthnot
Sara Joline Bedford
John G. Bernasconi
Douglas Blausten
Julia Boadle
Sarah Boardman
Marcia Brocklebank
Charles Booth-Clibborn
The Lord Browne of Madingley
David and Jane Butter
John Byford
Julian and Jenny Cazalet
Mary Ellen Cetra
Mr Colin Clark
Robert Compton Jones
Mark and Cathy Corbett
Nicholas Coutts
Samantha Darell
Amanda Deitsch and James Hochman
Nova Dobb
Mr Andrew P Duffy
Cindy Elden
Roger and Rebecca Emery
Eykyn Maclean Ltd
David Gibbons
Kathleen Gilfillan
Richard Green
Lucía V. Halpern and John Davies
Paula and Schuyler Henderson
Lady Heseltine
Joanna Hewitt
Jennifer and Bill Hicks
Andrew Hochhauser QC
Mike and Caroline Howes
David and Una Hudd
Philip Hudson
Monica Ishola
Nicholas Jones
Andrew Joy
James and Clare Kirkman
Norman A. Kurland and Deborah A. David
Lefevre Fine Art
Stuart Lochhead and Sophie Richard
Mark and Liza Loveday
Dr Chris and Mrs Gill Mallinson
Janet Martin
Mr Jay Massey
Clare Maurice
Mr Bruce McCoy
James McDonaugh
MCB Mellish
Norma and Selwyn Midgen
John and Jenny Murray
Mr Morton Neal CBE and Mrs Neal
Alan M Newton
Elizabeth Nicholson
John Nicoll and Laurence Colchester
Mr Michael Palin
Simon and Midge Palley
Lord and Lady Phillimore
Bridget Pinchbeck
Faith Pleasanton
Leslie Powell
Tineke Pugh
Lady Jennifer Rose
Mrs Janice Sacher
Dame Theresa Sackler
Richard and Susan Shoylekov
William Slee and Dr Heidi Bürklin-Slee
Christopher and Fiona Steane
Sara Stewart
Marjorie Stimmel
Sir Angus Stirling
Henry Tinsley
Johnny Van Haeften Ltd
The Rt Hon. Nicholas and Lavinia Wallop
Mr Richard West
George and Patricia White
Richard Wintour
Lynne Woolfson
Anita and Poju Zabludowicz

ASSOCIATES

Anonymous
Georgina Adam
Lord Jeffrey Archer
Mrs James Beery
Mr Oliver Colman
Richard Deutsch
Simon C. Dickinson Ltd
Caroline Doggart
David and Diane Frank
Cornelia Grassi
Mrs Kathryn Gyngell
Edward Harley
Mr Timothy D Llewellyn
Raymond and Penelope Locke
Anthony Loehnis CMG
Sir Frank Lowe
Sophie Mallinckrodt
Harriet McCalmont
Virginia Morck
Philip Mould Ltd
Richard Oldfield
Persephone Books
Mr Adrian Sassoon
Derek Searle
Anna Somers Cocks
Rex De Lisle Stanbridge
Jeremy Strachan
Mr Robert Stoppenbach
Professor Deborah Swallow
Yvonne Tan Bunzl
Diana and John Uff
The Ulrich Family
Cordula von Keller
The Weiss Gallery
Hugh Wilson

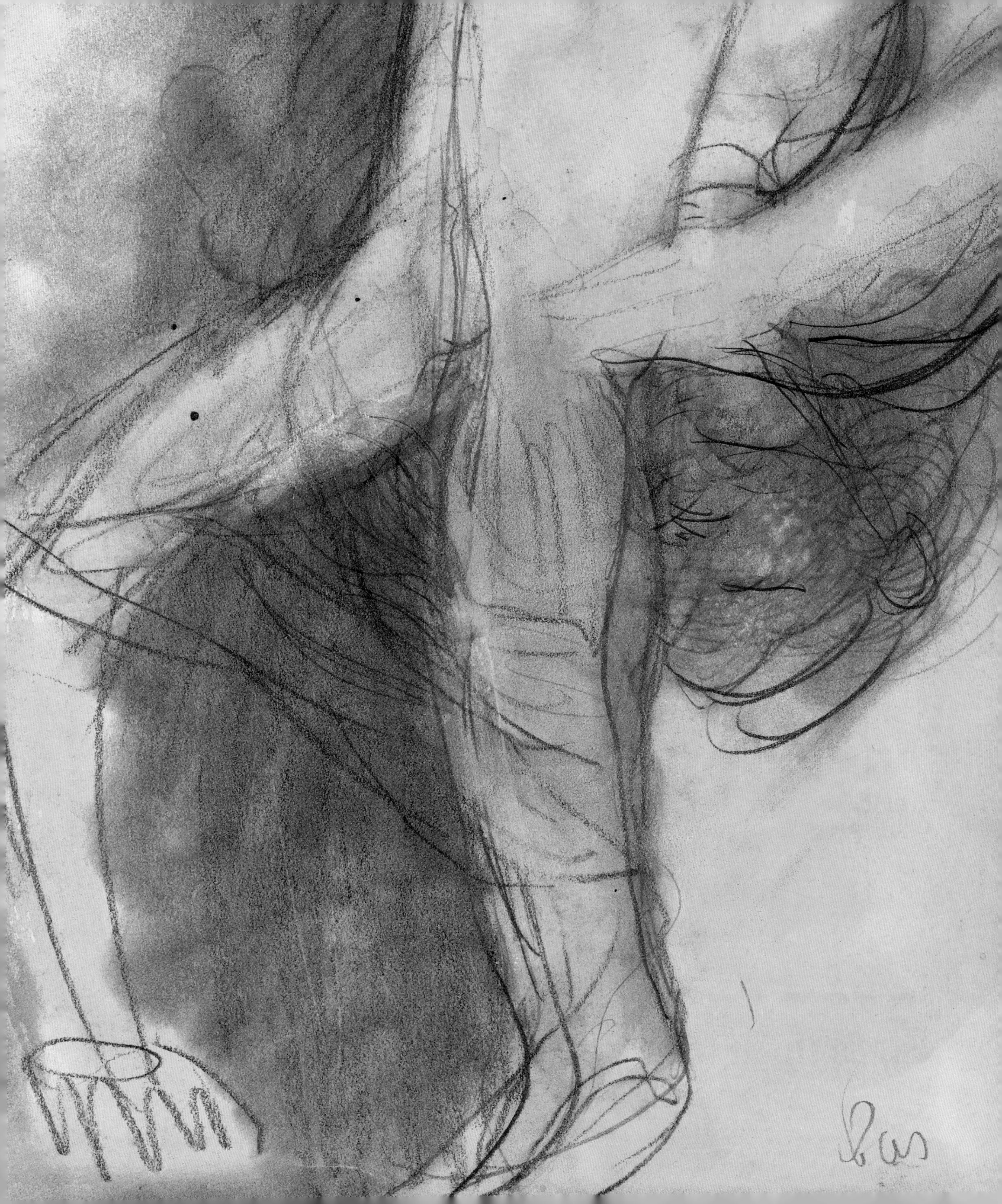

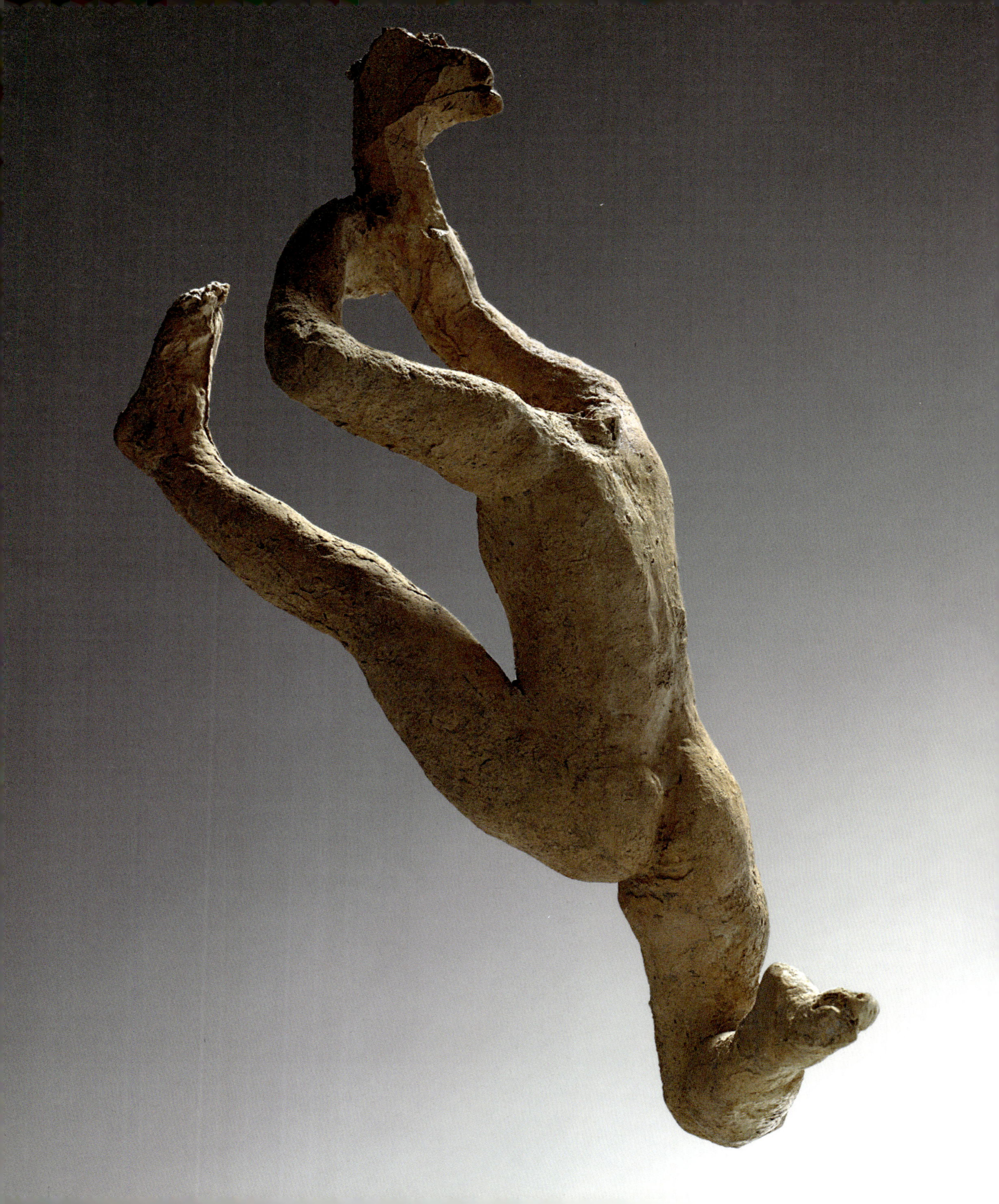

"HIGHER AND FURTHER": RODIN'S LATE WORKS

ANTOINETTE LE NORMAND-ROMAIN

On 27 May 1911, Rodin showed Count Harry Kessler, the German collector and patron who was one of his great admirers, "an entire glass case full of small clay figures which he had started after an acrobat – figures with astoundingly new lines and movements, more similar to his drawings than to the sculptures he has made hitherto". On 1 July Kessler returned to the studio and asked "when he was thinking of going back to working on the little acrobat figures. Rodin replied, 'It's not an acrobat. If it were an acrobat you would see it at once, it would be different. I haven't been able to work on them for a while because the model has been ill. And besides, I've stopped working on things unless I like them, I've stopped forcing myself to work.'" Kessler goes on, "I also asked him if he was intending to finish each of the many small figures or to combine them all into one. He said no, he wanted to combine them all in one figure. 'But I have so many pieces demanding attention that I can't say when I will finish this one. The work I have already done is demanding that I finish it – because I want to finish everything, I never shall finish it, but I want to.'" A year later (2 June 1912), Kessler went back to see Rodin with Nijinsky, and Rodin took out "a portfolio that he called 'the creation of woman'. These are study drawings of a very supple girl, a kind of acrobat, whose poses provide all kinds of entirely new and bizarre arabesques. Rodin told us he saw them as something like the early stages of an evolution, transitions leading from the animal world to woman – insects, varieties of frog, a creature resembling a sphinx – from which the woman crawls out as though from a cocoon: 'Some people find all this obscene. But it's almost pure mathematics. It's not driven by passion, or rather, it looks like the movements of unknown passions, which we can't imagine but might be possible – passions that are not human'. He keeps this portfolio very secret and had first to free it from all kinds of wrappings and ties before he could open it for Nijinsky." Then he showed them some "study sculptures after the same model as the one who inspired him for the 'creation of woman' – a number of small figurines of the most supreme beauty. In particular, they have the same architectonic rigour as his drawings, which he tends to obtain only rarely in his sculptures."[1]

RODIN IN THE 20TH CENTURY

The modelled studies known collectively today as *Mouvements de danse* (Dance movements), belong to Rodin's late period, a time when, aged nearly seventy and at the end of a long career that had seen many successes, he still had a capacity for renewal. The title by which this series is now known should really be abandoned, since it strongly suggests an interpretation that links it to works such as Degas's *Dancers*. Aside from the fact that Degas's works are much earlier – *Little Dancer Aged Fourteen* was presented at the Impressionist Exhibition of 1881 – the two artists' approaches are profoundly different. Although both start from observation of the life model, which Rodin closely records in drawings that have the quality of snapshots (D.1812, cat.62), Rodin goes further than Degas in the expression of movement, while keeping a sense of the raw material by using barely manipulated rolls of clay. Two other representations of dance, Bourdelle's metope for the Théâtre des Champs-Elysées (1912; fig.1) and Joseph Bernard's frieze for the Hôtel Nocard in Neuilly (1911–13; Paris, Musée d'Orsay) are slightly later than the *Mouvements de danse*, but they too reflect the distance between Rodin and these younger artists, whose aim was to make pieces for display, whether to a wider or more

Detail of S.118, cat.60

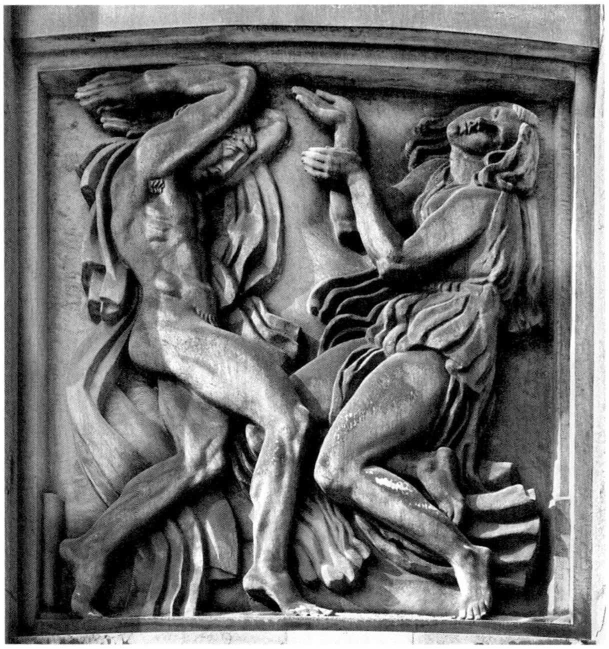

FIG.1
Antoine Bourdelle
The Dance, 1912
Marble relief on the façade of the
Théâtre des Champs-Élysées, Paris

restricted public, whereas Rodin kept his work secret. The figures modelled by Bernard and Bourdelle drew on the new forms of choreography practised by contemporary dancers such as Loïe Fuller with her whirling silks, or Nijinsky and Isadora Duncan, whose movements referred to Antiquity. They have nothing in common with the acrobatic poses of Rodin's statuettes, in which modelling stripped of any realist intent serves to emphasise the rigour of their construction. Rodin's pieces are comparable only to Picasso's *Acrobat* (oil on canvas, 1930, Paris, Musée Picasso). In the same period the theme of dance appears in the work of Archipenko (*Danseuse bleue* [Blue dancer], 1913), Kolbe (*Le Danseur* or *Nijinsky*, 1913) and Gaudier-Brzeska, who made a *Danseuse* in plaster, more naturalist in style like the other pieces mentioned above (1913; bronze version, Paris, Musée National d'Art Moderne), followed by another, carved directly from a block of red sandstone (fig.2), which acted as a manifesto for his new desire for geometricality. All these works are concerned with rhythm and are characterised by a strong presence in space, but they bear no relation to Rodin's pieces, which, moreover, their sculptors could not have known.

We should recall that Rodin's early period devoted to modelling figures for *La Porte de l'Enfer* (*The Gates of Hell*), had been followed by one in which he distanced himself from the hand that serves as the sculptor's primary tool. Heading a large studio employing assistants at many different levels, Rodin raised to the rank of creative processes certain activities more closely related to the techniques of production and reproduction, such as moulding, assemblage, enlargement and the composition of groups.[2] He did very little of this work himself, other than to direct his assistants. The mind had replaced the hand in all but his more personal works – the very free assemblages that he made using studies accumulated in his studio in combination with unusual elements such as dried branches, cobblestones and various ceramics, which inspired him and fuelled his imagination. He would also make sometimes humorous assemblages of female nudes and vases, the "little floral souls [rising from] ancient vases"[3] known only to a select few during his lifetime (fig.3). In fact, in this last phase of his career, Rodin divided his work sharply in two, keeping its freer element shrouded in the secrecy of his studio.

Conversely, in the early years of the twentieth century he showed a series of highly innovative works, primarily at the Salon of the Société Nationale des Beaux-Arts. These were the large, partial figures – *Ariane* (Ariadne), *Cybèle* (Cybele) and the *Torsos* of the 1910 Salon and the Victoria and Albert Museum – all of which were developed from figures born in the early 1880s, in the important period of the creation of *The Gates of Hell*. The most famous, *L'Homme qui marche* (*The Walking Man*), was made before 1900 from a study for *Saint John the Baptist* which in turn dated back to 1878–79. All had been through many different stages, notably reduction (in the culinary sense), through the removal of unnecessary elements and consequent simplification of the composition, and enlargement, which erases detail and modifies the relationships of the parts to each other and of the whole to the surrounding space, to the point where it is sometimes hard to recognise the source. How could one guess that the

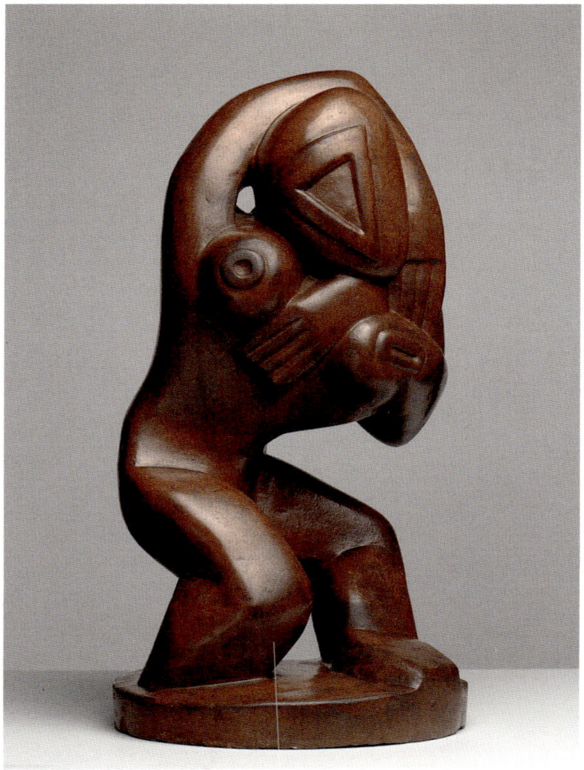

FIG.2
Henri Gaudier Brzeska
Dancer, 1913
Red sandstone,
43.2 x 22.9 x 22.9 cm
Tate, London

FIG.3
Auguste Rodin
Female nude with Head of the Slavic Woman (Tête de la femme slave), in a vase, c.1900–05
Plaster and ceramic, 22.7 x 12.2 x 13 cm
Musée Rodin, Paris, S.375

a movement that seems unfinished. The result is a pathos that has nothing to do with the subject but is intrinsic to the work itself, as can be seen in *Femme accroupie avec le masque d'Iris* [*Crouching Woman with the Head of Iris*], also known as *Grosse femme* [Large woman]), shown at the Salon of the Société Nationale des Beaux-Arts of 1911 (ex-catalogue). Rodin created this piece out of pre-existing elements diverted from their primary meaning: the head, recognisable as the mask known as *Iris*, is fixed atop a long neck that has been constructed very quickly; the join of the left leg remains very visible on the thigh, as do the seams; flattened rolls of clay can be seen here and there and the modelling is very uneven. In a previous

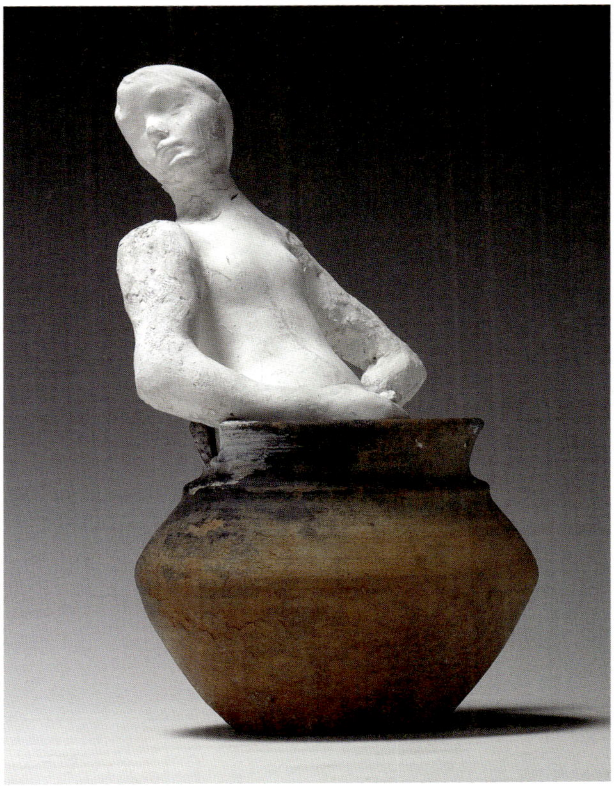

Torso in the V&A, simplified almost to the abstraction of a work by Arp, is derived from the pretty terracotta *Ève à la pomme* (Eve with the apple; Washington, D.C., National Gallery of Art), acquired by Kate Simpson, one of Rodin's leading American collectors, in the early years of the twentieth century? Through successive transformations the works acquire a monumentality that makes them a last resurgence of Antiquity. But they also acquire a kind of drama, as revealed by comparison of Maillol's *Méditerranée* (Mediterranean) and Rodin's *Cybèle*, both shown in 1905.[4] Leaving aside the absence of a head, the quivering modelling of the latter and its comparatively unstable pose are in complete contrast both to the plenitude and perfect balance of the former, in which every part has its place, and to its smooth surface over which the light skims unchecked. As Rodin so aptly said, Antiquity signifies "the happiness of being alive, tranquillity, grace, balance, reason".[5] In bringing Antiquity back to life Maillol gave sculpture an immutability that had an eternal aspect. Conversely, Rodin captured one instant in

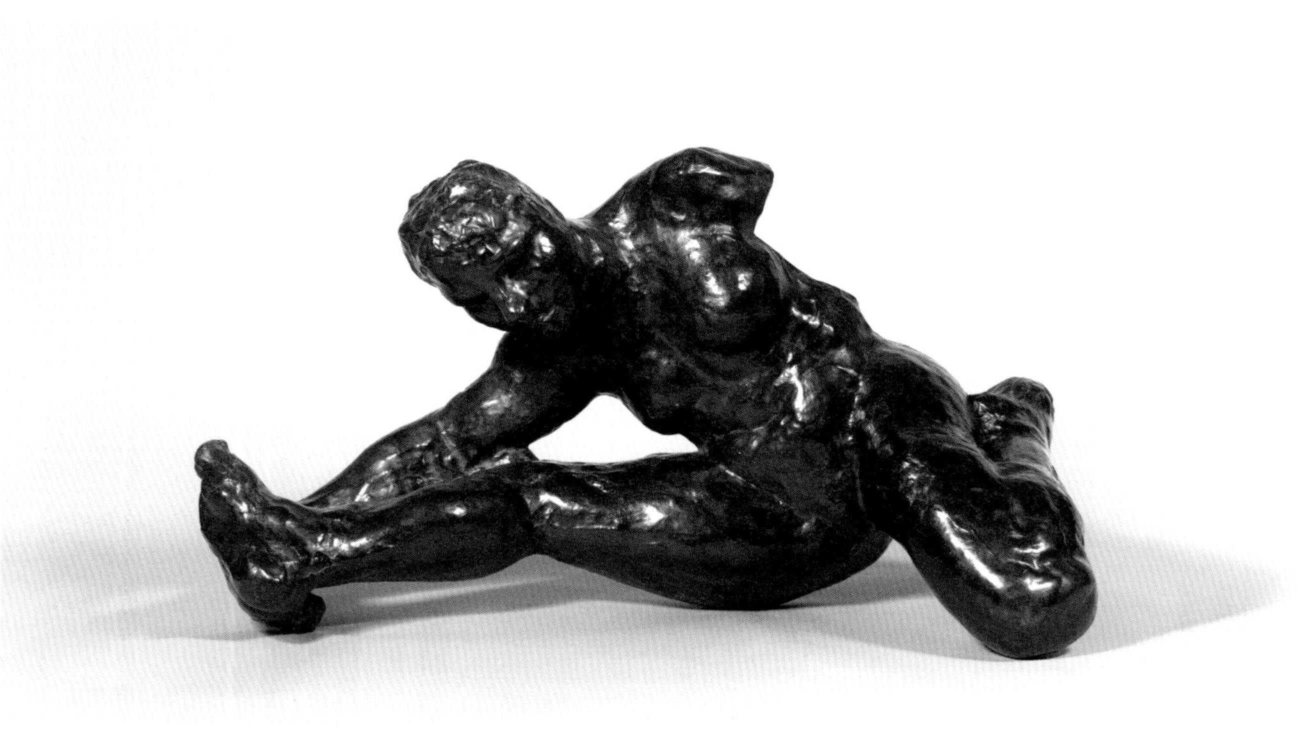

FIG.4
Auguste Rodin
Femme accroupie avec le masque d'Iris
(Crouching Woman with Head of Iris), 1911
Bronze, 53 x 96 x 53 cm
Victoria and Albert Museum, London

state, headless but with a left arm extending behind the back, this was a standing figure, but at some point Rodin decided it should lie down. This meant the left arm was in the way, so it was removed, leaving a gash in the left side. The toes were also cut from the left foot. The figure could then lie on its back with its right leg extending vertically upwards. However, Rodin was still not satisfied and gave it a quarter turn. A photograph by Druet (Musée Rodin, Paris, Ph. 361) shows that at the 1911 Salon it was held in the new position by plaster cones. This has been its position since then, with the right leg stretching before it and the torso leaning forwards. Rodin gave it the status of a fully finished piece, from which a single cast was taken in September 1911 (fig.4). *Femme accroupie* was exhibited at the Galerie Petit in 1912 and then in London in July 1914 as part of an exhibition of contemporary French decorative art, which showed the most modern aspect of Rodin's work.

"ENTIRELY NEW AND BIZARRE ARABESQUES"

The modelling that was the quintessential element of the sculptor's work in Rodin's period thus occupied only a limited number of the hours he spent in the studio. The time regained from sculpture, which his new approach left largely to his assistants, was devoted to drawing. But for drawing and modelling alike the presence of the life model was essential. Until the end of his career Rodin continued to bring in mainly female models to draw, allowing them to move around freely in his studio in a way that encouraged the renewal of the art of this "visionary", as described by Arthur Symons,[6] one of those who best understood him. Rodin forbade his models to adopt academic poses and was always looking out for everyday movements, often linked to functional necessities, for unconscious gestures and for positions in which he perceived the great flow of life. The contemplation of these female bodies that were for him the embodiment

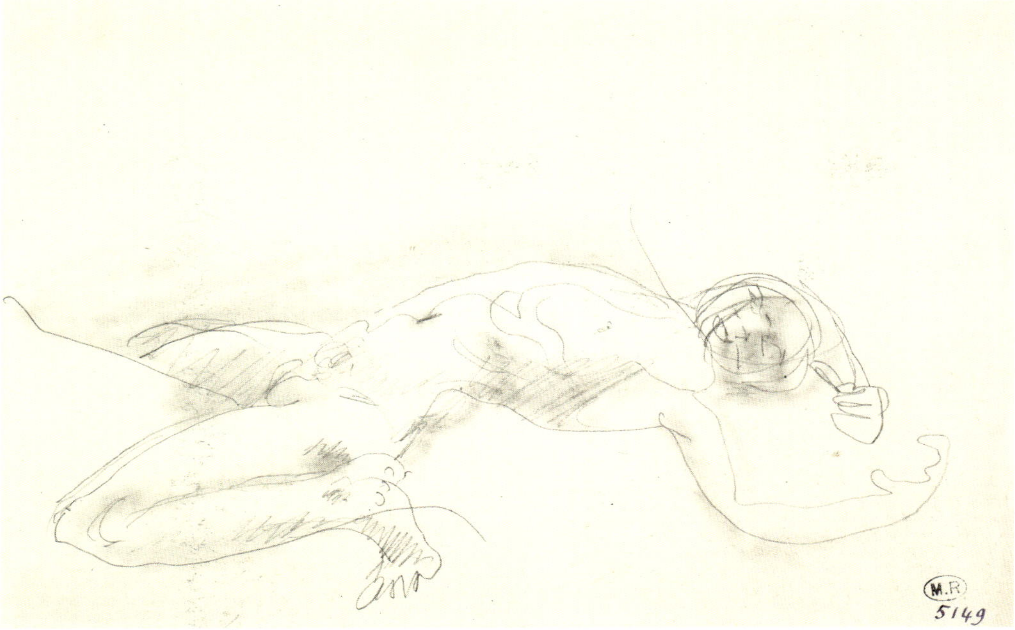

FIG.5
Auguste Rodin
Female nude lying, with legs folded under, 1909
Pencil with stumping on wove paper, 197 x 305 mm
Musée Rodin, Paris, D.5149

of nature itself stimulated Rodin's capacity to create. In drawing after drawing, this admirer of women – "with me you learn admiration", he wrote next to a study of a female nude (D.2885; "*chez moi on apprend l'admiration*") – explored their flesh with a voluptuous pencil, including the most intimate details of their sexual organs. However, around 1905 the studies for *Monument to Whistler* (1905–08) and the series of drawings of Cambodian dancers (1906) led him to take an interest in a new type of movement.

In the modelled and drawn studies for the *Muse* of the *Monument to Whistler* we recognise the slender silhouette of Gwen John, who had been posing for Rodin for a year and had become his mistress. She holds the pose with ease, one raised leg bent so that she could write on her knee. We recognise her in the significantly entitled statuette *La Gymnaste* (The gymnast), modelled in 1904 by the Finnish sculptor Hilda Flodin, who was present at the same time as John in Rodin's studio,[7] and indeed John had told Rodin, "I shall give you extraordinary poses as well as classical poses, because I'm supple! And they are all natural to me. They are the same as the ones I unthinkingly adopt at home".[8] Such "extraordinary" or acrobatic poses were also provided by Alda Moreno, an acrobatic dancer and artist's model who is generally thought to have inspired the *Mouvements de danse* (see Alexandra Gerstein's essay in this volume). Kessler said as much on 27 May 1911: the small clay figures were modelled "after an acrobat". And although Rodin denied this on 1 July – "It's not an acrobat. If it were an acrobat you would see it at once, it would be different" – on 2 June 1912 Kessler reported that the sculptures and drawings had been made after a "very supple girl, a kind of acrobat, whose poses provide all kinds of entirely new and bizarre arabesques". On that occasion Kessler was accompanied by Nijinsky, who had dazzled the sculptor a few days before, on 29 May 1912, with his performance of Debussy's *Après-midi d'un faune* (Afternoon of a faun). Rodin wanted to model a statue after him but we know from Nijinsky's journal that the sculptor found the dancer's body "badly put-together, that's why he crossed his sketches through. I realised he didn't like me and I left."[9] So Rodin abandoned his project, but he did make a few drawings and a sculpted sketch showing Nijinsky gathered into a core of energy before relaxing into weightlessness. He remained preoccupied with the fidelity to nature that had been his watchword throughout his career, but he was always searching for something new, and, just as partial figures and enlargement had shown him a different,

FIG.6
Auguste Rodin
Obsession, 1907
Marble, 57.5 x 43.3 x 46.5 cm
Musée Rodin, Paris, S.1395

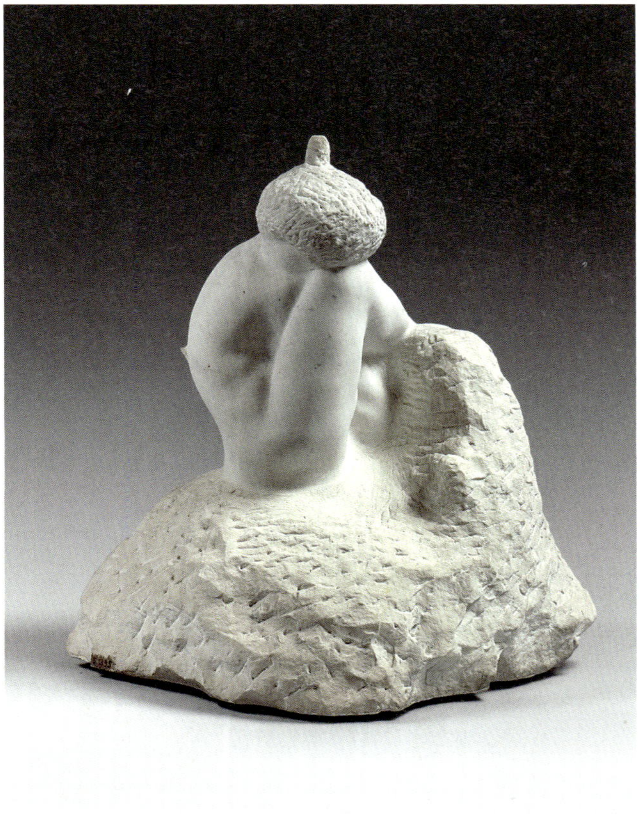

transcendent truth of form, so these models from the world of dance and acrobatics led him "higher and further". In 1906, having attended a performance by the Royal Ballet of Cambodia, he said to a journalist, "I am a man who has given his whole life to the study of nature and has been a constant admirer of the works of Antiquity. So imagine the effect on me of such a complete vision, which restored Antiquity to me while revealing mystery! ... For my own part, I know that in watching them my vision has expanded: I have seen higher and further; I have learned something."[10]

Both on paper and in clay Rodin was now completely free. In addition to Alda Moreno he undoubtedly had several acrobats and contortionists posing for him (D.5149, fig.5, and D.1310, cat.33; see detail facing), freeing him from the usual conventions to such a degree that some compositions appear clumsy. Yet he knew the human body better than anyone. On paper the results can sometimes be described as "bizarre arabesques" –figures with limbs strangely intertwined (D.1859, cat.68), far from the perfect organisation of Maillol's sculptures such as *Méditerranée* or *Désir* (Desire). Rodin's figures have a suppleness that runs counter to the laws of nature: their limbs seem jointed to bend the wrong way, their arms and legs to have interchangeable functions. The marble *Obsession*, "resting on the ground, legs crossed, the right leg bent very high, the foot resting on the left knee",[11] made in 1907 after a modelled piece that probably dated from around ten years earlier, appears as a direct translation of this approach (fig.6). Sometimes the figures are related to architecture, reinforcing the link between the two artistic fields and reasserting the trinity of human figure, architecture and sculpture in which Rodin profoundly believed. This trinity served as a fundamental leitmotiv for his book *Les Cathédrales de France* (1914), a hymn to the glory of medieval and Renaissance architecture, which was Rodin's major preoccupation in this period, and is reflected in the well-known drawings *Comme l'Egypte* (Like Egypt; D.5148), *Pluviôse* or *L'Architecture* (D.1813), *Ornement œuvre de l'homme* (Ornament the work of man; D.5147).

The last two drawings were among some sixty to be shown at the Salon du Gil Blas in 1910 and almost certainly reflected Rodin's recent work, or at least his preoccupations of the time. Among those that have been identified as shown there are a few sketches of women bent in two and curled in on themselves, bearing inscriptions such as *Avant la création de la femme. Le capricorne* (Before the creation of woman. The capricorn; D.2727) and *Le travail de la création. Les cherchements* (The work of creation. Searchings; D.1793), which lead us back to Kessler's reports of his visits to Rodin.

Detail of D.1310, cat.33

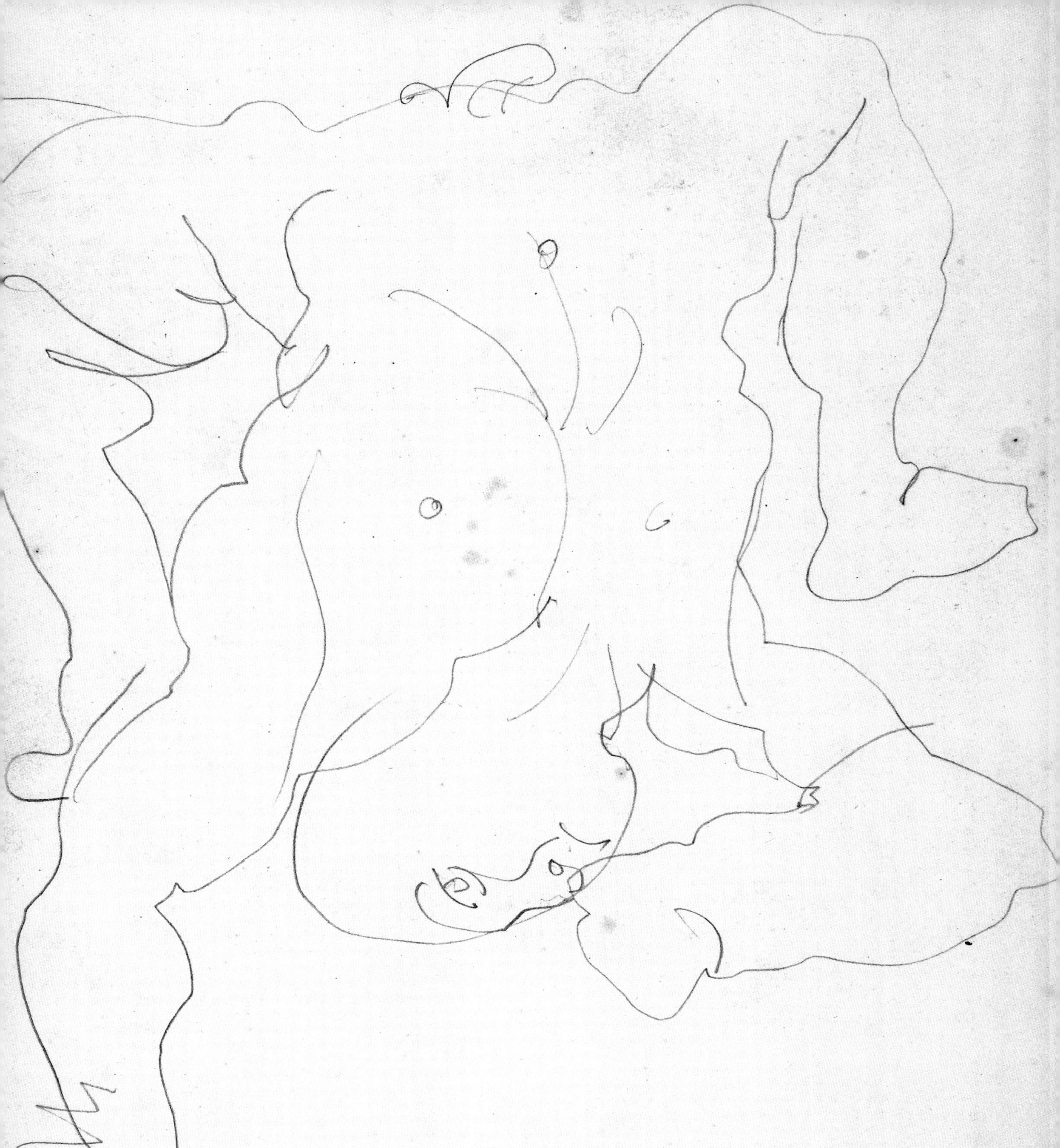

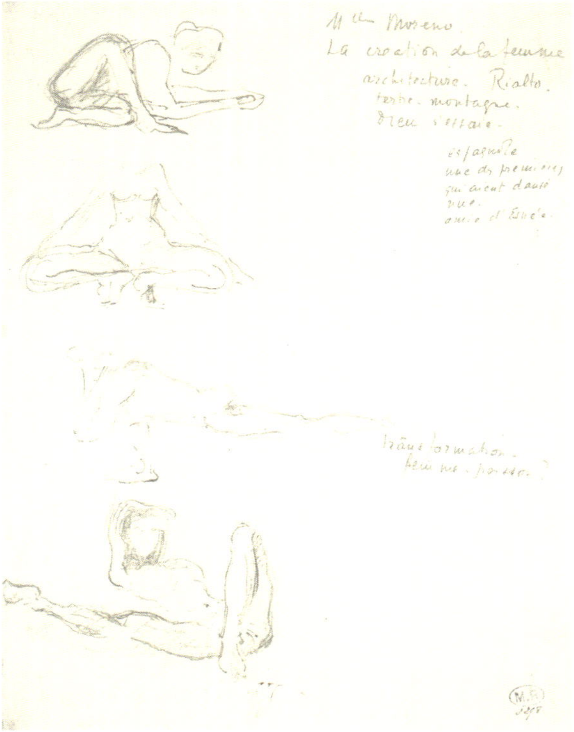

FIG.7
Louis Gillet
Four figures of dancers after Rodin's drawings, c.1910–13
Pencil with stumping on laid paper, 277 x 213 mm
Musée Rodin, Paris, D.2298

"MOVEMENTS OF UNKNOWN PASSIONS"

Some dozen of these drawings showing women in acrobatic poses were reproduced by Louis Gillet (1876–1943) on three large sheets of paper (D.2297–99, fig.7). These also show sketches after the *Mouvements de danse* and one bears the inscription *Mlle Moreno. La création de la femme. Architecture ... Dieu s'essaie ... Transformation femme poisson* (Mademoiselle Moreno. The creation of woman. Architecture ... God tests himself ... Transformation woman fish), while on one of the reproduced drawings is written, *On est en train de le créer* (It is being created; D.1849). This naturally links to the portfolio entitled *La création de la femme* (The creation of woman) described by Kessler: "These are study drawings of a very supple girl, a kind of acrobat, whose poses provide all kinds of entirely new and bizarre arabesques. Rodin told us he saw them as something like the early stages of an evolution, transitions leading from the animal world to woman – insects, varieties of frog, a creature resembling a sphinx – from which the woman crawls out as though from a cocoon: 'Some people find all this obscene. But it's almost pure mathematics. It's not driven by passion, or rather, it looks like the movements of unknown passions, which we can't imagine but might be possible – passions that are not human.'" His goal, we can guess, was thus closer to that of Henri Gaudier, who, writing to Sophie Brzeska in 1912, wondered "whether primitive forms might reveal a closer, greater and more intelligent understanding of nature than the sculptures of Pisani [sic], Donatello and Rodin",[12] seeming to echo the credo underlying *Les Cathédrales de France*. "The art of the Middle Ages comes from nature, in its ornamentation as in its constructions. So to understand it, we too must always return to nature."[13] In reality, Rodin had long ago embarked on this work, as noted in the 1880s by Octave Mirbeau, Gustave Geffroy and Edmond de Goncourt when they described *Femme accroupie* (*Crouching Woman*) as a "frog" or "batrachian", emphasising the impression of primitive sensuality emanating from the figure.

These forms folded over on themselves could be compared to chrysalids, while the Cambodian dancers and acrobats, and the ancient Indian sculpture revealed to Rodin by Victor Goloubev, took him to the next stage, that of opening and expanding. Their unadorned movements are gestures that, in Bourdelle's words, "have nothing to say ... that is anecdotal or literary",[14] bringing the composition back to primal forms, stripped of all aesthetic intent. These new sources of inspiration had enabled Rodin to discover a universal truth in which everything merged: "So the same thought had safeguarded art in Athens, Chartres, Cambodia, everywhere".[15] While some movements, notably the position with hands bent back, are typical of Eastern dance and indicate Rodin's nostalgia for his sessions with the Cambodian dancers, the *Mouvements de danse* are in a sense a culmination, a combination of models who could all perform exercises in balance, double-jointedness, muscular contraction and so on, with peerless physical control. The rejection of anatomical detail emphasises the movement in itself, reinforced by a materiality that remains as close as possible to the material used. The creative process moves into the foreground.

Baudelaire had defined modernity a few decades earlier, integrating into it the notions of newness and decadence, the latter understood in the sense of "art that has reached an extreme maturity in the oblique sunlight of aging civilisations".[16] In the generation after Baudelaire Rodin replaced the notion of decadence with a primitivism that is not that of Gauguin, but is rather a return to instinctive forms that remain close to natural elements. He admired the Japanese actress Hanako for being "so strong that she can stay as long as she wants on one leg while raising the other before her at a right angle. Standing in this way, she looks as if she were rooted to the ground like a tree."[17] We might also think of the statue *Balzac*, so often compared to a rock. It seems that the body expresses itself with all the more force if it is rid of all the codes to which artists had been made accustomed by a century of academic training in the fine arts.

DISCOVERY

Unable to choose from the series of modelled studies, Rodin – the late Rodin for whom slowness was a virtue – kept them all in the form of a series. If Kessler is to be believed, the sculpture he had planned was never made and the series was never shown. As one of the few to have been privileged to see them and the only one to have commented on them in Rodin's lifetime, Kessler wanted to obtain bronze casts of these figurines that had so astounded him. "But he gave me evasive answers, as he had the other times, eventually saying that he was afraid to give them up because he thought that in them he had found something new, which other sculptors would steal if he let go of them. I suggested simply having them moulded and he could keep the moulds in his studio, as belonging to me. But he thought even that was dangerous, because the founder might steal the moulds. He is so mistrustful of everything that it sometimes seems akin to a delusion of persecution."[18]

So the series long remained unknown to the wider public,[19] although some of the figurines were shown when the Musée Rodin opened (1919), as attested by the mention of three of them in the first catalogue.[20] Rodin's donation had given casting rights to the museum and it seems casting was quickly planned, since Mme Le Mancel, niece of the first curator Léonce Bénédite and the museum's secretary in the years following its opening, quoted a sale price of 3,500 francs alongside the notices describing the figures in the catalogue of 1921. However, casting was not begun until 1945, initially in the form of a few casts by Alexis Rudier[21] and, after his death in 1952, by his nephew Georges Rudier.

It was under the influence of Cécile Goldscheider, appointed museum secretary in 1945, assistant in 1952 and curator in 1960, that the casting of these pieces was developed. The bronzes were shown at the Louvre in 1962–63 at the exhibition *Rodin inconnu* (Unknown Rodin), where, among maquettes and sketches unearthed from the museum archives, visitors could see the *Mouvements de danse* – all those that had been cast to date, in other words the enlargement of *Mouvement A*, *Mouvements B, C, D, E, F, G* (nos. 83, 77, 78, 86, 87, 88, 79) and *Nijinsky* (no.101), alongside *Pas de deux B* in plaster (no.85) and *Mouvements H* and *I* in terracotta (nos. 89 and 90). To relaunch the sale of bronzes that was vital to the operation of the museum, Goldscheider had approached a few major dealers. The size and modernity of the *Mouvements de danse* made them very desirable objects for collectors and

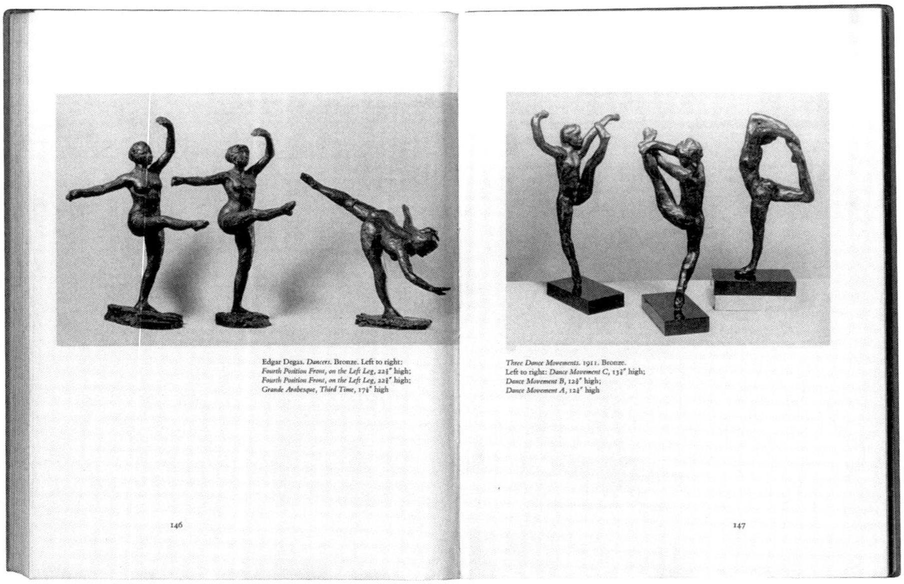

FIG.8
Three *Dance Movements* (recto) and (verso) three *Dancers* by Edgar Degas, in exh. cat. *Rodin*, Museum of Modern Art, New York, 1963, pp.146–47

galleries, who fought to have them, notably Curt Valentin in New York, Allan Frumkin in Chicago and New York, the Dominion Gallery in Montreal, Gerald Cramer in Geneva, Claude Bernard and Bérès in Paris and Roland, Browse & Delbanco in London – which was the gallery through which the figurines passed in greatest number (around fifty). In an article published in *The Burlington Magazine* in 1987, Lillian Browse noted the role she had played in the "revival of interest in one of the world greatest sculptors"[22] by mounting an exhibition in 1954 that was the first in London since 1932. She went on to report the discovery of the plaster of Nijinsky in 1957: "The directress (of the Rodin Museum) put a tiny plaster into my hands, asking me if I knew whom it represented. She was very excited over this wonderful thing. Although the two halves of the actual mould had lain in a drawer for years, they were far too intricate for it to be envisaged what the subject might turn out to be, and nobody dreamt of Nijinsky."[23]

The series was quickly exhausted – before 1960 for *Mouvements* A, small and large, *B, C, D, E*, F and G, and for *Nijinsky*, all casts of which were sold by the museum in 1958–59. However, the casting of *Mouvements* H and I was not undertaken until 1963, at which time the series was widely promoted in London at the exhibition *Rodin: A selection from the exhibition "Rodin inconnu" au Louvre* in July and August 1963,[24] while in New York the pieces were seen in the same year at the Museum of Modern Art as part of the *Rodin* exhibition mounted by Albert E. Elsen (fig.8),[25] and at the Slatkin Gallery.[26] The latter exhibition, which later travelled across the United States and Canada, gave rise to a celebrated review by Leo Steinberg. Already a noted critic of contemporary art at that time, Steinberg developed a new vision of Rodin, also advocated by Elsen. His piece is illustrated by reproductions of five of the *Mouvements de danse*, and closes with an analysis of these figurines in which Steinberg emphasises the determining role played by the material: "Rodin's modeling blinds itself to external anatomy. His subtle acquaintance with human surface is set aside for a deepening, inward-turned acquiescence. One feels as never before, an acceptance of the condition and shape of the material worked on; and a new willingness to let surface be no more than the track and passage of his own working hands."[27] For Steinberg this was the true sign of Rodin's modernity.

When, finally, the Musée d'Orsay – then still at the planning stage – negotiated an agreement with the Musée Rodin to have the most innovative aspects of the artist's work represented in its future display, three *Mouvements de danse* were selected, alongside *Balzac* and *L'Homme qui marche*, to reflect his position at the dawn of twentieth-century sculpture.[28]

NOTES

1 *"... eine ganze Vitrine voll angefangener kleiner Tonfiguren nach einer Akrobatin, Figuren von überraschender Neuheit der Linien und Bewegungen, seinen Zeichnungen näherstehend als allen seinen bisherigen Plastiken"; "... wann er an den kleinen Akrobatinnen Figuren weiterzuarbeiten gedenke. R: 'Ce n'est pas une acrobate. Si c'était une acrobate, ça se verrait tout de suite, ce serait différent. Je n'ai pas pu y travailler depuis quelque temps parce que le modèle a été malade. Et du reste, je ne travaille plus aux choses que quand elles me font plaisir, je ne m'astreins plus à aucun travail'. Ich fragte ihn noch, ob er die ganzen fertig machen wolle oder sie alle in einer einzigen zusammenfassen beabsichtige. Nein, er wolle sie alle in einer einzigen zusammenfassen. 'Mais j'ai tant de travaux qui me réclament que je ne peux pas dire quand je terminerai celui-ci. C'est le travail que j'ai déjà fait qui me réclame pour le compléter, car je voudrais tout compléter, je ne le compléterai jamais, mais je veux le compléter'"; "Rodin holte eine Mappe mit Zeichnungen heraus, die er die 'Création de la femme' nennt. Es sind Studien nach einem sehr gelenkigen Mädchen, einer Art von Akrobatin, deren Stellungen allerhand neue, sonderbare Arabesken ergeben. Rodin sieht in diesen Arabesken sozusagen Vorstufen zum Weib, Übergänge aus der Tierwelt zum Weib: Käfer, Froschformen, Sphinxartigen Gebilde, aus denen das Weib wie aus einer Puppe heraus kriecht: 'Il y a des gens qui trouveraient ça obscène. Et pourtant, c'est presque de la mathématique pure. Ce n'est pas passionné. Ou plutôt, on dirait les gestes de passions inconnues, de passions que nous ne pouvons imaginer mais qui seraient possibles, de passions en dehors de l'humanité'"; "Er hält diese Mappe sehr geheim und musste sie erst aus allerlei Hüllen und Bindfäden befreien, ehe er sie für Nijinski öffnete .... Rodin führte uns dann in die Kammer, wo er die plastischen Studien nach demselben Modell aufbewahrt, die ihm die 'Création' suggeriert hat: eine Anzahl kleiner Figürchen von grösster Schönheit; namentlich haben sie, was er sonst selten in seine Plastiken hineinkriegt, die gleiche architektonische Strenge wie seine Zeichnungen"*: Harry Graf Kessler, *Das Tagebuch*, ed. Jörg Schuster, 9 vols., Stuttgart (Cotta), 2004–10, vol.4, 2004 (1906–14).

2 See François Blanchetière, 'Hasards de l'atelier', in exh. cat. *Rodin. L'accident. L'aléatoire*, Musée d'Art et d'Histoire, Geneva, 2014, pp.124–29.

3 *"les petites âmes florales que vous avez fait surgir des vases antiques"*: Rilke to Rodin, Capri, 8 March 1908; Rainer Maria Rilke, *Lettres à Rodin*, Paris (Éditions Émile-Paul Frères), 1931, p.86–87.

4 *Cybèle* at the Salon National des Beaux-Arts, *La Méditerranée* at the Salon d'Automne.

5 *"Bonheur de vivre, quiétude, grâce, équilibre, raison"*: Auguste Rodin, *L'Art. Entretiens réunis par Paul Gsell*, Paris (Bernard Grasset), 1911, p.260.

6 Arthur Symons, 'Auguste Rodin' in *From Toulouse-Lautrec to Rodin with some Personal Impressions*, London (John Lane The Bodley Head), 1929, p.223.

7 Private collection, reproduced in Liisa Lindgren, 'Sigrid af Forselles and Hida Flodin, Rodin's Finnish students', in exh. cat. *Auguste Rodin and the Nordic countries*, Nationalmuseum, Stockholm, and Ateneum Art Museum, Helsinki, 2015–16, p.153, fig.4.

8 *"Je vais vous donner des poses extraordinaires aussi bien que les poses classiques car je suis souple ! et toutes sont naturelles pour moi. Elles sont les mêmes que je prends chez moi sans penser"*: Gwen John to Rodin, *"vendredi matin"*, Paris, Musée Rodin.

9 Vaslav Fomitch Nijinski, *Cahiers. Le Sentiment*, Paris (Actes-Sud), 1995, p.256; cited by Martine Kahane, in exh. cat. *Nijinsky (1889–1950)*, Musée d'Orsay, Paris, 2000, p.98.

10 *"Et dont les admirations constantes furent pour les œuvres de l'antique : imaginez donc ce que put produire en moi un spectacle aussi complet qui me restituait l'antique en me dévoilant du mystère! ... Pour moi, je sens bien qu'à les regarder, ma vision s'est élargie : j'ai vu plus haut et plus loin ; enfin j'ai appris"*: Georges Bourdon, 'Rodin et les petites princesses jaunes', *Le Figaro*, 1 August 1906. See also exh. cat. *Rodin et les danseuses cambodgiennes. Sa dernière passion*, Musée Rodin, Paris, 2006.

11 *"Assise sur le sol, les jambes croisées, la jambe droite repliée très haut, le pied posé sur le genou gauche"*: handwritten inventory entry; see Nicole Barbier, *Marbres de Rodin. Collection du musée*, Paris (Éditions du Musée Rodin), 1987, pp.132 and 257.

12 *"Si les formes primitives ne révèlent pas une compréhension plus étroite de la nature, plus grande et plus intelligente que les sculptures de Pisani* [sic], *Donatello et Rodin"*: Henri Gaudier to Sophie Brzeska, 1912, cited by Catherine Chevillot, 'Le problème c'était Rodin', in exh. cat. *Oublier Rodin? La sculpture à Paris 1905–1914*, Musée d'Orsay, Paris, 2009, p.21.

13 *"L'art du Moyen-Âge, dans son ornementation comme dans ses constructions, procède de la nature. C'est donc toujours à la nature aussi qu'il faut retourner pour le comprendre"*: Auguste Rodin, *Les Cathédrales de France*, Paris (A. Colin), 1914, pp.6, 125.

14 *"Qui ne laissent rien raconter ... d'anecdotique ou de littéraire"*: Antoine Bourdelle, 'Rodin et la sculpture', *Revue des Études franco-russes*, September 1909, p.381.

15 *"La même pensée avait donc sauvegardé l'art à Athènes, à Chartres, au Cambodge, partout"*: Rodin 1914, p.121.

16 *"Art arrivé à ce point de maturité extrême que déterminent à leurs soleils obliques les civilisations qui vieillissent"*: Roberto Calasso, *La Folie Baudelaire*, Paris (Gallimard, Folio), [2008] 2014, p.412.

17 Auguste Rodin, *Art: Conversations with Paul Gsell*, trans. Jacques de Caso and Patricia B. Sanders, Berkeley (University of California Press), 1984, p.51; *"... tellement robuste qu'elle peut rester aussi longtemps qu'elle le veut sur une seule jambe en levant l'autre devant elle à angle droit ; elle parait ainsi enracinée dans le sol comme un arbre"*: Rodin/Gsell 1911, p.152.

18 Kessler 2004, 2 June 1912.

19 To my knowledge none of the existing casts was made in Rodin's lifetime, which sometimes worries collectors. Gustav Delbanco advised Cécile Goldscheider to skate over the fact that the bronzes he showed in his gallery were recent casts (letter of 20 November 1956, cited by Catherine Lampert, exh. cat. *Rodin*, Royal Academy, London, 2006, p.266).

20 Léonce Bénédite, *Catalogue sommaire des œuvres d'Auguste Rodin et autres œuvres d'art de la donation Rodin*, Paris (Éd. Lapina Impr.) 1919, nos. 153–55.

21 Success led to a proliferation of false castings, mostly bearing the stamp of Alexis Rudier.

22 Lillian Browse, 'False castings of Rodin bronzes', *The Burlington Magazine*, December 1987, p.808.

23 Ibid., p.807.

24 *Mouvements* A, large model, and B-I, bronzes, nos. 15–23, of which F was that of the museum; *Nijinsky*, bronze, no.25.

25 A, B, C, D, part of the K. Delbanco collection in Larchmont, NY, supplemented by *Mouvement* E from the Musée Rodin and a *Nijinsky* from a private collection, all bronze; exh. cat. *Rodin*, New York, Museum of Modern Art, 1963, nos. 54–59.

26 *Mouvements* A, B, C, D, E and F, bronzes, exh.cat. *Rodin (1840–1917). An Exhibition of Sculptures and Drawings*, Charles E. Slatkin Gallery, New York, etc., 1963–65 (see note 33, p.76, below), no.85 (unique).

27 Leo Steinberg, 'Rodin', in *Other Criteria. Confrontations with Twentieth Century Art*, New York (Oxford University Press), 1972, pp.322–403, p.399.

28 Anne Pingeot, 'Rodin au musée du Luxembourg', *48/14. La Revue du musée d'Orsay*, no.11, Autumn 2000, p.71.

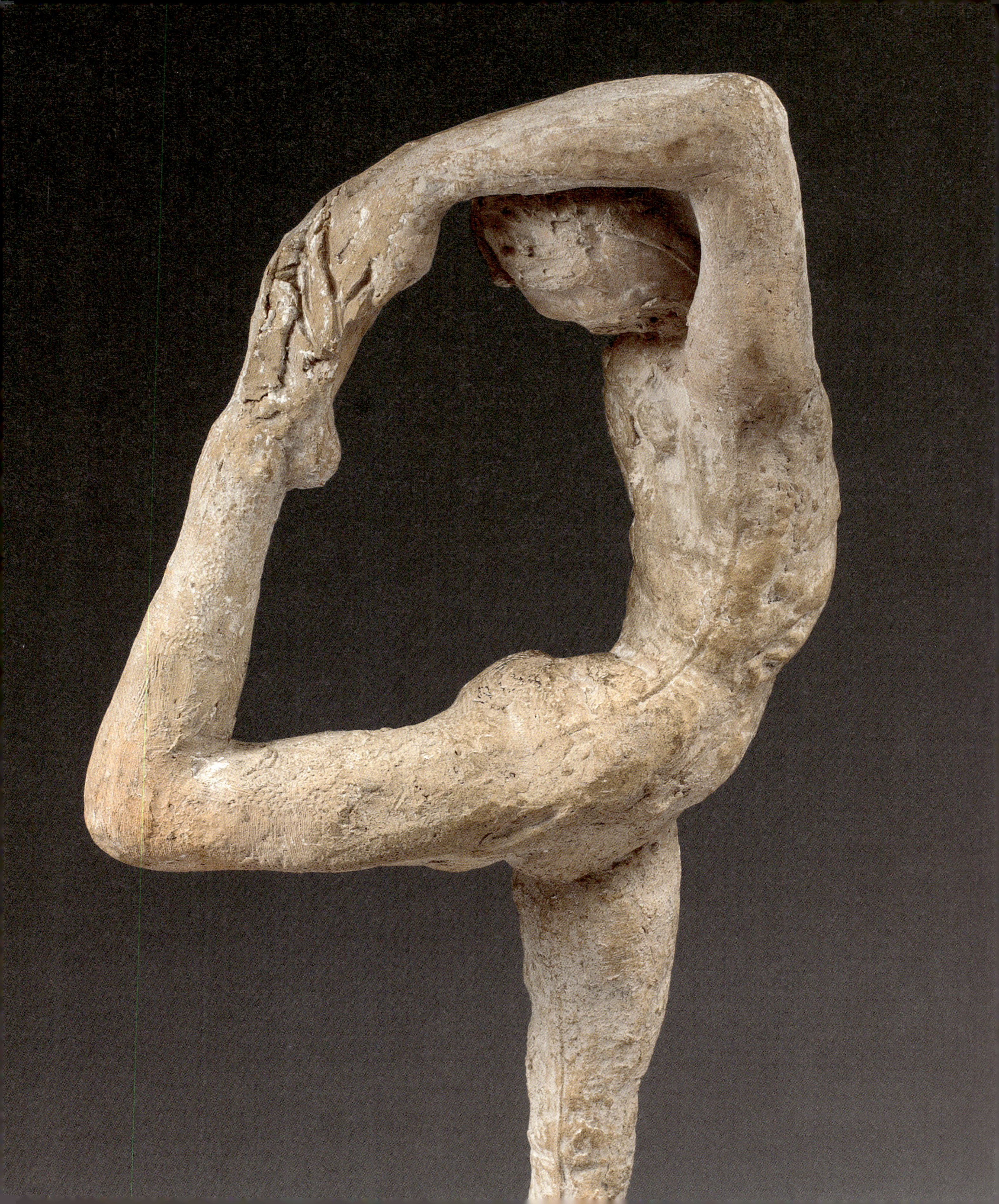

FLIGHT, ARABESQUE AND CANTILEVER IN RODIN'S MOVEMENT STUDIES

ALEXANDRA GERSTEIN

Auguste Rodin's interviews with the art critic Paul Gsell, published as *L'Art*, in 1911, contained a section entitled 'Movement in Art' in which he famously contrasted art and photography, praising the superior ability of artists to capture movement. Asked to compare artists to playwrights, he said that while the latter had the device of plot to allow action to unfold in real time, artists had to resort to other means. They could compress successive moments of an action into a single potent form or image and by so doing arrive, by 'sincerity' or 'instinct', at a true interpretation of the essence of movement.[1] Rodin's series of sculptural studies of these years, known posthumously as the *Mouvements de danse* (Dance movements), encapsulates these ideas beautifully. It provides a visual argument against photography's fragmentation of time into individual 'frozen' moments, and instead interprets 'movement in art' as a continuum of interconnected attitudes and postures. Not only does each figure compress several movements into one form, but altogether the series could be said to operate as a piece of theatre, with one figure enacting a sequence of loosely related actions which can be observed in real time.

The theatrical analogy can be taken a little further if one considers that, much like a director wishing to cast a particular actress in a part, Rodin seems to have been quite determined to work with one particular model in the development of the *Mouvements de danse*. This was an acrobat and model called Alda Moreno (d. before 1963), often called '*le petit modèle*' in Rodin's circle, in reference to her small stature.

Moreno was the model and companion of one of Rodin's closest collaborators, Jules Desbois (1840–1935), an accomplished sculptor whose aesthetic remained close to Rodin's. Desbois made a number of statuettes based on Moreno (fig.9) and a couple of busts of her, and he named her the executor of his estate. In the years around 1900, Moreno seems to have participated in the bohemian culture of Montmartre, with its mix of artists, illustrators, writers and music-hall performers. In May 1911, she danced in what must have been a minor role in a pantomime ballet called *Le Cœur de Floria* at the Théâtre de la Gaîté, usually referred to as the Opéra Comique. Beyond these facts very little is known about her.

There is, however, strong evidence that Moreno inspired Rodin's *Mouvements de danse*, from several inscriptions on some of the plaster moulds used for making the figures to mentions in the Musée Rodin's first inventories of the 1930s. This essay aims to shed some light on Moreno's role in the development of the *Mouvements de danse* by examining Rodin's drawings and sculpture in the light of her presence in the studio from about 1903 to about 1905 and from late 1910 to about 1913, and by considering archival sources, including two newly discovered photographs of Moreno, her letters to the sculptor and his secretaries' diaries for the relevant period, together with new information gained from the technical study into their fabrication (see Blanchetière, Cascio and Lévy in this volume, pp.60–76).[2]

This exhibition has benefited from a practice-based collaborative research project with movement practitioners under the auspices of the International Centre for Movement at the Royal Central School of Speech and Drama, London.[3] The project, which aimed to understand the *Mouvements de danse* from the perspective of physical movement, has involved embodying the postures of the sculpture and associated drawings. On a practical level, this research has confirmed what art historians have often written about the figures – that

Detail of s.5492, cat.47

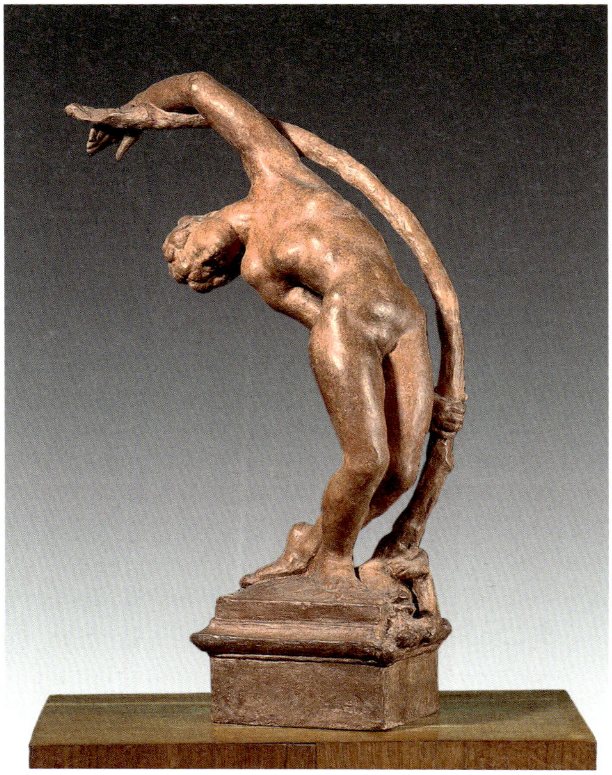

FIG.9
Jules Desbois
L'Arc, 1902
Terracotta, 45.8 x 30.4 cm
Musée Jules Desbois,
Parçay-les-Pins

they do not represent dance movements but rather acrobatic limbering exercises.[4] Indeed, the original title given to these works by the Musée Rodin's first curators in the years following the sculptor's death was '*études de mouvement*', or 'movement studies', and that title appears to be a more accurate reflection of the artist's intentions than the seemingly more market-orientated '*mouvements de danse*'.[5] On a more subtle level, this practice-based research provides a reading of the poses Rodin could have observed during the modelling sessions, and in particular of the movements in between the poses, reflected in the drawings but more difficult to discern in the sculpture.[6]

Until now, scholarly interpretation of these works has tended to focus on the apparent elasticity of the bodies and the high degree of invention in the postures, which is not an incorrect approach, as it is true that the figures appear absurdly supple and, for example, that joints are often positioned in impossible rotations (see, e.g., *Mouvement* B, cat.57 & 58). However, correlating our observations with the findings of the technical study yields an approach that allows one to focus instead on the quality and texture of the movements expressed.[7] Interestingly, in spite of its strangeness and its air of unreality, the series appears to involve the figures in a sequence of (potentially connected) postures, which can be described in the following terms: uplift (*Mouvements* A, B and E, cat.47 & 48, 57 & 58, 51 & 52), extension (*Mouvements* C, G and H, but also B and B+, cat.54, 59–61), twisting or gathering (*Mouvements* D and I, cat.63–65), leaping (*Mouvement* F, cat.75) and folding (cat.68, S.3845). That it is possible to extrapolate quite precise physical information from these abstracted figures shows how closely Rodin had observed Moreno's actions. It also suggests that by sketching her in these limbering exercises, presumably over and over again as she could have repeated them several times in a session and may have entered the poses in roughly the same way each time, Rodin could express the dynamics as well as the details of each of the poses.[8]

Thanks to the findings of the technical study, we now know that Rodin began his series by modelling two clay figures, which were sectioned into parts so that they could be cast in plaster (*Alpha* and *Beta*, cat.42). The original clay models (known to us only from the plaster casts) were simply rendered, neither had a head, and one of the figures had only one arm. Yet the poses themselves were naturalistic and perfectly plausible. One showed a standing figure holding her foot behind her head, and the other a lunging figure, like an non-balletic and more athletic version of Edgar Degas's *Grande arabesque* (fig.10). It was only later in the process that Rodin introduced bodily distortions. This occurred after the moulds used to make the plaster casts were reused to press-mould clay body parts ("*abattis*"), which Rodin then assembled together to make the dozen or so figures of the *Mouvements de danse*. It was in repurposing the clay parts that the figures acquired their strange appearance. Limbs and torsos that were originally modelled to express the texture, depth and quality of a particular movement lost their logic when he attached them to a figure in

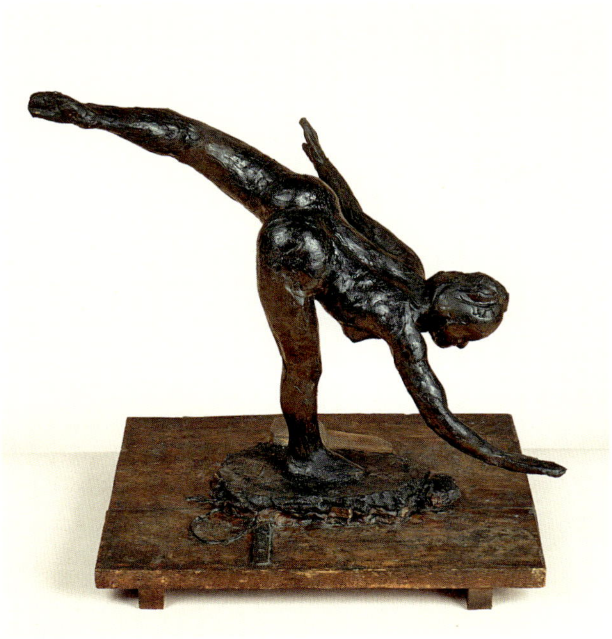

FIG.10
Edgar Degas
Grande arabesque, troisième temps, première étude, c. 1882–95
Wax, 46.5 cm high
Musée d'Orsay, Paris

another position. This idea was not new in Rodin's practice. Working on *The Gates of Hell*, his major project of the 1880s, had already led him to experiment with amalgamating disparate bodies and fragments into new works. As Le Normand-Romain discusses in her essay in this catalogue, in the late years Rodin's approach became increasingly experimental, as he assembled together elements that seemed even less 'finished'. Examples of this are the *Femme accroupie* (*Crouching Woman*) of 1911 (fig.4, p.16) and *L'Homme qui marche* (*The Walking Man*), conceived in 1899–1900, enlarged in 1905–06, and cast in bronze in 1910, both of which show a preoccupation with creating simplified forms. In *L'Homme qui marche* Rodin brought together two halves of the same sculpture but positioned them slightly off axis to each other, creating a work that expresses the essence, rather than the physiology, of walking. A similar principle of expressive dislocation is found in the *Mouvements de danse*, albeit on a smaller scale and shared by a dozen figures.

Throughout his oeuvre, Rodin had explored the essence of human movement in its most extreme forms. The modelling sessions with Moreno offered him the opportunity to study these attitudes in the studio with a model who was not only capable of producing and maintaining a range of difficult postures, but for whom dislocation and contortion would have been second nature. As has often been noted, Rodin's imaginative and practical processes were so entwined that his ideas were often the direct result of experiments in the studio. He often changed the meanings of his works simply through re-orientating them, i.e. turning them upside down, on their side or otherwise, a process allied to Albert Elsen's notion of 'inventive economy'.[9] Acrobatics offered a particularly rich seam for this practice, which is hinted at in small-scale experimental works such as *L'Acrobate*, also known as *Le Jongleur* (of c.1892–95?). Working with the creative energy and technical skill of an acrobat like Moreno could have fuelled this process further since she could herself offer permutations of postures – being upside down is an integral aspect of the art of acrobatics, as is the creation of contorted, extreme shapes or 'arabesques' and postures requiring a 'dynamic equilibrium', such as standing on one leg, whilst holding the other leg extended behind or to the side of the head.[10] These positions jettison the quotidian by reversing the normal order of things, pushing the body to extreme shapes and heightening the eroticism of the poses.[11]

Attendant to the practice of acrobatics in general, and to balancing poses in particular, is the risk factor of falling. Minute adjustments need to be made to maintain balance in a particular pose, to counter the gravitational pull. These are not necessarily visible in the body of an experienced acrobat but they are no less present.[12] In this context it is helpful to recall Rodin's interest in the architectural principle of the cantilever, which he seems to have understood as a counterpoint to imbalance. Always alive to the analogy between architecture and the human body, he turned specifically to the principle of cantilever in the opening page of his book on Gothic cathedrals, *Les Cathédrales de France*, published in 1914 but prepared over a long time and considered to be one of the major achievements of his late years. "Everyone knows that the human body, in movement, is cantilevered and that equilibrium is re-established through compensations. The bearing leg, directly under the body, is the only pivot for the whole body, and, during that instant, it alone makes makes all the effort. The non-bearing leg serves only to modulate the stance, to modify it, either slowly or rapidly, if need be, until it has replaced, and freed, the bearing leg".[13] In some of the figures of the *Mouvements de danse* and in many of the associated drawings this idea of cantilever is present, as a way of exploring the threshold between stability and instability and the precariousness at the edge of balance. Acrobats are a particularly apt subject for this exploration, as they inhabit this fine line for several moments each time they enter a pose.

The sessions with Moreno would have provided Rodin with a set of predictable parameters within which he could have been free to experiment with the forms of the poses, much in the same way that he often liked to model a roughly similar size of clay or, in his late figure drawings, use a similar size of paper. Observing a variety of poses embodied by the same person would have provided likewise a shortcut to the movements he wanted to capture. If, therefore, the modelling sessions with Moreno can be thought of as the material of the *Mouvements de danse*, then Moreno herself might be considered as a collaborator in the studio. As Rodin said to a journalist in the late 1880s: "A model is, therefore, more than a means whereby the artist expresses a sentiment, thought or experience; it is a correlative inspiration to him. They work together as a productive force."[14] The notion of collaboration in relation to Rodin's creative process is particularly relevant to the sculptor's late years.[15] As the head of a large studio, his role was often that of a director of operations, collaborating with his assistants on practical and aesthetic matters. Moreno, like Rodin's technical assistants, possessed a particular set of skills that he required in order to develop and refine his ideas.

Although a friend of Rodin's asserted that she was a Spanish dancer,[16] in fact Moreno was French, possibly from Anjou or Touraine. Alda Moreno was a stage name most likely reflecting the vogue for Spanish dancers in Paris at the time. In the sources, it is spelled Moreno, Morena, Morano, Morennot, Morenno, Moréno, Moreño, and in her letters to Rodin she mostly signed 'Morẽno'.[17] Her given name was Noémie Chevassier.[18] The earliest record of her in the archives of the Musée Rodin is a note by Rodin's secretary René Chéruy: "*modèles femmes 1903/ Alda Moreno/ modèle acrobate/ 41 rue de la Tour d'Auvergne*". Her address was in the 9th *arrondissement*, not far from Montmartre. If she performed as an acrobat in Montmartre, it could have been at a circus such as the Cirque Médrano or at one of the music-halls, like the Moulin Rouge or the Folies-Bergère, which offered acrobatic entertainments as a supplement to the ballet numbers. Acrobats were apt to find employment at either. The most talented were the "independent artists who appear on the stage of the music-hall or in the big fixed circuses of the capital cities", according to *L'Acrobatie et les acrobates* (Paris, 1904).[19] As the life of an acrobat was financially precarious, she seems to have supplemented her income by posing for nude photographs.[20]

Rodin must have met Moreno in the studio of the sculptor Jules Desbois. It was common for Rodin and the assistants in his studio to share models.[21] As well as being one of Rodin's marble carvers, Desbois was an old friend from the time they worked together at the Sèvres porcelain manufacture.[22] It is not known how often Moreno visited Rodin's studio since no diaries survive for these years,[23] but by June 1905 she was no longer modelling for him and seems to have disappeared. Rodin's friend, an eccentric navy captain and collector called Edmond Bigand-Kaire (1847–1924), known as '*le capitaine des arts*', who liked to send Rodin delicacies such as fresh oysters and almonds, seems to have taken it upon himself to try and find Rodin's missing model. He wrote to him on at least six occasions to relate his various ideas on how to find her, mainly by enlisting the help of artist friends in Montmartre. In

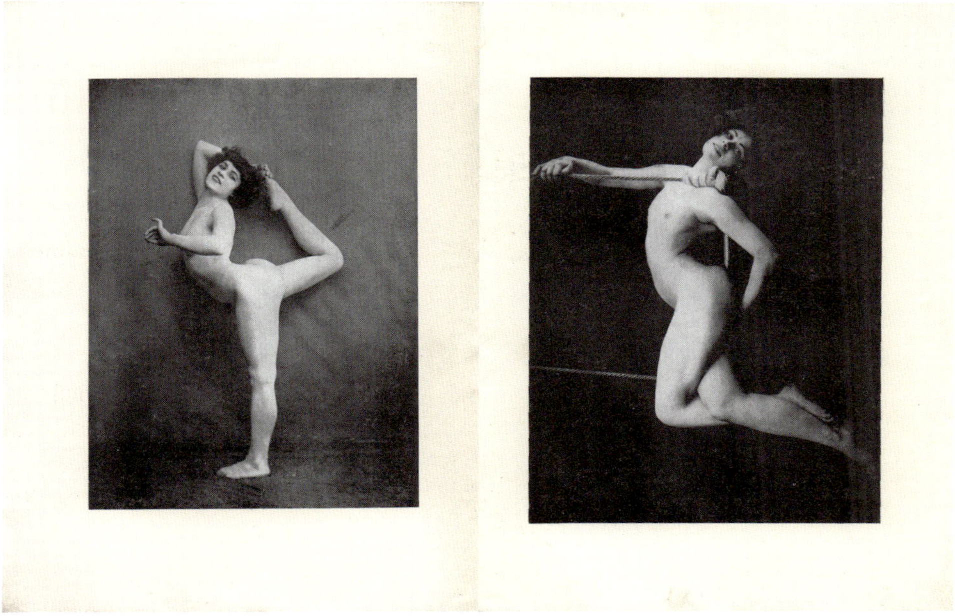

FIG.11
Alda Moreno, photographs from Le nu académique. Publication de documents photographiques à l'usage des artistes,
1 November 1905
Musée Rodin, Paris

the first of these letters, probably dating to the autumn of 1905, one learns that the "acrobat-model" had been missing since June and that photographs of her were on sale in a stationer's shop "on the Boulevard Clichy near the café Coquet not far from the Moulin Rouge". He explained that he could not go to the shop himself and asked whether Rodin wanted him to involve the painter and denizen of Montmartre Adolphe Léon Willette to help him in his search.[24] Rodin's secretary at the time, the German poet Rainer Maria Rilke, responded to Bigand-Kaire: "You are referring to the acrobat-model; Monsieur Rodin would be in fact grateful to you if you would continue your search by contacting Mr. Willette as you propose".[25] Willette, a fixture of bohemian Montmartre, knew everyone; he promised to help find "the young person in question", whom he thought had stopped modelling because of a serious operation.[26] Bigand-Kaire himself enlisted the help of another artist, who found out that Moreno had in fact recently married and for that reason had decided to stop modelling.[27] Although he had not discovered her whereabouts, Bigand-Kaire wrote again to inform Rodin that "some poses that were obviously taken by the acrobat in question" appeared in an erotic review called *Le nu académique*. As he was writing from his home in Marseille, he provided details of where Rodin could purchase the magazine,[28] which he obviously did since the Musée Rodin preserves his copy (fig.11).

In the photograph, Moreno is obviously in an acrobatic posture, which presumably could have been performed either at a circus or at a music-hall (see figs.12–15). The photograph shows clearly that she was not struggling to maintain the position, and that she had an unusually flexible back, which would have allowed her to execute difficult postures like this one with ease. It may represent a stage towards a more advanced posture, known, according to the British Symbolist poet and chronicler of nightlife entertainment Arthur Symons (1865–1945), a friend and admirer of Rodin's, as '*la jambe derrière la tête*', or 'leg behind the head'. In that position the raised leg is held straight up in a reverse standing splits behind the head, "a position which requires the most elaborate acrobatic training, and which is perhaps as painful to see as it must be to do".[29] The facing photograph needs to be turned clockwise to be seen in the correct orientation, with Moreno shown as though swinging on a tightrope or trapeze cord, possibly a reference to her acrobatic profession or more likely just a prop in the photographer's studio. The deep curve of her back is also noticeable in this photograph.

From the 1880s, the cabaret, circus and music-hall entertainments of Montmartre provided artists with

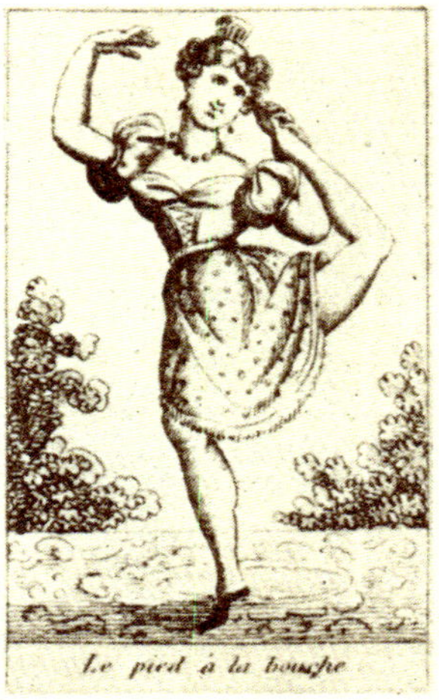

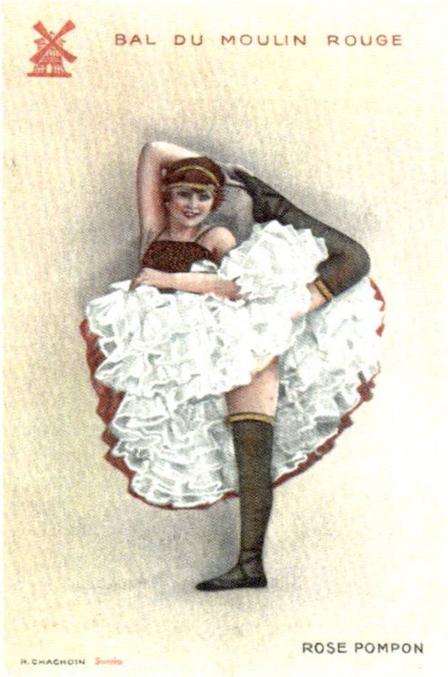

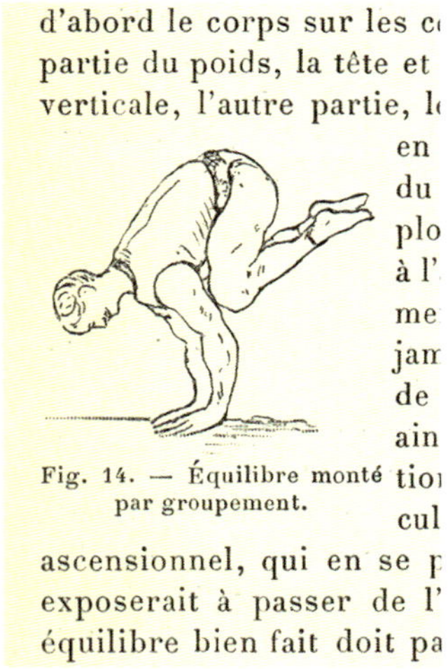
d'abord le corps sur les c
partie du poids, la tête et
verticale, l'autre partie, l
en
du
plo
à l'
me
jan
de
ain
tio
cul
Fig. 14. — Équilibre monté par groupement.
ascensionnel, qui en se p
exposerait à passer de l'
équilibre bien fait doit pa

FIG.12
'Le pied à la bouche' from an engraving showing various exercises of the Franconi Circus, early 1800s, in Denys Amiel, *Les spectacles à travers les âges*, Paris, Éditions du Cygne, 1931, p.214

FIG.13
Albert Chazelle
'Rose Pompon', postcard from the Moulin Rouge, *c.*1925
Collection Gérard Jouhet, Paris

FIG.14
Balance pose, from G. Strehly, *L'Acrobatie et les acrobates*, Paris, 1904, p.80

subjects from modern life, for example, Edgar Degas's *Miss La La at the Cirque Fernando* (1879, National Gallery, London) shows the famous trapeze artist performing her act high above the heads of spectators. Artists like Toulouse-Lautrec and less well-known painters and illustrators, such as Willette or Ferdinand Rops, depicted the seamier side of Montmartre nightlife. Rodin appreciated the music-hall spectacle with its provocative high-kicking dances like the *chahut*, but his drawings of models in acrobatic poses were sketched in his studio rather than in situ, showing figures, both male and female, usually nude and abstracted from any setting. Rodin focused on how these athletic bodies "twine into exquisite arabesques", as Symons once wrote of a music-hall dancer.[31] This spirit of focused interest in extreme body shapes is seen in Kees van Dongen's series of single-figure paintings of about 1909, such as *L'Acrobate* (fig.15), in a pose very similar to the one taken by Alda Moreno, depicting performers at the Cirque Médrano (successor to the Cirque Fernando)[32] and at the Folies-Bergère.

In his last letter to touch on this subject, along with the present of a live eel for Christmas, Bigand-Kaire sent Rodin the address of the stationer's shop, which elicited the following response from the sculptor: "My dear friend, Many thanks for your kindness: your package arrived in an excellent state. – The animal still alive frightened everyone. – Concerning the model, thank you for the information, I will take note and maybe in time we will find her again."[30]

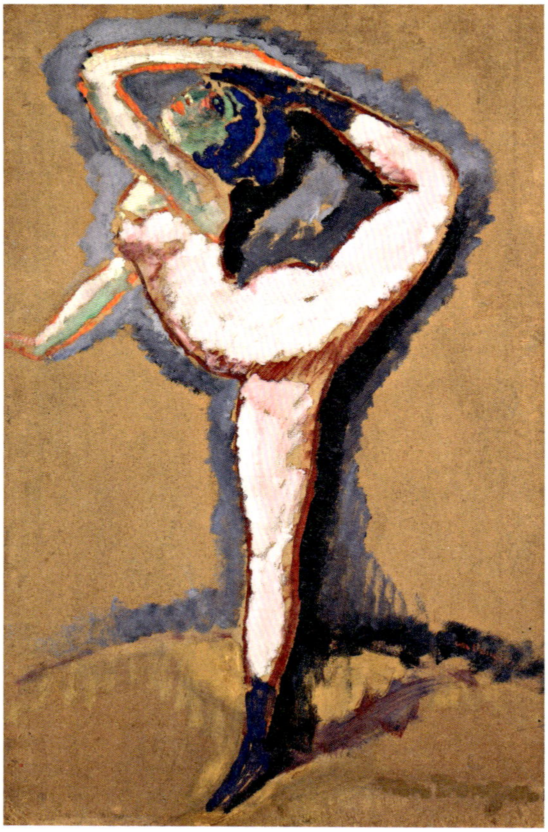

FIG.15
Kees van Dongen
L'Acrobate, *c.*1909–10
Oil on board laid on panel, 79 x 52 cm
Private collection

FIG.16
Auguste Rodin
Female nude holding her leg behind her head, c.1903–05
Pencil and watercolour on paper, 362 x 250 mm
Musée Rodin, Paris, D.4405

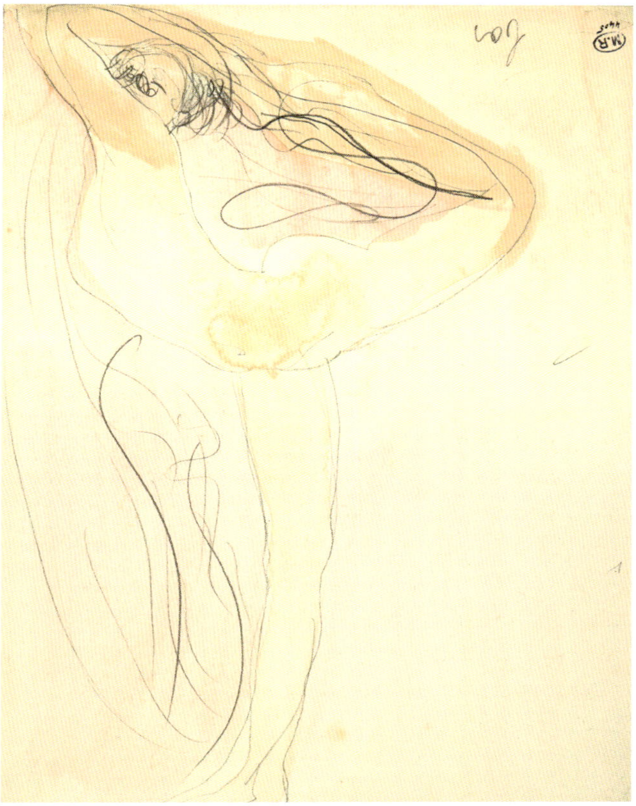

It was only in the summer of 1910 that Rodin seems to have seen Moreno again, and we learn from Bigand-Kaire that a small party was thrown in Desbois's studio in honour of her reappearance: "Dear friend, What an unforgettable day it was yesterday and how happy I am that your pretty model from before, whom I thought dead, has been found! Since the day before I knew the surprise that was reserved for you but Desbois made me swear not to say anything, finally this pretty Greek body has made us all joyful with artistic lyricism and the little party finished in the studio of Rivière, who would have liked you to be among us".[33] It seems Rodin was present in Desbois's studio before the party was taken to the studio of (presumably) the Montmartre artist Henri Rivière. Desbois then wrote to Rodin to tell him not to expect Moreno to pose immediately: "Dear friend, The little model has written to me that she is still unwell. She is leaving to take the waters as she is not strong. As soon as she returns you will see her and you will be able to work from her as much as you would like."[34] A couple of months, later Desbois confirmed that she was now free to model for Rodin: "Dear friend, The little model has returned and [is] completely at your disposal. Here is her address: Madame Morenno/ 58 Rue Michel Ange (16e)".[35] Moreno had evidently left Montmartre for the 16th *arrondissement*, and thereafter remained in that vicinity.[36]

Modelling sessions resumed some time towards the end of 1910, which coincided, apparently, with a new style of drawing for Rodin, abandoning colour for the silvery grey of pencil with stumping, which creates the effect of more softly modelled figures. In early 1911 he was also working on making the *Mouvements de danse*. Before turning to this phase, it is worth briefly comparing a group of drawings Rodin made with the photograph of Moreno in *Le nu académique* of 1905 (fig.11).

The pose Moreno displays in the photograph is almost exactly that of a delicate watercolour dedicated to his American patron Kate Simpson and dated 11 October 1905 (see fig.46, p.106). The watercolour is one of a group of over a dozen drawings of this pose (see, for example, fig.16 and cat.25–29). That all these drawings show a figure so close in proportion and in detail to the photograph of Moreno suggests that Rodin had fully developed the composition while she was still present in the studio. There is another group, comprising about a dozen drawings, showing a figure in a tripod position, another pose that seems equally to have fascinated him (see, for example, fig.17 and cat.39–41). Of all Rodin's late drawings, these two poses bear the closest relationship to the *Mouvements de danse*, notably *Mouvement A* (cat.47) and *Mouvement C* (cat.54). Interestingly, neither of the

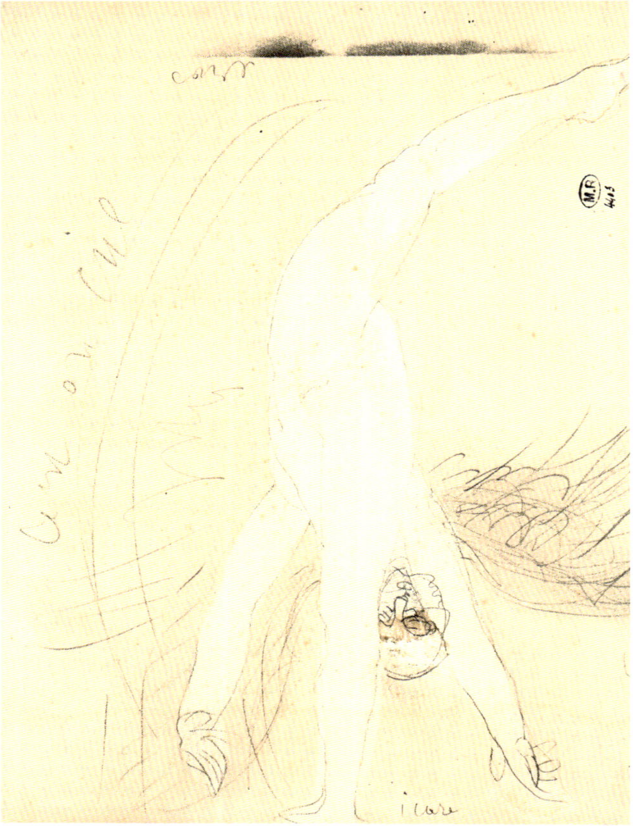

FIG.17
Auguste Rodin
Female nude in a tripod position,
*(Arc en ciel), c.*1900–05
Pencil with stumping and gouache
on paper, 329 x 245 mm
Inscribed *arc en ciel* (rainbow),
icare (Icarus) and *eros*
Musée Rodin, Paris, D.4403

two poses appears in the later group of stumped pencil drawings thought to be after Moreno (dated *c.*1910–13), which strongly suggests that Rodin had worked out the particularities of these two positions, at least on paper, before he lost sight of his model and that he only returned to them to make his little sculptural figures five or six years later. However, there is another possibility – that the pair of modelled clay figures mentioned earlier were in fact made at roughly the same time as these drawings, and that work on them was cut short by the disappearance of his model. The standing figure, *Alpha*, and the drawings of that pose are strikingly similar, particularly as both the drawings and the sculpture, which has only one arm, really only function as profile views. *Beta*, a figure lunging forward, is more loosely connected to the tripod drawings in so far as it shows one of the actions on the way to the tripod position represented in those drawings.[37]

In late 1910, Moreno seems to have resumed modelling sessions with Rodin. Her name thereafter appears relatively regularly in the diaries, showing appointments in 1911 on 24 February, 15 March, 15 and 17 June, and then not until November (on three occasions) and December (on five occasions). Between January and May 1912 there were apparently 14 visits (two in January, six in March, four in April, one in May), followed by one in December.[38] Sessions seem to have carried on through to late 1913, but Moreno, who seems to have been prone to cancelling anyway (often apologising for a variety of small mishaps, such as having twisted her foot or forgetting an appointment) was evidently suffering from what appears to have been a low-grade, then chronic appendicitis.[39] She had an appendectomy in early 1914, which was followed by post-operative complications lasting some months and again disabling her from posing.[40] If she ever modelled for Rodin again after this, there is no record of it, although he wrote her a couple of letters in which he expressed the hope that they would resume their work together one day (discussed below).

Few people seem to have seen the sculptural series during Rodin's lifetime. The first mention we have of them is dated 27 May 1911, by the Irish-German diarist Count Harry Kessler, who is the only person to have left a precise account of the works and of Rodin's ideas about them. Kessler described having seen "an entire glass case full of small figures which he had started after an acrobat". According to Kessler, they were a development from his drawings after this same acrobat, and had to do with the theme of the creation of woman.[41] Rodin told him that he had been lately unable to work on his figures because his model was ill. From about mid March to 7 May 1911 she was also, it seems, busy rehearsing a pantomime-ballet at the Théâtre de la Gaîté-Lyrique (better known under name of its managing theatre, the Opéra Comique), but perhaps her participation as a dancer in a ballet, in a boulevard theatre, was not something Rodin wished to convey about his model, considering that he later protested when Kessler said that his figures showed an acrobat (see below).

Female acrobats inspired an ambivalent reception in *fin-de-siècle* literary and artistic Paris, appearing often in the works of writers and novelists from Flaubert and Balzac to Théophile Gautier, Félicien Champsaur and Edmond de Goncourt, and with a rather nastier streak in the writings of Jean Lorrain and Alphonse Daudet. Many of the novels of the *fin de siècle* featured protagonists who were infatuated with the sexually provocative dancers of Montmartre and with the '*monde du cirque*' (the circus world), in particular acrobats, whose extraordinary power and man-like strength fascinated and repulsed in equal measure.[42] The trapeze or high-wire performer, nicknamed a *sylphide*, drew perhaps more admiration than disdain but it was not unmixed admiration and much of the thrill of watching them rested on the inherent danger of their performance: "nothing is airier, lighter or of a more graceful peril", wrote Lorrain.[43] A more poignant image is conjured in Rilke's *Fifth Elegy* from his long poem, *The Duino Elegies* (1923), on the tragic futility of acrobats' unnatural poses and death-defying leaps in the air.[44] Rodin betrayed his own ambivalent attitude towards the genre when he told Kessler that his figures did not represent an acrobat, and that if they did, "you would see it at once, it would be different".[45] It is interesting that, while we know Rodin sought models with athletic and acrobatic abilities, only Moreno and one other woman (an acrobat called Marie Dion who solicited him for modelling work and may have posed for him in 1906) are in fact identified as acrobats in his register of models.[46]

The ballet Moreno danced in was a new piece called *Le Cœur de Floria*, which premiered on 7 May 1911 at la Gaîté-Lyrique (following a performance of *La Dame Blanche*). It was described in the newspaper *Comœdia* as "*un ballet pantomime à grand spectacle*" and included a cast of at least eleven named performers and the whole of the corps de ballet. Set in medieval Florence and featuring a love triangle with at its heart a statuette of a dancer, the ballet was choreographed by Madame Mariquita, written and produced by André de Lorde, with Georges Ménier as composer. Moreno is mentioned, in one short note in *Comœdia*, on 19 May 1911: "*Dance now* .... A smile on her lips ... lively and graceful, she went to rue de Varennes [sic; Rodin's studio] .... She posed in front of the great sculptor who is M. Rodin. The charming Mlle Moréno was the model for numerous works, and her harmonious lines were reproduced often in little statuettes. Today, Mlle Moréno is one of the sweet interpreters of the *Cœur de Floria*; supple and playful, the little model is made for being a graceful dancer."[47]

Other than this one mention, Moreno's name does not appear in any of the reviews of the ballet in *Comœdia*, which is not surprising given how small a role she would have had. That her name is not in the archives of the Opéra Comique, however, makes one wonder if her appointment was not the result of a casual personal arrangement (perhaps with another dancer), and that is why it was not recorded in the books.[48] In any case, the crossover from music-hall acrobatics to ballet was an easy one and there was a great deal of overlap in these years. This was especially true for the Opéra Comique, the Théâtre de la Gaîté-Lyrique and the Folies-Bergère, which were all three owned by the Isola Brothers and shared the accomplished choreographer Madame Mariquita as their ballet mistress. Under Mariquita it was common for dancers to move back and forth between these venues.[49]

Returning to Rodin's studio, we can now put forth a proposed date for the making of the *Mouvements de danse*. This is based on a note he wrote to his mould-maker Eugène Guioché on 17 March 1911, which may refer to the process of making press-moulds of the body parts that the sculptor would assemble together to create the *Mouvements de danse* figures: "My dear Guioché, Could you please make me about ten heads, no matter which, to go with the figurines you are press-moulding".[50] As has been recently noted, it is characteristic of Rodin in his late years that he readily delegated minor aesthetic decisions, such as the choice of a head, to one of his trusted technical assistants, as this would save him time for other activities.[51] Guioché chose the so-called *Tête de la femme slave*, developed by Rodin twenty years earlier. That head had already been used for Rodin's sculptural figures combined with ancient ceramics of around 1900–05 (fig.3, p.15), and one can only speculate that Guioché chose it perhaps because a mould of the right size existed already.

It seems plausible that this note refers to the *Mouvements de danse* (even if Rodin speaks of "little figures" rather than of body parts or *abattis*), considering that Moreno had just returned to the studio and could therefore have provided Rodin with the modelling sessions he needed to reactivate his project. If Guioché was press-moulding the parts in mid March, then to do the whole group (of about 75 pieces) could have taken a few days or at most a week. Once the parts were ready, Rodin could not have waited long to begin assembling them, as otherwise they would have dried out, and, likewise, he could not have spent too long on making them, perhaps a couple of weeks at the most. This would mean that by early April he could have finished with this part of his research into the *Mouvements de danse*. Some of the late drawings in pencil with stumping relate closely to the sculptural figures, such as the drawing of a huddled figure (D.1859, cat.68) with elongated limbs stretching over the body in a position that seems to echo that of the terracotta of a huddled figure (S.3845, cat.67), or the drawing of a stretching (or lunging) figure (D.1837, cat.37) whose angular shoulders and forward-leaning torso are strikingly close to a headless figure in a similar position (S.5491, cat.61). If Rodin assembled his figures in one go (which seems likely, since Kessler mentioned having seen a vitrine full of figures in late May), then the modelling sessions with Moreno after this date, and there were many, need not relate to the making of the *Mouvements de danse* directly, but rather, indirectly, to the development of his ideas from his initial clay assemblages, taking them in another direction.

In an undated letter thought to be of about 1916, Rodin addressed Moreno as "*petite victoire adorable*": "little adorable victory/ be patient, you have my artist's heart, you need to make masterpieces with me. We must. Take care of yourself."[52] An original term of affection, 'victory' recalled the winged statues of antiquity for which he had a particular fondness, as well as his transformation of a number of his drawings of Cambodian dancers into "*quelque Victoire, inconnue et toujours nouvelle*" (some Victory, unknown and always new) several years earlier.[53] But above all Rodin's use of this expression for Moreno seems to relate quite clearly to a plan we now know he had with respect to the main figure of the series, *Mouvement A*, which, at some point, he decided to develop into a monument to aviation or aviators. The monument was never executed but what must be the maquette for it is known today as *Pas de deux ailé A sur colonne* (*Winged Pas de*

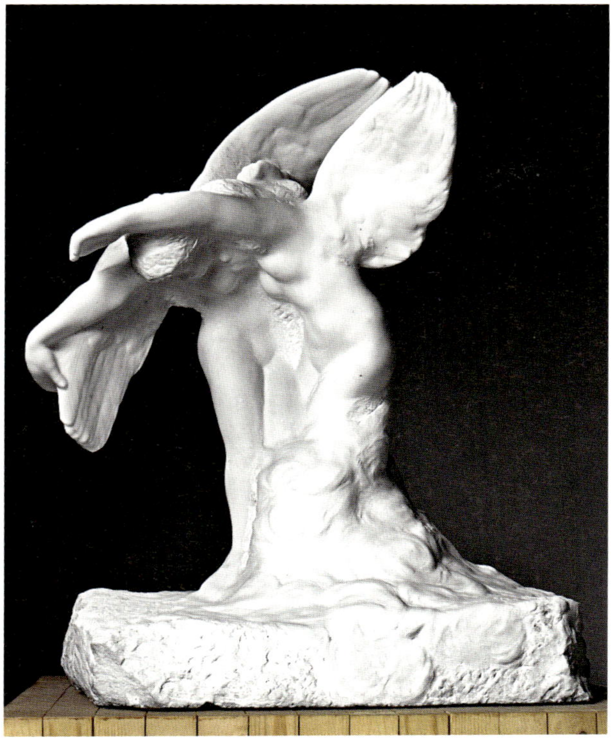

FIG.18
Auguste Rodin,
Bénédictions, before 1894 (the small model) to 1911 or later (this marble)
Marble, carved by Victor Peter,
80 x 75.5 x 66.5 cm
Musée Rodin, Paris, S.428

Deux A on a Column).[54] Had it materialised, the monument would have been in support of the military aeronautical industry and would have expressed the nationalistic and revanchist values that Rodin fully embraced towards the end of his life.[55]

Les victoires (The victories) was also one of the three subtitles Rodin gave his marble group *Les Bénédictions*, the others being *L'Envolée* (Flight) and *Les gloires* (The glories). Although the work was started many years earlier, the carving of two of the marble versions was probably still in progress around 1912–13 (fig.18). The connection with flight was obvious from the subject matter – two winged female nudes gently touching down to land like a pair of birds, to paraphrase a critic's contemporary description[56] – and, by 1910, Rodin had decided to give it a modern meaning as a reference to the hazards and glories of aviation. In January 1911 Rodin told *Paris-Journal* of his admiration for pilots and of his wish, which he said was sadly ignored, "to build a monument to these sublime martyrs. I had a project: the Benedictions that come from the sky. Erect [them] on the tomb of the modern Icaruses!"[57] In a brief note in the newspaper *L'Homme Libre*, of 7 May 1913, a journalist reported that Rodin had called his sculpture "*mon biplan*", in reference to the biplanes popular in aeronautics in the first decade of the twentieth century.[58] It is interesting to note, in connection with the idea of a planned monument to aviation/ aviators, that Rodin re-used the wings from his *Bénédictions* for his *Pas de deux ailé* A, seen in a photograph of Rodin at the Hôtel Biron of about 1913 or 1914 (fig.19).

Developments in aviation captured the popular imagination in the years 1900 to 1914. Artists, dancers and performers, high, low, avant-garde or mainstream – all were captivated by flight, from Valentine de Saint-Point writing a poem on Nijinsky which referenced aeronautics to music-hall ballets bearing titles such as 'L'Aéroplane' or 'Les Ailes'.[59] Press coverage from about 1912 insisted on the military aspect of progress in aviation in the context of the preparations for war with Germany, and Rodin was in sympathy with these ideas.[60] A couple of accounts of visits to Rodin's studio, one by the avant-garde theorist Ricciotto Canudo in 1913, and another by the art critic and writer Michel Georges-Michel, undated but probably around the same time, relate the sculptor's enthusiasm for both the technical and patriotic aspects of aviation.[61] Rodin told Georges-Michel that he admired aviators because they were like artists, crafting their "birds" in the way sculptors carved their marble. He mentioned that he often had lunch with aviators and finished by inviting his guest to see his "biplane".[62] From his description, one guesses that he may have shown him both *Les Bénédictions* and *Pas de deux ailé A sur colonne*, and that the journalist (and possibly Rodin) mixed up the two. One is downward-facing, and landing (or crashing); one is upward-facing (and lifting off), the latter corresponding to Georges-Michel's account of the foot barely touching the sphere (the egg).

Flight had troubled and fascinated Rodin for years,[63] and, implicitly at least, seems to have been present in Rodin's research into acrobatic postures from the start. One example of this is the drawing of a figure in a tripod

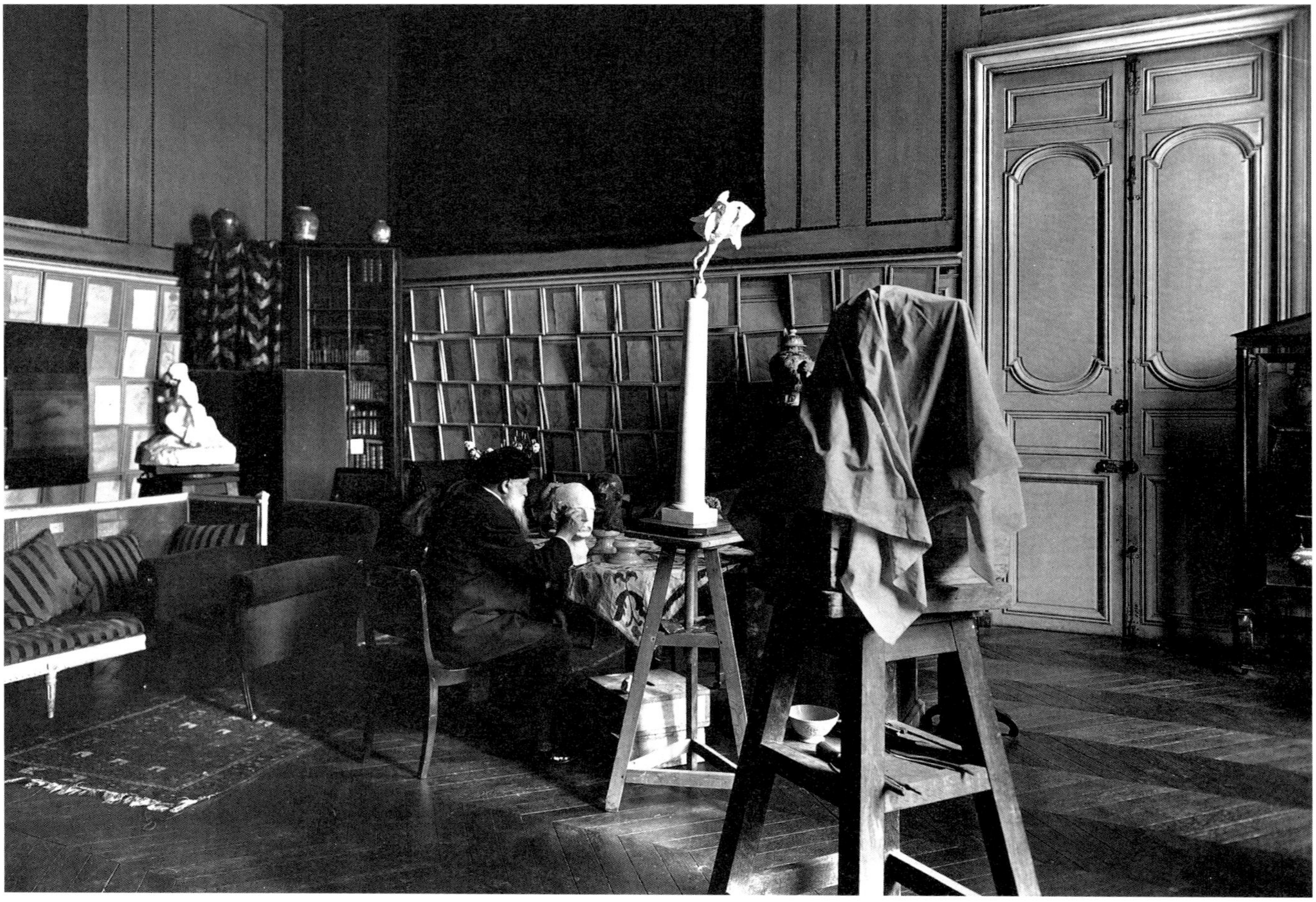

FIG.19
Rodin at the Hôtel Biron, Paris, with the *Pas de deux ailé A sur colonne*, in the foreground, *c.*1913–14
Musée Rodin, Paris, PH.10371

position which has wings and bears the inscription Icarus (see fig.17). The inscription on another drawing (cat.53) showing a figure holding a pose virtually identical to one of his *Mouvements de danse* (E, cat.51 & 52) is much more contemporary in its evocation of flight, illustrating a turn towards a more optimistic and less complex interest in the theme of flight through the filter of the mechanics of aviation. The drawing has three separate inscriptions, *aviation*, *souveraine équilibre* (sovereign equilibrium) and *emblème de puissance* (emblem of power), which, together with the pose, show that in this drawing flight was associated with stability. It may be interesting to note that the inscription seems to echo the contents of a letter Rodin received from an aviator based nearby in Meudon, in early 1911, in which he explained the principle of aviation in terms of "positive stability".[64] Another drawing, bearing the annotation *aéroplane* on its verso, shows a seated figure with long lateral arms at the top (D.3021), and Rodin exhibited a drawing entitled *Aéroplane* in 1910.[65]

Working on the *Mouvements de danse* gave Rodin the opportunity to explore an astonishing range of postures without being tied down to a commission, and, as he often did, to overlay a variety of themes on to the work as they came to him. Like much of the small-scale work produced in his late years, it was highly experimental and open-ended, and in this case, since Moreno could no longer provide the attitudes, postures and movements required, the project seems to have remained unfinished.

NOTES

1 A. Rodin, *Art. Interviews with Paul Gsell* (Rodin 1911), trans. de Caso and Saunders, Berkeley (University of California Press), 1984, 'Movement in Art', pp.27–39, at p.33. See also Rodin's expression of the same idea in Henri Dujardin-Beaumetz, *Entretiens avec Rodin*, Paris, 1913, in Augustin de Butler, ed., *Éclairs de pensée. Écrits et entretiens de Rodin*, Paris, Éditions du Sandre, 2008, pp.97–190, at p.113.

2 As noted in the technical study in this volume, there is no documentation recording the actual making of the *Mouvements de danse*, so the proposed chronology relies on the interpretation of often indirectly relevant archival sources and on current knowledge of Rodin's studio practices. For the latter, I am particularly grateful to François Blanchetière for sharing his unmatched knowledge of Rodin's sculptural practices with me over the course of the research into this exhibition. I would also like to thank Agnès Cascio and Juliette Lévy for discussing these aspects with me on several occasions, and providing insights on the material properties of Rodin's clay and plaster works, and thanks are also due to Dominique Brisset of the Musée Rodin for sharing her expert knowledge on Rodin's casting processes. I am grateful to Sophie Biass-Fabiani for facilitating and encouraging my repeated visits to the Musée Rodin to study Rodin's late drawings of dancers and for sharing her knowledge of Rodin's graphic practice.

3 Over a period of 16 months a series of encounters with actor movement practitioners generated physical and observational investigations of the sculptures and drawings. Vanessa Ewan and Ayse Tashkiran (co-course leaders of the MA/MFA Movement), and graduates Ana Marambio and Rachel Nouchi are trained in a collective movement background that includes Laban, contemporary dance, ballet, yoga, social dance and Lecoq practices. Our collaboration has involved investigating movement heritage, fragmentation of body parts and postures represented in this exhibition. In its pilot phase, the International Centre for Movement was founded by course leaders of the MA/MFA Movement: Directing and Teaching at Royal Central School of Speech and Drama, London.

4 See for instance, Cécile Goldscheider, exh. cat. *Rodin inconnu*, Paris, Musée du Louvre, December 1962 – January 1963, in which some of the *Mouvements de danse* are described as "exercises": for balance (C), for a particular posture (G), or for warming up the thighs to make them more pliable, known as '*le brisement des cuisses*' (B); Antoinette Le Normand-Romain, 'Un nouveau Mouvement de danse de Rodin (1840–1917)', in *La Revue du Louvre et des musées de France*, 1996, no.4, pp.59–62, at p.59; and Raphael Masson and Véronique Mattiussi, *Rodin*, Paris, Flammarion, 2004, p.177.

5 In the earliest catalogues of the Musée Rodin, covering 1919 to 1931, the terracotta figures are identified as '*Études de mouvements*' (with the subtitle '*d'après une figure de danseuse*' and, from 1922, '*d'après une danseuse*'). From 1926 three of the figures are illustrated, with a synopsis on their genesis in 1911 whilst Rodin was working on "*une foule de croquis relatifs à des études de mouvements, d'après une artiste en chorégraphie, aux fins de créer des figures volantes, ou encore des attitudes de danse*" (1926, p.135, and repeated in subsequent catalogues). In 1938, they become '*Études de mouvements de danse*' and then '*Mouvements de danse*' in 1944. Bronze casting began in 1946.

6 It was noted that during the workshops, as the researchers entered Rodin's *Mouvements de danse* postures, they frequently, and inadvertently, reproduced postures which Rodin had also drawn but which had not been the subject of the study.

7 This is discussed in detail in the catalogue entries for each of the *Mouvements*.

8 I am grateful to Chloe Le Tissier for discussing the practice of life drawing with me, and for adding that dimension to the movement research workshops.

9 Albert Elsen, in exh. cat. *Rodin Rediscovered*, National Gallery of Art, Washington, D.C., 1981, p.137. Although referring specifically to dip casting in plaster, the notion explains many areas of Rodin's studio practice, including re-orientations and inversions, which Elsen went on to discuss on the same page.

10 Myriam Peignist, 'Histoire Anthropologique des Danses Acrobatiques', *Corps*, vol.2, no.7, 2009, pp.29–38, at p.30.

11 See Peignist 2009 for an anthropological perspective on acrobatics at the turn of the nineteenth century, which she interprets as a challenge to conventional norms about the body and the social order and above all as a space for exploration of the erotic at its most raunchy. See Jean Starobinski, *Portrait de l'artiste en saltimbanque*, Geneva (Albert Skira), 1970, especially pp.57–81, for the acrobat's erotic appeal and the dark underside of the fascination with acrobatics.

12 See Agathe Dumont, 'Interprètes au travail: danseurs et acrobats, de l'indiscipline à la désobéissance', in *memento* (published by HorsLesMurs – Centre national de ressources des arts de la rue et des arts du cirque), no.3, October 2011, pp.2–9, especially pp.5–7 for a discussion of balancing poses.

13 "*Tout le monde sait que le corps humain, dans le mouvement, porte à faux et que l'équilibre se rétablit par des compensations. La jambe qui porte, rentrant sous le corps, est seule le pivot du corps entier et fait seule, en cet instant, l'unique et total effort. La jambe qui ne porte pas sert seulement à moduler les degrès de la station, à la modifier, soit lentement, soit rapidement s'il le faut, jusqu'à ce qu'elle se soit substituée, pour la libérer, à la jambe qui portait*": Auguste Rodin, *Les Cathédrales de France*, with an introduction by Charles Morice, Paris (A. Colin), 1914, p.1. This idea had already been expressed, with slightly different wording, in Auguste Rodin, 'Pour faire aimer les cathédrales', *Le Matin*, 1901, p.1, reproduced in J. Paul Morel, ed., *Faire avec ses mains ce que l'on voit*, Paris (Éditions Mille et une nuits), 2011, pp.106–09, at p.107.

14 Rodin to Truman Howe Bartlett, *The American Architect and Building News*, vol.XXV, 1 June 1889, all instalments published in full in Nathalie Bondil and Sophie Biass-Fabiani, edd., exh. cat. *Metamorphoses. In Rodin's Studio*, Museum of Fine Arts, Montreal, 2015, pp.218–54, p.249. On collaboration with models see Catherine Lampert, *Rodin: Sculpture and Drawings*, London (Arts Council of Great Britain), 1987, p.82. Generally on Rodin's relationship with models see Hélène Pinet, 'Comédie ou Lever de Rideau. Rodin et ses modèles', in D. Viéville, ed., exh. cat. *Figures d'Éros, dessins et aquarelles 1890–1917*, Musée Rodin, Paris, 2006, pp.12–29. Still the key text for Rodin's conception of female sexuality, including his relationship with models, is Anne M. Wagner, 'Rodin's Reputation', in Lynn Hunt, ed., *Eroticism and the Body Politic*, Baltimore (Johns Hopkins University Press), 1993, pp.191–242.

15 See Le Normand-Romain's essay in this volume.

16 See the inscription on Louis Gillet's drawing copying Rodin's sketches of poses taken by Moreno, D.2298 (in this volume, fig.7).

17 To add to the confusion Rodin had another model, Suzanne Demars, known as 'Suzanne Morenna'. All the letters from Moreno to Rodin referred to in this essay are in the archives of the Musée Rodin, in Moreno's 'dossier scripteur' (MOR 4504). Many of her letters to him are undated, though they have tentative dates ascribed to them. On Moreno, the best documented sources are Antoinette Le Normand-Romain, *The Bronzes of Rodin*, Paris (Éditions du musée Rodin and RMN), 2007, pp.540–43, and Christina Buley-Uribe, *Mes Sœurs Divines. 99 Femmes de l'Entourage de Rodin*, Paris (Éditions du relief), 2013, pp.280–82. An early note of Moreno, which, although inaccurate in detail, is interesting for its ring of truth in the general description, was written by someone who knew the sculptor: "Rodin had a certain degree of affection for some of his models, especially for one young woman; she was the wife of a talented artist, and posed only for Rodin and Desbois. He heard one day that she had undergone an operation for appendicitis; he was loud in lamentation. 'Those doctors are butchers,' he declared …. 'What do you call her disease?' 'Appendicitis, Maître.' 'Ah yes, appendicitis. They've opened up that young body which they ought to be worshipping, to take out a bit of gut. It makes me sick to think of it!': Marcelle Tirel, *The Last Years of Rodin*, trans. R. Francis, London (A.M. Philpot), 1925, pp.74–75. See p.32 in this volume.

18 I am very grateful to Sophie Weygand, the founding curator of the Musée Jules Desbois in Parçay-les-Pins near Angers, for her generosity in sharing the information she was able to gather about Moreno, including the record of an interview of 2011 with a neighbour of Moreno's in Paris in the post-war years.

19 At the top of the pyramid were: "*Les artistes indépendents qui s'exhibent sur la scène des music-halls ou dans les grands cirques à demeure des capitales*": George Strehly, *L'Acrobatie et les acrobates. Textes et dessins*, Paris (Librairie Ch. Delagrave), [1904], p.47. Strehly noted that in the last twenty years acrobatics had "migrated" from circus to theatre, with the latter, in the form of the music-hall, becoming the preferred venue for acrobats, and attributed the change to the fact that music-halls were able to pay performers more: see pp.53–54.

20 Ibid., pp.56–57.

21 For example Desbois asked Rodin for the addresses of models, and vice versa; most notably, the same model posed for Rodin's *Celle qui fut la belle heaulmière* as for Desbois's *La Misère*; similarly Rodin asked his then assistant Antoine Bourdelle for the name of one of his models. See Hélène Pinet, in exh. cat. *Rodin et ses modèles. Le portrait photographié*, Musée Rodin, Paris, 1990, at p.16.

22 Moreno, who at some point became Desbois's companion, is identified as his "*légataire universelle*" in the papers relating to payments for state commissions in 1936, Arch. Nat. F 21 6786, cited in V. Wiesinger, 'Desbois et Rodin' (mémoire de maîtrise Paris IV, Sorbonne, 1983). Moreno shared the inheritance of Desbois's studio with a collector called Eugène Laporte, and together they made gifts of his sculpture to three museums in his native Anjou and the neighbouring Loire Valley. She also was involved in commissioning a bust of Desbois for his home town of Parçay-les-Pins in 1950. I would like to thank Claire Bray of the Musée des Beaux-Arts in Tours and Jacqueline Mongellaz of the Château-Musée of Saumur.

23 Moreno does not figure in the diary for 1902, which could suggest 1903 was indeed the first year she posed for Rodin. No diary survives for 1903.

24 The letter is dated before 4 October 1905 (the date of Rodin's response); transcribed in full as letter 127 in exh. cat. *A notre ami Bigand, Rodin, Redon et Moreau*, Musée Ziem, Martigues, 1992. I am grateful to Sophie Biass-Fabiani for alerting me to the importance of Bigand-Kaire in the context of Moreno and Desbois, with whom he was evidently close, as the dedication on a plaster statuette of Desbois's *L'Arc*, which Bigand-Kaire owned (now in the Musée Ziem in Martigues) reads *à toi mon vieux Bigand*. As equals, these people were much more familiar with each other than any of the three could be with Rodin. A couple of letters on the market recently (at http://www.delcampe.net) attest to this familiarity.

25 Alain Beausire and Florence Cadouot, edd., *Correspondance de Rodin*, 1860–1917, Paris (Musée Rodin), 4 vols., 1985–92, vol.2, p.167, quoted in Martigues 1992 after letter 127.

26 It may be worth noting that, although she is referred to as an acrobat in these letters, only her modelling is discussed, not her work as an acrobat.

27 Undated letter (the proposed date is late November/early December 1905), in Martigues 1992 as letter 130. Perhaps this is the Labole from whom she is known to have been divorced.

28 Published by the Nouvelle librairie artistique at 7 and 9 rue de la Boétie; letter 128 in Martigues 1992.

29 Arthur Symons, 'Dancers and Dancing', in *The Lotus Magazine*, vol.8, no.7, April 1917, pp.314–18, gives the French names and English translations for many poses in an article in which he described attending a training session for students of the music-hall star Nini Patte-en-l'Air in Paris in 1892. Somewhat confusingly, the term '*le port d'armes*' is often used to describe the position that Symons described as '*la jambe derrière la tête*' (see, for example, the image of a dancer in that position, from a programme of the Folies-Bergère of 1929, reproduced in Peignist 2009, p.35). Symons defined '*le port d'armes*' as a held high kick, "in which the leg is held upright, one hand clasping the heel of the boot – a position of great difficulty". Symons's article is briefly discussed in Anna Gruetzner-Robins, '"J'arrive de London": Jane Avril and Britain', in exh. cat. *Toulouse-Lautrec and Jane Avril. Beyond the Moulin Rouge*, The Courtauld Gallery, London, 2011, pp.27–41, at p.31.

30 Rodin's letter of 28 December 1905, in response to Bigand-Kaire's letter of 25 December, in Martigues 1992, after letter 132: "*Mon cher ami Merci mille fois pour votre amabilité: votre colis est arrivé en excellent état. – L'animal encore vivant a effrayé tout le monde. – Pour ce qui est du modèle, je vous remercie du renseignement, j'en prends note et peut-être d'ici quelque temps le retrouverons-nous.*"

31 Arthur Symons, quoted in Jane Pritchard, '"More Natural than Nature, More Artificial than Art": the Dance Criticism of Arthur Symons', *Dance Research: The Journal of the Society for Dance Research*, vol.21, no.2, winter 2003, pp.36–89, p.65. Rodin's contemporaries often used the term 'arabesque' to describe his late drawings of dancers. For example, see Harry Kessler's journal entry of 1912, quoted on p.13 of this volume.

32 "*Le meilleur cirque de Paris*": Strehly [1904], p.55. The comparison with *L'Acrobate* was made in Le Normand Romain 2007, p.540.

33 Letter 159 in Martigues 1992.

34 Desbois to Rodin, letter dated 27 July 1910, post-stamped 28 July, Archives of the Musée Rodin. In 1914, Rodin's mould-maker Eugène Guioché wrote to inform him that Moreno's address was 58 rue Michelange, as he had found out having just been to Desbois's studio. He was apparently unaware that the sculptor had found his model several years before. Guioché's correspondence file in the archives of the Musée Rodin. I would like to thank Antoinette Le Normand-Romain for passing this detail on to me.

35 Desbois to Rodin, 24 September 1910, Archives of the Musée Rodin.

36 Moreno seems to have remained at the same address for many years; a letter probably of late 1913 was written on headed paper with the address 2, Hameau Boileau, and after World War II she is known to have lived on Boulevard Exelmans, also in the 16ème *arrondissement*.

37 *Alpha* and *Beta* were assembled together with plaster slip at some point; it is not known when Rodin did this but there is no reason why it could not have been done years later.

38 24 February 1911; 15 March 1911; 15 July 1911; 17 July 1911; 7 November 1911; 25 November 1911; 30 November 1911; 5 December 1911; 9 December 1911; 14 December 1911; 21 December 1911; 26 December 1911 (?); 2 January 1912 with a model called Yvonne d'Ars; 4 January 1912; 11 March 1912; 12 March 1912 at the Panthéon (perhaps to see *The Thinker* installed in 1906?); 15 March 1912 (?); 19 March 1912; 22 March 1912; 28 March 1912; 19 April 1912; 24 April 1912; 26 April 1912; 27 April 1912; 23 (or 24) May 1912; 6 December 1912.

39 On 3 December 1913 she wrote to say that her health was becoming more and more precarious and that she could no longer travel by automobile: discomfort in seated positions is consistent with appendicitis.

40 The surgeon who operated on Moreno wrote up the operation in *Bruxelles-Médical, Revue hebdomadaire des sciences médicales et chirurgicales*, no.23, 7 April 1940, a cutting of which is in the archives of the Musée Rodin. Mindful of not leaving a large scar on her stomach considering that she was Rodin's model, he described how he used a novel positioning technique, initially developed for greater diagnostic accuracy, which enabled him to get a better cosmetic result by a smaller incision. Modern medicine relies on radiology for diagnostic accuracy. I am grateful to Dr Olivia Geraghty for explaining his technique to me.

41 This is discussed in detail in Le Normand-Romain's essay in this volume, which quotes in full Kessler's diary entries relating to these visits to Rodin (above, p.13).

42 See Linda Wolk Simon, *Mis La La at the Cirque Fernando*, New York (Morgan Library and Museum), 2013, especially Nancy Ireson, 'New Arenas: Degas's Legacy at the Cirque Fernando', pp.23–38, in that volume. This vast literature is analysed in Guy Ducrey, *Corps et graphies. Poétique de la danse et de la danseuse à la fin du XIXe siècle*, Paris (Champion), 1996. Rodin was evidently not alien to this kind of writing, since one of the books in this genre, Félicien Champsaur's *L'Amant des danseuses* (1888), was in fact dedicated to him. I am grateful to Aline Magnien for this suggestion. See also N.A. Haxell, 'Ces dames du cirque', *Modern Language Notes*, no.4, September 2000, pp.783–800. See also Starobinski 1970, especially pp.43–55 and 102–03.

43 "*… rien n'est plus aérien, plus léger, et d'un péril plus gracieux*", quoted in Haxell 2000, p.793. Jean Lorrain was discussing the dangerous pleasure

of watching the trapeze artist – "woman's eternal weakness and woman's eternal suffering, exploited", from 'L'Acrobate', *L'Écho de Paris*, 15 December 1890, quoted in Haxell 2000, p.792. See also Starobinski 1970, pp.27–41, on the attractions of the acrobat, especially the aerial displays.

44 The Fifth Elegy was dedicated to his friend Hertha Koenig, who owned Picasso's *Family of Saltimbanques* (1905; National Gallery, Washington, D.C.). I would like to thank my colleague Rachel Sloan for bringing Rilke's poem to my attention.

45 Kessler's diary (Kessler 2004), 27 May and 1 July 1911.

46 Marie Dion, identified in a note of 1906 in the archives of the Musée Rodin as "Modèle femme acrobate", wrote a couple of letters asking Rodin for modelling work (this was not in itself unusual); "*je suis très souple je suis une acrobate*". She was apparently recommended by Baron Joseph Vitta, a patron and friend of Rodin's and she mentioned having come to see Rodin (but does not seem to have posed?) in November 1905: Musée Rodin archives.

47 *Comœdia*, 19 May 1911: "*Dansez maintenant .... Le sourire aux lèvres ... vive et gracieuse, elle se rendait rue de Varennes* [sic] *.... Elle posait devant le grand sculpteur qu'est M. Rodin. La charmante Mlle Moréno a servi de modèle à de nombreuses œuvres, et ses lignes harmonieuses ont été reproduites souvent dans de petites statuettes. Aujourd'hui, Mlle Moréno est une des gentilles interprètes du* Cœur de Floria*; souple et enjoué, le petit modèle était tout désigné pour faire une gracieuse danseuse*"; clipping in the Musée Rodin. Somewhat confusingly, Marguerite Moreno (who would later become a distinguished actress at the Comédie Française) played the role of the cat. According to a descendant of Marguerite Moreno's, the two women were not related. I would like to thank Claudette Joannis for finding this out for me. Alda Moreno was rehearsing from at least mid-March and explained to Rodin that the rehearsals were taking place every morning and that for that reason she could now only work on Sundays.

48 She should appear in one of the *registres d'appointement du personnel* (personnel registers) of the Opéra Comique at the Archives Nationales: AJ/13/1598 (1910–11) or AJ/13/1599 (1911–12).

49 On the porous relationship between music hall and ballet during these years, see Gutsche-Miller 2015, and specifically pp.72–73 on Madame Mariquita.

50 "*Mon cher Guioché, Pourriez-vous me faire, je vous prie, une dizaine de têtes, n'importe lesquelles qui aillent avec les figurines que vous estampez.*" It may be a coincidence but there are in fact only ten heads for the 13 figures in the *Mouvements de danse*. This letter is cited in François Blanchetière, 'Mouler, tirer, modifier, mouler à nouveau. Rodin et le moulage', *In Situ*, no.28, 2016: 'Le moulage. Pratiques historiques et regards contemporains': https://insitu.revues.org/12743.

51 Blanchetière 2016.

52 *Correspondance de Rodin* 1986, vol.4, letter 228. The full letter reads: "*petite victoire adorable/ prend patience, tu as mon cœur d'artiste, tu dois faire avec moi des chef-d'œuvre. il le faut Soustient toi./ A Rodin/ Je suis pourtant malade.*" In another slightly more formal letter (227), also tentatively dated 1916, Rodin expresses a similar desire to continue to work together: "*Mademoiselle Moréno/ Comment allez vous? ma grande belle, ma première belle. / Votre sculpteur va mieux et espère en votre patience. / quelle belle œuvre que je porte dans mon Cœur. / A faire avec vous Dieu nous le permettra/ Je vous embrasse affectueusement/ Rodin.*"

53 Rodin, in 'Fresques de danse' (1914), published in *Faire avec ses mains ce que l'on voit*, pp.134–37. The full sentence is: "*Lorsque j'ai voulu les dessiner, j'ai vu qu'en ajoutant à leurs mains une statuette ou une couronne, on avait l'image parfaite de quelque Victoire, inconnue et toujours nouvelle*" (When I wanted to draw them, I saw that by adding a statuette or a crown in their hands, one had the perfect image of some Victory, unknown and always new).

54 In fact there are two of these *Pas de deux ailé A sur colonne*. The genesis of the monument to aviators is discussed in the technical essay by Blanchetière, Cascio and Lévy, in this volume, pp.72–73.

55 This may be linked to Rodin's offering to the nation, as part of the National Movement in Favour of Military Aeronautics, a bronze cast of his sculpture of *La Défense*. See Guillaume Gaudet, *La Réception critique des monuments français d'Auguste Rodin*, Rennes (Presses universitaires de Rennes), 2014, pp.325–32.

56 Gustave Geoffroy, 'Rodin', *Art et décoration*, October 1900, no.10, pp.108–09, "the bénédictions are figures of women [flying] in a gentle movement of birds that are about to land": "*les bénédictions sont des figures de femmes planantes d'un doux mouvement d'oiseaux qui vont se poser*". I am grateful to Julie Davodet for this reference.

57 "*Mil Neuf Cent Dix. Ce que l'Année dernière lègue à l'Année qui vient*" (1910. What the last year has bequeathed to the coming year), in *Paris-Journal*, 1 January 1911, pp.1–2, p.2. "*Je voudrais bâtir un monument à ces martyres sublimes. J'avais un projet: les Bénédictions qui viennent du ciel. L'élever sur la tombe des Icares modernes!*" See Le Normand-Romain, 2007, vol.2, pp.199–202, and Marie-Pierre Delclaux, *Rodin : éclats de vie*, Paris, Musée Rodin, 2003, pp.55–56.

58 The newly founded newspaper *L'Homme Libre* included a brief notice on Rodin and aviation in its 'Échos' section, entitled 'Rodin et l'aéroplane' (7 May 1913). The description is unmistakably the *Bénédictions*, two marble versions of which were indeed carved in 1911 and 1912, respectively at the Musée Rodin, Paris (fig.18, p.35 in the present volume), and the Ny Carlsberg Glyptotek, Copenhagen. The author of this notice may be Georges-Michel as his account of an (undated) visit to Rodin's studio (see the quote in Blanchetière, Cascio et Lévy in this volume, pp.72–73) is very similar in detail.

59 Nijinsky performed *Le Spectre de la rose*, with Tamara Karsavina, at a Ballets Russes gala in honour of the Aéro-club de France held at the Paris Opéra on 19 December 1911, to raise money for a monument glorifying French aviation and for a fund to help families of fallen aviators. Saint-Point's poem 'Nijinski' referencing aeronautics and Nijinsky's powerful leaps, appeared on the front page of *Comœdia* soon after. See Philippe de Lustrac, 'Nijinski et ses sources : la chronophotographie, l'art assyrien et l'aviation', *Ligeia*, nos.49–52. Jan–June 2004, pp.5–27, at pp.22–24.

60 L. Robène and D. Bodin, 'Le feuilleton aéronautique à la Belle Époque', *Le Temps des médias*, vol.2, no.9, 2007, p.47, cited in Gaudet 2014, p.325.

61 "*On dirait que l'ingénuosité humaine s'est concentrée dans l'industrie. Cela a aboutit à l'étonnante, – aviation*": R. Canudo, *La revue hebdomadaire*, April 1913. Canudo was the editor of avant-garde publications and author of a manifesto on 'cerebrism', and his numerous visits to Rodin's studio (often in the company of his companion the Futurist dance theorist and choreographer Valentine de Saint-Point, who wrote an article on Rodin) are attested in Rodin's secretaries' diaries. Georges-Michel's account is very close to the notice in L'Homme Libre of 1913. See above note 58.

62 For example, Rodin's secretary's diary for 1908 records that he had lunch with Wilbur Wright on 5 November 1908. Four pilots appear as correspondents of Rodin's in the archives of the Musée Rodin, including the pioneering Brazilian-born aviator Alberto Santos Dumont (1873–1932).

63 On flight and falling, see Philippe Junod, 'Rodin et les métamorphoses d'Icare', *La Revue de l'Art*, no.96, 1992, pp.31–39.

64 In the archives of the Musée Rodin there are three letters from André Dumoulin, an aviator based in Meudon, near Rodin. This one is dated 2 January 1911. Rodin bought as an investment a future share in the development of the 'Aéroplane Dumoulin Jacquin' in December 1911. Dumoulin's company invented a 'gyroplane': *Notes sur la machine volante imaginée par André Dumoulin et construite en collaboration de Auguste Jacquin.*, Paris, n.d. [c.1911].

65 This recalls the anecdote recounted by Marcelle Tirel in her book *The Last Years of Rodin*, trans. R. Francis, preface by Judith Cladel, London (A.M. Philpot), 1925, p.102, of Rodin and his mistress the duchesse de Choiseul looking at a drawing of a figure: "... and the Muse remarked: 'One would almost say it was an aeroplane!' Rodin, delighted with the idea, exclaimed: 'Quick! Quick! Write Aéroplane on the back'". Was D.3021 the drawing shown under that title at the exhibition of Rodin's drawings at the headquarters of the Gil Blas, in 1910? Another drawing in the collection, D.4498, showing a figure holding her leg behind her head in a pose similar to fig.16 in this volume, is also traditionally known as 'aéroplane', but it is not known when this title was given to it. I am grateful to Sophie Biass- Fabiani for alerting me to Tirel's passage and for information on the drawings and inscriptions.

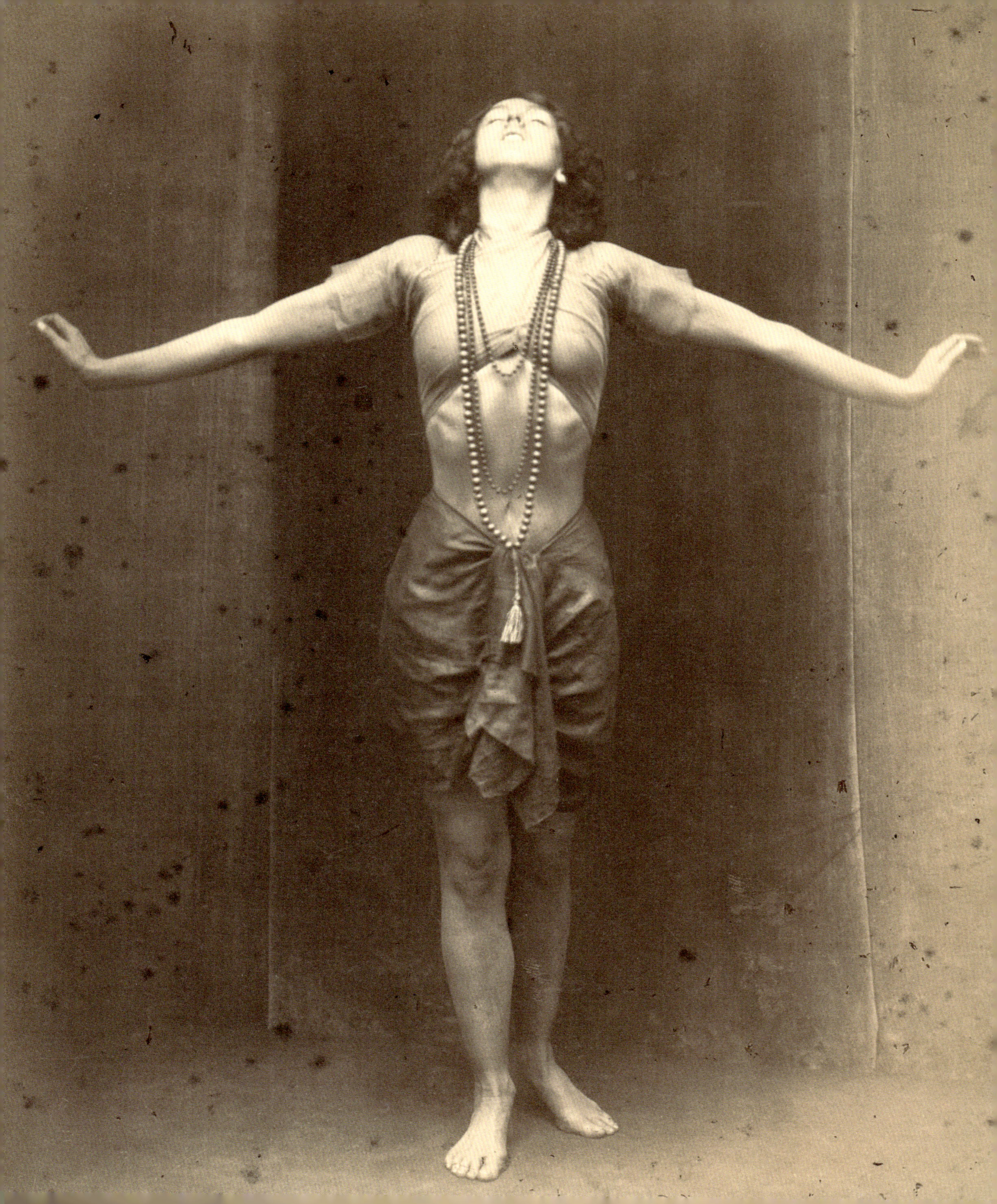

BEYOND MOVEMENT: AUGUSTE RODIN AND THE DANCERS OF HIS TIME

JULIET BELLOW

"Dance, which in France always has privileged the erotic, now finally is becoming worthy of the other arts, which it summarises." (Auguste Rodin, 'Fresques de danses', 1914)

Over the final 25 years of his career, Auguste Rodin frequently praised dance in interviews and articles published in the mass media, waxing eloquent on the way it capitalised upon the human body's expressive possibilities.[1] During that time, he also promoted the work of a select number of choreographers and performers – an eclectic group that included Loïe Fuller, Valentine de Saint-Point, Isadora Duncan, Ruth St. Denis, Vaslav Nijinsky and the Cambodian Royal Ballet troupe – thus allusively associating these dancers' practice with his own artistic endeavours. We know that several, and possibly all, of these performers modelled for Rodin at one time or another. However, his dance images often depart visibly from the work of the dancers he admired, making it difficult to tie a given representation directly to a specific choreographic referent (fig.20).[2] Moreover, unlike several other sculptors of his day, Rodin never created a life-sized exhibition piece on the subject of dance.[3] He also showed his dance images somewhat selectively: while his drawings of dancers frequently appeared in exhibitions and in the press, his small-scale models (including the *Mouvements de danse* assembled for the present exhibition) remained in the semi-private precinct of his studio (see, for example, fig.19).[4]

Dance proves an elusive element in Rodin's oeuvre. While the medium figured prominently in the sculptor's public image, dance formed a relatively minor part of his artistic production – or so it would seem.[5] In this

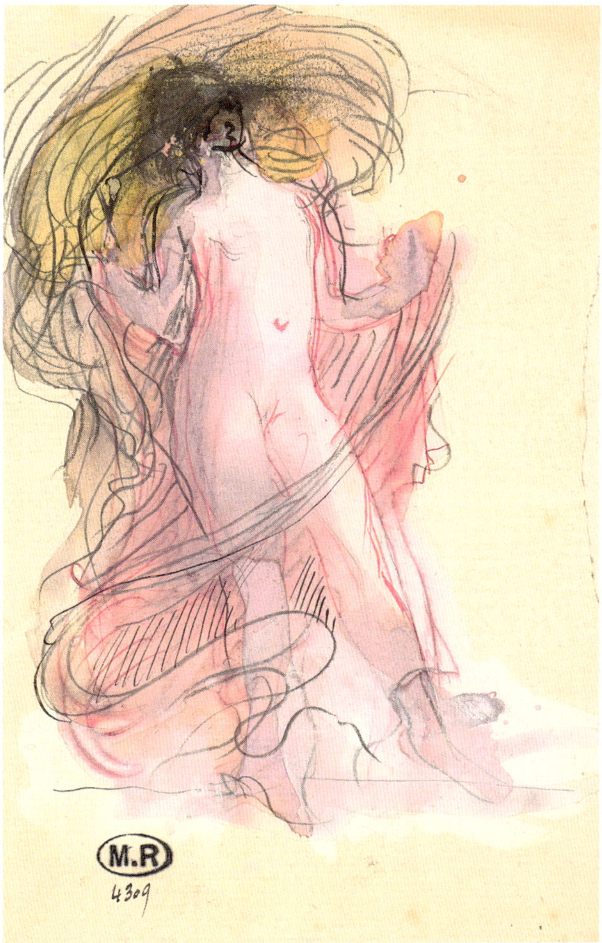

FIG.20
Auguste Rodin
Woman with veil (Loïe Fuller?), c.1895
Pencil, pen and ink, watercolour and gouache on laid paper, 175 x 110 mm
Musée Rodin, Paris, D.4309

Detail of *Ruth St. Denis in The Yogi*, cat.20

essay I propose instead that dance played an expansive, albeit largely implicit, role in the artist's work. Dance provided Rodin with far more than a motif to represent: the medium also acted as a partner in his development of a modernist sculptural idiom, deepening his ongoing exploration of unclassical poses, open form and non-finito rendering. One aspect of this argument has long been noted in the scholarly literature, where the implied movement of Rodin's sculptures is attributed to his interest in dance.[6] To be sure, the sculptor was fascinated by the mechanics of dancers' motions, and by the ephemerality of the aesthetic effects those motions achieved. However, a near-exclusive focus on movement has obscured how other, equally salient constitutive principles of the dance of his time also resonated in Rodin's work. In what follows, I take a close look at the dances Rodin favoured, highlighting innovations not only in movement style, but also in the body's relation to its spatial envelope, to the pull of gravity, and to the enactment of stillness – innovations that dovetailed, as I argue, with the most radical dimensions of Rodin's sculptural practice.

In claiming that dance reshaped Rodin's understanding of his sculptural aesthetic, this essay articulates an alternative to a medium-specific view of his late career. The traditional reading of this period holds that Rodin arrived at a modernist approach to sculpture through a searching process of self-examination. He altered, multiplied and recombined his sculptures in progressively unorthodox configurations, introducing changes in both shape and meaning of a given composition over successive iterations.[7] That is, Rodin treated his sculptural corpus not as a collection of objects, but as a conceptual gallery of bodily configurations, properties and operations subject to continual revision and adjustment (fig.21). Building on this account, I hold that the open-endedness of Rodin's process allowed him to integrate insights generated by watching dance into his existing sculptural lexicon.

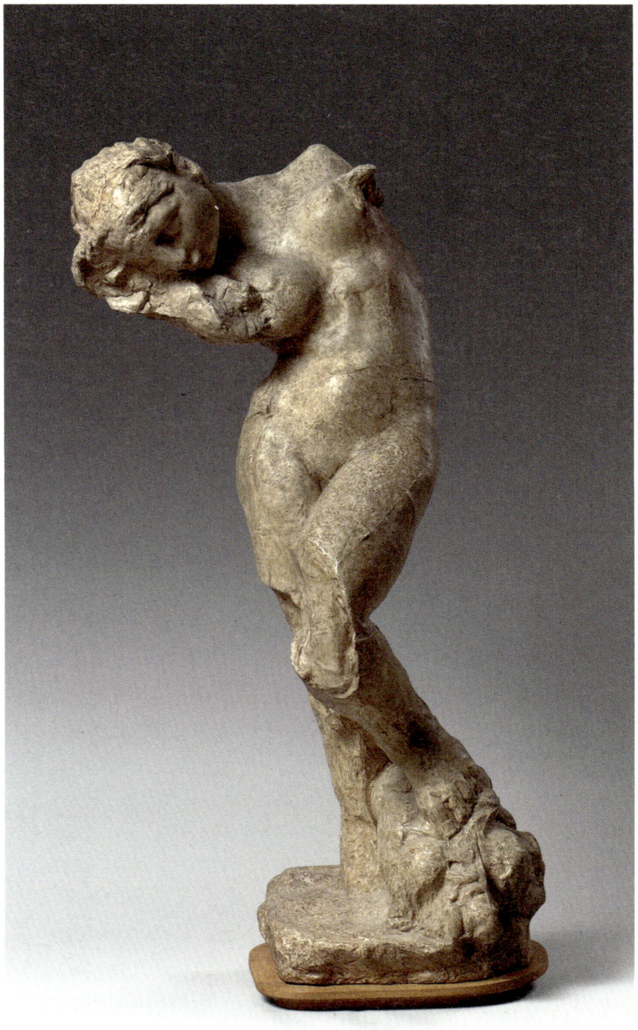

FIG.21
Auguste Rodin
Meditation, 1896
Plaster, 147 x 76 x 55 cm
Musée Rodin, Paris, S.1125

From the 1890s onward, as Rodin became increasingly interested in dance, he witnessed choreographic techniques in which he recognised strong analogies with his sculptural practice. Those dances, which re-presented to Rodin aspects of his own aesthetic principles in live, vivid, intensely embodied form, became intertwined with his sculpture over time.[8] In so far as this reading of Rodin's work points to ways that dance exerted external pressure on his creative process, it reframes that process as dialogic – perhaps even collaborative.[9]

Though this essay concentrates primarily on artistic parallels between Rodin's sculpture and dance performance around the turn of the twentieth century, the alignment of these two media also encompassed, and responded to, extra-aesthetic questions. In this period, Rodin increasingly operated outside official artistic institutions: he participated more frequently in non-juried exhibitions and competed more rarely for the sorts of monumental commissions that had previously occupied much of his time.[10] This shift permitted Rodin to show stylistically daring work, but necessitated an enterprising attitude: he had to create his own exhibition opportunities, use the mass media to shape his public image, and tap into new audiences for his art.[11] The dancers with whom Rodin forged relationships had experience developing their careers in just this way. Nearly all of the performers listed above were unaffiliated with established dance companies; several performed in unusual venues such as art galleries, private salons and universal expositions; a few, including Fuller, Duncan and Saint-Point, directed their own publicity campaigns and stage-managed the imaging of their performances.[12] That is, at least in some measure, why many of these dancers actively sought out Rodin: his name lent credibility and prestige to their work.

To understand fully what dance meant to Rodin – and what Rodin meant to dancers – therefore requires a new approach to situating dance within his oeuvre, one that attends to the complex, oblique relationships between his sculpture and the dances of his time.[13] The ephemeral nature of dance underscores the difficulty of its analysis in relation to Rodin's work: none of the dances described here survive today in the precise form that Rodin saw them.[14] Indeed, the instability of dance as an object of study may explain why the correlations that I trace between modernist experiments in dance and sculpture were not noticed earlier: they were essentially hiding in plain sight.

MODELLING DANCE

Like many other members of his generation, Rodin's intense fascination with dance led him to perceive, and to capitalise upon, a link between his artistic practice and the new dance forms of this period. Around 1900, sculptors, painters, poets and playwrights looked to dance as they mounted challenges to the conventions of the arts they practised, and struggled to make those arts responsive to the conditions of modernity. The dance scholar Gabrielle Brandstetter notes that "on the one hand, as a transitory art of the body, which is subject to mortality, and on the other as a culturally stable set of techniques for symbolic representation", dance offered a potent model for modernist forms in other media.[15] In addition, through its longstanding association with popular culture, dance helped practitioners of other arts to envision alternative modes of distributing and displaying their work, thus opening up ways to resolve modernism's fraught relation to the public sphere.

While these broad historical factors may explain Rodin's engagement with dance writ large, they do not fully explain the particular affiliations he made within the dance world. The extreme heterogeneity of Rodin's tastes compounds this problem: it is difficult to find many commonalities among a group of dancers that differed so widely in their level of training and the style that they practised, as well as in their national identities and socio-cultural backgrounds. However, that such a range of dance forms was available to Rodin is a significant fact in itself: it speaks to the fecund experimentalism of this moment in the history of dance, and to the importance of Paris as a hub and incubator for innovative dance practices around the turn of the twentieth century.[16]

During the 1860s and 1870s, when Rodin began his career, two types of dance were on offer for Parisian audiences, ballet and social dance. In terms of dances created specifically for the stage, the primary form in this period was ballet, employed in *divertissements* between the acts of operas as well as in autonomous productions of varying length.[17] The institution best known for staging ballet was the Paris Opéra, which from 1821 to 1873 occupied a theatre on the rue le Peletier, not far from the popular theatre district centred on the Boulevard du Temple; in 1875, the Opéra moved into the lavishly decorated Palais Garnier to cater to the haut-bourgeois moving into apartment buildings recently erected nearby.[18] However, ballet was also a staple of less elevated venues on or near the Boulevard du Temple, such as the Opéra Comique and the Théâtre Lyrique, and increasingly featured in the city's music-halls and circuses. Though a small number of ballets from this period survive – such as *Coppelia*, which premiered at the Opéra in 1870 – most do not. Relative to the way the genre is practised today, the ballets of that era employed less 'classical' dancing, with the ballerina on pointe. Choreographers relied heavily on mime to convey the plot, typically a melodramatic or comedic love story.

As this description attests, ballets then were regarded as a form of light entertainment, and were thus not entirely distinct from popular social dances like the cancan, quadrille or waltz.[19] Most such social dances originated as partnered or participatory genres, and some were staged on open dance-floors where members of the audience could mingle with the performers. But this loose category also encompassed acrobatic dances by professionals capable of extreme bodily contortions – figures like the Moulin Rouge star La Goulue (née Louise Weber) and Alda Moreno (née Noémie Chevassier) of the Opéra Comique, the model for Rodin's *Mouvements de danse*.[20] It seems telling that, while Rodin evidently found artistic inspiration in the way Moreno used her body, he never publicly identified himself with the déclassé genre she practised in his writings on dance.

Beginning in the 1890s, Parisian audiences witnessed a veritable explosion of different types of dance. In the first phase of this phenomenon, new forms of solo art dance by a group of female performers born in North America – including Loïe Fuller, Isadora Duncan and Ruth St. Denis – came to Paris.[21] Each of these figures, who served as both choreographer and performer, employed a distinctive style of dance. Generally speaking, though, the techniques these women practised appeared simpler and more natural than ballet: their vocabularies derived from everyday movements such as walking, running and skipping. Their work also bore a seriousness of purpose and theme that contrasted directly with the frothy eroticism of period ballets (as Rodin indicated in the passage quoted at the beginning of this essay). Over a short span of time, these performers pioneered various new uses of the human instrument, thus expanding the very definition of dance and empowering subsequent solo dancers, like Valentine de Saint-Point, to further experimentation. Indeed, the performance styles these women invented departed so radically from dance as it was then conceived that some critics contested the very categorisation of these genres as dance.

During the same years, so-called 'exotic' dances adapted from traditions originating in South and South-East Asia, the Middle East and Africa appeared in Paris at temporary expositions as part of displays of France's colonial holdings. By and large, such 'exotic' dances were made for export: originally created for a variety of distinct purposes, from temple ritual to court entertainment, they were carefully recalibrated to suit European performance venues and audiences. The Exposition Universelle held in Paris in 1889 featured two such genres, a *danse du ventre* ('belly dance') performed as part of the Egyptian exhibition and a Javanese-style dance by a troupe assembled by Dutch entrepreneurs from the East Indies.[22] Widely taken to be authentic, unadulterated forms, these two dances proved enormously popular, ensuring that subsequent expositions prominently featured troupes of indigenous peoples from France's colonies. In 1906, for example, the French colonial ministry worked with the newly crowned King of Cambodia to bring a troupe of dancers to perform at the Exposition Coloniale held in Marseille.[23] Contact with these forms proved inspirational not only for visual artists like Rodin but also for dancers such as La Goulue, the ballerina Cléo de Mérode and the performer Mata Hari, each of whom began to feature adapted versions of these dances in their acts.[24]

A second phase of this dance explosion developed in the second decade of the twentieth century, as choreographers across Europe began to experiment with new forms of group dancing, either by reforming ballet practice or by inventing alternatives to ballet. The first such troupe to arrive in Paris was the Ballets Russes, created in 1909 by Serge Diaghilev and a cohort of Russian-born choreographers, composers and designers dedicated to reshaping ballet composition and practice.[25] To carry out this ambitious goal, the company built a new repertoire of short, one-act works that reformulated balletic technique and, inspired by Richard Wagner's concept of an operatic *Gesamtkunstwerk* ('total work of art'), aimed to integrate dance, music and décor on stage. Michel Fokine and Vaslav Nijinsky, who served as the troupe's first two choreographers, both had trained as ballet dancers in the Russian Imperial (now Maryinsky) Theatre. In different ways, their choreographies deconstructed ballet's rigid rules of bodily comportment; some of their works blended ballet steps with non-balletic styles of movement, while others dispensed with the balletic vocabulary altogether. Nijinsky and Fokine also helped to devise scenarios that widened ballet's range of geographic settings and cultural references, from ancient Egypt to rural Russia.[26] Enhanced by dazzlingly colourful designs by painters such as Léon Bakst and Nicholas Roerich, and by daringly avant-garde musical accompaniments by Claude Debussy, Igor Stravinsky and others, Fokine's and Nijinsky's choreographies helped to establish ballet as a legitimate art form, thereby recalibrating Parisian viewers' attitudes toward the genre.

Thus, while each of the different strands of dance that emerged in Paris around 1900 helped to propel Rodin's interest in the medium, the techniques employed by these dancers and choreographers varied widely. Other than Rodin himself, however, one factor unites the disparate figures that Rodin admired: their choreographies were all either intended or perceived as alternatives to existing ballet practice. Rodin certainly cast their work this way, meanwhile characterising the French ballet tradition as a barrier to the development of dance as a true art form. In his 1914 essay 'Fresques de Danses', Rodin claimed that "watching our ballets at the Opéra, I could not understand at all how the Greeks could have put dance above everything else".[27] Though Rodin did not spell out precisely what made ballet so problematic, part of his opposition surely stemmed from its codification of bodily positions and of choreographic sequences.[28] The dance forms that interested him did not employ the bravura footwork characteristic of the Opéra's ballets (such as pointe work, pirouettes or leaps). Indeed, most of the idioms he supported de-emphasised the legs and feet, instead privileging other body parts, such as the torso. These new choreographies also refigured the dancer's posture and habits of carriage, replacing ballet's five positions and strict rules of comportment with other ways of holding and moving the body. Many viewers, including Rodin, described these choreographies as less rule-bound and more improvisatory than traditional ballet – and thus, paradoxically, more artful.[29]

More fundamentally, though, as Rodin noted in 'Fresques de Danses', what distinguished these dance genres from traditional ballet was their makers' push to make the medium "worthy of other arts" – even as they profited literally and figuratively from dance's links with popular culture.[30] All of the dancers and troupes that Rodin admired moved self-consciously to elevate the medium, in part by forging alliances with other art forms. In many cases, they reworked dance's relation to narrative, turning away from the typical marriage plots of period ballets.[31] Duncan and Nijinsky drew themes from epic and myth; St. Denis and the Cambodian Royal Ballet worked from religious and folkloric texts; Saint-Point employed poetic accompaniment to her performances; Fuller created a non-narrative form of pure dance. Many of these performers set their dances to concert music, a genre perceived as more weighty than scores made to a choreographer's specifications. Their work also frequently quoted or paraphrased well-known works of visual art: for example, Duncan's *Marseillaise* (1914) paid homage to François Rude's famous sculpture, while Nijinsky's *L'Après-midi d'un faune* (1912) emulated ancient Greek bas-relief. Finally, several of these figures explicitly positioned dance as an intellectual endeavour by writing manifestos explaining their philosophies, delivering or soliciting lectures and essays about their craft, and stressing the archival basis of dance composition with well-publicised visits to museums and libraries. At the same time, these performers found ways to maintain the popular appeal of dance through risqué eroticism, titillating exoticism or the shock value of vanguardism (and sometimes all of these).[32]

It was partly as a result of this push by dancers to transform perceptions of their métier that so many figures in Rodin's orbit came to uphold dance as an example for other arts – particularly Stéphane Mallarmé, who, in a series of essays published in the 1890s, and through weekly gatherings of intellectuals in his apartment on the rue de Rome, disseminated his belief that dance constituted the most ideal iteration of Symbolist poetics.[33] As Susan Jones notes, Mallarmé drew conceptual parallels between the two arts, "credit[ing] dance with an economy of form akin to that of poetry" and musing that dance, as a form of "*écriture corporelle*" (corporeal writing), "might offer alternative forms of communication to the written word".[34] For Mallarmé, that is, dance held the potential to revolutionise the form and practice of poetry, opening up new ways to conceive of language and to approach the act of writing.

Rodin was deeply embedded in the poet's circle, and, while he did not personally attend Mallarmé's Tuesday gatherings, the discussions about dance that took place in that milieu proved formative in the sculptor's developing views of the medium.[35] Several of Rodin's closest friends and most vocal supporters – including Roger Marx, Camille Mauclair, Georges Rodenbach and Charles Morice – were frequent visitors to the famous *mardis*, and espoused Mallarmé's ideas about dance in critical and poetic texts.[36] Marx and Mauclair wrote extensively on Fuller and the Ballets Russes, directly relating these dances to Mallarmé's theories, and Marx helped Rodin to craft his published statements on dance.[37] In those texts, Rodin positioned dance as a model for sculpture in a manner parallel to Mallarmé's concept of dance as "corporeal writing". Rodin repeatedly pointed to the "reform" of dance practice introduced by Fuller, Duncan, Nijinsky and the Javanese and Cambodian troupes: by breaking with existing formulae, he argued, these dancers had "retaught us to love the beauty of the body, of movement and of gesture".[38] These new techniques had not only allowed dance finally to become "worthy of other arts", but also underscored the fundamental relatedness of dance to other artistic forms: as Rodin put it, dance

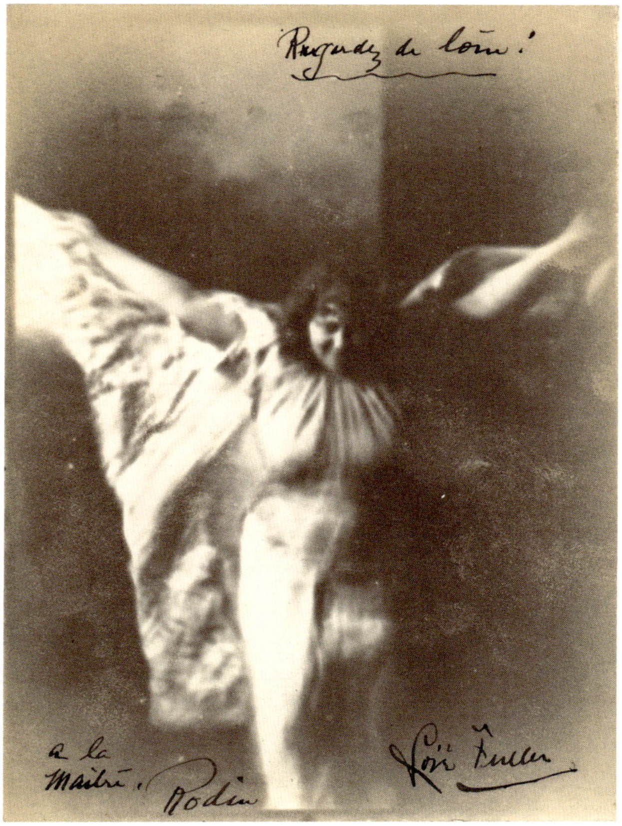

FIG.22
R. Moreau
Loïe Fuller
Photograph inscribed by Fuller to Rodin
Musée Rodin, Paris, PH.1537

"summarises" the arts.[39] We can extrapolate from this characterisation of dance that Rodin viewed the medium as uniquely positioned to provide new perspectives on other arts – particularly on sculpture, at that time the only art form other than dance so closely identified with the human body.

ELECTRIFYING SPACE

One key characteristic of Rodin's art is a tendency to energise the relation of the sculpted figure to its physical surroundings. Both his single figures and his group compositions, as Alex Potts notes in *The Sculptural Imagination*, "impinge actively on the space around them" with projections away from the body's core, with a "lively flow of surface" that disrupts the literal boundaries of the sculpted figure, and through the fragmentation of body parts, which invites the viewer imaginatively to complete his figures in the voids around them.[40] While this quality pervades Rodin's oeuvre, it is most visible in his *Gates of Hell* (begun 1880) and many of the compositions drawn from that massive project over subsequent decades. In an extended analysis of the *Gates*, David Getsy points out that the molten, rippling interstitial material of the background acts as "an active participant rather than a passive backdrop" to the bodies it surrounds.[41] To date, scholars have not connected these aspects of Rodin's sculpture to striking parallels in the work of the dancer/choreographers Loïe Fuller (1862–1928) and Valentine de Saint-Point (1875–1953). Both women developed forms of synthetic theatre that forged equivalences between concrete objects (such as body, costume and setting) and more immaterial presences (including light, sound and rhythm). By encouraging viewers to make synaesthetic connections between these various elements, Fuller and Saint-Point treated the stage environment as a material entity, thus dramatising the shapes and patterns created around the edges of the dancing body as it cut through that space.

Rodin and Fuller met some time in the mid to late 1890s, probably through Marx, a keen advocate of both artists.[42] Surely, Rodin knew of the celebrity performer soon after her November 1892 premiere at the Folies-Bergère, which garnered her an immediate following among critics, artists and the general public. Fuller's fame stemmed from her invention of a genre of dance-spectacle premised upon the dynamic interaction of her costumed body with coloured light.[43] The first of these choreographies, her plotless *Serpentine Dance* (1892), set to Ernest Gillet's popular waltz 'Loin du Bal' (*c.*1886), made the extension of sinuous line into three dimensions the explicit subject of her dance.[44] Performing on a stage lined in black fabric, Fuller wore a long white silk robe with a pair of hidden bamboo rods that extended the reach of her arms (see cat.1). Her relatively simple movement vocabulary, rooted in the torquing of her torso, sent the garment fluttering into motion to form a shifting series

FIG.23
Valentine de Saint-Point, 'Poème de l'amour', from *La Métachorie*, 1913

of asymmetrical patterns.[45] Stage lamps fitted with tinted gelatin filters, controlled by a legion of stage-hands – purportedly up to 38 at a time – made her dance into a live performance of abstract form and colour that blurred distinctions between body, costume and scenography.[46]

Across a span of about a decade, Rodin collected about a hundred photographs that represent (or, rather, approximate) the spatial effects obtained in Fuller's performances. Clearly, this large, varied group of pictures – many likely to have been made at Rodin's behest – evinces his desire for images of Fuller's act.[47] But, more broadly, photography functioned as a site of exchange

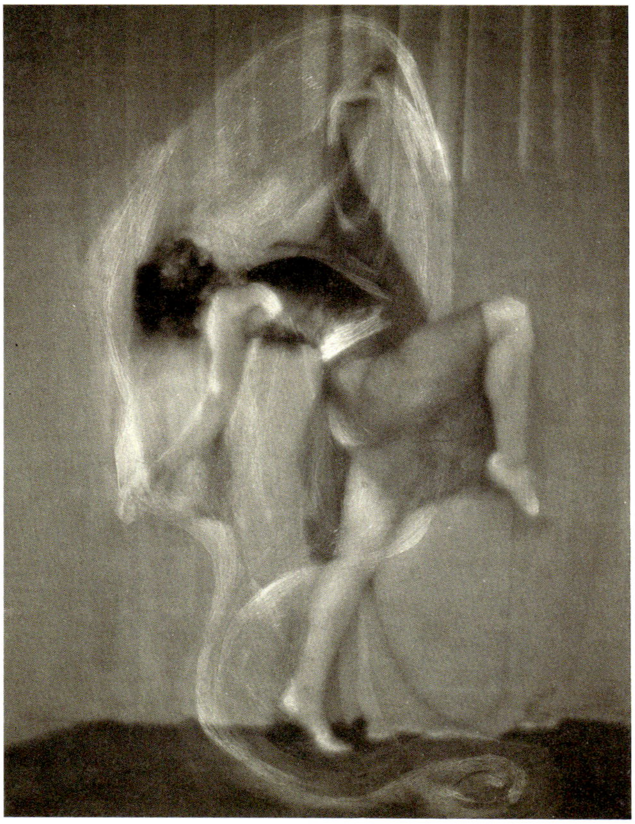

between Fuller and Rodin, and as a forum for exploring the relation of sculpture to dance. In these images, many containing written explanations or instructions for Rodin, Fuller communicated ideas about her practice, often with pointed reference to his sculpture. In one such picture (fig.22), she appears with her arms outstretched, running toward the camera lens; the force of her body presses her garment against her torso and creates rippling waves in its fabric. Fuller here imitates the famous *Victory* of Samothrace (*c.*190 BCE), the sculptural avatar of a body poised on the verge of motion.[48] Yet she seems less concerned with her pose in itself than with the way it is transfigured by the row of footlamps positioned beneath the picture's bottom edge: as they partly dissolve her form, those lights reconfigure our perceptions of solid and void. This hauntingly pictorialist mise-en-scène bears remarkable similarities to photographs of Rodin's sculptures made around the same time (in several cases, created by the same photographers Fuller employed). Such parallels between photographs of his sculptures and her dance become more pronounced when this image is viewed from a distance – as Fuller advised Rodin to do in the message she scribbled to him in the top right corner of the image.

As Fuller was reaching the end of her performing career, Valentine de Saint-Point conceived a related form of multimedia performance that she called *métachorie* ('beyond dance').[49] Saint-Point was a poet, critic and visual artist with no dance training. Rodin first came to know her as the author of *Poèmes de l'Orgueil*, a section of which, subtitled 'Le Penseur' (The thinker) after his most famous work, she dedicated to the sculptor.[50] Subsequently, Saint-Point began to conceive of a hybrid form of dance poetry, culminating in the presentation of her *métachorie* in December 1913 at the Salle Léon-Poirier (fig.23).[51] The performance consisted of four tableaux: Saint-Point danced while an offstage actor read twelve of her poems and a live orchestra played.[52] Like Fuller,

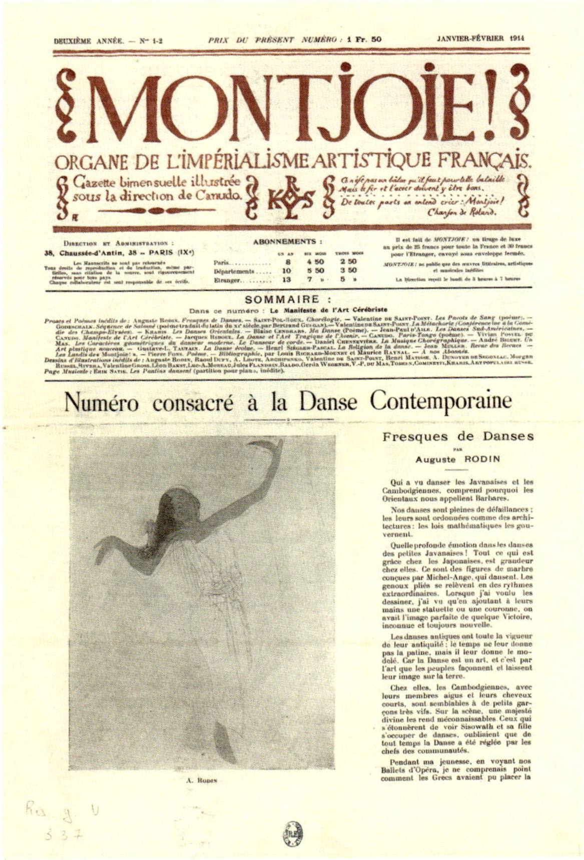

DEUXIÈME ANNÉE. — Nos 1-2 PRIX DU PRÉSENT NUMÉRO : 1 Fr. 50 JANVIER-FÉVRIER 1914

MONTJOIE!

ORGANE DE L'IMPÉRIALISME ARTISTIQUE FRANÇAIS.

Gazette bimensuelle illustrée sous la direction de Canudo.

Ce n'est pas un bâton qu'il faut pour telle bataille
Mais le fer et l'acier doivent y être bons.
De toutes parts on entend crier : Montjoie!
Chanson de Roland.

DIRECTION ET ADMINISTRATION :
38, Chaussée-d'Antin, 38 – PARIS (IXe)

Les Manuscrits ne sont pas retournés
Tous droits de reproduction et de traduction, même partielles, sans citation de la source, sont rigoureusement réservés pour tous pays.
Chaque collaborateur est seul responsable de ses écrits.

ABONNEMENTS :

	UN AN	SIX MOIS	TROIS MOIS
Paris	8	4 50	2 50
Départements	10	5 50	3 50
Etranger	13	7 »	5 »

Il est fait de MONTJOIE ! un tirage de luxe au prix de 25 francs pour toute la France et 30 francs pour l'Etranger, envoyé sous enveloppe fermée.

MONTJOIE ! ne publie que des œuvres littéraires, artistiques et musicales inédites

La Direction reçoit le lundi de 5 heures à 7 heures

SOMMAIRE :

Dans ce numéro : Le Manifeste de l'Art Cérébriste

Proses et Poèmes inédits de : Auguste RODIN. *Fresques de Danses.* — SAINT-POL-ROUX. *Chorélogie.* — Valentine DE SAINT-POINT. *Les Pavots de Sang* (poème). — GODESCHALK. *Séquence de Salomé* (poème traduit du latin du XIe siècle par Bertrand GUÉGAN). — Valentine DE SAINT-POINT. *La Métachorie (Conférence lue à la Comédie des Champs-Elysées).* — KHARIS. *Les Danses Orientales.* — Blaise CENDRARS. *Ma Danse* (Poème). — Jean-Paul D'AILE. *Les Danses Sud-Américaines.* — CANUDO. *Manifeste de l'Art Cérébriste.* — Jacques REBOUL. *La Danse et l'Art Tragique de l'Avenir.* — CANUDO. *Paris-Tango* (poème). — Vivian POSTEL DU MAS. *Les Caractères géométriques du danseur moderne. Le Danseur de corde.* — Daniel CHENNEVIÈRE. *La Musique Chorégraphique.* — André BIGUET. *Un Art plastique nouveau.* — Gustave-L. TAUTAIN. *La Danse évolue.* — Henri SIÉGLER-PASCAL. *La Religion de la danse.* — Jean MULLER. *Revue des Revues* — *Les Lundis des Montjoie! ».* — Pierre FONS. *Poème.* — *Bibliographie*, par Louis RICHARD-MOUNET et Maurice RAYNAL. — *A nos Abonnés.*
Dessins d'Illustrations inédits de : Auguste RODIN, Raoul DUFY, A. LHOTE, ARCHIPENKO, Valentine DE SAINT-POINT, Henri MATISSE, A. DUNOYER DE SEGONZAC, Morgan RUSSEL, RIVERA, Valentine GROSS, Léon BAKST, Luc-A. MOREAU, Jules FLANDRIN, BALDO, Gerda WEGENER, V.-P. DU MAS, TOBEEN, COMINETTI, KHARIS, ART POPULAIRE RUSSE.
Page Musicale : ERIK SATIE. *Les Pantins dansent* (partition pour piano, inédite).

Numéro consacré à la Danse Contemporaine

A. Rodin

Fresques de Danses

PAR

Auguste RODIN

Qui a vu danser les Javanaises et les Cambodgiennes, comprend pourquoi les Orientaux nous appellent Barbares.

Nos danses sont pleines de défaillances ; les leurs sont ordonnées comme des architectures : les lois mathématiques les gouvernent.

Quelle profonde émotion dans les danses des petites Javanaises ! Tout ce qui est grâce chez les Japonaises, est grandeur chez elles. Ce sont des figures de marbre conçues par Michel-Ange, qui dansent. Les genoux pliés se relèvent en des rythmes extraordinaires. Lorsque j'ai voulu les dessiner, j'ai vu qu'en ajoutant à leurs mains une statuette ou une couronne, on avait l'image parfaite de quelque Victoire, inconnue et toujours nouvelle.

Les danses antiques ont toute la vigueur de leur antiquité ; le temps ne leur donne pas la patine, mais il leur donne le modelé. Car la Danse est un art, et c'est par l'art que les peuples façonnent et laissent leur image sur la terre.

Chez elles, les Cambodgiennes, avec leurs membres aigus et leurs cheveux courts, sont semblables à de petits garçons très vifs. Sur la scène, une majesté divine les rend méconnaissables. Ceux qui s'étonnèrent de voir Sisowath et sa fille s'occuper de danses, oubliaient que de tout temps la Danse a été réglée par les chefs des communautés.

Pendant ma jeunesse, en voyant nos Ballets d'Opéra, je ne comprenais point comment les Grecs avaient pu placer la

FIG.24
Auguste Rodin, 'Fresques de Danses',
Montjoie!, January–February 1914
Bibliothèque nationale de France, Paris

Saint-Point employed electric-light projections that threw geometric forms on to the gray backcloth; she added clouds of incense that wafted into the hall.[53] As the art historian Nell Andrew notes, this multisensory experience transformed such ineffable properties as sound, smell and empty space into palpable realities.[54] Weeks after her premiere, Saint-Point collaborated with Ricciotto Canudo, publisher of the journal *Montjoie!*, to print a special issue on dance that featured her manifesto and several images of her *métachorie*. Emblazoned on the front page was Rodin's 'Fresques de Danses', illustrated with his drawings of the Cambodian Royal Ballet; their play with the relation of figure to ground resembles several pictures of Saint-Point published in the journal (fig.24). Thus while Rodin's essay never directly refers to or pictures Saint-Point, their juxtaposition would have primed readers to align his ideas about dance with her choreography and her theoretical writings.

SENSING GRAVITY

Another hallmark of Rodin's sculptural idiom is his tendency to experiment with bodily position, distribution of weight, and muscle contraction and release. His poses throw the figure out of plumb and put it visibly under stress, showing with tensed sinews the work of holding a given pose. As a result, these bodies often appear either as if suspended, evincing an "evasive relationship to a supporting ground" – as in the case of his *Iris messagère des dieux* (*Iris, Messenger of the Gods*; 1890–91; first exhibited 1898) – or as if emphatically rooted, acquiescing to gravitational pressure, in works like his *Les Trois Ombres* (*Three Shades*, 1885; enlarged 1898; first exhibited 1902).[55] Scholars rarely relate these properties of Rodin's work to the concept of kinaesthesia, a core principle in the choreographies of Isadora Duncan (1877–1927) and Ruth St. Denis (1879–1968).[56] Kinesthesia, or proprioception, refers to the sensations associated with an awareness of posture and movement: the term applies both to muscular experience within the body and to a spectator's perception of another body.[57] Duncan and St. Denis's interest in the aesthetic possibilities of kinesthetic sensation was manifest in their choreographic use of "arm and leg swings, lateral bends, spirals and twists of the torso, and experimentation with shifts in the centre of gravity".[58] Like Rodin, moreover, both Duncan and St. Denis related their explorations of the body's external mechanics to inner processes of the mind and spirit – thus elevating and sanctioning dances whose degree of bodily liberation and exposure otherwise could be construed as licentious.[59]

In her autobiography, Duncan recounts her visit to Rodin's pavilion at the 1900 Exposition Universelle, followed by an erotically charged encounter with the sculptor in his studio on the rue de l'Université.[60] She claims to have danced for him "an idyll of Theocritus", possibly a foretaste of the *Dance Idylls* (1900) Rodin witnessed in April 1901, when Duncan staged a recital in her studio on the Avenue de Villiers, with a lecture on

Greek art delivered by Rodin's close friend the painter Eugène Carrière.[61] Set to sixteenth- and seventeenth-century concert music rendered in piano accompaniment, her *Dance Idylls* evoked a series of famous paintings including Botticelli's *Primavera* (c.1482) and Titian's *Bacchus and Ariadne* (1520–23).[62] Duncan wore her characteristic costume – a simple, loose garment – and danced barefoot, deliberately rejecting the balletic corset and blocked slippers. Her movement vocabulary, which originated in the solar plexus, also constituted a polemic against pointe work: she acknowledged the weight of her body in her skips, leaps and falls.[63] Calibrating her actions to the pattern of her breath, Duncan viewed her dances as physical manifestations of the invisible forces that governed the natural world.

Rodin and Duncan employed a shared vocabulary to describe their artistic practices, weaving references to nature together with evocations of high culture.[64] Like Duncan, who described her dance as originating in "the study of nature", Rodin claimed to draw his sculptural poses from the free movements of his models' bodies, seizing "only that which reality offers me spontaneously".[65] At the same time, both artists positioned their work as reviving classical principles of corporeal harmony, and characterised themselves as the true inheritors of the great art of antiquity.[66] Such a careful calibration of "nature" and "art" is manifest in a drawing by Rodin that purportedly depicts Duncan (D.2892). The slight cock of her head, drooping arm and casually bent leg lend this pose an air of apparent artlessness, as if struck without intention or design.[67] However, a closer look reveals that this body is torqued in a spiral that would require muscular effort to strike and maintain: her bent leg, passing in front of her body, twists her hips to follow it while her shoulders, dragged by her elongated right arm, swivel in the opposite direction. This subtly complex pose bears relation to the postures of Rodin's *Adam* (1880) and *Méditation* (1885–98), in which the torso serves as a fulcrum for the rotation of the upper and lower body in different directions. The drawing thus not only underscores fundamental links between Rodin's sculptural practice and Duncan's approach to dance, but also demonstrates how Rodin actively absorbed the choreographies he witnessed into his sculptural corpus: the image, a portmanteau of sorts, fuses his archive of poses with hers.

Whereas we can document Rodin's attendance at several of Duncan's performances up until 1914, we do not know how much exposure he had to the work of St. Denis during her three-year European tour of 1906–09. It seems that she visited Rodin's studio in late 1907. He may have seen her performance of *Radha* at the Théâtre Marigny in 1906.[68] Dancing to Leo Delibes's *Lakmé* (1883), St. Denis embodied a sculptural idol who, descending from her pedestal, awakens each of her senses in succession. Throughout, St. Denis played with her body's relation to its vertical and horizontal axes, partnering with gravity to express a range of internal sensations. Rodin must have drawn parallels between his precariously top-heavy sculptures – many of them named for states of mind – and St. Denis's cantilevering of her body as she moved from side to side, whirled in spirals, craned into vertiginous backbends (fig.25) and crashed to the floor.[69]

PERFORMING STILLNESS

Movement is a key attribute of Rodin's sculpture and an overt theme in many of his late works, including his *L'Homme qui marche* (*Walking Man*; 1900) and *Flying Figure* (1891). In these and many other sculptures of this period, he achieved the appearance of movement through unstable poses, exaggerated oppositions in the body, and by melding parts from differently posed sculptures into a single figure. Indeed, Rodin animated his figures so effectively that it can be easy to overlook the degree of vivid stasis that they project. Stillness is, as Getsy has pointed out, a form of passive resistance that structures viewers' encounters with sculpture.[70] It is also an essential – though often unnoticed – component of dance performance.[71] In 1906 and 1912, Rodin encountered two types of dance that marked stillness as a choreographic material, the slow, deliberate performance style of the Cambodian Royal Ballet troupe and the succession of hieratic poses in *L'Après-midi d'un faune*, the choreographic debut of Vaslav Nijinsky. Rodin's images of these dances investigate their quasi-sculptural alternation between immobility and movement; the fact that both dances claimed direct affiliation to ancient sculptural precedents could only have made their parallels with his craft more evident to the sculptor.

The Cambodian Royal Ballet troupe, which numbered around 45 young female dancers, formed part of the entourage of King Sisowath during the royal visit to France for the Exposition Coloniale held in the summer of 1906.[72] A trip sponsored by the Colonial Ministry brought the dancers to Paris in early July, where Rodin attended a performance at the Pré-Catelan theatre in the Bois de Boulogne; returning to Marseille with the troupe, he embarked upon a sketching campaign of three or four days during which he produced more than 150 drawings.[73] Derived from a style of court and temple dance common throughout South and South-East Asia, the dance he saw this troupe perform did not feature the propulsive movements that give nineteenth-century European ballet its most distinctive, climactic moments. (Its musical accompaniment, largely percussive, likewise lacked the harmonic progression characteristic of balletic accompaniment in that period.)[74] The scholar Paul Cravath describes Cambodian dance as achieving a "hypnotic balance of stillness and movement" by juxtaposing "large movements" of the legs (including turning, walking and kneeling) with periods in which the dancer stays in place, tapping her feet and making "small" movements of the head, arms, hands and feet.[75] The performer also

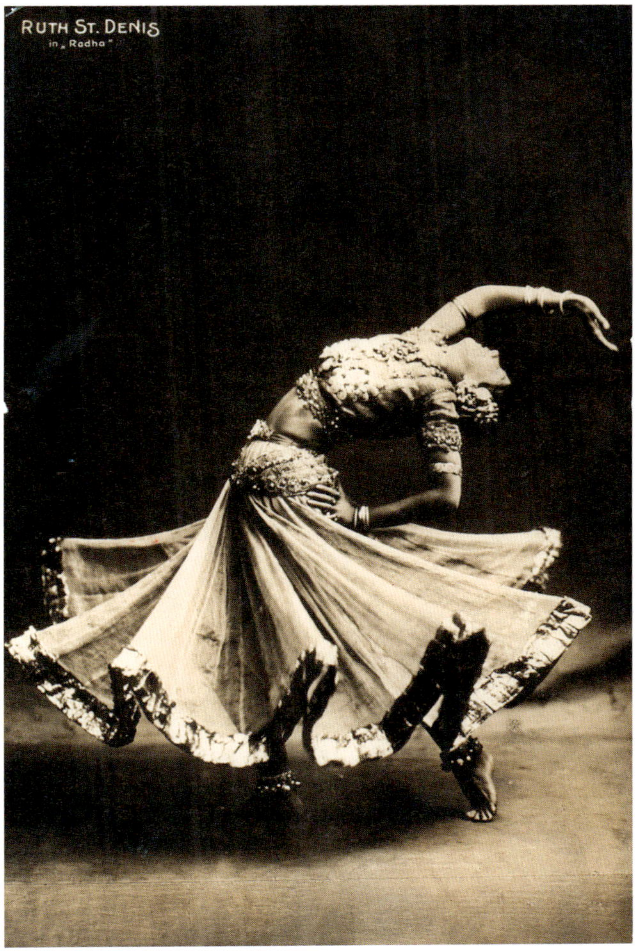

FIG.25
Ruth St. Denis in *Radha*, 1906
The New York Public Library

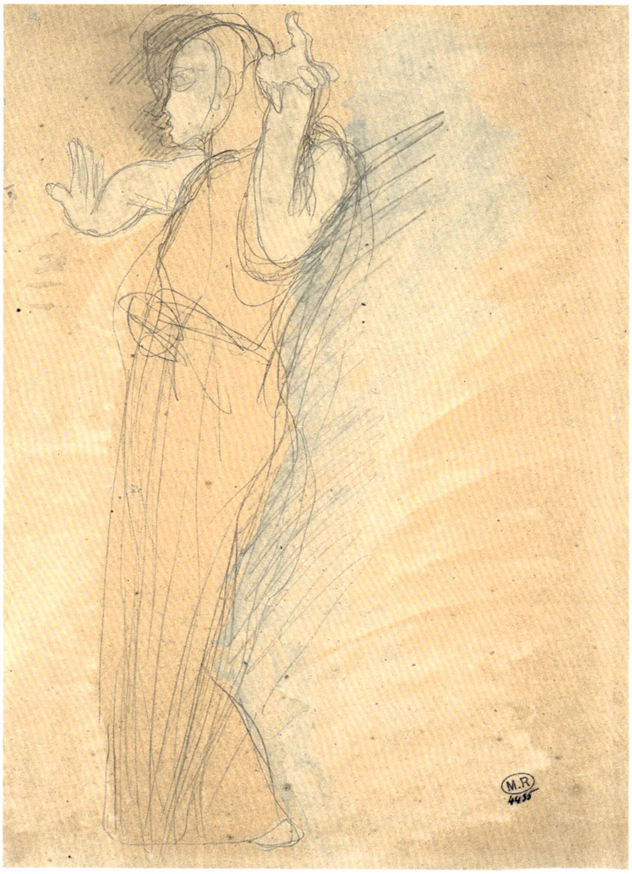

FIG.26
Auguste Rodin
Cambodian dancer in profile, 1906
Pencil and watercolour on paper,
342 x 240 mm
Musée Rodin, Paris, D.4435

maintains a fairly consistent bodily carriage throughout the dance, keeping her knees strongly bent while the arms alternate between hyperextension and straightening in a serpent-like flow.[76] To some extent, this relatively limited range of motion stemmed from costuming introduced in the mid nineteenth century: these garments were worn so tightly that the dancers had to be sewn into them for each performance.[77]

To European audiences unfamiliar with the technique, Cambodian dance appeared simultaneously static and continuous. In many of Rodin's drawings of the troupe, he exploits the varied effects and associations of line both to arrest the dancers in time and space and to convey the duration and flux of their performance. In some places, he demarcates bodily contours, creating the illusion of solid, bounded form; in others, he deploys line in repeated patterns to connote action, as if tracking the positions of the dancer's body over time. That the troupe performed in view of the Exposition's Cambodian pavilion, made from plaster casts of the twelfth-century Bayon Temple at Angkor, played a significant role in shaping Rodin's perceptions of the dance.[78] Several of his drawings conflate the dancers' poses with visual references to examples of Cambodian bas-relief and free-standing sculpture on display at the fair and in collections Rodin knew well. For example, at least four of his drawings show a dancer seated, legs folded in or under the body, the arms bent in opposing angles. Several photographs of the Cambodian Royal Ballet in 1906 show dancers assuming variants of this pose, possibly suggesting that he drew these images from a live model. Yet the pose also closely resembles statues of the seated Buddha; several examples were on view in public collections in Paris at that time, and Rodin himself owned several casts of seated Buddha figures.[79] Another reference to typologies of Cambodian sculpture may be seen in the many drawings that portray the dancers' arms multiple times in a single image. This motif simultaneously suggests sequentiality (that is, the

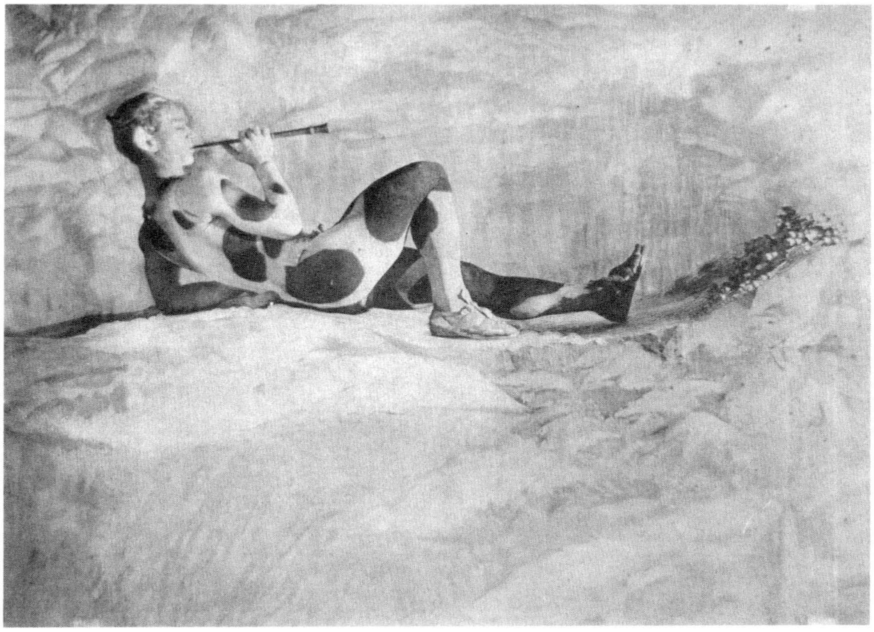

FIG.27
Adolphe de Meyer
Nijinsky in the first tableau
of *L'Après-midi d'un faune*, 1912
Collotype, 147 x 197 mm
Musée d'Orsay, Paris

motions of a dance) and alludes to images of the multi-armed god Shiva; one such statue took pride of place in the Musée Indochinois, which Rodin is known to have frequented. And, in at least one instance (fig.26), Rodin entwined a Cambodian dancer's pose with quotations from his own sculptural corpus. The position of the figure's draped legs in the drawing mirrors the figure of Andrieu d'Andres from Rodin's *Burghers of Calais* (1884–95); her torqued, hyperextended arm echoes the gesture of Pierre de Wissant from the same monument.

Six years later, the year after Rodin had begun to assemble his *Mouvements de danse*, he was present at the premiere of Nijinsky's *L'Après-midi d'un faune*, a dance expressly aimed to render the body as sculpture (fig.27).[80] As I note above, Nijinsky had come to prominence as the star male dancer for the Ballets Russes, and several critics close to Rodin declared the troupe's synthetic approach to ballet composition a realisation of Mallarmé's poetic ideal. In apparent dialogue with this critical reception, Nijinsky based his *choreo-poème* on Mallarmé's 1876 poem *Prélude à l'après-midi d'un faune*, underscoring his act of homage by using Claude Debussy's chromatic symphony *Prélude à l'après-midi d'un faune* (1892–94) as musical accompaniment. Nijinsky conjured Mallarmé's dreamlike, Arcadian vision in concrete, sexually explicit terms: the faun's thwarted desire for the nymphs that elude his grasp culminated in the ballet's final, masturbatory act. In an equally controversial move, Nijinsky staged the dancers' bodies to mimic the style of Greek bas-relief, thereby producing a "two-dimensional 'choreographic picture'".[81] Occupying only the edge of the stage, the dancers oriented their feet in parallel, torsos to the audience, their hips and faces in profile, illusorily compressing the body into a flat plane. The "limb shapes", dance scholar Stephanie Jordan writes, were markedly "angular, indicating the joints at elbows and wrists and, in the case of the Faun" – played by Nijinsky himself – "at the knee and ankle."[82] As Jordan also notes, the choreography frequently required the dancers to stop and hold a given position, sometimes to remain motionless for an extended period, including the climactic moment when the Faun encounters the nymph that is his object of desire.

The morning after the ballet's premiere, Rodin published a front-page editorial in the newspaper *Le Matin* praising the "deliberately awkward", "jerky" effects achieved as the dancers alternated between rapid motion and maintaining a pose.[83] Describing the ballet's initial scene, in which Nijinsky lay on the ground, one leg folded, a pipe at his lips (see fig.27), Rodin told his readers, "you might think him to be a statue". That Rodin cast Nijinsky in such terms makes his depiction of the dancer all the more surprising (cat.79 & 80). Standing on one footless leg, holding the other in his hand, leg hiked up to nestle in the armpit in an adaptation of Rodin's *Iris*, this figure at first seems unrelated to Nijinsky's choreography.[84] In fact this contradictory arrangement of the body condenses several choreographic points into a single pose, and those moments unfold as the viewer moves round the sculpture.[85] When the sculpture is oriented as Nijinsky appeared on stage, with the dancer's chest facing forward and his head in profile, its upper body appears as in the ballet's first tableau in which Nijinsky, in repose, leans back on his elbow. From this same point of view, though, his lower body alludes to a different part of the ballet: his bent leg recalls the moment when Nijinsky leaned down to retrieve a scarf dropped by the nymph who fled his pursuit. Moving around the sculpture towards the right, Nijinsky's body seems to fold, accordion-style, flattening into an almost straight line. Viewed at an angle that puts Nijinsky's face in full view, the standing leg is visibly oriented in two different positions: the sheared-off calf is shifted markedly further to the left than the thigh in an allusion to the ballet's "bas-relief" choreography. Moving further around to view the figure from behind, Nijinsky's back appears to heave upward, and his arms gradually disappear behind his torso in an evocation of the ballet's scandalous climax. Through Rodin's complex recasting of *L'Après-midi d'un faune*, Nijinsky's choreography travels full circle back into the medium of sculpture, situating itself directly at the place where the two arts meet. In this figure – as in the *Mouvements de danse* – we see a configuration of the body possible only through a total convergence of dance and sculpture.

CHOREOGRAPHING FRAGMENTS

Reading Rodin's late work through the lens of dance – with specific attention to the qualities of the dances he knew well – transforms our understanding not only of the sculptures he made and showed at that time, but also of his broader approach to his creative process. In so far as he conceived of his sculptures as in a perpetual state of becoming, they served as open receptacles for his observations of dance, which accumulated in sedimentary layers over time. As Rodin paid ever closer attention to dance, he would have noted the quasi-choreographic nature of his own process: his conceptual gallery of poses was akin to a repertoire in which the dancer's body functions as an archive, conserving memories of past performances and, in each successive iteration, introducing changes to the original work.

Just as Rodin looked to dance at a moment when he hoped to breach the given limits of sculpture, several choreographers of this era looked to sculpture, including Rodin's, as they reinvented the medium of dance. This free migration of ideas and images between sculpture and dance is the explicit subject of Loïe Fuller's *Hand Dance* (1914), made in homage to Rodin's fragmentary, disembodied hands – works that defy corporeal wholeness and the statue's conventionally vertical orientation.[86] Masking most of her body with black fabric, Fuller left only her hands visible, performing with them a series of expressive gestures. In a series of photographs that Fuller gave to Rodin – the only remaining record of this work – we see that the transfer of his original concept into dance sharpened its challenge to sculptural (as well as choreographic) convention. Activating Rodin's hands, Fuller intensifies their uncanny mix of incompletion and self-containment, animation and lifelessness. Using the medium of photography to make this transitory dance durable, she then added them to his collection – joining her hands to his so that they all together formed a single corporeal archive.

NOTES

1 I am grateful to several interlocutors for their responses to the ideas presented here, including Linda Kim, Mary Hunter and Emmelyn Butterfield-Rosen. I am also grateful to Jennifer Homans and the staff and 2015–16 cohort of fellows at the Center for Ballet and the Arts, New York University, for the role the Center played in incubating and shaping this essay.
Rodin's published statements on dance include several interviews about the Cambodian Royal Ballet published in summer 1906: see especially Georges Bourdon, 'Rodin et les petites princesses jaunes', *Le Figaro*, 1 August 1906, pp.1–2, and George Bois, 'Le Sculpteur Rodin et les danseuses cambodgiennes', *L'Illustration*, no.3309, 28 July 1906, pp.64–65; his defense of Nijinsky's *L'Après-midi d'un faune*, 'La Rénovation de la danse: Loïe Fuller, Isadora Duncan, Nijinski', *Le Matin*, 30 May 1912, p.1; reprinted in *Comœdia*, vol.6, no.1707, 2 June 1912, p.2; and his two-page article 'Fresques de Danses', published in the journal *Montjoie!*, vol.2, nos. 1–2, January–February 1914, pp.1–2. He also discusses the Cambodian Royal Ballet in his *Cathedrals of France* [1914], trans. Elizabeth Chase Geissbuhler, Boston (Beacon Press), 1965.

2 Nearly all Rodin's images that recognisably represent a specific dancer manipulate that performer's choreography in one way or another. I discuss several examples in this essay; for a more lengthy analysis of Rodin's process of shaping the *Nijinsky*, see my essay 'Reforming Dance: Auguste Rodin's *Nijinsky* and Vaslav Nijinsky's *L'Après-midi d'un faune*', *Cantor Arts Center Journal*, vol.3, 2002–03, pp.172–85.

3 Prominent examples of sculptures of dance, all likely to have been well known to Rodin, include Jean-Baptiste Carpeaux's *Danse* (1865–69) on the façade of the Paris Opéra; Edgar Degas's *Little Dancer Aged Fourteen* (1878–81), shown at the Impressionist exhibition of 1881; Camille Claudel's *La Valse* (1883–1901), shown at the Salon of the Société des Beaux-Arts in 1893; and Alexandre Falguière's *Dancer* (1896), shown at the Salon of 1897.

4 The one group of dance images that Rodin showed publicly with some regularity was his suite of drawings of the Cambodian Royal Ballet. In addition to displaying them prominently in his studio, he published several examples in illustrated journals (see footnote 1 for a list of those publications) and subsequently exhibited them on a few occasions, as in his October 1908 exhibition at the Galerie Devambez in Paris.

5 Hélène Pinet discusses the apparent "marginality" of dance to Rodin's work in *Ornement de la durée: Loïe Fuller, Isadora Duncan, Ruth St. Denis, Adorée Villany*, Paris (Musée Rodin), 1987, p.2.

6 The issue of movement in Rodin's sculptures is discussed widely; examples include Pinet 1987, p.2; Herbert Read, *The Art of Sculpture*, Washington, D.C. (National Gallery of Art) and New York (Bollingen), 1956, pp.92–98; Jacques de Caso and Patricia B. Sanders, *Rodin's Sculpture: A Critical Study of the Spreckels Collection*, San Francisco (The Fine Arts Museums of San Francisco) and Rutland, VT (Charles E. Tuttle), 1977, p.139; Albert E. Elsen with Rosalyn Frankel Jamison, *Rodin's Art: The Rodin Collection Iris & Gerland B. Cantor Center for Visual Arts Stanford University*, ed. Bernard Barryte, Oxford (OUP), 2003, pp.573–78.

7 This process is described in Leo Steinberg, 'Rodin', in *Other Criteria: Confrontations with Twentieth-Century Art*, New York (OUP), 1972, especially p.371; Rosalind Krauss, 'The Originality of the Avant-Garde: A Postmodernist Repetition', *October*, vol.18, 1981, pp.47–66; and David Getsy, *Rodin: Sex and the Making of Modern Sculpture*, New Haven (Yale UP), 2010, pp.101–22.

8 Important here is the issue of chronology, which is extremely complicated in Rodin's case, not only because he often replicated and revised his work but also because many of his most convention-defying sculptures were not exhibited until years after they were first made. See Alain Beausire, *Quand Rodin Exposait*, Paris (Musée Rodin), 1988.

9 The importance of intermedial dialogue to the development of modernist idioms is fundamental to my book *Modernism on Stage: The Ballets Russes and the Parisian Avant-Garde*, Farnham (Ashgate), 2013, as well as my forthcoming book on Rodin. See also Juliet Bellow and Nell Andrew, 'Inventing Abstraction? Modernist Dance in Europe', in Stephen Ross and Allana C. Lindgren, eds., *The Modernist World*, London and New York (Routledge), 2015, pp.329–38. Several of the dances described here are discussed in this essay.

10 On Rodin's exhibition history, see Beausire 1988; on his role in the splintering of the annual Salon in 1890, see Constance Cain Hungerford, 'Meissonier and the Founding of the Société Nationale des Beaux-Arts', *Art Journal*, vol.48, no.1, Spring 1989, pp.71–77.

11 A key aspect of Rodin's keeping tabs on his public image was his subscription to a clippings service in the early 1880s. David Getsy discusses Rodin's awareness of his own public image more broadly in Getsy 2010.

12 Loïe Fuller's pursuit of patents for her choreography is a fascinating example of the way she approached the business side of her craft. See Anthea Kraut, *Choreographing Copyright: Race, Gender, and Intellectual Property Rights in American Dance*, Oxford (OUP), 2015.

13 In some ways, my approach echoes that of Gabrielle Brandstetter's *Tanz-Lectüren: Körperbilder und Raumfiguren der Avantgarde* (1995), recently published in English as *Poetics of Dance: Body, Image, Space in the Historical Avant-Gardes*, trans. Elena Polzer and Mark Franko, Oxford (OUP), 2015. Brandstetter discusses the relationship between dance and literature (and, to a lesser degree, visual art) through Aby Warburg's concept of the 'pathos formula'.

14 The analyses of dance that I provide below draw upon a variety of sources, including period reviews, memoirs of dancers and of witnesses, secondary-source analyses, later films and reconstructions of the dances. My thoughts about the difficulties endemic to studying dance are indebted to Kate Elswit's introduction to her book *Watching Weimar Dance*, Oxford (OUP), 2014, especially pp.xvi–xxi.

15 Brandstetter 1995, p.2.

16 The most comprehensive, wide-ranging text on this period in dance history is Nancy Reynolds and Malcolm McCormick, *No Fixed Points: Dance in the Twentieth Century*, New Haven (Yale UP), 2003.

17 For discussions of ballet in this period, see Ivor Guest, *The Ballet of the Second Empire* [1953], Middletown (Wesleyan University Press), 1974; Barbara Barker, *Ballet or Ballyhoo: The American Careers of Maria Bonfanti, Rita Sangalli, and Giuseppina Morlacchi*, New York (Dance Horizons), 1984; and Sarah Gutsche-Miller, *Parisian Music-Hall Ballet, 1871–1913*, Rochester (URP), 2015. The ballet 'classics' we know today were by and large developed by Marius Petipa and Lev Ivanov in Russia in the late nineteenth century, and were not known in Europe or America until the 1920s and 1930s. See Beth Genné, 'Creating a Canon, Creating the "Classics" in Twentieth-Century Ballet', *Dance Research*, vol.18, no.2, Winter 2000, pp.132–63.

18 On the construction of the Palais Garnier and the social and political associations of the building, see Christopher Mead, 'Urban Contingency and the Problem of Representation in Second Empire Paris', *Journal of the Society of Architectural Historians*, vol.54, June 1995, pp.138–74; the

histories of the Salle le Peletier and Palais Garnier are also discussed at length in Jill DeVonyar and Richard Kendall, *Degas and the Dance*, New York (Harry N. Abrams), 2002, and in Isabel Smith, 'The Politics of Location in Edgar Degas's Depictions of the Paris Opéra', M.A. Thesis, American University, 2016.

19 On the history of the cancan, see David Price, *Cancan!*, Cranbury, NJ (Fairleigh Dickinson University Press), 1998; a more general history of popular performance in this period is provided in Catherine Pedley-Hindson, *Female performance practice on the fin-de-siècle popular stages of London and Paris: Experiment and Advertising*, Manchester (MUP), 2007.

20 On acrobatic dance, see Myriam Peignist, 'Histoire Anthropologique des Danses Acrobatiques', *Corps*, vol.2, no.7, 2009, pp.29–38.

21 As their careers progressed, each of these women performed with other dancers, but each originally came to prominence as a solo performer. A fourth dancer of this type, less famous now, was the Canadian-born dancer Maud Allan. For a description of her work, see Amy Koritz, 'Dancing the Orient for England: Maud Allan's "The Vision of Salomé"', *Theatre Journal*, vol.46, no.1, March 1994, pp.63–78.

22 On the performance and reception of the *danse du ventre* in 1889, see Zeynep Çelik and Leila Kinney, 'Ethnography and Exhibitionism at the Expositions Universelles', *Assemblage*, no.13, December 1990, pp.34–59; on the Javanese troupe, see Matthew Isaac Cohen, *Performing Otherness: Java and Bali on International Stages, 1905–1952*, London (Palgrave Macmillan), 2010. For a general survey of 'exotic' dance in France in this period, see Anne Décoret-Ahiha, *Les danses exotiques en France 1880–1940*, Pantin (Centre nationale de la danse), 2004.

23 The only full-length published source to deal directly with Rodin's encounter with the Cambodian Royal Ballet is an exhibition catalogue published by the Musée Rodin, ed. Jacques Vilain et al., *Rodin et les danseuses cambodgiennes: Sa dernière passion*, Paris, 2006. The Cambodian dancers also form a major chapter in the earlier exhibition catalogue *Rodin et l'Extrême-Orient*, Paris (Musée Rodin), 1979. More recently, the subject was treated in a short exhibition catalogue by Stephen Feeke and Ramsay Burt, *Rodin: Rhythm and Ritual*, Leeds (The Henry Moore Sculpture Trust), 1998, and in a chapter of Marco Deyasi's doctoral thesis 'French Visual Culture and "Indochina": Modernism, Primitivism, and Colonialism, 1889–1931', Ph.D. dissertation, Duke University, 2007).

24 On Cléo de Mérode, see Michael Garval, *Cléo de Mérode and the Rise of Modern Celebrity Culture*, Farnham (Ashgate), 2012; on Mata Hari, see Cohen 2010; on La Goulue's adaptation of the belly dance, see Danielle Sensabaugh, 'Between Poster and Painting: Artistic and Cultural Hybridity in Henri de Toulouse-Lautrec's Panels for "La Goulue"', M.A. Thesis, American University, 2015.

25 For a lengthy discussion of the reasons behind this reform and the way the troupe carried it out, see Bellow 2013, ch.1, as well as Lynn Garafola, *Diaghilev's Ballets Russes*, New York (OUP), 1989.

26 I discuss issues of national identity in relation to the Ballets Russes and its repertory in 'When Art Danced with Music', in Jane Pritchard, ed., *Diaghilev and the Golden Age of the Ballets Russes, 1909–1929*, London (V&A) and Washington, D.C. (National Gallery of Art), 2013, pp.186–203, and in 'The "Sacre au Printemps": Parisian Audiences and the Ballets Russes', in Karen L. Carter and Susan Waller, eds., *Foreign Artists and Communities in Paris, 1870–1914: Strangers in Paradise*, Farnham (Ashgate), 2015, pp.155–68, and in Bellow 2013.

27 The title of Rodin's essay is difficult to render in English; the best translation might be 'dance frescoes' – which positions the text as a sort of ekphrastic exercise. See Rodin 1914, pp.1–2.

28 During the period under discussion (as, to some degree, today) ballet was structured around the five positions of the arms and legs, as well as the sequencing of solo, pas de deux and ensemble appearances. On this issue, see Brandstetter 1995, p.270, as well as Marion Kant, ed., *The Cambridge Companion to Ballet*, Cambridge (CUP), 2007.

29 Fuller's, Duncan's and St. Denis's work appeared spontaneous, but was often far more scripted than it might at first appear. On this issue, see Ann Daly, *Done Into Dance: Isadora Duncan in America*, Middletown, CT (Wesleyan University Press), 1995.

30 See the epigraph to this essay, drawn from Rodin 1914, p.2: "*Et la danse, qui a été chez nous toujours un apanage érotique, tend enfin de nos jours à devenir digne des autres arts, qu'elle résume*".

31 On the 'marriage plot' in nineteenth-century ballet and its evolution over the course of the following century, see Sally Banes, *Dancing Women: Female Bodies Onstage*, London and New York (Routledge), 1998.

32 For a nuanced interpretation of modern art's complex relation to mass culture, see Jeffrey Weiss, *The Popular Culture of Modern Art*, New Haven (Yale UP), 1993.

33 Importantly, unlike Rodin, Mallarmé gave equal praise to ballet and 'modern" dance (especially Loïe Fuller's performance style). His essays on dance, 'Ballets' (1886), 'Crayonné au théâtre' (1887), and 'Autre étude de danse: les fonds dans le ballet d'après une indication récente' (1893–96) all appear in his *Divagations* (1897); see Mallarmé, *Igitur, Divagations, Un coup de dés*, ed. Bertrand Marchal, Paris (Gallimard), 2003, or Mallarmé, *Divagations*, trans. Barbara Johnson, Cambridge, MA (Belknap Press of Harvard UP), 2007.

34 Susan Jones, *Literature, Modernism and Dance*, Oxford (OUP), 2013, p.13; on Mallarmé and dance, see also Mary Lewis Shaw, *Performance in the Texts of Mallarmé: The Passage from Art to Ritual*, University Park (Pennsylvania State UP), 1993, and Dee Reynolds, 'The Dancer as Woman: Loïe Fuller and Stéphane Mallarmé', in Richard Hobbs, ed., *Impressions of French Modernity: Art and Literature in France 1850–1900*, Manchester (Manchester UP), 1998, pp.155–72. Though Mallarmé viewed dance in less fraught terms than he did the genre of the newspaper, there are nevertheless marked parallels between his use of these two 'popular-cultural' sources. On Mallarmé and the newspaper, see Anna Sigrídur Arnar, *The Book as Instrument: Stéphane Mallarmé, the Artist's Book, and the Transformation of Print Culture*, Chicago (UCP), 2011.

35 Ruth Butler, in her biography of Rodin, dates their friendship back to at least the early 1890s, when Mallarmé tried to help Rodin to obtain a commission to commemorate the poet and critic Charles Baudelaire. See Butler, *Rodin: The Shape of Genius*, New Haven (Yale UP), 1993, p.259; Claudine Mitchell discusses Rodin's relationship to Mallarmé in greater depth in 'Metaphor and Metamorphosis: Rodin in the Circle of Mallarmé', *Cantor Arts Center Journal*, vol.3, 2002–03, pp.111–27. For an in-depth history of Mallarmé's *mardis*, see Gordon Millan, *Les "Mardis" de Stéphane Mallarmé: Mythes et Réalités*, Saint-Genouph (Librarie Nizet), 2008.

36 Rodin's connections in the dance world strengthened after 1900 when he became enmeshed in German intellectual circles through Rainer Maria Rilke (who worked for a time as his secretary) as well as Helene von Nostitz and Count Harry Kessler.

37 See, for example, Marx's lengthy essay

on Fuller, 'Une Rénovatrice de la danse' [1892–1907], republished in Marx, *L'Art social*, Paris (Bibliothèque-Charpentier), 1913, which undoubtedly influenced Rodin's similarly titled 'La Rénovation de la danse: Loïe Fuller, Isadora Duncan, Nijinski' (Rodin 1912). Mauclair related the Ballets Russes to Mallarmé in 'Karsavina et Mallarmé', *Le Courrier musical*, vol.15, no.11, 1 June 1912.

38 Rodin 1912.

39 The word Rodin used was *résumer* (see note 30).

40 See Alex Potts, *The Sculptural Imagination: Figurative, Modernist, Minimalist*, New Haven (Yale UP), 2000, pp.90, 98. In addition to Potts's astute analysis, my understanding of this aspect of Rodin's work is indebted to Leo Steinberg, who discusses the way "solids and voids interact as modes of energy" in Rodin's late sculpture: Steinberg 1972, p.351.

41 Getsy 2010, pp.126–27.

42 Marx was the author of an essay on Fuller in the *Revue encyclopédique* published in 1893. Rodin's first recorded mention of Fuller came in a letter sent to Marx on 26 November 1897, in which he signalled his regret for having missed "the lovely modern tanagra of the beautiful Loïe Fuller", perhaps indicating that Marx had invited Rodin to one of Fuller's performances. For a discussion of Marx's writings on Fuller, see Bellow, 'Reforming Dance: Auguste Rodin's "Nijinsky" and Vaslav Nijinsky's "L'Après-midi d'un faune"', *Cantor Arts Center Journal*, no.3, 2002–03, pp.172–85.

43 On Fuller's technique and reputation, see among the many publications on the dancer Giovanni Lista, *Loïe Fuller: danseuse de la belle époque*, Paris (Éditions Stock), 1994; Ann Cooper Albright, *Traces of Light: Absence and Presence in the Work of Loïe Fuller*, Middletown, CT (Wesleyan University Press), 2007; and Rhonda K. Garelick, *Electric Salomé: Loïe Fuller's Performance of Modernism*, Princeton (PUP), 2007.

44 Sally Sommer is one of few scholars to address Fuller's choice of musical accompaniment for this early work; her selections later veered toward concert music. See Sommer, 'Loïe Fuller's Art of Music and Light', *Dance Chronicle*, vol.4, no.4, 1981, pp.389–401.

45 Her movement vocabulary itself was simple, consisting of rushes across the stage, turns and undulations of the arms and torso, and waltz steps and skips. Ann Cooper Albright discusses at length the experience of trying to re-create Fuller's dance, noting how much effort this apparently simple technique required. See Albright 2007, p.30. Fuller herself describes the technique in her slightly premature autobiography, *Fifteen Years of a Dancer's Life, With Some Account of Her Distinguished Friends*, London (Herbert Jenkins), 1908.

46 Brandstetter characterises Fuller's performance as a form of "moving scenography" (1995, p.271); see also Bellow and Andrew 2015, pp.331–32. As I note above, Fuller applied for patents for several elements in her staging, including the costume and the lighting technology she used. See Kraut 2015. She was dubbed the 'electric fairy' for her purported use of electric lights in her act, but it seems likely that she actually used more traditional gas lighting, at least at the beginning of her career. I am indebted to the research of Jaimie Holman, '*La fée gazeuse?* Light blindness and the historiography of Loïe Fuller', unpublished paper prepared for a seminar led by S. Hollis Clayson, Northwestern University, 2010.

47 For example, a whole series of photographs was created by Eugène Druet, Rodin's 'in-house' photographer, and were set in the sculptor's garden. (Druet, an amateur photographer, worked only for Rodin at this time.) On Rodin and photography, see Hélène Pinet, *Les Photographes de Rodin*, Paris (Musée Rodin), 1986; Pinet, ed., *Rodin et la Photographie*, Paris (Gallimard/Musée Rodin), 2007; Pinet, '*Montrer est la question vitale*: Rodin and Photography', in Geraldine Johnson, ed., *Sculpture and Photography: Envisioning the Third Dimension*, Cambridge (CUP), 1999, pp.68–85; and Natasha Ruiz-Gómez, 'Auguste Rodin and the "scientific image": the sublime copy versus the photograph', in Minsoo Kang and Amy Woodson-Boulton, eds., *Visions of the Industrial Age, 1830–1914: Modernity and the Anxiety of Representation*, Farnham (Ashgate), 2008, pp.109–36.

48 Rodin owned four subtly different iterations of this image; for the whole series, see Pinet 1987, nos. 24–27. On the appeal of the *Nike* sculpture (in the collection of the Louvre) around the turn of the century, see Sophie Basch and Fabrice van der Kerkhove, 'La Victoire de Samothrace, Muse Fin de Siècle', *Revue des Deux Mondes*, September 2014, pp.33–45. The authors relate Fuller's act generally to the Nike statue, but do not discuss this particular image. Likewise, Brandstetter discusses Rilke's use of the *Nike* as a metaphor for Rodin's work, and echoes of the *Nike* in Fuller's as well as Duncan's choreography, but does not directly connect them, or discuss this particular photograph: see Brandstetter 1995, pp.124–42.

49 'Valentine de Saint-Point' was the pseudonym of Anne-Jeanne-Valentine-Marianne Desglans de Cessiat-Vercell.

50 Saint-Point's 'Poèmes de l'Orgueil' (Poems of pride) were published in the journal *L'Europe Artiste* in July 1904; a copy was sent to Rodin through his clipping service, Le Courrier de la Presse. In 1906, Saint-Point authored an in-depth work of criticism on Rodin's sculpture entitled 'La Double Personnalité d'Auguste Rodin'; it appeared in the *Nouvelle Revue* in November 1906 (pp.29–42). The two corresponded intensively about this article and other ideas for publications that did not materialise.

51 In 1911–12, Saint-Point invited the dancer Ariane Hugon to interpret her poems: see Nell Andrew, 'Bodies of the Avant-Garde', Ph.D. dissertation, University of Chicago, 2007, p.89. The Salle Léon-Poirer was an adjunct to the Théâtre des Champs-Élysées.

52 The orchestra played music by Roland Manuel, Florent Schmitt, Claude Debussy and Erik Satie. For in-depth descriptions of this performance, see Andrew 2007 and Günter Berghaus, 'Dance and the Futurist Woman: The Work of Valentine de Saint-Point', *Dance Research*, vol.11, no.2, Autumn 1993, pp.27–42.

53 Andrew 2007 discusses the dismissal of Saint-Point's technique as a form of rhythmic gymnastics; Brandstetter describes Saint-Point's dance as comprising "various movements of the arms, twists of the torso, small steps forward and backward, frequent forward bends": Brandstetter 1995, p.303.

54 Andrew (2007, pp.81–146) discusses in depth the issue of space in a chapter on Saint-Point. As Andrew also notes, Saint-Point was a painter and printmaker and made several images of her act.

55 Steinberg 1972, pp.346–49.

56 Jacques de Caso (de Caso and Sanders 1977, p.19) uses the term "kinesthetic awareness". My discussion of kinaesthesia is indebted to the introduction of Dee Reynolds's book *Rhythmic Subjects: Uses of Energy in the Dances of Mary Wigman, Martha Graham and Merce Cunningham*, London (Dance books), 2007, particularly to her observation that "Movement events that disrupt normative, habitual ways of using energy in movement and produce innovations in production, distribution, expenditure and retention of energy in the body are acts of 'kinesthetic imagination'" (p.4). On this issue as it relates to Duncan, see also Sarah Kennel, 'Bodies, Statues, and Machines: Dance and

the Visual Arts in France, 1900–1925', Ph.D. Dissertation, University of California, Berkeley, 2003, pp.32–34, and Hillel Schwartz, 'Torque: The New Kinaesthetic of the Twentieth Century', in Jonathan Crary and Sanford Kwinter, eds., *Incorporations*, New York (Zone Books), 2003, pp.71–126.

57 Reynolds 2007, p.4.

58 Brandstetter 1995, p.49. See also Carrie J. Preston, 'The Motor in the Soul: Isadora Duncan and Modernist Performance', *Modernism/modernity*, vol.12, no.2, 2005, pp.273–89, and Robin Veder, *The Living Line: Modern Art and the Economy of Efficiency*, Hanover, NH (Dartmouth UP), 2015.

59 On the complex role of eroticism in Rodin's art and identity, see Anne Wagner's landmark essay 'Rodin's Reputation', in Lynn Hunt, ed., *Eroticism and the Body Politic*, Baltimore (Johns Hopkins UP), 1993, pp.191–242, as well as Getsy 2010.

60 Isadora Duncan, *My Life* [1927], New York and London (Liveright), 1995, pp.68–69. Many of Duncan's statements on dance are collected in *Isadora Speaks: Writings and Speeches of Isadora Duncan*, ed. Franklin Rosemont, Chicago (Charles H. Kerr), 1994. On Duncan's theory and practice, see Daly 1995, as well as Kennel 2003.

61 Duncan's 'Idyll of Theocritus' may refer to Theocritus's Idyll 18, which is presented as a choral song performed by a group of maidens celebrating the marriage of Helen, and in which the maidens describe their own dance. I am grateful to Deborah Stein for suggesting this reference. It should also be noted that most of Duncan's early work was performed in intimate salons and in art galleries; later, she began to stage dances more frequently in theatres.

62 For a description of the *Dance Idylls* and the reaction of Netherlandish audiences to Duncan's 1905 performances of that piece, see Lillian Lowenthal, 'Isadora Duncan in the Netherlands', *Dance Chronicle*, vol.3, no.3, 1979–80, pp.227–53.

63 She opposed ballet in part for "vainly striving against the natural laws of gravitation", as she wrote in her 1903 manifesto 'The Dance of the Future', reprinted in Sheldon Cheney, ed., *The Art of the Dance*, New York (Theatre Arts), 1928, pp.62–63.

64 In her discussion of the similarities between Duncan's and Rodin's conceptions of the 'natural', Ann Daly emphasises the influence of Rodin on Duncan (see Daly 1995, p.95); I believe that Duncan's ideas, especially as expressed choreographically, also influenced Rodin.

65 Duncan 1995, p.126; Auguste Rodin, *Art: Conversations with Paul Gsell* [1911], trans. Jacques de Caso and Patricia B. Sanders, Berkeley (University of California Press), 1984, pp.11–12; see also the similar language he used in his interview with Henri Dujardin-Beaumetz, reprinted in Albert Elsen, ed., *Auguste Rodin: Readings on His Life and Work*, Englewood Cliffs, NJ (Prentice-Hall), 1965, pp.158. Ann Daly discusses with great nuance the relationship between 'nature' and 'art' in her book on Duncan, also noting that the dancer "used strategies of difference and exclusion, exploiting the conventional distinctions between high and low." See Daly 1995, p.111; this issue is also discussed in Reynolds 2007, p.37.

66 For example, in an interview about her 1903 trip to Greece published in the *New York Sunday World*, Duncan argued that "Of all the thousands of figures of Greek sculpture, bas-reliefs and vases there is not one but is in exquisite bodily proportion and harmony of movement .... I came to Greece to study these forms of ancient art, but above all, I came to live in the land which produced these wonders, and when I say 'to live,' I mean to dance." (This passage is quoted in Daly 1995, p.101.) Rodin frequently invoked classical antiquity in his writings on dance; see the sources cited in footnote 1 for examples.

67 In a short piece on Duncan for the Dance Heritage Coalition's online collection of essays, Ann Cooper Albright notes that "although she speaks of dancing, Duncan rarely calls herself a choreographer. Most of her descriptions, in fact, talk of 'finding' movements, almost as if she were simply channeling the motion of the universe through her body." See http://www.danceheritage.org/duncan.html.

68 This encounter with Rodin is recounted in Suzanne Shelton, *Ruth St. Denis: A Biography of the Divine Dancer* [1981], Austin (University of Texas Press), 1990, p.75. Very few traces of his contact with St. Denis exist in the Rodin archive: there is an undated note from St. Denis, from an address at 4, Avenue Matignon, accepting an invitation from one Mme de Kozmutza to visit Rodin's studio; a telegram sent from St. Denis in London in October 1908 asking if she could list Rodin as a patron for an upcoming fête; and a photograph in Rodin's collection of St. Denis in *The Yogi* (1908), one of a suite of images made by Stephanie Ludwig.

69 For a description of *Radha*, see Shelton 1990, p.61; on the relation of *Radha* and other St. Denis works to 'nautch' dancing from northern India and Sri Lanka, see Priya Srinivasan, *Sweating Saris: Indian Dance as Transnational Labor*, Philadelphia (Temple UP), 2011; on St. Denis's later career, see Paul Scolieri, 'Rhythms of Resurrection: The Comebacks of Ruth St. Denis', *Women and Performance: A Journal of Feminist Theory*, vol.22, no.1, March 2012, pp.89–107, and Susan Teneriello, 'The Divine Spaces of Metaphysical Spectacle: Ruth St. Denis and Denishawn Dance Theatre at Lewisohn Standium, the Esoteric Model in American Performance', *Performance Research*, vol.13, no.3, 2008, pp.124–38. On the importance of cantilevering to Rodin's sculpture, see Elsen 2003, p.573.

70 David Getsy, 'Acts of Stillness: Statues, Performativity, and Passive Resistance', *Criticism*, vol.56, no.1, Winter 2014, pp.1–20.

71 On the centrality of stillness to dance, see André Lepecki, 'Still: On the Vibratile Microscopy of Dance', in Gabriele Brandstetter and Hortensia Völckers, eds., *ReMembering the Body*, Ostfildern-Ruit (Hatje Cantz), 2000, pp.334–65.

72 Obtaining a precise account of the members of the troupe and of the works performed in France has proved difficult. The number of 45 comes from the official *Rapport Général* of the Marseille exhibition, authored by M.J. Charles-Roux, Commissaire général (*Rapport Général, Exposition Coloniale de Marseille*, Marseille [Barlatier] 1907); Gaspard Galy, the reporter who covered the fair daily for the *Petit Marseillais*, put the number of dancers at 42, and claimed that they were "between 16 and 26 years old"; the troupe also consisted of "4 spoken-word performers [*lectrices*], 8 percussionists, 4 dressers, 2 clowns [*bouffons*], 12 musicians, 2 jewellers and 3 guards": 'Le roi du Cambodge à Marseille', *Le Petit Marseillais*, 12 May 1906); copies of both documents are now held in the archives of the Musée Rodin, Paris.

73 A full programme of the performance at the Pré-Catelan is in the archives of the Musée Rodin, Paris. The troupe performed a "Fan Dance", "Bird Dance" and a narrative folkloric work entitled 'The Legend of Prince Ounaroth'. Importantly, these works appear not to be drawn from the *Reamker*, the source of the mostly narrative dance-drama works performed in the Cambodian tradition. The *Reamker* is the Cambodian variant of the *Ramayana*, a Hindu epic that originated in India and tells the story of the exploits of Prince Rama, the earthly incarnation of the god Vishnu, in his quest to rescue his wife Sita from the demon-king Ravana. Sources on

Cambodian dance include Toni Samantha Phim and Ashley Thompson, *Dance in Cambodia*, Oxford (OUP), 1999; Hideo Sasagawa, 'Post/colonial Discourses on the Cambodian Court Dance', *Southeast Asian Studies*, vol.42, no.4, March 2005, pp.418–41; Paul Cravath, *Earth in Flower: The Divine Mystery of the Cambodian Dance Drama*, Holmes Beach, FL (DatASIA), 2007; Denise Heywood, *Cambodian Dance: Celebration of the Gods*, Bangkok (River Books), 2008. On the relation of this form to other Southeast Asian dance and theatre, see Jukka O. Miettinen, *Classical Dance and Theatre in South-East Asia*, Oxford (OUP), 1992.

74 Jonathan Kramer provides a useful, if also problematic, discussion of the temporality of European music versus that of "non-linear cultures" in his essay 'New Temporalities in Music', *Critical Inquiry*, vol.7, no.3, Spring 1981, pp.539–56.

75 See Paul Cravath, 'The Ritual Origins of the Classical Dance Drama of Cambodia', *Asian Theatre Journal*, vol.3, no.2, Autumn 1986, p.190. To some extent, this relatively limited range of motion stemmed from the costuming introduced in the mid nineteenth century: these garments were worn so tightly that the dancers had to be sewn into them for each performance (Cravath 2007, p.112).

76 The serpentine motions of the arms are often said to relate to the legend of the Naga, the snake-like embodiment of the spirit of the waters, in the *Reamker*. See Cravath 2007, p.46.

77 Cravath 2007, p,.112.

78 A report in the *Petit Journal* claimed that the dances were presented in the Cambodian pavilion, but official reports place them in the music-hall and Grand Palais as well as an outdoor terrace in view of both the Cambodian pavilion and the 'Théâtre Indo-Chinois', both designed by the French architect Henri Vildieu. The *Rapport Général* characterised the Cambodian pavilion as a "faithful reproduction of a part of Bayon at Angkor-Thom ... possibly the most original monument that Khmer art produced" (p.141). On the relation of this structure to its original Cambodian referent, see Isabelle Flour, 'Orientalism and the Reality Effect: Angkor at the Universal Expositions, 1867–1937', *Getty Research Journal*, vol.6, 2014, pp.63–82.

79 For a discussion of Rodin's Buddhas, see Bénédicte Garnier, 'Vivante immobilité, une collection de gestes antiques', in Katia Légeret, ed., *Rodin et la danse de Çiva*, Saint-Denis (Presses Universitaires de Vincennes), 2014, pp.133–50, and Deyasi 2007, p.113. The Musée Guimet also owned a work now referred to as *Ornamented Buddha protected by the Naga*, which was brought to France in the late 1870s as part of a group of original sculptures and plaster casts retrieved by the explorer Louis Delaporte in an expedition to Cambodia in 1873–74. On Delaporte's expedition, see Pierre Baptiste and Thierry Zéphir, *Angkor: Naissance d'un mythe, Louis Delaporte et le Cambodge*, Paris (Musée national des arts asiatiques Guimet), 2013.

80 Rodin evidently attended the premiere that took place on Wednesday 29 May 1912; the fact that his article came out so soon after the premiere suggests that he may have written it (or had it ghostwritten) in anticipation of the scandal that materialised. In his diaries, Count Harry Kessler documents a session in which Nijinsky modelled for Rodin on Sunday 2 June 1912: see *Journey to the Abyss: The Diaries of Count Harry Kessler, 1880–1918*, ed. and trans. Laird M. Easton, New York (Alfred A. Knopf), 2011, pp.602–03.

81 On this novel technique, see Stephanie Jordan, 'Debussy, the Dance, and *Faune*', in James Briscoe, ed., *Debussy in Performance*, New Haven (Yale UP), 1999, pp.119–34; Kennel 2003; Hanna Järvinen, 'Dancing without Space: On Nijinsky's *L'Après-midi d'un faune* (1912)', *Dance Research*, vol.27, no.1, April 2009, pp.28–64; Emmelyn Butterfield-Rosen, 'The Disposition of Persons: Conventions of Pose and Modern Figural Art, 1886–1912', Ph.D. dissertation, Princeton University, 2015; and Bellow 2013, pp.50–55.

82 Jordan 1999, p.126.

83 Rodin 1912.

84 I relate Rodin's *Nijinsky* to *Iris* in Bellow 2002–03, p.182.

85 In his interview with Paul Gsell, conducted the year before he made the *Nijinsky*, Rodin negatively compared chronophotographic representations of movement with the sculptor's ability to convey movement in a single pose. See Auguste Rodin, *L'Art: Entretiens réunis par Paul Gsell* [1911], Paris (Bernard Grasset), 1999, p.63. The fact that Rodin did not affix this small figure to a base means that one way of viewing it would be to hold it, thus allowing the viewer to turn it around and set its poses into successive motion. See Bellow 2002–03, p.180, and Steinberg 1972, pp.338–39.

86 The history of their hand exchange includes Rodin's dedication of a version in plaster of his sculpture *Hand of God* (*c.*1898) to Fuller, a work often characterised as a self-portrait of sorts. Fuller's version of this sculpture is now in the collection of the Maryhill Museum of Art, along with many other Rodins that she owned.

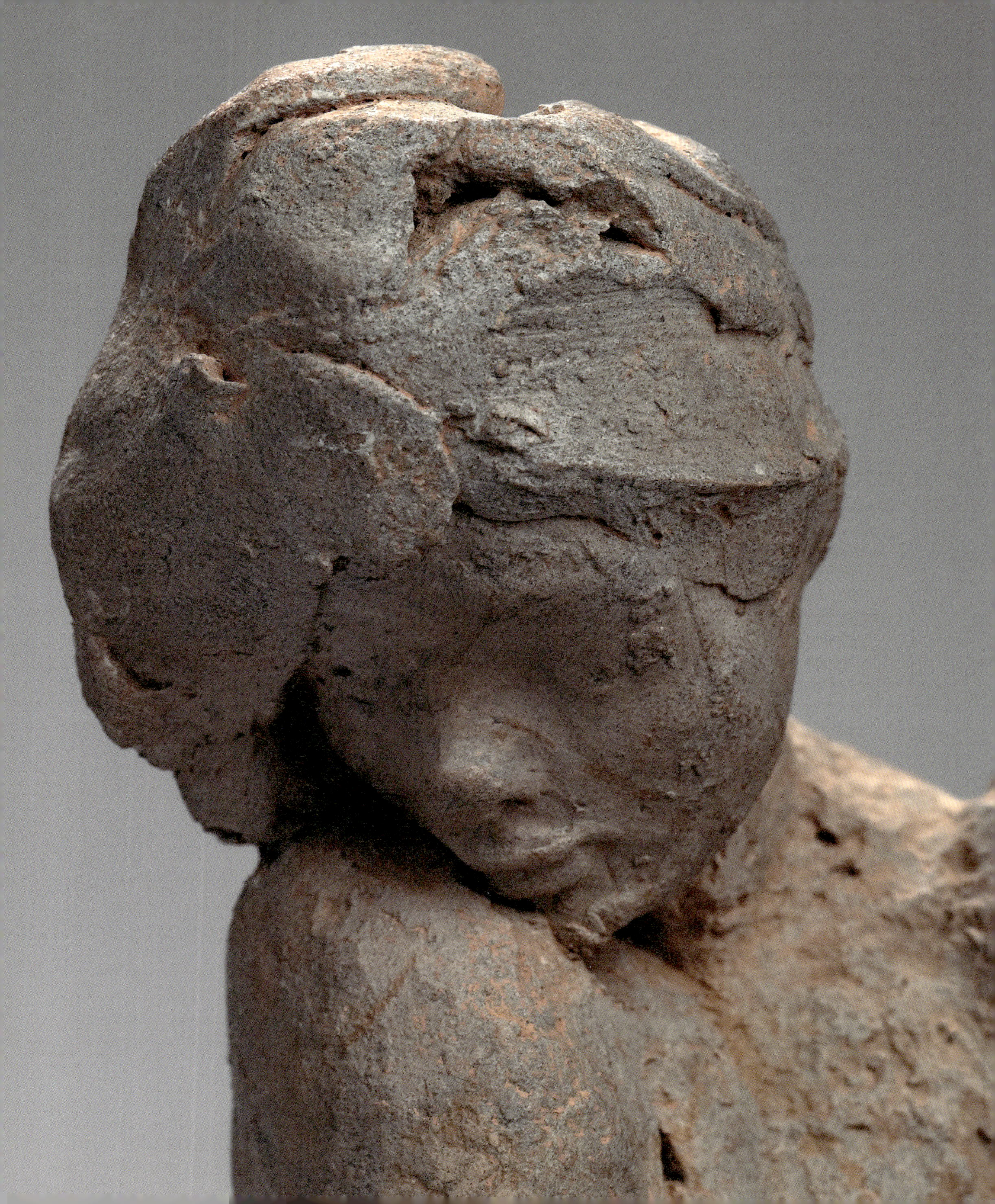

A MATERIAL AND TECHNICAL APPROACH TO RODIN'S MOUVEMENTS DE DANSE

FRANÇOIS BLANCHETIÈRE, AGNÈS CASCIO AND JULIETTE LÉVY

"In many of his late figurines, such as the *Jugglers*, the *Nijinsky*, the *Dance Movements*, Rodin's modeling blinds itself to external anatomy. His subtle acquaintance with human surface is set aside for a deepening, inward-turned acquiescence. One feels, as never before, an acceptance of the condition and shape of the material worked on; and a new willingness to let surface be no more than the track and passage of his own working hands. His little *Dance Movements* must have looked gauche in 1911 when they emerged. They are so frankly made of crude rolls of clay of nearly uniform thickness; their modulations are so naively the imprint of Rodin's thumb and the pinch of his fingers. And the marvel is that they too, the figures, their clay irradiated by movement, consent. For they dance. Accepting perfunctory surfaces and awkward limbs, they are oblivious of self and body, of style and beauty – to be only what the dance is."[1]

This paragraph forms the conclusion to the brilliant essay on Rodin written by the American critic and art historian Leo Steinberg in 1962. An expert on the Italian Renaissance and champion of modern art, in this now famous article he crystallised the main elements of the new vision of Rodin's art that was then emerging in the United States, spearheaded by Albert E. Elsen.[2] Steinberg recommended leaving the sculptor's best known works aside to focus on the studies in plaster and terracotta, which he regarded as the only works that offered access to the truth of the artist, since they had been made directly and personally by Rodin, unlike the bronzes and above all the marbles (which had been worked by marble carvers under his direction). According to Steinberg, the plaster and terracotta pieces reveal all Rodin's power of invention, indisputably establishing him as one of the fathers of modern art: "he invented a new concept of modelling which propels the septuagenarian Rodin into this century's avant-garde".[3]

Steinberg was right to draw attention to Rodin's creative processes, and it is noteworthy that he gave such an important place to the *Mouvements de danse* at the end of his discussion. In their formal freedom these small figures undeniably differ from the art of the nineteenth century and belong fully to the twentieth. However, we need to revise the terms in which he describes the technique Rodin used to create the *Mouvements*: "They are so frankly made of crude rolls of clay ... their modulations are so naively the imprint of Rodin's thumb and the pinch of his fingers". Steinberg refers to the "marvel" of "clay irradiated by movement" so that these works come alive, "to be only what the dance is". Swept along by these lyrical descriptions, the reader imagines Rodin modelling clay at the speed of the acrobatic dancer's movements, and we seem to see it shaped in seconds, as though by magic.

But there is an element of this story that is not quite right. Examination paying even a minimum of attention to the material and technical characteristics of the works reveals that the *Mouvements* in terracotta were not modelled but assembled from pre-existing pieces.[4] This does not make them any less interesting – quite the reverse, as we hope to show here.[5]

RODIN AT WORK

Let us start by recalling Rodin's usual working method, common to all the sculptors of his day.[6] The creation of a work would usually begin with a model made in clay, a malleable material that cannot be kept for a long time, since it cracks as it dries. So it was usual to cast the piece

Detail of s.5493, cat.63

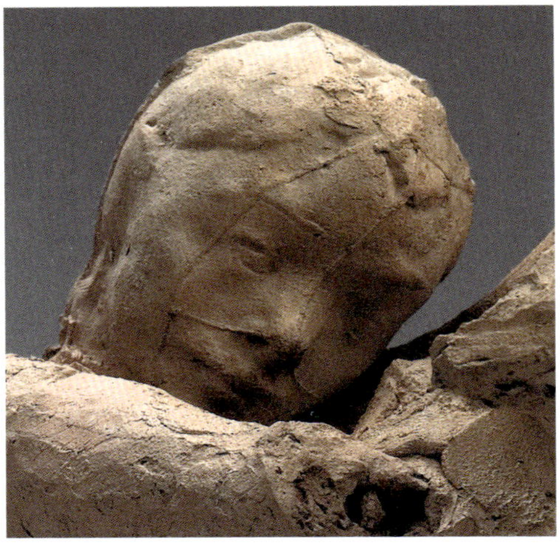

FIG.28
Network of seams on the face, *Mouvement I*

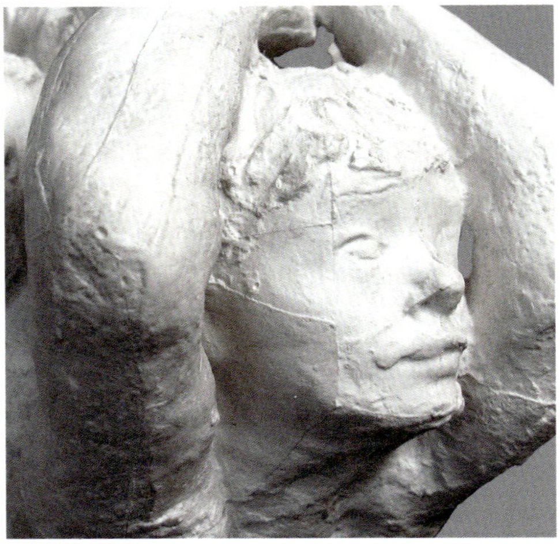

FIG.29
Double network of seams on the arms, *Pas de deux A*

that had been modelled, in other words to create a fairly rudimentary mould that would enable the form created by the sculptor to be reproduced as precisely as possible, in all its detail. The making of the plaster mould brought about the destruction of the clay model, and only one plaster could be cast from a mould made in this way since the mould itself was destroyed in the process (hence its name, *moule à creux perdu*, with its suggestion of a 'lost' mould). However, this plaster cast, which faithfully reproduced the modelling of the original work, was also much more robust, which meant it could be used to make a second, more complex mould from which several copies could be cast.

In the last part of his career, however, Rodin adopted a wide range of different techniques, which he did not necessarily invent himself, but which he readily used in combination or took further than other sculptors. He notably developed practices of fragmentation, assemblage and variation, which made it possible to create new versions of pre-existing works by removing, adding or modifying some of their elements, repeating some or all of a sculpture, or combining works that had previously been considered separate. Rodin made great use of casting techniques in order to retain the traces of particular states of his work, which meant he was always able to add another variation to the many ramifications of his art.[7]

DECODING THE SURFACE OF THE WORKS

Where the *Mouvements de danse* are concerned, in the absence of eye-witness accounts or archives documenting the progress of Rodin's work, our understanding of the process of creating these terracotta sculptures is based solely on a detailed examination of their surface. The traces of fingers and tools reflecting stages of shaping and moulding are clues that enable us to grasp the sculptor's technique and creative process. Luckily Rodin set little store by the finish of his works and did not seek to erase their imperfections or the traces left by the work of making them. On the contrary, in the last twenty years of his career he tended to see the visible signs of a work's creation as integral to the piece.

One of the first clues to catch the eye is the presence of seams – lines in slight relief marking the junction where two pieces of the mould meet. They immediately indicate that a terracotta piece was made not by modelling but rather by pressing in a mould (the raw clay was pressed inside the mould to take its shape; fig.28). Close observation of these seams enables us to identify the type of mould used – a mould *à creux perdu* (as described above)[8] or *à bon creux*, known in English as a piece mould,[9] or a gelatine mould[10] – and potentially to deduce the number of casts obtained. Sometimes the discovery of a double or even triple network of seams, resulting from successive operations, sheds valuable light on the genealogy of

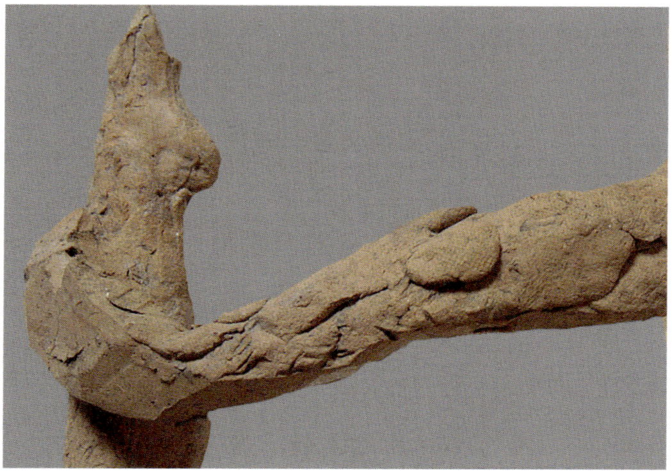

FIG.30
Addition of small balls of clay and removal of clay from the arm using a spatula, *Mouvement E*

the cast and its relationship to the lost initial clay model (fig.29).

All the terracotta *Mouvements de danse* show seams, proving that they were made by press-moulding rather than modelling. In a second stage of the process, Rodin reworked the raw clay figurines as he wished, of which there is evidence in the presence of fingerprints. He developed their forms either by adding small balls of clay or by removing clay with a spatula, turning each of the clay *Mouvements de danse* into a unique model (fig.30).

Our examination of the surface has more to tell us: the imprint of the fabric weave that the sculptor used to wrap the freshly made clay sculpture and keep it moist, so that he could modify it later if he chose, reflects the passing of time in the studio while it was made (fig.31). The marks of various tools – incisions made with a spatula, or fine ribbing indicating the use of a fine-toothed scraper (fig.32) – allow us to imagine Rodin's working movements. Similarly we see that he frequently used a small plaster rasp – an otherwise unusual tool in sculpture – lightly to strike the clay surface, which relates to his way of modifying planes and volumes to obtain a material texture that catches the light. Lastly, small areas of flattened clay, indicating the contact points on which the sculpture rested, enable us to deduce the orientation in which Rodin placed the sculpture once he had shaped it. So we can see that the terracotta *Mouvement B+* (cat.61)

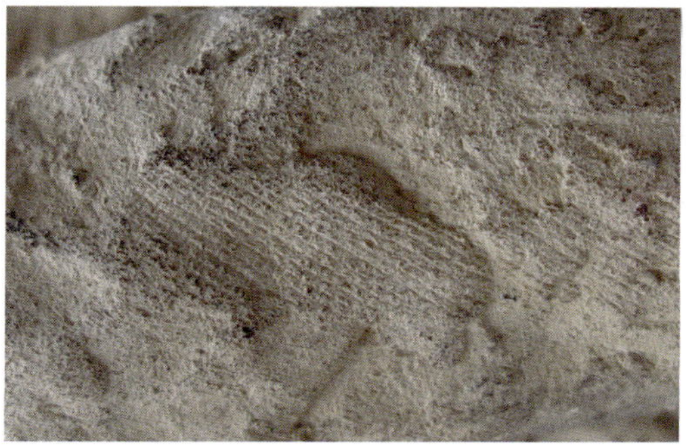

FIG.31
Imprint of the weave of the fabric used to keep the clay moist from one session to the next, s.3845, cat.66

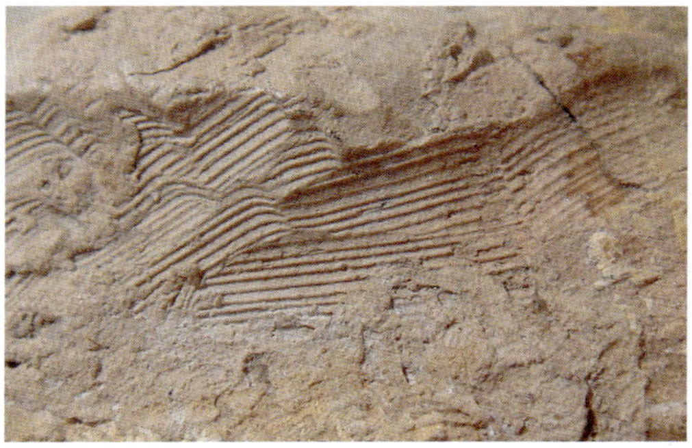

FIG.32
Traces of a toothed scraper in the clay, *Mouvement E*

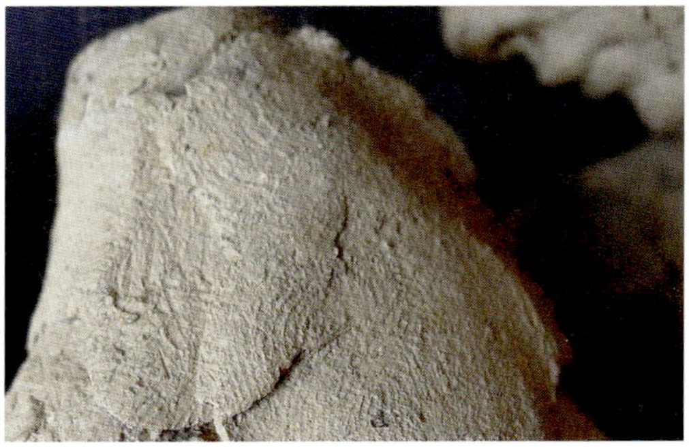

FIG.33
Finger print, *Mouvement I*

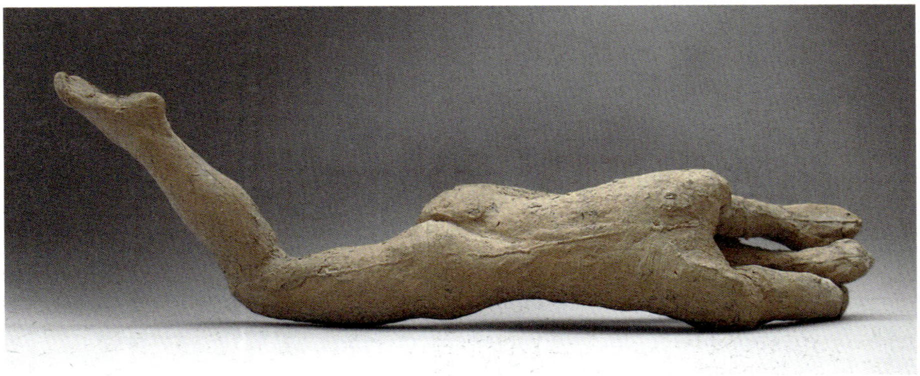

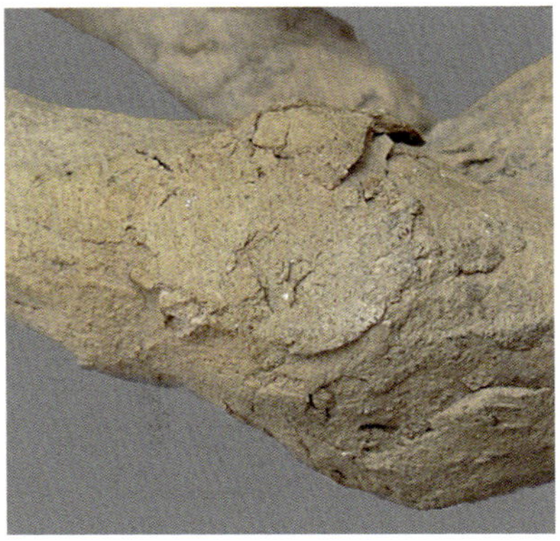

FIGS.34 & 35
Flattening of the clay under the right shoulder, *Mouvement B+*

was lying down and resting on its right shoulder and thigh, which bear the marks of this position (figs.34 and 35). The same applies to *Nu féminin ramassé sur lui-même* (Huddled seated figure; cat.68), which has a particularly complex form.

MOUVEMENTS DE DANSE: THE CREATIVE PROCESS
Of the many models and casts of the *Mouvements de danse*, two in particular enable us to retrace the early stages of Rodin's developing research around this theme. These are two headless figures in plaster, assembled into a very dynamic group, which Rodin did not, however, pursue (cat.42; see facing). These plaster casts are unique; we have neither the modelled clay pieces used to cast them, nor any identical reproductions in the form of plaster casts. In this late period of his career, Rodin often made a mould of a piece in progress from which he had several casts made, simply to document a stage of his work. As we shall see, these two figures reflect an earlier stage than all the other *Mouvements* and in the light of this should be given a specific name. We have chosen to call them respectively *Alpha* and *Beta*.

That these two plasters reflect an early stage of work is revealed first by their dimensions – they are slightly larger than all the other known *Mouvements*. They were cast using moulds taken from two figurines modelled in fresh clay, before any shrinkage caused by drying and firing.

In line with his usual practice of keeping one example of each stage of his work, Rodin decided to make moulds of the two small headless figurines that he had modelled while their clay was still fresh (see diagram overleaf). He had several skilled mould-makers and plaster casters on hand in his studios to carry out his requests. The mould-making process was facilitated by sectioning the torsos of these two modelled pieces from the arms and legs, which were referred to as "*abattis*" (meaning both 'limbs' and 'giblets'). For *Alpha* the left leg and the right arm connected to the right leg were detached from the arching torso; for *Beta*, the lower right leg, left leg and both arms were cut off and separated from the torso, which remained attached to the right thigh. Before cutting, two small incisions were made to mark the point where the limbs were attached, so that the mould-maker could later reposition the arms and legs very precisely on the torsos (fig.36).

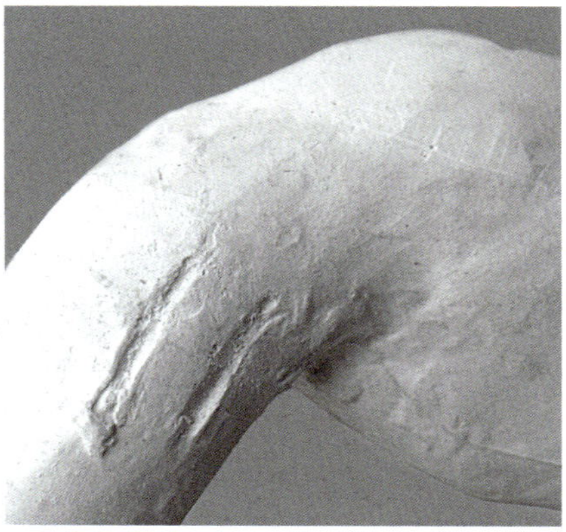

FIG.36
Registration marks on the *Beta* torso and its left arm

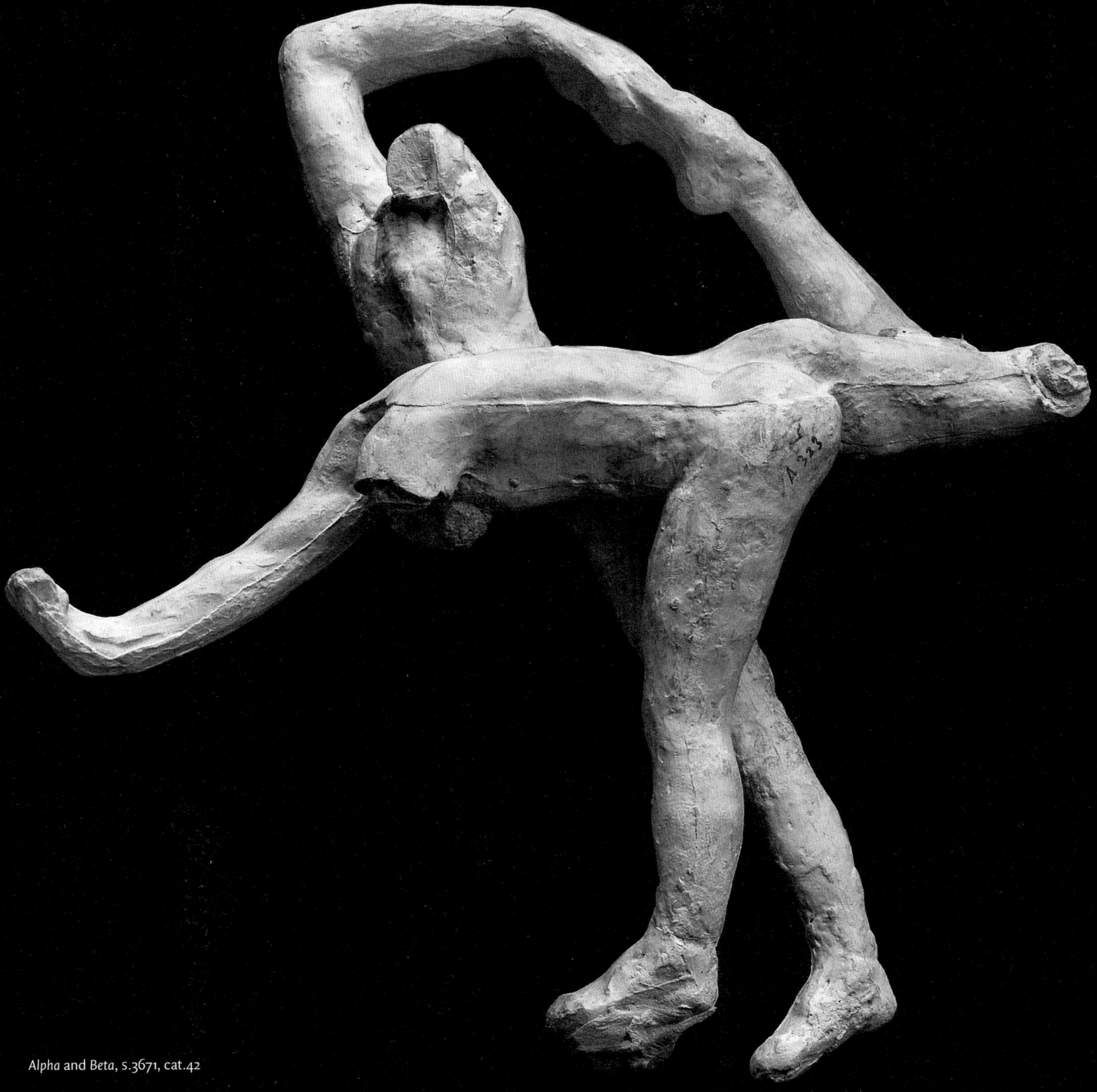

Alpha and *Beta*, S.3671, cat.42

STAGES IN THE CREATION OF THE MOUVEMENTS DE DANSE

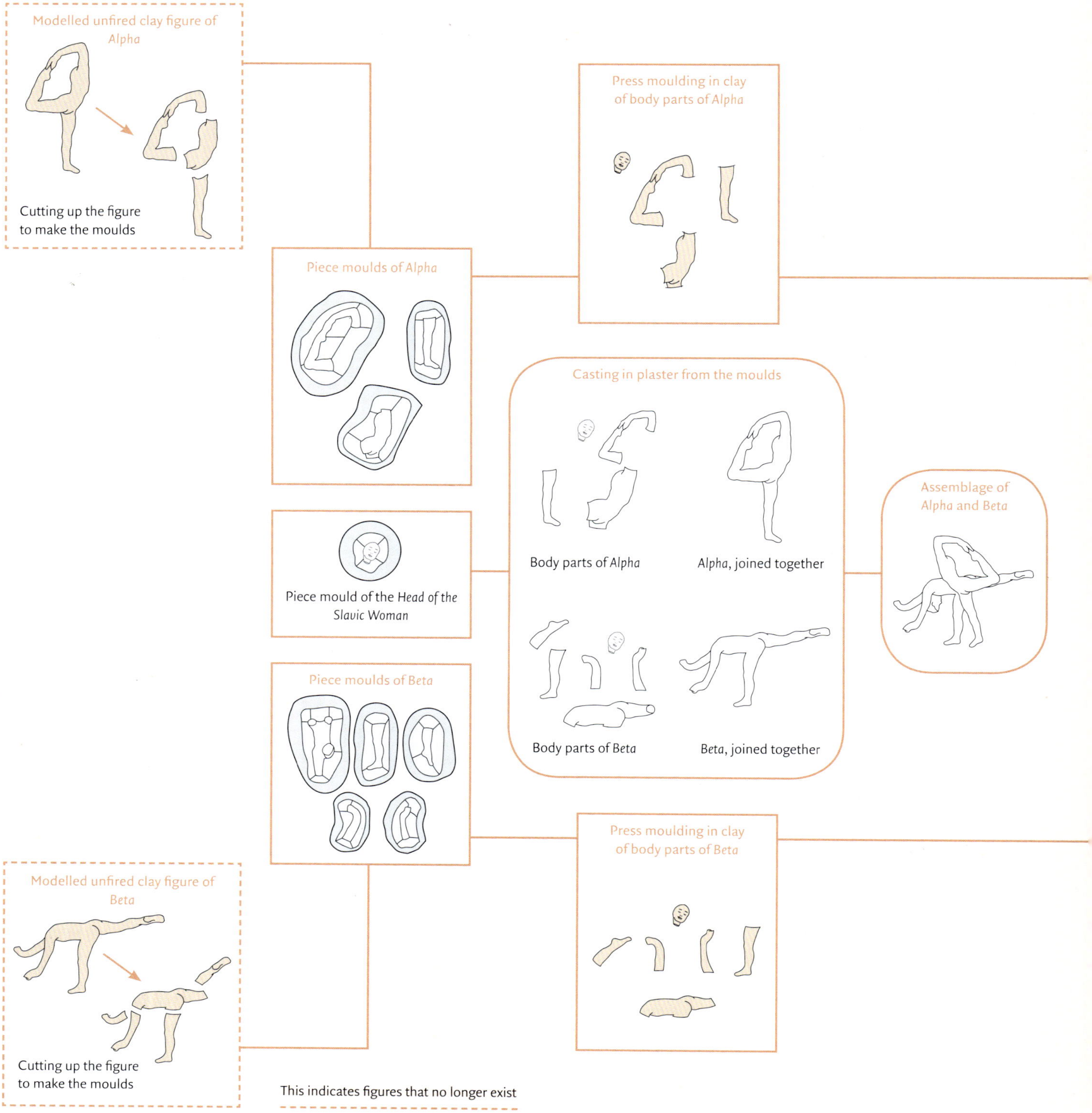

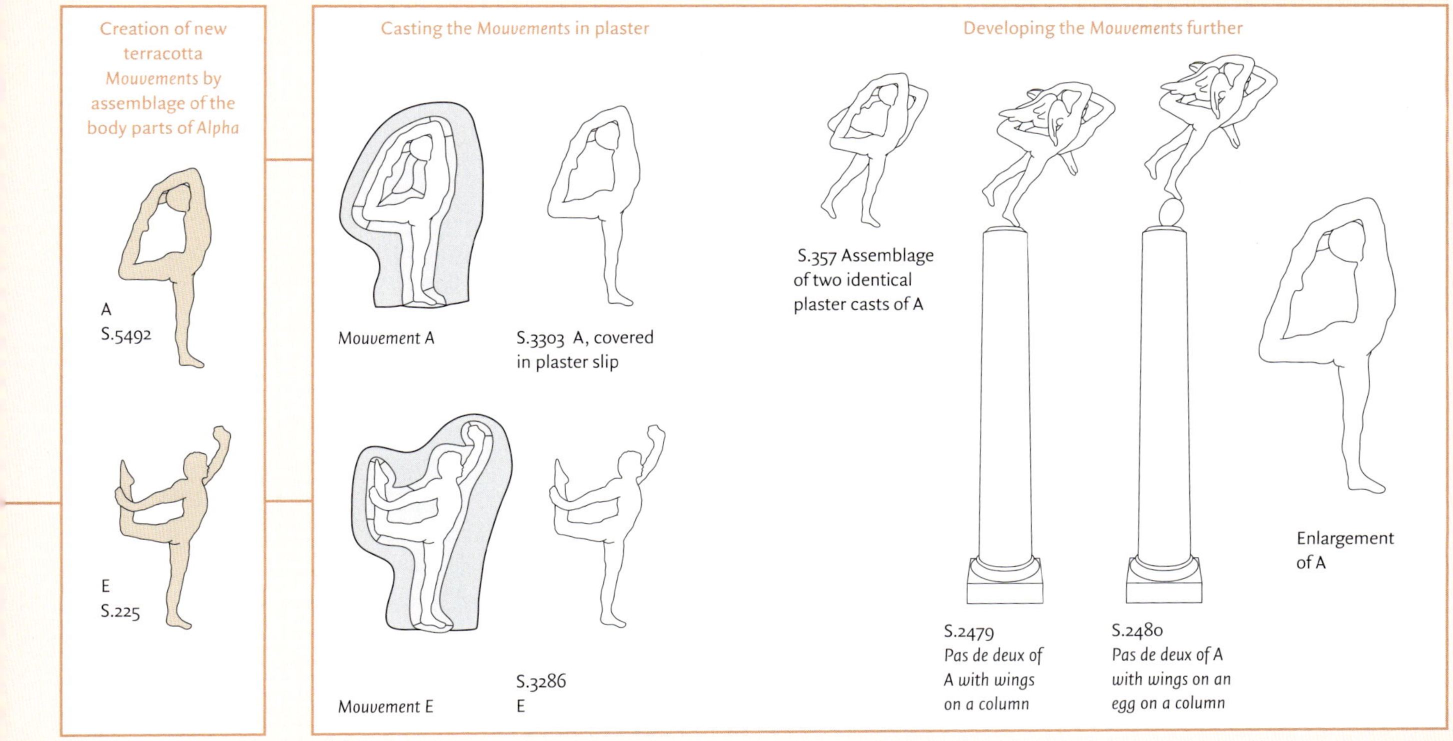
Creation of new terracotta *Mouvements* by assemblage of the body parts of *Alpha*
A
S.5492
E
S.225
Casting the *Mouvements* in plaster
Mouvement A
S.3303 A, covered in plaster slip
Mouvement E
S.3286
E
Developing the *Mouvements* further
S.357 Assemblage of two identical plaster casts of A
S.2479
Pas de deux of A with wings on a column
S.2480
Pas de deux of A with wings on an egg on a column
Enlargement of A

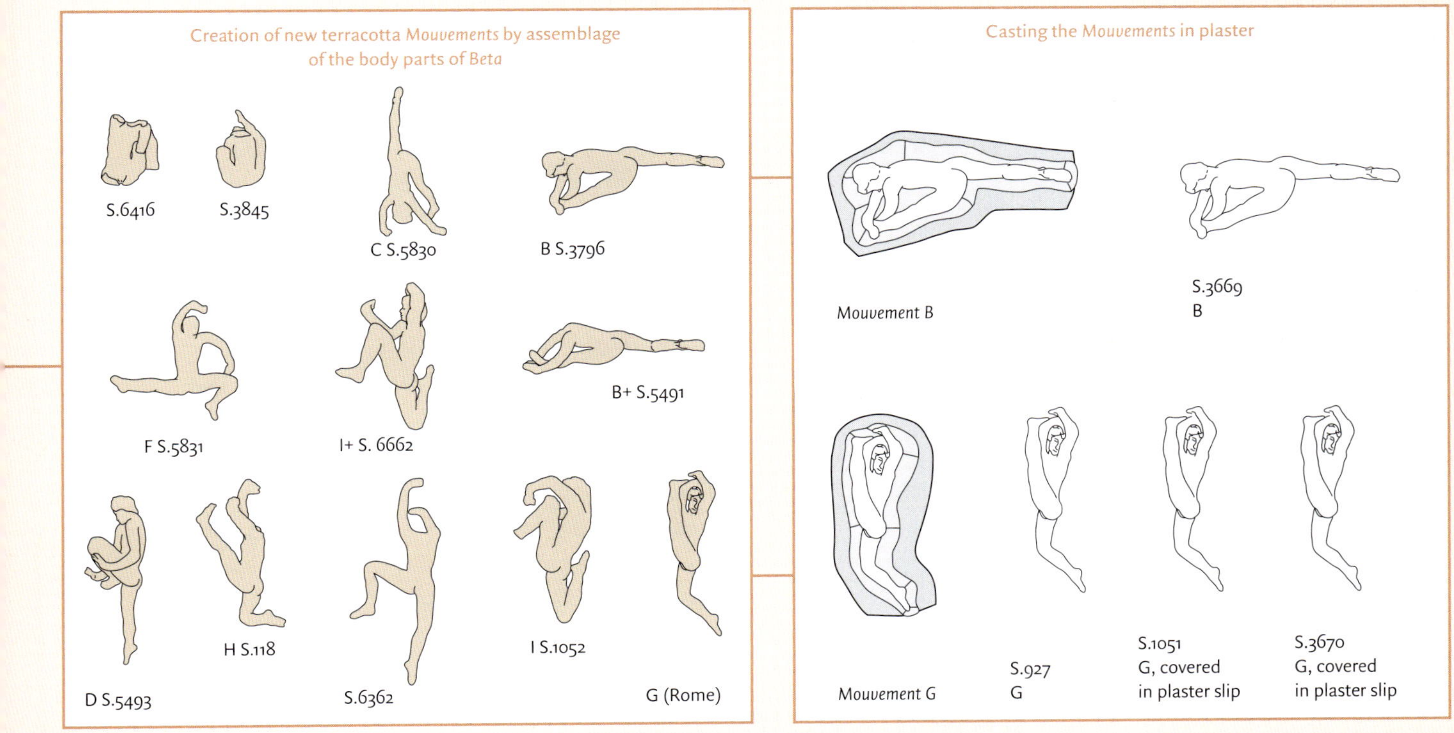
Creation of new terracotta *Mouvements* by assemblage of the body parts of *Beta*
S.6416
S.3845
C S.5830
B S.3796
F S.5831
I+ S. 6662
B+ S.5491
D S.5493
H S.118
S.6362
I S.1052
G (Rome)
Casting the *Mouvements* in plaster
Mouvement B
S.3669
B
Mouvement G
S.927
G
S.1051
G, covered in plaster slip
S.3670
G, covered in plaster slip

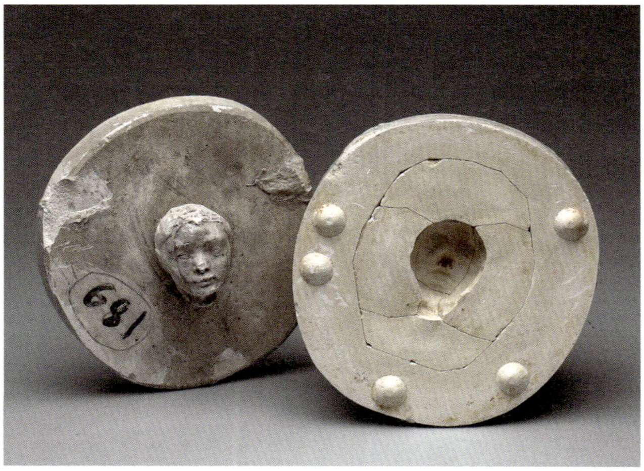

FIG.37
Mould for the face, top and inside, with plaster cast of the head on the top

Each of the limbs was reproduced in a piece mould. The use of this type of mould, called in French *moule à bon creux* and also known as *moule à pièces*, meant that as many casts as necessary could then later be made by either press-moulding in clay or casting in plaster. The Musée Rodin is fortunate to have nine moulds made during this first stage of the work (fig.37). We should also remember that these two initial models were headless. Rather than model one or two new heads, Rodin decided to use the piece known as *Tête de la femme slave (Head of the Slavic Woman)*, which he had made previously and used in *The Gates of Hell*. He had it cast in a piece mould, which he then used to create all the figures of the *Mouvements de danse*.[11]

Once the mould-makers had made the moulds for the eight limbs and head, Rodin was able to continue his explorations from these two figures, which comprised all the elements he later used for each of the other *Mouvements*.

THE FIRST STAGE

As noted above, in the first stage of the process the moulds were used to cast the limbs in plaster. Once removed from the moulds, they were then carefully assembled to create the bodies of the *Alpha* and *Beta* casts, faithfully reproducing the two original modelled pieces, which were consumed in the process (see diagram). These plaster casts are the record of the first stage of Rodin's research. The sharpness of the sculpted volumes on each of the figures is a sure sign of an early work by Rodin.

We do not know exactly when Rodin put together the plaster figures to obtain the group we are now calling *Alpha and Beta* (cat.42). This group clearly reflects his concern with the arrangement of limbs in space, evoking a wheel or a sun's rays. Its composition is remarkably similar to that of the very fine group *Zephyr and Psyche* by Henri-Joseph Rutxhiel (marble, 1814; Musée du Louvre), in which Zephyr stretches forward, leading Psyche, whose body is more upright with her right arm bent over her head (see fig.57, p.141).

Its importance had not been noted before our study, since the two casts had previously been regarded as variants of *Mouvements* A and H, whereas, as we shall go on to see, they are in fact earlier, primary stages of these two *Mouvements* and gave rise to all the other *Mouvements* as well. An addition of slightly granular plaster shows that Rodin almost certainly tried to affix a head, no doubt that of the *Femme slave*.

MANY EXPERIMENTS AND THE CREATION OF A SERIES

Rodin used the moulds again to press-mould several series of limbs, this time in fresh clay (see diagram). We should remember that he had only one head and two sets of limbs, those of *Alpha* (an arched torso, an extended left leg and a right leg connected to a right arm) and *Beta* (a left arm, a right arm, a straight torso connected to a right thigh and a very slightly bent left leg).

He could then work more freely. The cast clay limbs were still very malleable and he attached them to the torsos, twisting and reshaping them as he wished. Like letters combined into words, the limbs were freely assembled and fixed with slip to make the bodies of a dozen figures representing different movements, which can be divided into two main groups, those based on the *Alpha* movement, in other words *Mouvements* A and E (cat.47 and 51) – type A then giving rise to two further

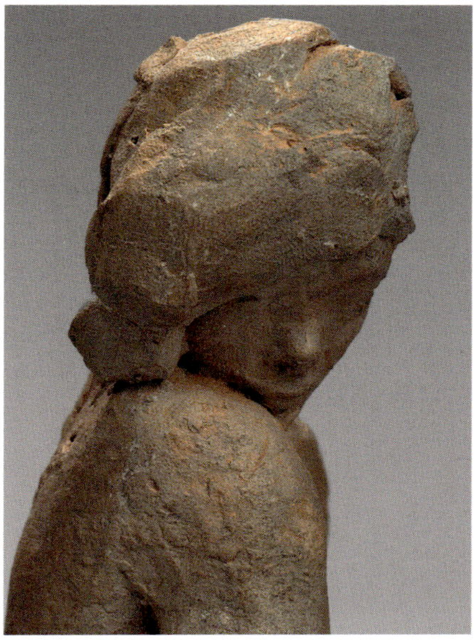

FIG.38
Detail of head of *Mouvement D*

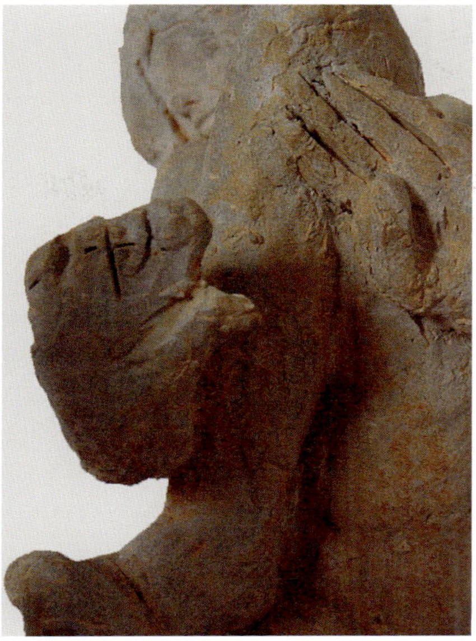

FIG.39
Detail of hands of *Mouvement D*

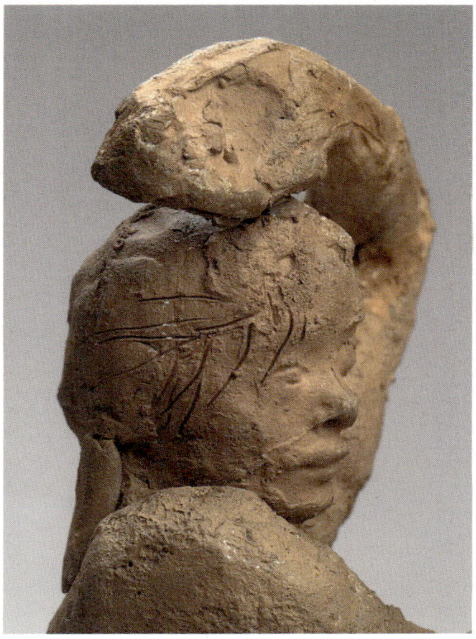

FIG.40
Incisions made in fresh clay with the point of a spatula to indicate locks of hair on *Mouvement I+*

sculptures known as *Pas de deux ailé A* (*Winged Pas de Deux A*) – and those derived from *Beta*, identified by the letters *B* (cat.56), *B+* (cat.61), *C* (cat.54), *D* (cat.63), *F* (cat.75), *G* (see fig.60, p.160), *H* (cat.60), *I* (cat.64) and *I+* (cat.65)

The similarity between the *Mouvements* obtained in this way and the initial models *Alpha* and *Beta* varies from one figure to the next. *Mouvement H*, which looks very similar to *Beta*, was obtained by folding back the initially extended right leg of *Beta*, while the left leg is lifted higher towards the chest.

In *Mouvement B+*, Rodin raised the left leg so that it was closer to the torso, enabling the hands to grasp the foot. The pose then becomes reminiscent of the well-known splits position, suggesting the statuette should be placed – and viewed – lying horizontally on its back, front or side.

Not content with reshaping the cast limbs, Rodin also removed some of the fresh clay, slicing it with a sharp implement, or increased its volume by adding clay in small balls.

An examination of *Mouvement E* (cat.51) reveals that it is clearly related to *Alpha*. The right leg, held at the ankle by the right hand, extends further back, while the right arm has been reshaped with a spatula and differently arranged, so that it is hardly recognisable (see fig.30 above). *Mouvement D* (cat.63) is another which differs most from the prime models *Alpha* or *Beta*. Here, although all the component limbs of *Beta* are present, the two arms come down to clasp the bent left leg, while the right leg is fully extended as though in preparation for a movement. Having created this pose, Rodin completed the figure by rapidly adding the clay pellets that form the bun of hair, its mass accentuating the movement of the head (fig.38).

Having finished the composition, Rodin would sometimes add new details in fresh clay, cutting into it with his spatula to suggest fingers (fig.39) and locks of hair on the head (fig.40). He also drew with the point of the spatula.

All his actions – reshaping and removing or adding clay – reflect the spontaneity of his approach and his almost feverish desire to capture the tension and expression of movement.

In creating the *Mouvements* in this way he was clearly not concerned with anatomical precision. Although none of the poses is imaginary and some suggest known positions, all are composite, Rodin being interested primarily in their dynamic forms.

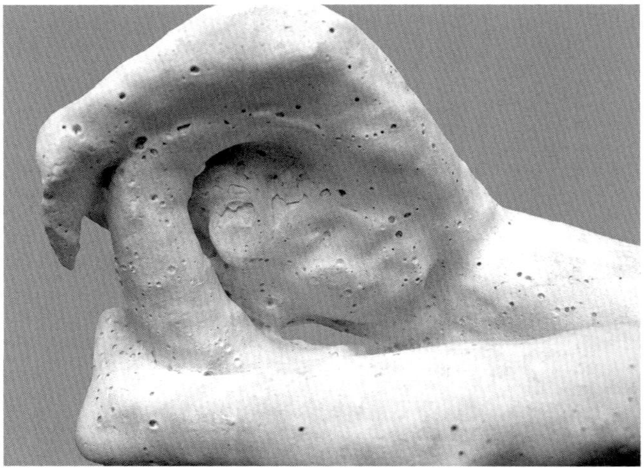

FIG.41
The plaster cast has been dipped in plaster slip (*lait de plâtre*), forming small surface bubbles, *Mouvement G*

FIRING THE CLAY AND A NEW SERIES OF MOULDS

The figurines were preserved by firing, which also led to a final modification, since the heat caused them to shrink, as the water which represents 7–12% of the volume of clay is lost in firing. Thus the fired *Mouvements* are smaller than the plaster casts of the *Alpha and Beta* group, even though they were made using the same moulds.

Rodin created twelve *Mouvements* in terracotta, of which it seems he used only four (types A, B, E and G) in pursuing his research further. He took these four terracotta *Mouvements* as the basis for a new series of piece moulds, which were in turn used to make plaster casts for use in further experiments.

APPLYING THE LAIT DE PLÂTRE (PLASTER SLIP)

Using a process with which he was familiar, Rodin coated the surface of three plaster casts taken from these new moulds with *lait de plâtre.*[12] This is a very thin, liquid solution of plaster, made with far more water than would be added for normal uses, into which objects can be dipped. The thickness of the resulting plaster film depends on how set the plaster is. The solution can also be poured over an object, producing drips. As it dries it forms a layer of variable thickness, with a surface that is always matt, porous and even sometimes granular, containing bubbles that can appear as small craters (fig.41). Rodin liked the somewhat random nature of this process, which afforded him surprises each time he used it.[13]

In visual terms, the result is an envelopment of forms, since the modelling of the cast is masked and enveloped by the liquid plaster. '*Enveloppement*' is also a studio term used metaphorically to describe the softening of the modelling of works in marble obtained by a process described as '*soutenir les points*' (keeping the points), which meant leaving an additional thickness of a few millimetres in the marble version as compared with the plaster model from which it was carved.[14]

TRANSLATION INTO MARBLE

The aesthetic convergence of the effects obtained through the use of *lait de plâtre* or plaster slip and the so-called 'envelopment' of marble forms is particularly interesting since Rodin translated one of the type B *Mouvements de danse* into marble, listed in the inventory with the title *Danseuse debout, le pied dans la main (Standing Dancer, Holding One Foot*; fig.42).[15] The accounts of the technician Aristide Rousaud show that Rodin asked him to make this marble "for an American buyer" in 1914. The piece was still in progress in 1916 and was included in Rodin's donation to the French state of that year. In May 1917 he took the marble back to Rousaud to continue the work, but the piece remained unfinished in Rousaud's studio and was not taken to the museum until 1927.

So here the unfinished aspect so characteristic of Rodin's marbles was intended only in part, since the cutting of the marble was not taken as far as he expected. However, we should note that, while the proportions of *Mouvement B* have been respected in terms of limb length, their thickness was greatly altered in the process of transposition from plaster to marble. We should also note that Rodin asked his technician to enlarge the figure considerably – almost tripling it in size using the three-compass method. The plaster model (lost, but undoubtedly analogous to the preserved examples) must have been about 35 cm tall, whereas the marble is 114 cm.

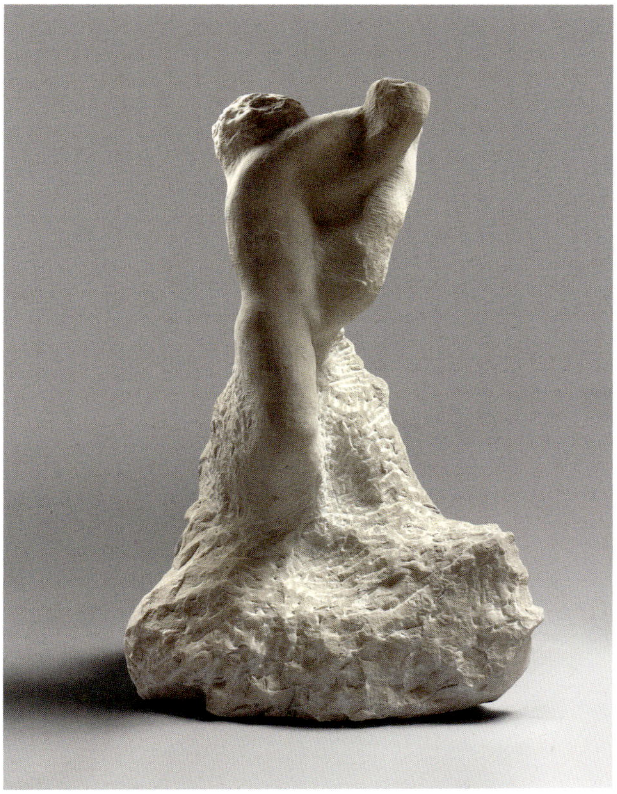

FIG.42
Auguste Rodin
Danseuse debout, le pied dans la main, 1914
Marble, carved by Aristide Rousaud,
114 x 70.2 x 47.3 cm
Musée Rodin, Paris, S.2226

PANTOGRAPH ENLARGEMENT

Rodin also enlarged another *Mouvement*, A, but this time by mechanical means using a pantograph, with the assistance of Henri Lebossé, a specialist in the use of this machine (see cat.51 for the bronze).[16] The pantograph has two rotating plates connected to a single screw thread, which turns them at exactly the same angle. The operator places the model to be enlarged on one of the plates and, on the other, the malleable material (clay or soft plaster), which is then cut to the contours of the model by means of a needle attached to a bar, which is connected to another bar holding a needle. The second needle shapes the malleable material by transposing the enlarged movements of the first.

The result is a *Mouvement* doubled in size (more or less – 72 cm as opposed to 31 cm – the larger version having a round base which is absent from the original), with modelling that is modified in the process. All the original details are recreated in the 'augmented' version (in Lebossé's term), but with a loss of sharpness due both to the change of scale and to the technical limitations of the tool. The salient parts are softened, the hollows are a little less deep and the angles a little less sharp. However, far from complaining, Rodin accepted these imperfections, particularly as the result reflected the aesthetics he was then trying to develop, as we have seen with the *lait de plâtre* and the envelopment of forms in marble.

DUPLICATION BY ASSEMBLAGE AND PLACEMENT ON A PLINTH

In parallel to the explorations described above, which remained unfinished or were not pursued, Rodin used the same figures to take his research in other directions. His interest in assembling identical figures is a well-documented phenomenon. The first known example dates from the mid 1880s, with the *Trois Ombres* (*Three Shades*) crowning *The Gates of Hell*. Twenty-five years later, he brought together two *Mouvements de danse A* to make what has been called (probably posthumously) a *Pas de deux* (cat.49). He was satisfied with the result and asked his mould-makers to devise a way for him to make identical reproductions of such groups. They made small pencil marks on the model and created two 'reminder' or registration pieces ('*pièces de rappel*') in the form of simple plaster wedges on which impressions of two parts of the group were taken, so that the exact position of each figure in relation to the other could be checked.

New groups of paired casts of *Mouvement A* were made using this system. Rodin added wings and placed each group on a small plaster column, on which the foot of one of the figures rested (S.2479 and S.2480; fig.43). Each has a slightly different relationship to the vertical in an exploration of balance – or imbalance, since Rodin was seeking to create an effect of movement suggesting flight. On one of these, *Pas de deux ailé A* (S.2480), he inserted a small egg (obtained from making a mould of a hen's egg) between the column and the winged figures, making the whole even more strange and poetic.[17]

FIG.43
Auguste Rodin
Pas de deux ailé A, 1911 or after
(this cast, later 20th century)
Plaster, 39.3 x 18.2 x 23.3 cm
Musée Rodin, Paris, S.933

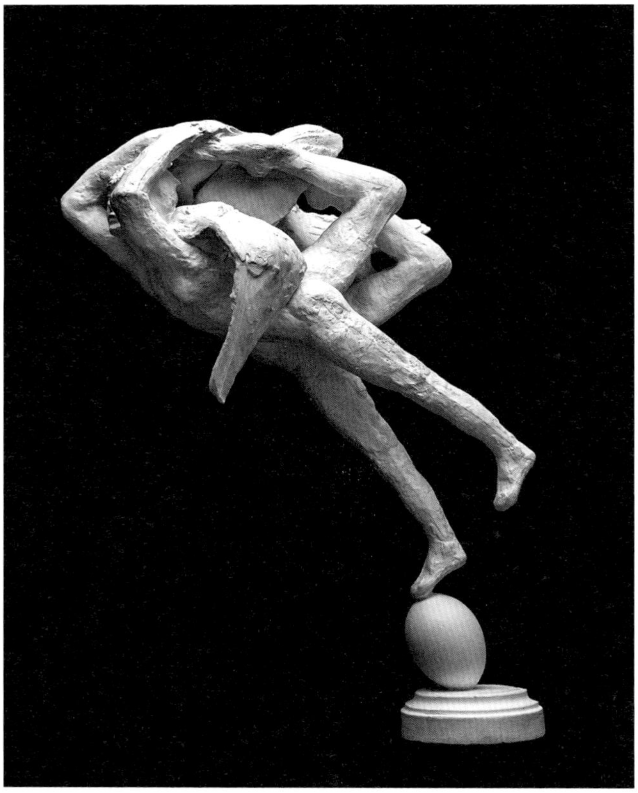

Rodin seems also to have assembled two examples of *Mouvement B*, creating a group that was later called *Pas de deux B*. There are no surviving examples that would enable us to be sure that they were made during Rodin's lifetime,[18] but an entry in the old Musée Rodin inventory[19] tells us that a group of this kind existed in the 1930s.

PROJECT FOR A MONUMENT TO AVIATORS

Several inscriptions on moulds and entries in the old inventory suggest that Rodin planned to make this *Pas de deux ailé A* into a monument to aviation – or aviators. In the inventory of moulds, which goes back to the 1930s, no.592 consists of the moulds of three different figures (A, B and G) grouped under the title "*Morena* [sic] *3 figures de mouvement de danse – 1e figure / 2e figure / 3e figure*", with the comment: "*pour le monument aux aviateurs / Aviation*". The third figure of this group, which corresponds to *Mouvement de danse A*, is described as: "*592 n° 3 Morano* [sic] *groupe aéronaute*" (Morano aeronaut group), while the two 'reminder' or 'registration' pieces which belong to this mould are wrapped in brown paper on which is written: "*Pièce de rappel monument aéronaute / Morano n° 3 / Pièce de rappel pour l'assemblage de deux épreuves Morano N° 3 en un groupe monument des aéronautes*" (Aeronaut monument reminder piece / Morano no.3 / Reminder piece for the assemblage of two Morano no.3 casts into a group for the monument to aeronauts).

We know that in 1912 Rodin offered a work, *La Défense*, or *L'Appel aux armes* (*The Defence* or *The Call to Arms*), to the newspaper *Le Matin* to be a monument to the glory of French aviation.[20] He had made it in 1879 for the competition to design a monument to the defence of Paris in 1870 during the Franco-Prussian War, but it had not been selected.[21] However, it seems that Rodin had previously planned to offer a new piece, original in every sense of the term, which the journalist Michel Georges-Michel described with the title *Biplane* in his account of a visit to Rodin that can probably be dated to 1913:

'There's Da Vinci's dream flying by! ...' murmured Rodin. The plane glided over us without casting a shadow .... These planes that fly past are a Renaissance .... 'Come with me, I'll show you my biplane, you'll be the first to see it.'

...

A column without ornamentation and surmounted by an elongated sphere, if I can call it that, and which seemed almost .... You know Houdon's *Diana*, resting on one toe and so gracious you're afraid you'll see her run towards you .... You know Giambologna's *Mercury*, *Mercury taking Flight*, raised heel and raised arm ... you've heard about the lovely *Nike* of Paeonius, which virgins were told to look at with bated breath ....

Wait till you see Rodin's biplane! ... It is two marble twins with solid bodies, curved like rushes. The light bounces off their foreheads turned skywards, leaps on the broad, airy modelling of their busts and scatters on their wings. They are a duo, joined at the sides, just one foot touching, brushing, scratching the sphere ....

The wings ... do you think Rodin has done them by the book? You imagine them open, wide and classical .... Not at all. They are half folded, quivering feathers intertwined, quills crossing, almost in each other's way, but flapping, with energetic effort, pushing, aiding, clattering into each other .... One of them seems to hang down, it looks broken .... I was surprised not to see a snow of feathers.[22]

The description leaves no doubt: this is the *Pas de deux ailé A sur un œuf* (*Winged Pas de Deux A on an Egg*). However, we have to admit that the journalist has somewhat embellished his memory: there is no trace of a marble by Rodin made after this composition, either in the collections of the Musée Rodin or in the archives or photographs of his studios, of which many were taken at this time. It is possible that in the memory of M. Georges-Michel the composition of the *Pas de deux ailé A*, recognisable in detail from his text, became muddled with the marble group of *Bénédictions* (*Blessings*; fig.18), of which there are several examples,[23] and which shows two female figures joined and leaning forwards, with exactly the wings reused by Rodin for the *Pas de deux ailé A*.

From this we can conclude that the memory of this project for a monument to aviators, aeronauts or aviation had been preserved by those who drew up the inventory of moulds, and that the piece later called *Pas de deux ailé A* had been envisaged by Rodin as a kind of maquette. The placement of this group on a column was intended to give it a new monumentality, anticipating the effect that the group would have had once enlarged. We may wonder whether the pantograph enlargement of *Mouvement de danse A* discussed above was not in fact made as a design for this proposed monument, which came to nothing.

LATER AWARENESS OF THE MOUVEMENTS DE DANSE

In Rodin's lifetime the *Mouvements de danse* (or *Études de mouvement* [Movement studies], as they were long known) do not seem ever to have been exhibited. A few visitors to Rodin's studio – Michel Georges-Michel, as we have just seen, and Count Kessler, accompanied by Nijinsky[24] – saw them and have left more or less trustworthy descriptions.

At the time of Rodin's death in November 1917, it seems the preserved *Mouvements* can be identified as follows:

- ten terracottas[25] intended for the collections of the Musée Rodin, which was then being founded;
- 14 or 15 plasters,[26] almost certainly including plasters covered in *lait de plâtre* (three), groups (four, including two on columns) and enlargements (two);
- one marble[27] left unfinished.

When the Musée Rodin opened its doors in August 1919, visitors could admire three "*Études de mouvement*" in terracotta, as we are informed by the museum's very first catalogue, published that year by the curator Léonce Bénédite.[28] These small works were presented in a glass case on the first floor of the Hôtel Biron, the main building of the museum, with some studies of masks after the face of the Japanese actress Hanako,[29] and other pieces including a few vases decorated by Rodin and small bronze pieces related to *The Gates of Hell*. There was no coherence to this agglomeration, in which the *Mouvements* must have tended to go unnoticed. The new catalogue published in 1927 by Bénédite's successor Georges Grappe again identifies three terracottas (the same ones, presumably) and the illustrations show them to be types C, D and F.

It seems that the museum's curators tried to establish a classification for the *Mouvements* in the 1930s, but it was clearly not until immediately after the Second World War that the types were identified and attributed with letters, in the classification still in use today. Moreover, it is clear that the alphabetical order follows the sequence of the reproduction of each of these types in bronze: type *A* in 1946, *B* in 1951, *C*, *D* and *E* in 1952, *F* in 1953, *G* in 1958, *H* and *I* in 1963.[30]

In late 1962 and early 1963 the Louvre hosted a major exhibition curated by Cécile Goldscheider, director of the Musée Rodin. It was called *Rodin inconnu* (Unknown Rodin)[31] and resulted from a visit by André Malraux, then Minister of Culture, to the museum's reserves in Meudon. Impressed, like all visitors to the reserve, by the scale of Rodin's vast output, and fascinated by some works he had never seen, since they had never been shown to the public, Malraux asked Goldscheider to put on an exhibition that would update the vision of Rodin and assert his modernity. It was at this exhibition that the wider public discovered the *Mouvements de danse* in the form of seven bronzes and two terracottas,[32] accompanied by drawings[33] and other works completing the section entitled 'Rodin et la danse'. The exhibition also provided an opportunity to foreground *Nijinsky*,[34] the mould for which had almost certainly been identified in the reserves around 1953 and which Cécile Goldscheider had quickly had cast in bronze.[35] The exhibition was a great success, in which the *Mouvements de danse* played an undeniable part. Their lightness, sense of upward movement, formal simplicity and serial nature were perfectly suited to the tastes of the time.

So we return now to 1963, the year of publication of Leo Steinberg's text with which we began. Steinberg, who was then aged 43 and had never previously worked on Rodin, later said that he could never have imagined the reception given to this introductory essay for the catalogue of what was a comparatively modest exhibition, even though it travelled all over North America for eighteen months.[36]

However, Steinberg's influence on the vision, reception and understanding of the *Mouvements de danse* was to prove lasting, and possibly definitive, since his musings on Rodin's near-magical modelling are so brilliantly set out and so stimulating to the imagination that once read they are, and were, hard to forget. We do not question Steinberg's ultimate conclusions, which are very astute concerning the aesthetics of the series. We simply hope to have made a contribution to a more detailed material and technical approach to this famous series, and to a better understanding of Rodin's creative processes in the as yet incompletely explored context of his prolific later work.

NOTES

1 Leo Steinberg, 'Rodin', in *Other Criteria: Confrontations with Twentieth-Century Art*, New York (Oxford UP), 1972, pp.399–402. This is a slightly modified version of the piece written in the summer of 1962 following a visit to the Musée Rodin, Meudon, and first published in 1963 as the introductory essay to the catalogue of an exhibition of Rodin's work at the Charles E. Slatkin Gallery, New York (*Rodin. Sculptures and Drawings*, 6 May–26 June 1963, etc.; see note 36 below).

2 The year 1963 also saw a major Rodin exhibition at the Museum of Modern Art, New York, which Elsen curated. At the same time in France Cécile Goldscheider, director of the Musée Rodin, mounted the exhibition *Rodin inconnu* (Unknown Rodin) at the Louvre (see below, note 31).

3 Steinberg 1972, p.399.

4 This observation is not new: see A. Le Normand-Romain, 'Un nouveau Mouvement de danse de Rodin (1840–1917)', in *La Revue du Louvre et des musées de France*, no.41, 1996, pp.59–62. However, until now the consequences of this fact for the design and genealogy of the works have not been appreciated.

5 The present study was undertaken in the second half of 2015, in two stages. In the first François Blanchetière and Alexandra Gerstein worked separately from Agnès Cascio and Juliette Lévy; we then pooled our observations and questions in relation to the works. The present essay is the result of this highly stimulating process, made possible by the exceptional riches of the collections of the Musée Rodin. The authors would like to thank Alexandra Gerstein and The Courtauld Gallery for facilitating this research and for funding the technical study. As always when in comes to moulds at the Musée Rodin, Dominique Brisset's assistance proved invaluable and we owe her many thanks.

6 On these technical aspects, see Marie-Thérèse Baudry, ed., *La Sculpture: méthode et vocabulaire*, Paris (Imprimerie nationale et Ministère de la Culture) [1978], 7th edn, 2011; and Jeanne L. Wasserman, ed., exh. cat. *Metamorphoses in Nineteenth Century Sculpture*, Fogg Art Museum, Cambridge, 19 November 1975 – 7 January 1976, Cambridge and London (Harvard University Press).

7 Good examples of these processes can be found in N. Galissot, ed., exh. cat. *Rodin, Les Ombres*, Musée des Beaux-Arts, Quimper, 5 March – 7 June 2010, Paris (Somogy), 2010 (on the repetition of the figure from the group *Les Ombres*); F. Blanchetière and B. Garnier, edd., exh. cat. *Rodin. Le Rêve japonais*, Musée Rodin, Paris, 16 May – 9 September 2007 (on the series of face studies after the Japanese actress Hanako); Agnès Cascio and Juliette Lévy, 'Généalogie d'un portrait: Clemenceau par Rodin', *Patrimoines*, no.9, 2013 (on the thirty or more versions of the bust of Clemenceau).

8 Plaster mould in few parts (usually two), based on a modelled (raw or unfired) clay figure. When the mould-maker opens the mould, the modelled piece is destroyed and plaster is poured in. The mould-maker then has to break the mould to take out the cast, which reproduces the modelled piece from which the mould was made. This cast is known as the 'original plaster' and has very few seams (usually a single, thick lateral seam).

9 Plaster mould formed of several elements placed together and held in place by a screed. This mould can be taken apart to remove the model on which it was cast (usually in plaster). It is then reassembled by the mould-maker, who may use it to make several casts. The surface of each cast shows a network of seams corresponding to the separation between the pieces of the mould.

10 Mould made of animal gelatine, a flexible material (as opposed to rigid plaster), which makes it easy to remove the mould from the finished piece. A mould of this kind does not therefore need to be made of many parts. Several casts can be made, but in a short space of time, since gelatine does not keep. The seams on the surface of these prints are not usually as straight as on a plaster mould in pieces.

11 Although this mould of a version of *Tête de femme slave* is very similar, it is probably not the one used to cast the heads of the *Mouvements de danse*. Our work did not include a comparison of the moulds of the *Femme slave*, which would have been of limited interest for our research.

12 The plaster figure S.3303 is based on type A, and S.1051 and S.3670 are derived from *Mouvement G*. We should note that S.3670 differs from S.1051 because Rodin reworked the left forearm slightly.

13 On this see A. Le Normand-Romain and L. Madeline, edd., exh. cat. *Rodin. L'accident, l'aléatoire*, Musée d'Art et d'Histoire, Geneva, 20 June – 24 September 2014, Milan (5 Continents), 2014, notably F. Blanchetière, 'Hasards de l'atelier', pp.124–29.

14 Correspondence between Rodin and his technicians reveals that the artist gave these instructions to the assistants who had the job of carving the marble under his direction and on the basis of the modelled pieces he gave them, using the three-compass technique. On this see F. Blanchetière, 'Metteurs aux points et praticiens de Rodin', in A. Magnien, ed., exh. cat. *Rodin. La chair, le marbre*, Musée Rodin, Paris, 8 June – 3 March 2013, Paris (Éditions du musée Rodin and Hazan), 2012, pp.57–69, notably pp.65–67.

15 Musée Rodin, S.2226 (114 cm high; 70.2 cm long; 47.3 cm across). See N. Barbier, *Marbres de Rodin, Collection du musée*, Paris (Éditions du musée Rodin), 1987, no.92.

16 On pantograph enlargement and its consequences for forms, linked to the envelopment of marble sculptures and the use of plaster slip, see F. Blanchetière, 'Larger Figures, Simpler Forms', in A. Feldman, ed., exh. cat. *Moore Rodin*, The Henry Moore Foundation, Leeds, 29 March – 27 October 2013, and Compton Verney, Warwickshire, 13 February – 31 August 2014, Leeds (The Henry Moore Foundation), 2013, pp.118–25.

17 We might wonder whether Rodin was thinking of the famous *Spirit of Liberty* by Auguste Dumont (gilt bronze, 1836); this winged spirit mounted on a sphere and balancing on one leg tops the column erected on the Place de la Bastille in Paris to commemorate the Revolution of 1830. We should add that some of Rodin's drawings dating from the 1880s, entitled, for example, *Démon en espace* (Demon in space, D.5669), and sculptures such as *Esprit prenant le vol* (Spirit taking flight; S.17, plaster; figure included in *The Gates of Hell*, almost certainly *c.*1888) reflect his early interest in compositions representing one or several bodies leaping upwards.

18 The only plaster examples now conserved were used as foundry models in the early 1960s to create the bronze of *Pas de deux B*, cast by the Musée Rodin from 1964. The same is true of *Pas de deux G*, of which there is only one plaster example in the collections of the Musée Rodin (S.879, a cast made for the version in bronze, almost certainly *c.*1965).

19 This inventory is held in the archives of the Musée Rodin. It was drawn up in 1936–37 by the museum's archivist, Jean-Paul Hippeau, almost certainly with the help of the mould-maker Paul Cruet. It lists the moulds held by the Musée Rodin, and also the works in plaster and terracotta, classified by category and subject, with a note of the number of casts preserved for each subject. The pieces here are nos. A 321 (*"Étude de danse, femme un pied à terre, une jambe relevée côté gauche près du pied haut et la tête de ¾"*

[Dance study, woman standing on one foot, one leg raised on the left side near the raised foot and head ¾], with the comment, "*Danse / exp provenant / de Rousaud. Moreno*", indicating that this must be the model for the three-compass reproduction in marble cut by Aristide Rousaud, for which see above) and A 322 ("*Groupement de 2 figures A 321 dans un mouvement de danse*" [Group of 2 figures A 321 in a dance movement]).

20 See Guillaume Gaudet, *La Réception critique des monuments français d'Auguste Rodin*, Rennes (Presses universitaires), 2014, p.325–28.

21 It was the design by Ernest Barrias that was selected, and the monument still stands on the roundabout in La Défense, the area in the west of Paris to which it gave its name. In 1879 Rodin was still a fairly obscure sculptor and unlikely to win a competition of this kind. The expressive vigour of his maquette made it unlikely to be chosen by the jury, but this did not stop the group finding success as a work in its own right in the 1880s. See A. Le Normand-Romain, *The Bronzes of Rodin*, Paris (Éditions du musée Rodin and RMN), 2007, pp.299–305.

22 Michel Georges-Michel, *En Jardinant avec Bergson*, Paris (Albin Michel), 1926; republished 1942 (with some modified details) New York (Brentano), as *Peintres et sculpteurs que j'ai connus, 1900–1942*, in the chapter 'Rodin', pp.261–70. We are grateful to Alexandra Gerstein for drawing our attention to this text.

23 Musée Rodin, Paris, S.428; see Barbier 1987, no.98; Lisbon, Calouste Goulbenkian Foundation; Copenhagen, Ny Carlsberg Glyptotek; see Le Normand-Romain 2007, pp.199–202.

24 See the essay by Antoinette Le Normand-Romain in this volume, pp.13 and 17.

25 Type A (S.5492), type B (S.3796 and S.5491, which latter is a variant of type B we have called B+), type C (S.5830), type D (S.5493), type E (S.2225), type F (S.5831; S.6362 was listed as a variant of type F, but in fact is rather different), type H (S.118) and type I (S.1052); in 1995 the Musée Rodin acquired a variant of type I on the Paris art market (provenance: Georges Depeper, a mould-maker who worked for Rodin and then for the museum from 1916 to 1919; see Le Normand-Romain 1996, pp.59–62). The Galeria Nazionale d'Arte moderna e contemporanea, Rome, also has a terracotta *Mouvement* of type G, taking the number of known terracottas to twelve. It would be interesting to know more about the provenance of this last terracotta, a bequest of Countess Fourton in 1955, widow of Count Enrico di San Martino e Valperga, a Roman senator who played an important part in spreading awareness of Rodin's work in Italy, briefly discussed in relation to cat.59, p.160 in this volume.

26 This number is obtained by comparing the data in the old inventory (which gives the number of casts for each type) and the works conserved today, which can be classified as follows: type A (S.3303, with *lait de plâtre* – hereafter ldp; S.933 and S.2479, *Pas de deux ailé A sur colonne*; S.122 and S.1996, enlargements), type B (S.3669, with ldp, and a work currently being added to the inventory, which may have been an element of *Pas de deux* B), type E (S.3286), type G (S.1051 and S.3670, both with ldp).

27 Type B (S.2226; see above).

28 L. Bénédite, *Catalogue sommaire des œuvres de Rodin et autres œuvres d'art de la donation Rodin*, Paris, 1919, nos.153–55, p.29: "*Études de mouvement. (D'après une figure de danseuse; figurines terre cuite)*" (Movement studies. (After the figure of a dancer; terracotta figurines).

29 See F. Blanchetière, 'Rodin und Hanako', in exh. cat. *Auguste Rodin und Madame Hanako, Der französische Bildhauer und die Emanzipations-geschichte der japanischen Tänzerin*, Georg Kolbe Museum, Berlin, 9 June – 18 September 2016, pp.42–49.

30 We should add that the enlarged version of *Mouvement A* was first cast in 1955, *Pas de deux B* in 1964, *Pas de deux G* in 1965 and *Pas de deux ailé A* in 1970. See the essay by A. Le Normand-Romain in this volume.

31 C. Goldscheider, exh. cat. *Rodin inconnu*, Paris, Musée du Louvre, December 1962 – January 1963. The archives of the Musée Rodin have a large album of press cuttings about this exhibition, providing a good idea of the very positive reception given to this display of works that had long been held in store and which reflected practices seen as modern. See D. Viéville, 'Introduction', in exh. cat. *L'Invention de l'œuvre. Rodin et les ambassadeurs*, Musée Rodin, Paris, 6 May – 4 September 2011, pp.10–27 (on the importance of this exhibition and its reception, pp.12–13).

32 In the catalogue nos. 77, type B, bronze (*Exercice pour 'le brisement des cuisses'*); no.78, type C, bronze (*Exercice pour 'le balancement'*); no.79, type G, bronze (*Exercice pour 'le port d'armes'*); no.83, type A, enlargement, bronze; no.85, *Montage de deux mouvements de danse* B (Assemblage of two dance movements B), plaster; no.86, type D, bronze; no.87, type E, bronze; no.88, type F, bronze; no.89, type H, bronze; no.90, type I, terracotta (the bronze casting of these last two types began a little later in 1963).

33 Nos.80 (D.1832, *Le Grand Écart* [The splits]), 81 (D.1799, *Mouvement de danse*), 82 (D.4419, *idem*) and 84 (D.4418, *idem*).

34 No.101, *Étude d'après Nijinsky* (Study after Nijinsky), bronze (but the photograph on p.55 shows one of the plasters held by the museum); the short text on Rodin and Nijinsky states that this was "a recently identified small sketch", which was discussed in the press. On this see Lillian Browse, *Duchess of Cork Street, The Autobiography of an Art Dealer*, London, 1999, p.163. Our thanks to Philippe de Lustrac for our exchanges on this subject; he is preparing a book on the Russian ballet, which will deal with the complex question of the history of Rodin's *Nijinsky*, from the posing sessions of 1912 to the bronze casting undertaken by the Musée Rodin.

35 Minutes of the session of the Board of the Musée Rodin on 30 November 1957 (archives of the Musée Rodin): "Madame Goldscheider presents plasters that have never been cast: *Petit danseur (Nijinski), Danseuse, Baigneuse accroupie*, 3 *petits torses de femme*. The Board approves the choice. Cast no. 0 will go to the museum's collections." The casting of 12 bronzes (plus one, no. 0) was entirely carried out in the years 1958 and 1959 by the Georges Rudier foundry.

36 Shown at the Charles E. Slatkin Gallery, New York, in May – June 1963, the exhibition *Rodin. Sculptures and Drawings* travelled until January 1965 and was shown at the Musée des Beaux-Arts de Montréal, Art Gallery of Toronto, Winnipeg Art Gallery, William Rockhill Nelson Gallery (Kansas City), Cleveland Museum of Art, Baltimore Museum of Art, North Carolina Museum of Art (Raleigh), Dallas Museum of Art, Minneapolis Museum of Art, Seattle Museum of Art, Fogg Art Museum (Harvard University, Cambridge) and the National Gallery of Canada (Ottawa).

NOTE ON THE CATALOGUE

Catalogue by Alexandra Gerstein
with contributions by Kate Edmondson
and Sophie Biass-Fabiani

The discussions of the postures of the *Mouvements de danse* and associated drawings in the catalogue are the result of a collaborative research project with the Royal Central School of Speech and Drama in London (International Movement Centre). I am especially grateful to Ayse Tashkiran and Vanessa Ewan for their expertise regarding this section of the exhibition catalogue.

Titles of drawings: titles are English adaptations of the titles in the Musée Rodin's inventory of drawings (Judrin 1984–92).

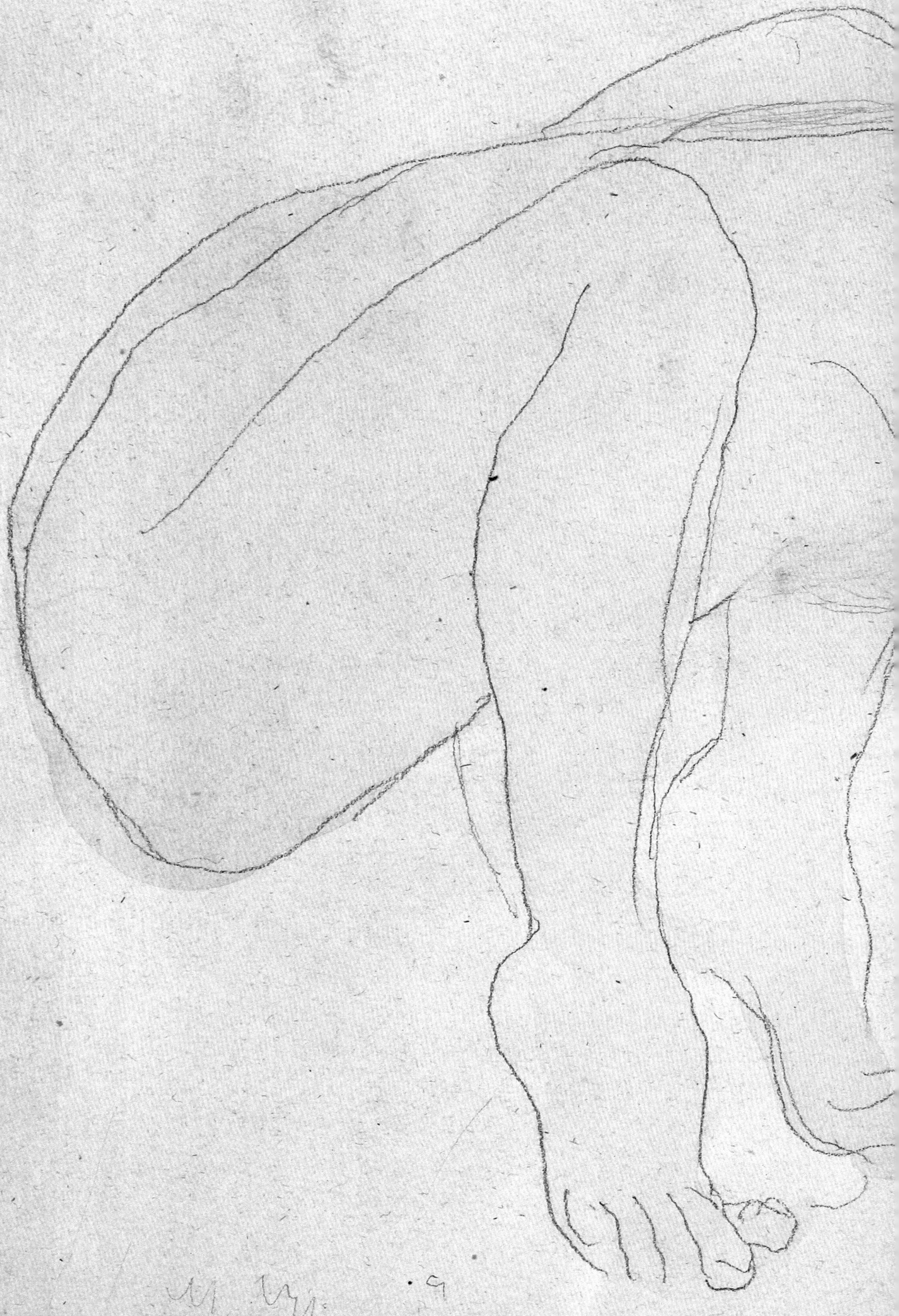

CATALOGUE

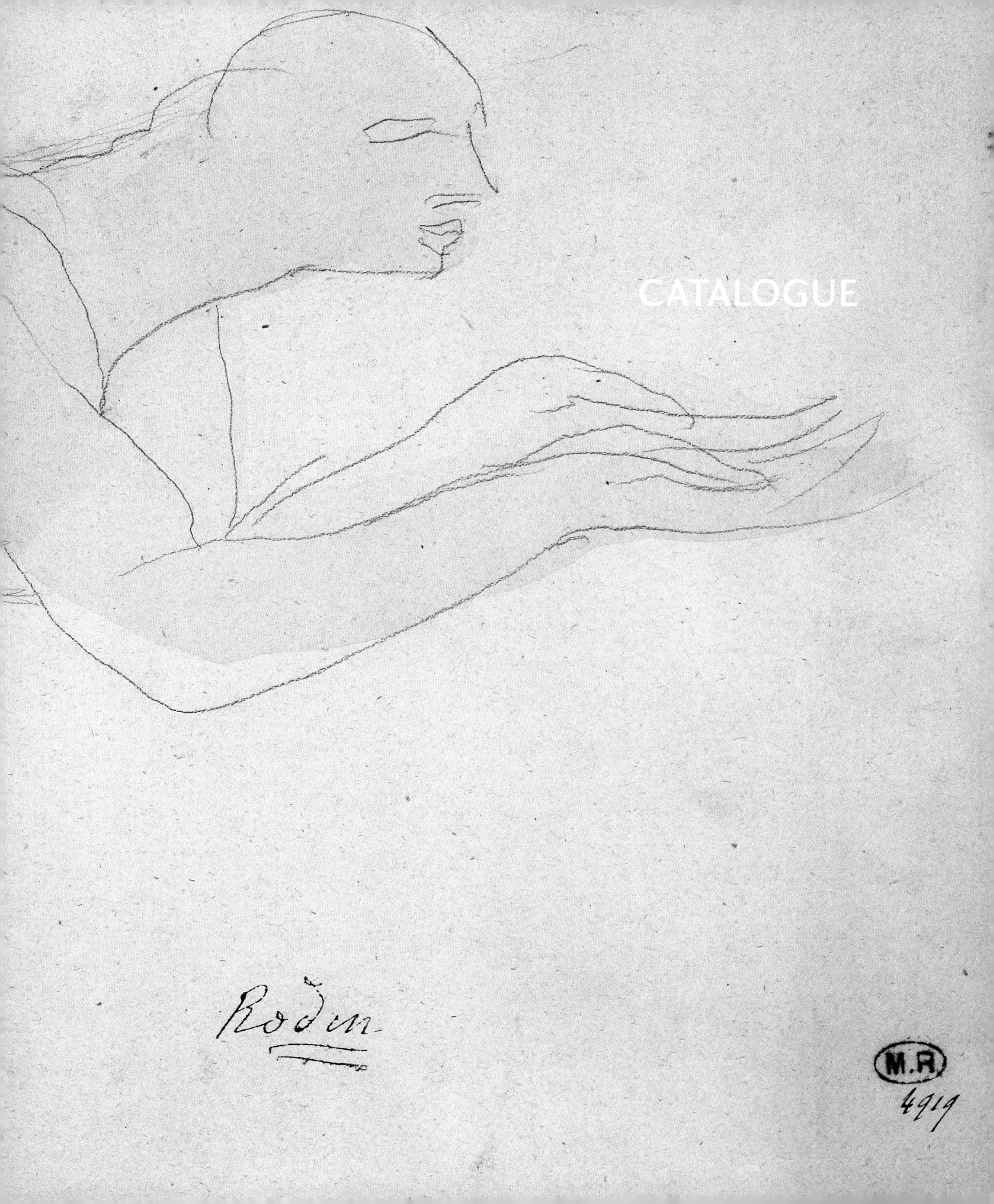

I

EUGÈNE DRUET

Loïe Fuller dancing, c.1900

Gelatin silver print, 400 x 300 mm
Musée Rodin, Paris, PH.1745

Loïe Fuller (1862–1928), née Marie-Louise Fuller, was the most innovative dancer on the Parisian stage at the turn of the century, and one of the founding figures in the history of modern dance in the twentieth century. She first performed at the Folies-Bergère in 1892, remaining the music-hall's star attraction for many years, and introducing a new form of dance into its repertoire of acrobatic numbers and popular ballet pieces. Although described at the time as an acrobatic dancer,[1] unlike conventional acrobats Fuller was not interested in showing off the body through feats of athleticism. Instead she made her body disappear behind metres of translucent silk fabric, which she manipulated with tall bamboo rods tucked inside her sleeves, to create images of insects, flowers, butterflies and clouds. The evocative patterns produced by her draperies, which she further enhanced with jewel-like colours filtered through the stage lights, were a mine of inspiration for Art Nouveau artists and decorators. Symbolist writers, in the wake of the poet Stéphane Mallarmé, admired Fuller's ethereal and abstract choreographies, such as her famous Serpentine dance.

Rodin owned about one hundred photographs of Fuller. Most, like this one by Eugène Druet, who worked closely with Rodin for several years, were set outdoors because Fuller was wary of allowing the camera to capture her on stage. The blurred lines of fabric in this image (with the presence of the rods just visible at the straight edges of her sleeves) could only hint at the extraordinary visual effects of her performances, in which her brightly tinted draperies traced her movements in space, as though cutting through the solid substance of the air. Her dances were often interpreted in terms of the *fin-de-siècle* belief that all living organisms were governed by an energy, termed '*l'élan vital*' by the French philosopher Henri Bergson in his book *L'Évolution créatrice* of 1907. The concept of '*élan vital*', which is sometimes translated as 'vital force', was influential in the natural sciences, astronomy, art, architecture and literature. Fuller's performances, with their constant flow of images borrowed from nature, encapsulated the essence of this philosophy, of which she would have known through her friendship with one of its distinguished exponents, the astronomer Camille Flammarion. Rodin was equally attuned to vitalist ideas of flux, metamorphosis and transformation, as suggested by his fascination with plaster as a shape-shifting material whose fluidity and protean qualities he could endlessly manipulate and rework.[2]

Although Fuller posed for Rodin from about 1899 to 1901, and continued to be a frequent visitor to Meudon for many years afterwards, it was to no avail that she pressed him to make a sculpture of her. On a more profound level, however, her radical approach to dance and the body undoubtedly influenced and helped shape Rodin's interest in capturing movement in his drawings after the life model from the 1890s.[3] She also provided introductions to some of the period's most original avant-garde performers, who came to model in his studio and in this way contributed to renewing Rodin's late oeuvre (see cat.19–23). With respect to the reception of Rodin in the United States and his presence in American collections, it is worth noting that Fuller was instrumental in persuading collectors and museums to acquire his work. AG

1 For example, in de Ménil 1905, p.338.
2 See C. Chevillot, 'Le plâtre: un univers rodinien', in Montreal 2015, pp.42–51, p.48, who points out that Leo Steinberg was the first to appreciate this, in his seminal text later published in *Other Criteria* (Steinberg 1972). On Fuller and vitalist thought in the sciences, see for example A.H. Gomez, *Body Stages: The Metamorphosis of Loie Fuller*, Madrid, La Casa Encendida, 2014.
3 Fuller's influence on Rodin is discussed in Juliet Bellow's essay in this volume.

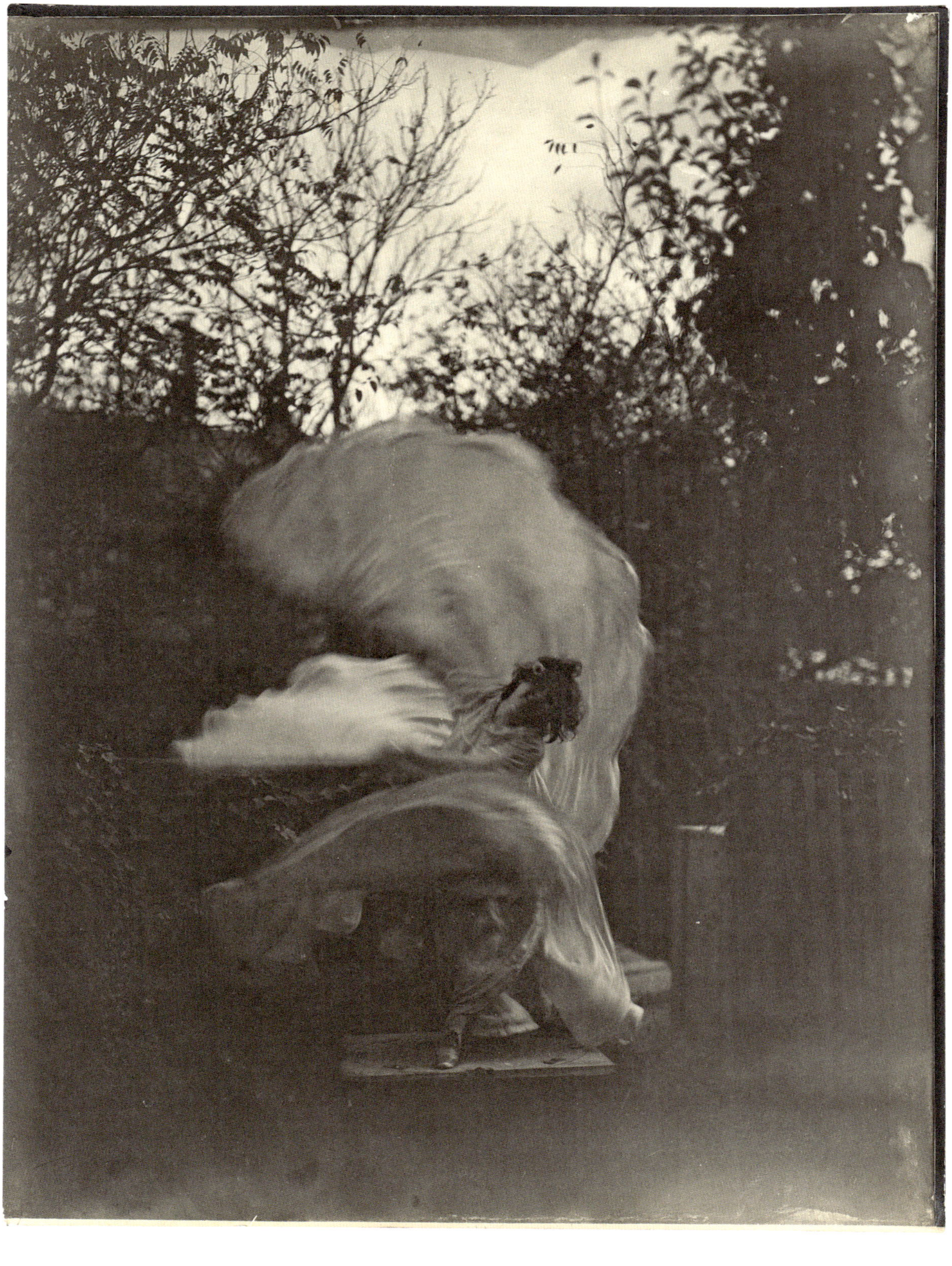

2–5

Woman dancing, c.1889

Pen and black ink and grey ink wash over gouache on laid paper, 177 x 115 mm
Musée Rodin, Paris, D.4349

Woman dancing with folded arms and bent knees, c.1900

Pencil with stumping on wove paper, 305 x 200 mm
Musée Rodin, Paris, D.2363

Cambodian dancer, 1906 or after

Pencil with stumping, watercolour and gouache on wove paper, 348 x 267 mm
Musée Rodin, Paris, D.4455

Cambodian dancer in profile, 1906 or after

Pencil, watercolour and gouache on wove paper, 300 x 197 mm
Musée Rodin, Paris, D.4468

These drawings were all made from life and show Rodin capturing a dancer's movements in various media. Their sense of animation derives from the free and spontaneous appearance of the lines, whether in pen and ink or brush and watercolour. The drawing of a woman dancing (D.4349, cat.2) is dated to Rodin's 'transitional' period of the early 1890s when he began to do extensive sketching directly from the model. Its sombre tonality and the use of grey with white to model and set the figure in space tie it to his drawings for *The Gates of Hell*, his major artistic project of the 1880s.

The dancer's movements, especially her straight left arm and flexed hands, low bent knees and flat feet, are alien to European dance traditions of the time. They seem instead to record something of the gestures of the South-East Asian dances, notably Javanese, that were seen for the first time in Europe at the Great Exhibitions of 1889 and 1900. Beginning with a light gouache background, Rodin built up the figure with layers of pen and black-grey ink and grey wash applied with a brush. The variety of swirling pen and brush strokes contributes to the sense of movement of the figure and her drapery. This is particularly apparent in the long flowing strokes that taper to a point around the figure's head and upper body. The continuous and rapidly drawn zigzag pen strokes around the outside of the figure and within the folds of the drapery create shadow and depth. The forked metal nib at the bottom right of the sheet (detail below) is an indication of both pressure and speed of draughtsmanship.

Rodin's final application of broad parallel brush strokes in black ink across the upper body and thighs and around the head, however, compromises the sense of movement in the

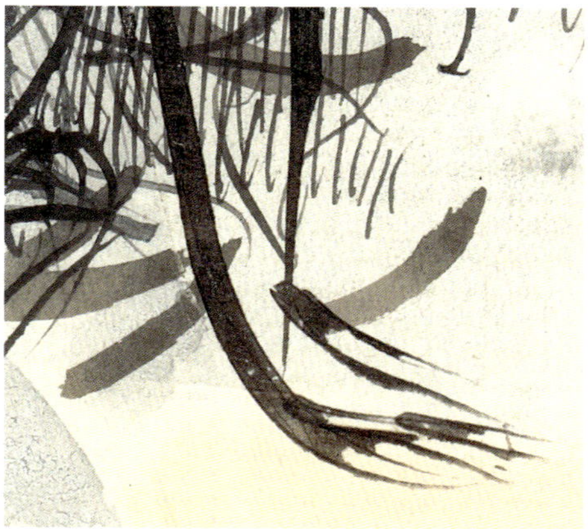

Detail of D.4349, cat.2

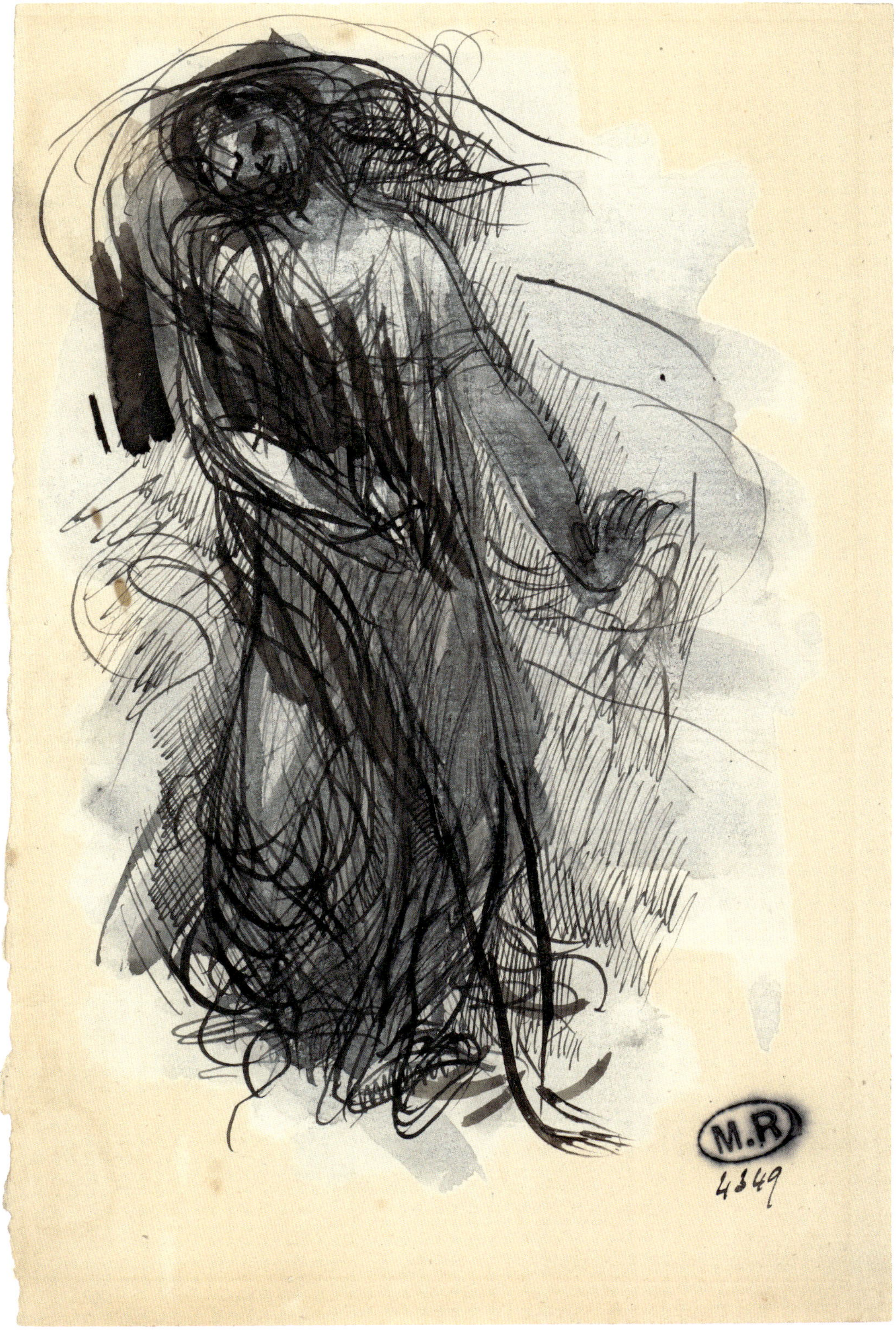

2

drawing, resulting in the head appearing fixed in position. Yet there can be little doubt that the figure was moving as Rodin sketched her. This is confirmed by the existence of a very similar drawing in the Musée Rodin's collection showing the same figure in a slight variation of the pose and seen from the side rather than the front (D.4363). The two drawings, which share a watermark, were originally part of the same sheet.[1]

Rodin's dynamic style of capturing the model's movements was considered at the time one of his major achievements of these years. To sketch at speed, Rodin developed a working method which was described by the writer Clément-Janin in 1903: "Equipped with a sheet of ordinary paper posed on a board, and with a lead pencil – sometimes a pen – he has his model take an essentially unstable pose, then he draws spiritedly, without taking his eyes off the model .... In less than one minute, this snapshot of movement is caught."[2] The critic Louis Vauxcelles also described the process in his preface to an exhibition of Rodin's drawings in 1908: "He follows them with his eyes, and, pencil in hand, captures the being in full movement and throws a silhouette on to the paper".[3]

Sketches such as *Woman dancing* (D.2363, cat.3) illustrate this technique, with long continuous pencil strokes extending across the sheet and capturing the movement of the figure. The figure is naked, holding some kind of drapery, and is captured dancing, possibly turning and tapping her feet quickly. Curved pencil lines indicate a rhythmic motion whilst stumping with hatched lines give volume and a sense of weight to the body. This sketch is thought to represent the Spanish dancer and artists' model Carmen Damedoz, referred to as '*la petite espagnole*' in the studio archives, who posed for Rodin between about 1898 and 1902 and with whom he also seems to have had an intimate relationship.[4]

Rodin's drawings of royal dancers from the French Protectorate of Cambodia (D.4455, cat.4, and D.4468, cat.5) were sketched from life over the course of a few days in July 1906. The dancers travelled as part of the entourage of King Sisowath, Cambodia's French-friendly king, to perform traditional court dances at the Exposition Coloniale in Marseille from April of that year. Towards the end of their stay, they accompanied the king on a diplomatic visit to Paris, performing at a presidential garden party at the Elysée Palace on 1 July and at the Pré-Catelan, a venue in the Bois de Boulogne, ten days later. At the Pré-Catelan the frenzy was such that a midnight performance was added at the last minute to allow a further 1500 people to attend the show.[5] Rodin, who saw the public performance, was granted a private audience to sketch the dancers at their hotel in Paris. He was then given official permission to travel by train with them to Marseille, where he spent a few days sketching before they sailed back to Phnom Pen (cat.6, 7 and 11).

Rodin executed the drawing of a Cambodian dancer (cat.4) initially in light pencil, with some areas such as the figure's right hand appearing exaggerated and distorted as he may have drawn it without looking down at the paper. He added tone with stumped pencil, watercolour and gouache washes and then used broader, darker pencil strokes to reinforce the position of the legs and the movement of the draped fabric behind the figure's left arm. In the drawing of a Cambodian dancer in profile (cat.5), Rodin's treatment of the background adds a further sense of movement. The broad brush strokes of dilute blue watercolour are clearly visible, applied in a free and vigorous way. For example the swirl to the right of the figure and the curved strokes around the raised leg echo the dancers' 'wave'-like motions so admired by Rodin.[6] KE & AG

1 The left edge of D.4349 (cat.2) lines up with the left edge of the drawing D.4363. Our thanks to Sophie Biass-Fabiani for verifying this.
2 Clément-Janin 1903, pp.286–87, quoted in K. Varnedoe, 'Rodin as a Draftsman – A Chronological Perspective' in Elsen and Varnedoe, 1971, pp.25–120, p.76. See Paris 2011 for a complete bibliography of Rodin's drawings, and Martigny 1994, pp.179–83, for a précis of contemporary sources.
3 "*Il les suit du regard, et, le crayon à la main, saisit l'être en plein mouvement, jette la silhouette sur le papier*": Vauxcelles 1908, p.4.
4 Buley-Uribe 2005, p.172. See also Paris 1990, pp.31–37. Damedoz would later become one of France's first female aviators.
5 Décoret-Ahiha 2004, p.44.
6 'Rodin et les petites princesses jaunes', *Le Figaro*, 1 August 1906, published in Rodin 2011, pp.130–34.

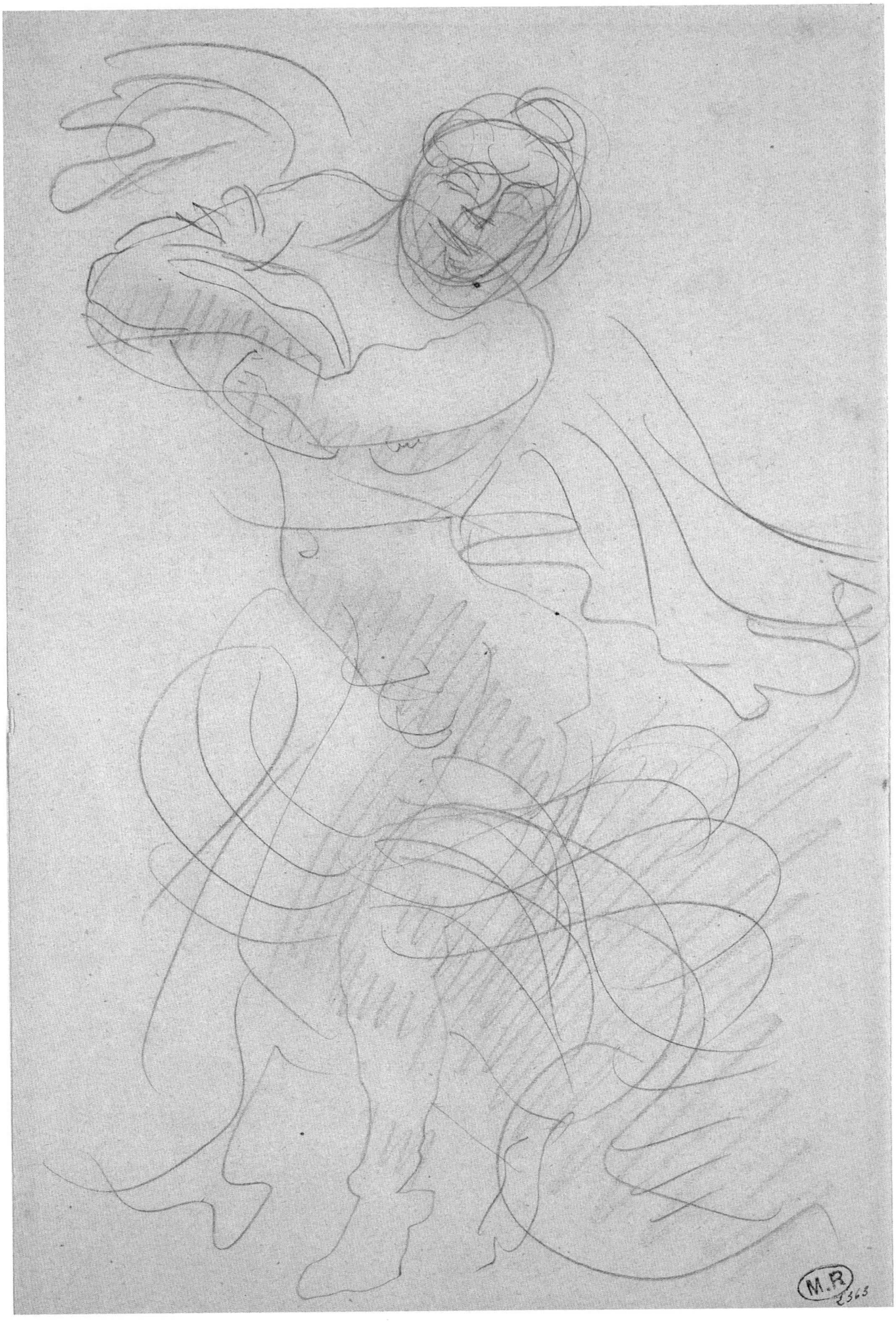

3

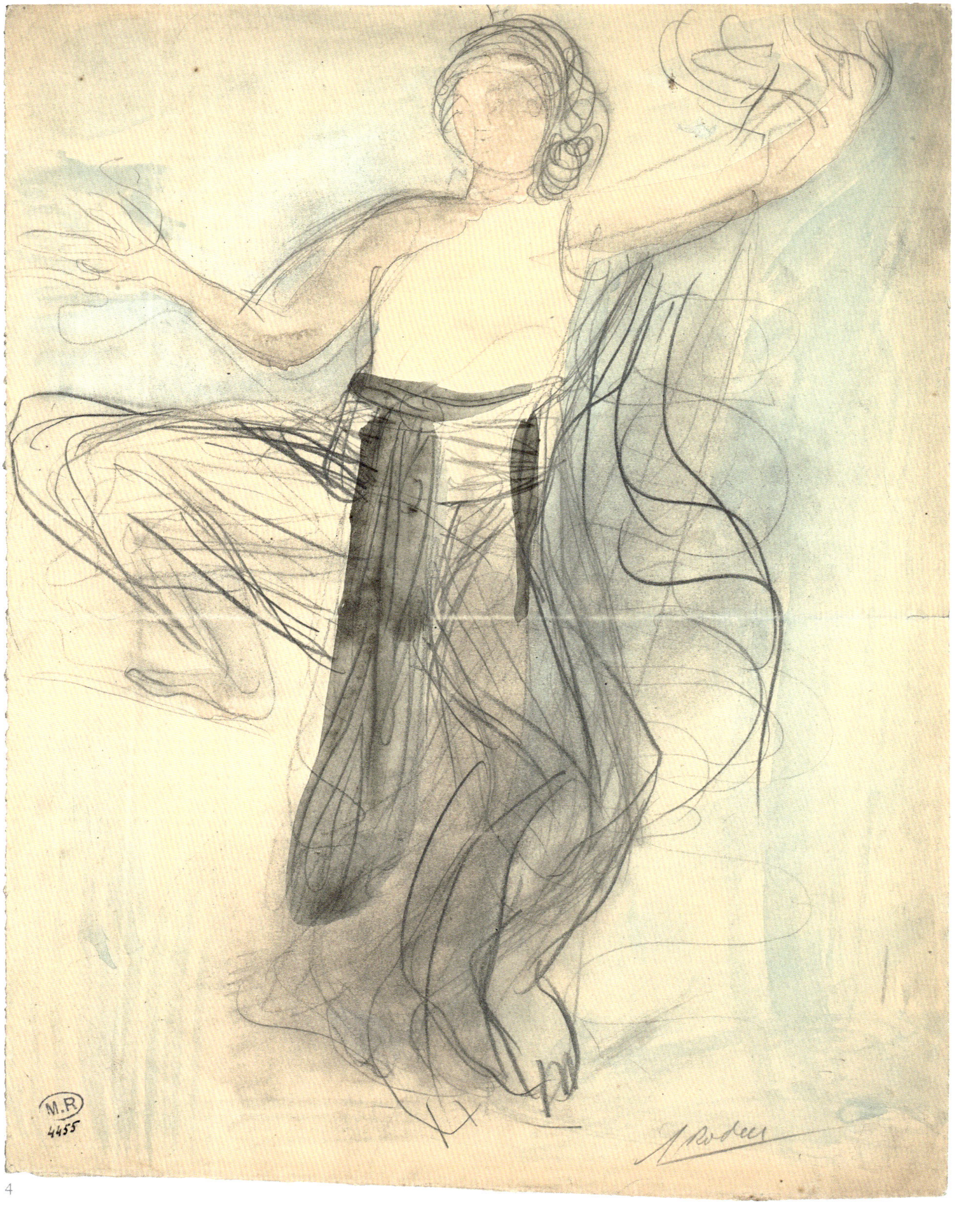
M.R
4455

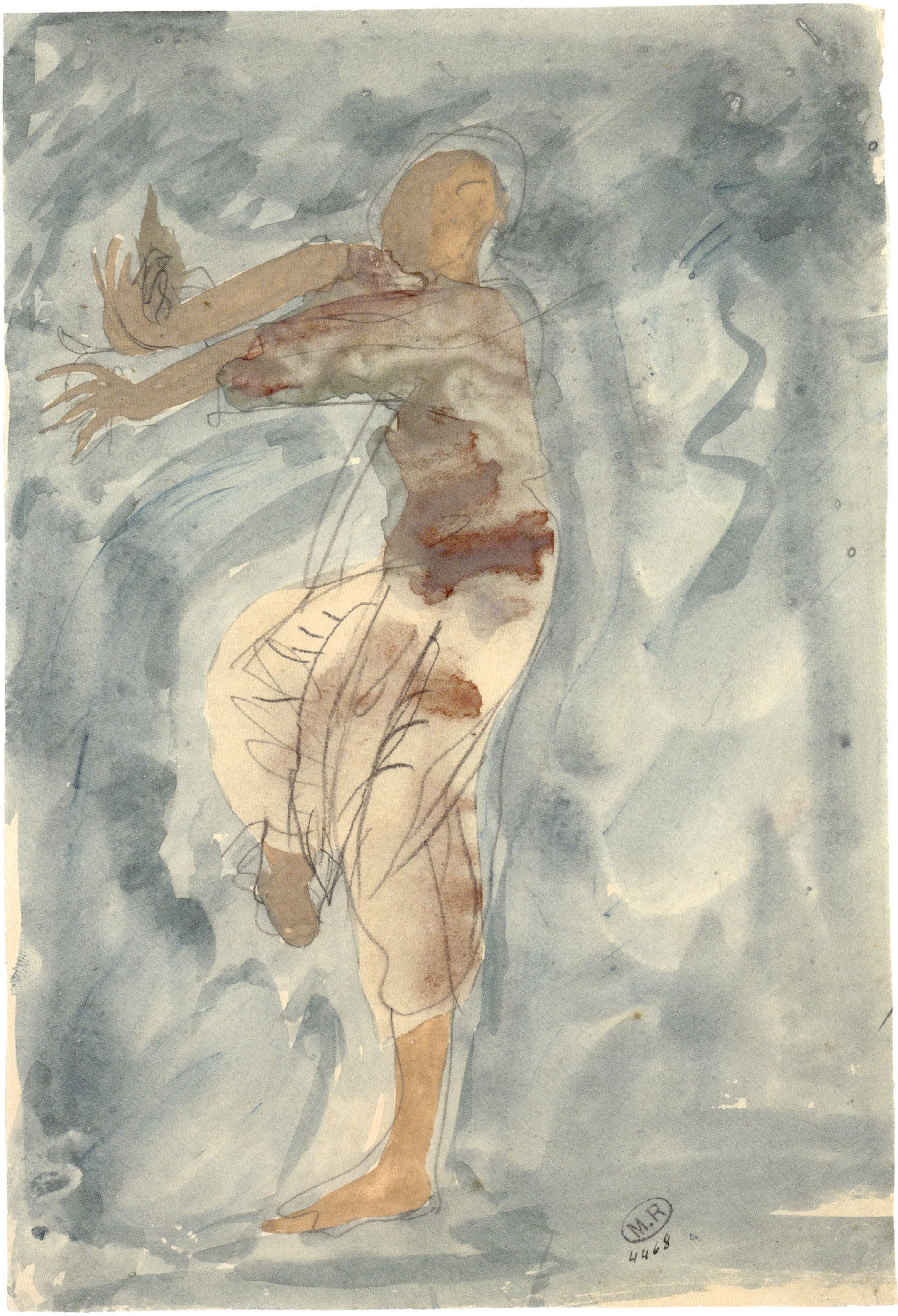
M.R
4468

6–7

EMILE SANREMO

Rodin drawing the Cambodian Royal Dancers in Marseille, July 1906

Gelatin silver print, 118 x 169 mm
Musée Rodin, Paris, PH.14379

EMILE SANREMO

Rodin adjusting a pose, July 1906

Gelatin silver print, 120 x 170 mm
Musée Rodin, Paris, PH.14910

8–10

Three postcards of the Royal Cambodian Dance Troupe, 1906

Each 90 x 140 mm
Musée Rodin, Paris

11

'Le Sculpteur Rodin et les danseuses cambodgiennes', *L'Illustration*, 28 July 1906

420 x 308 mm (closed)
Musée Rodin, Paris

These photographs show Rodin seated simply on a bench in the garden of the Villa des Glycines in Marseille, where the troupe of royal Cambodian dancers was housed during the Exposition Coloniale, sketching the young dancers as they posed for him. The photographer captured him, paper on his knees, observing the dancers and drawing (cat.6 & 7). The encounter between France's greatest living artist and these 'exotic' young dancers was covered in both local and national papers (cat.11).

In the press the dancers were often described as the living manifestations of the ancient stone sculptures from Cambodian temple complexes. Rodin reiterated many clichés about them, yet his published statements analysing the quality of movement of the Cambodian dances (and of the Javanese dancers he had seen several years earlier) show a thoughtful and original response, which of course informed his drawings of them. Rodin noted in particular the 'wave'-like undulation of their bodies, which starts from the shoulder blades and descends into the spine and then the knees. This impression of a serpentine line that flows from top to bottom is indeed present in many of the 150 or so drawings of Cambodians he is known to have produced around 1906. Rodin's drawings capture the dancers' movements in various ways, but mostly their motions, gestures and postures were transformed. This approach is close to Debussy, who created musical scores borrowing, incorporating and transforming elements of Javanese music.[1]

L'Illustration (cat.11) records an interview with Georges Bois, the Inspector of Professional Education in Indo-China and Fine Arts Delegate to the Exposition Coloniale in Marseille. Rodin began it by saying he had just spent "three days from three thousand years ago". He then went on to say:

1 Seee M.I. Cohen, *Performing Otherness: Java and Bali on the international stages, 1905–52*, Basingstoke (Palgrave Macmillan), c.2010, pp.1–22. Generally on exoticism in dance in France during this period, see Décoret-Ahiha 2004.

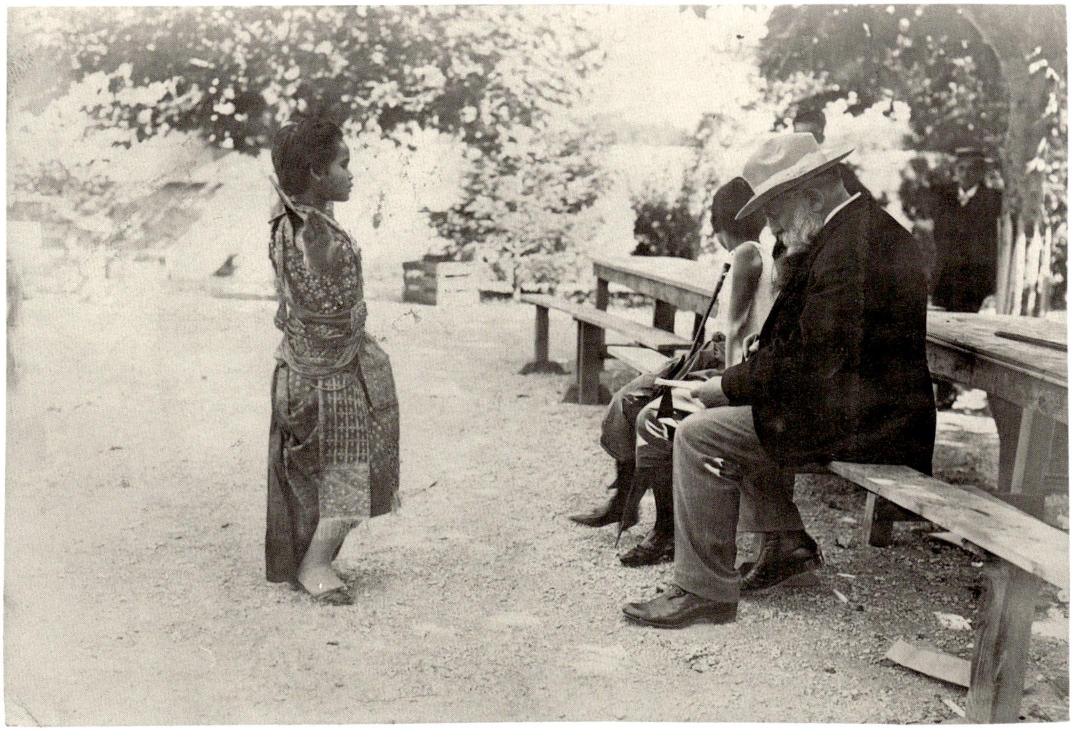
6

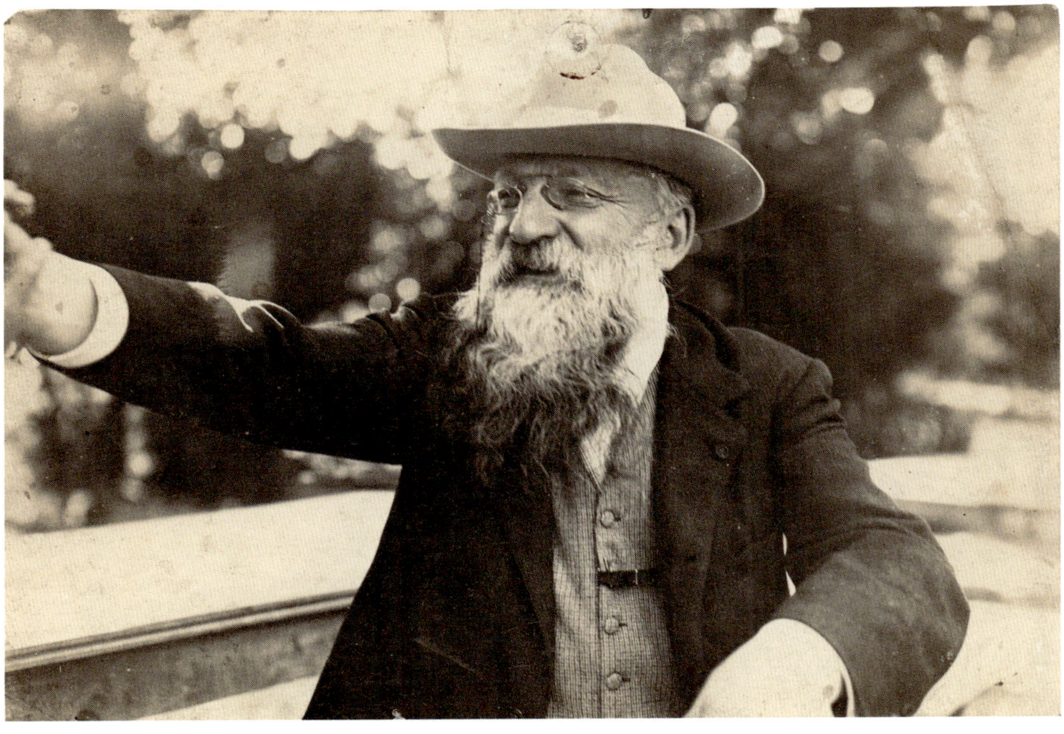
7

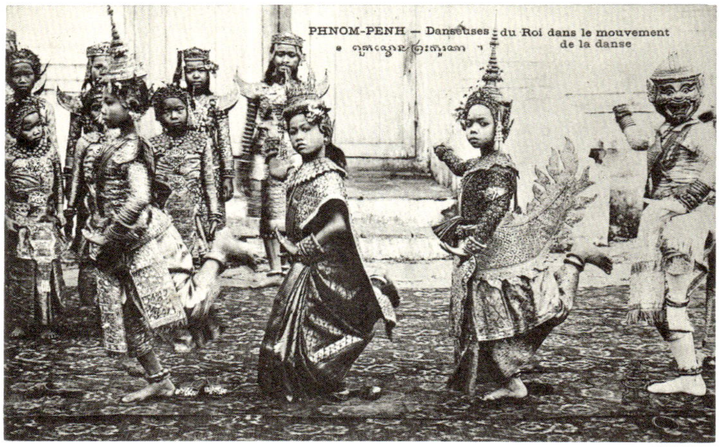

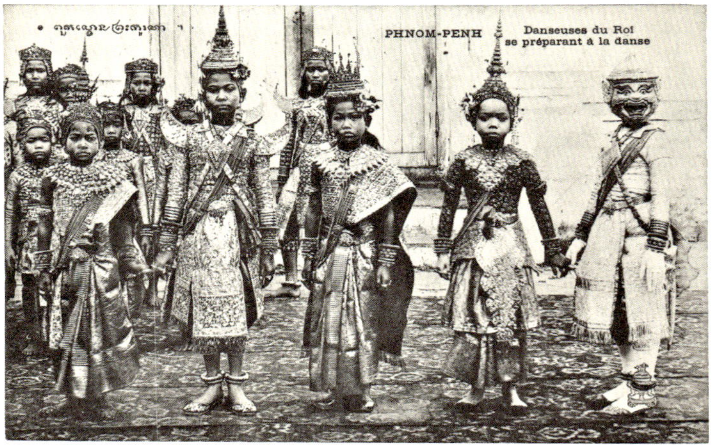

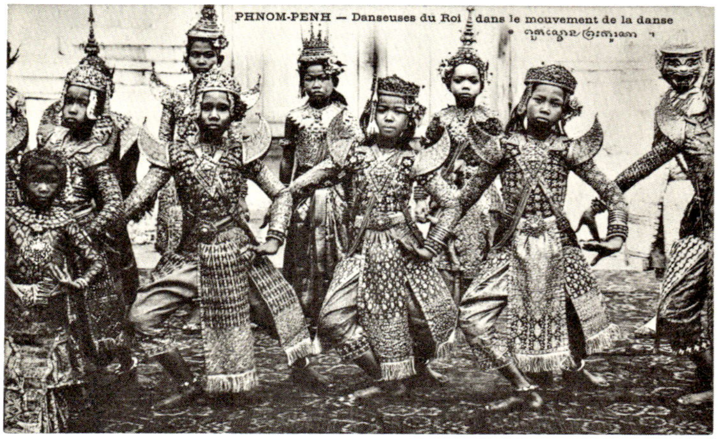

8–10

> They even found a new movement, which I did not know: these are the shudders that the body gives and into which it descends. And then, the great resource, is that they have almost permanently bent knees, and it's a receptacle of leaps that they model as they wish and which allows them to lift themselves, to grow at a certain point. / Another movement of theirs, unknown to the Ancients and to us: when the arms are extended as in a cross, they give a movement which snakes from one hand to the other, passing by the shoulder-blades. This movement belongs to the Far East, unknown, never seen, that is, when a movement of the left arm makes a concave arc, the other makes a convex arc, and they play these arms, and the spark of movement travels into the shoulder-blades. / The posture of bent knees is a movement that belongs to them, and these bent knees are a store of expressions; because one can elevate the body from time to time, according to the rhythm of the music. And the articulations of the fingers which are capable of being elongated, very flexible and which can in addition also be made to tremble! ... They are solicited from an early age.[2]

A few days later, speaking with *Le Figaro*, Rodin's analysis of their dances was slightly more precise:

> These monotonous, slow dances to the rhythms of strange music have an extraordinary, a perfect beauty, like the beauty of Greece but with its own special quality. The Cambodian dancers have revealed movements to me that I have never found anywhere before, either in the art of sculpture or in nature. For instance, that longitudinal motion they create by stretching out their arms, turning their hands up, and spreading their fingers, producing a slow undulation from one end of the cross they

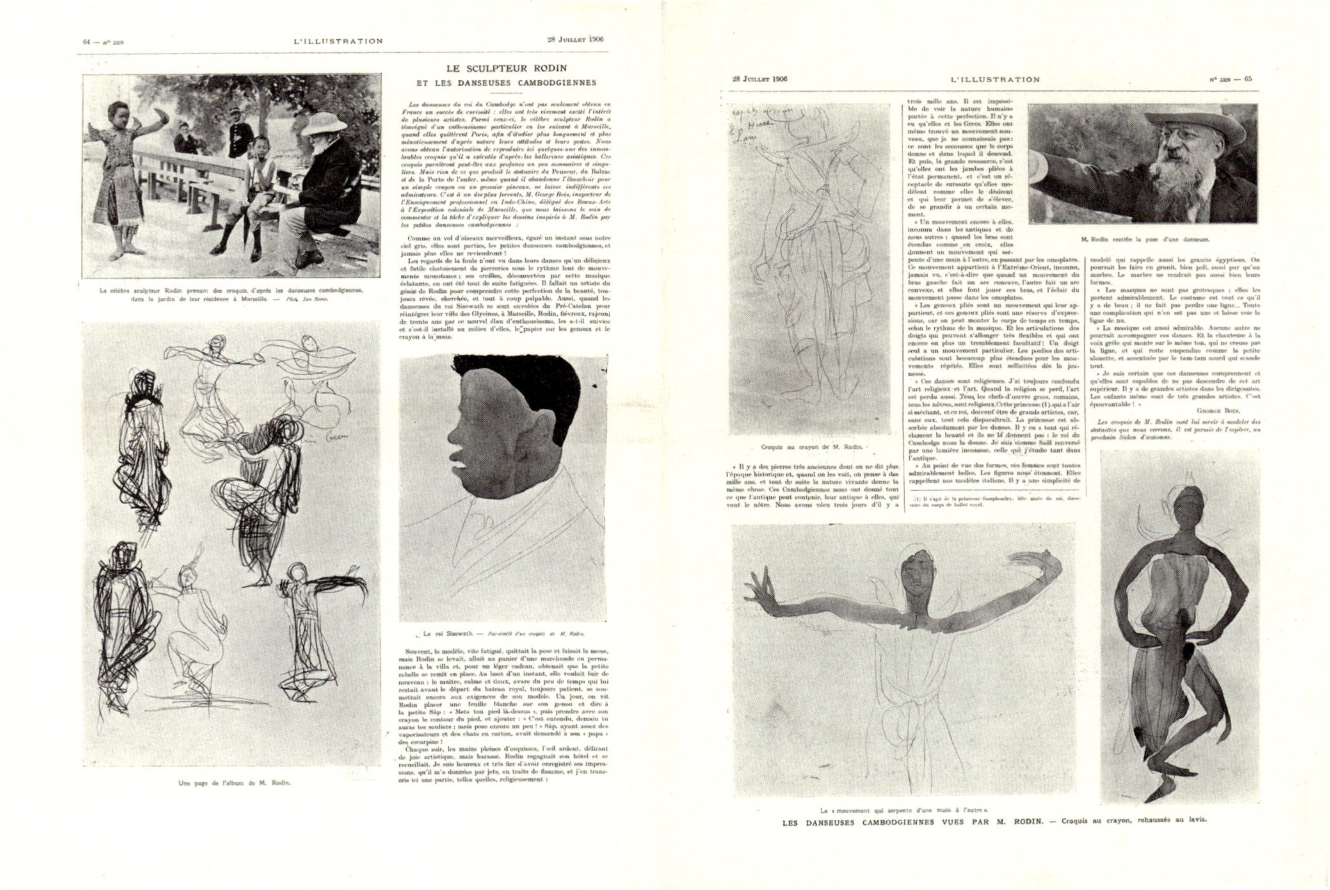
64 — Nº 3309 L'ILLUSTRATION 28 JUILLET 1906

LE SCULPTEUR RODIN
ET LES DANSEUSES CAMBODGIENNES

Le célèbre sculpteur Rodin prenant des croquis d'après les danseuses cambodgiennes, dans le jardin de leur résidence à Marseille.

Une page de l'album de M. Rodin.

Le roi Sisowath. — Portrait d'un croquis de M. Rodin.

28 JUILLET 1906 L'ILLUSTRATION Nº 3309 — 65

Croquis au crayon de M. Rodin.

M. Rodin rectifie la pose d'une danseuse.

GEORGE BOIS.

Le « mouvement qui serpente d'une main à l'autre ».
LES DANSEUSES CAMBODGIENNES VUES PAR M. RODIN. — Croquis au crayon, rehaussés au lavis.

11

form to the other, a wave motion that is also transmitted to chest and shoulders and which creates a continual opposition of the curves of their arms, one forming a convex and the other a concave arc .... All you can say is that all movements of the body, if they are harmonious and right, can be inscribed within a geometric pattern whose lines are simple and few.[3]

It seems the drawings were ends in themselves. Although Bois stated that Rodin's sketches were preparatory for "statuettes" (which he was apparently intending to present at the following Salon d'Automne in Paris), when he was asked the same question by *Le Figaro* Rodin answered firmly that no, he was too old.[4] Nonetheless, this intense episode of sketching the dancers was a catalyst for Rodin, which would bear fruit in years to come, notably in the creation of the *Mouvements de danse* of 1911. In subsequent interviews he would often refer to this as a time of wonderment and enrichment. Although Rodin complained in a letter to the German poet Rainer Maria Rilke, who had been his secretary in 1905–06, that he had not been able to capture the essence of the Cambodian dancers, his sketches do home in on the essential structure and shape of their movements.[5] Rodin's drawings transform the Cambodians' angular gestures into soft curves and flowing lines, their joints disappearing inside elastic limbs, and the slow pace so characteristic of the dance is replaced by an almost ecstatic vigour (especially in drawings like the Musée Rodin's D.4487 whose swirling lines encircle and cross over the dancers), with figures in positions that are often just on the edge of stability (D.4455, cat.4). AG

2 Rodin's interview is republished in Rodin 2011, pp.127–29.
3 'Rodin et les petites princesses jaunes', *Le Figaro*, 1 August 1906, published in Rodin 2011, pp.130–34, and translated into English in Güse 1985, p.271.
4 Further, Anthony Ludovici, Rodin's secretary in 1906, argued against this idea: Ludovici 1926, pp. 137–38.
5 Rodin to Rainer Maria Rilke (Paris or Meudon), 8 November 1907; *Correspondance de Rodin*, vol.2.

12 & 13

Three Cambodian dancers, 1906 or after

Pen and brown ink, watercolour and gouache on wove paper, 340 x 216 mm
Musée Rodin, Paris, D.4467

Female figure, right arm bent toward the chest, c.1900–06

Terracotta, 29 x 14.8 x 12.1 cm
Musée Rodin, Paris, S.6359

While many of Rodin's drawings of Cambodians concentrate on representing motion (cat.4 & 5), others focus more particularly on capturing a pose, and in the latter group are a few sheets populated with multiple small figures in a variety of poses, sometimes in more than one orientation (D.4467, cat.12). Rilke wrote to Rodin, upon seeing one such sheet with multiple drawings at the Galerie Bernheim-Jeune exhibition of his drawings in 1907: "The most tender flowers, having bloomed on the happy soil of your immense labour, are preserved for ever as in a herbarium, where plants, carefully dried, have taken a definitive gesture which contains in essence the fragile and yet eternal rhythm of their life".[1]

The three figures are executed in pen and brown ink; the uniformity of the ink colour suggests they were drawn at the same time. Rodin reinforced and modified their poses, as seen in the changes to the position of the hands and legs, these adjustments evoking a sense of movement. He then applied layers of dilute watercolour over the draperies and reinforced the position of the figures with a combination of light pink gouache underneath a brown tint. For example, a small flash of pink is visible on the arm of the figure on the lower left. The choice of a darker black-brown wash over the drapery on the upper figure gives it more prominence, drawing the eye away from the muted tones of the pair of figures below.

Rodin has connected the figures by adding a background that seems to suggest sky and ground. A single brushstroke drawn across the sheet, and dragged towards the bottom right, gives the area beneath the pair of upright figures weight and volume. It is thought that Rodin reworked many of his Cambodian drawings in relation to a commission between 1907 and 1910 to produce frescoes on the theme of Paradise for a new space in the Musée du Luxembourg dedicated to him, and providing a counterpoint to *The Gates of Hell*.[2] Rodin's reworking of this drawing by adding a unifying background to the figures seems to be connected to this aborted project.

The quickly modelled clay sketch of a nude in what appears to be a dance pose (S.6359, cat.13) seems to capture a movement from a non-European, possibly South-East Asian dance of the type Rodin was known to admire at least since he first saw the Javanese dance troupes in Paris in 1889. According to Edmond de Goncourt, Rodin was captivated by them, saying that he rated their dances far higher than the "jumpy" rhythms of the ballet, and showing him sketches he had made after the dancers.[3] Years later, Rodin would write: "Whoever has seen the Javanese and the Cambodians dance, understands why the Orientals call us Barbarians. [Their dances] are ordered like architecture: mathematical laws govern them. What profound emotion in the dances of the little Javanese!"[4]

The figure has the low bent knees, the flattened feet with upturned toes and the bent arm position familiar from Rodin's drawings of Cambodian dancers, for example the two upright figures in the drawing of three Cambodian dancers (cat.12). As the figure is nude, the muscles and angles

1 3 November 1907, in Rilke 1931, p.73: "*Les fleurs les plus tendres écloses sur le sol bienheureux de votre immense travail y sont conservées pour toujours comme dans un herbarium, où les plantes, soigneusement sèchées, ont pris un geste définitif qui contient en essence le rythme fragile et pourtant éternel de leur vie*".
2 Paris 2006, pp.63–69.
3 "*Il trouve nos danses trop sautillantes, trop brisées …*": Edmond de Goncourt, Journal entry for 23 July 1891, quoted in Paris 1979, p.101.
4 "*Qui a vu danser les Javanaises et les Cambodgiennes, comprend pourquoi les Orientaux nous appellent 'Barbares'. [Leurs danses] sont ordonnées comme des architectures: les lois mathématiques les gouvernent. Quelle profonde émotion dans les danses des petites Javanaises!*": 'Fresques de danses', in *Montjoie!* 1914, pp.1–2, published in Rodin 2011, pp.134–37.

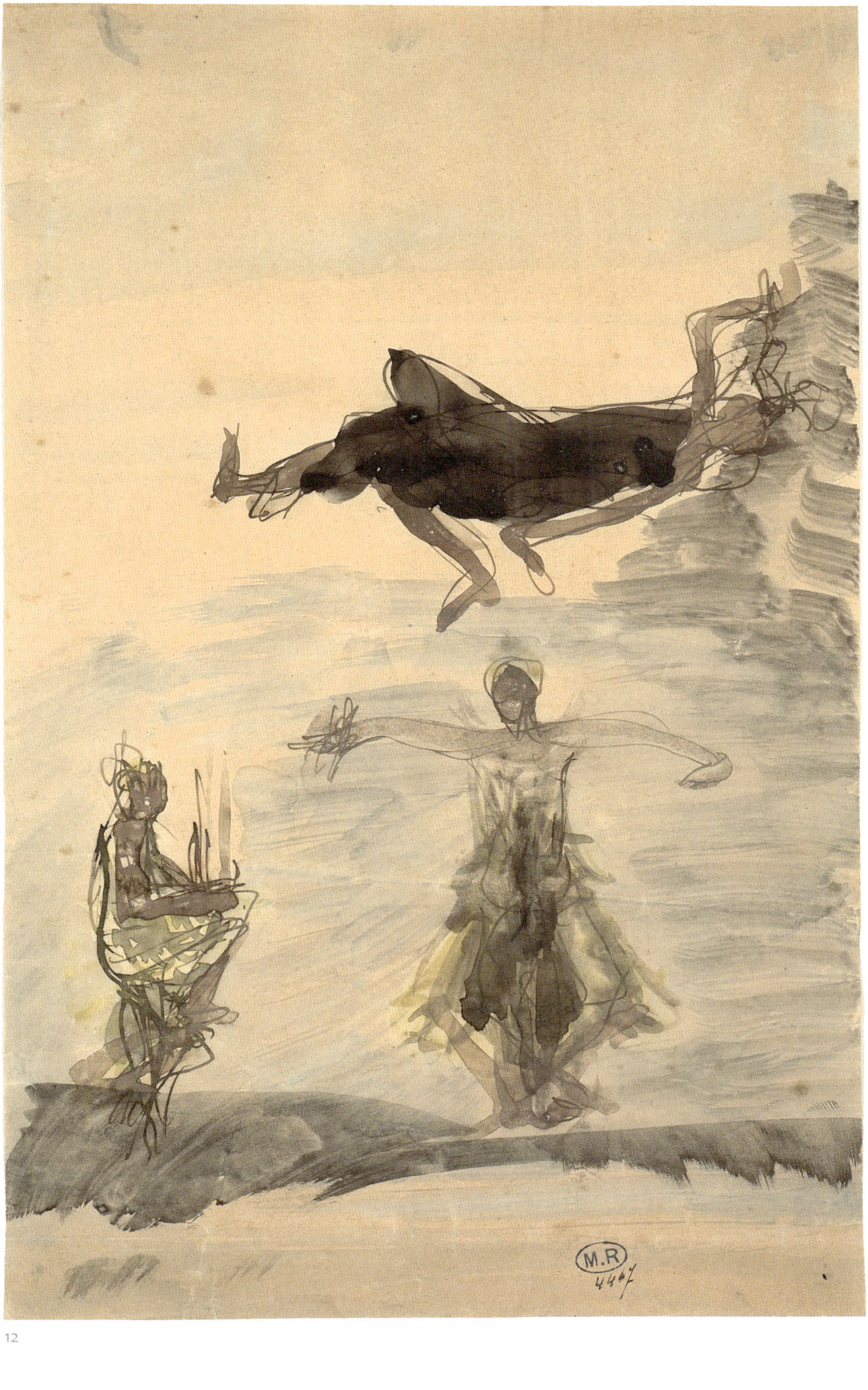
M.R
4467

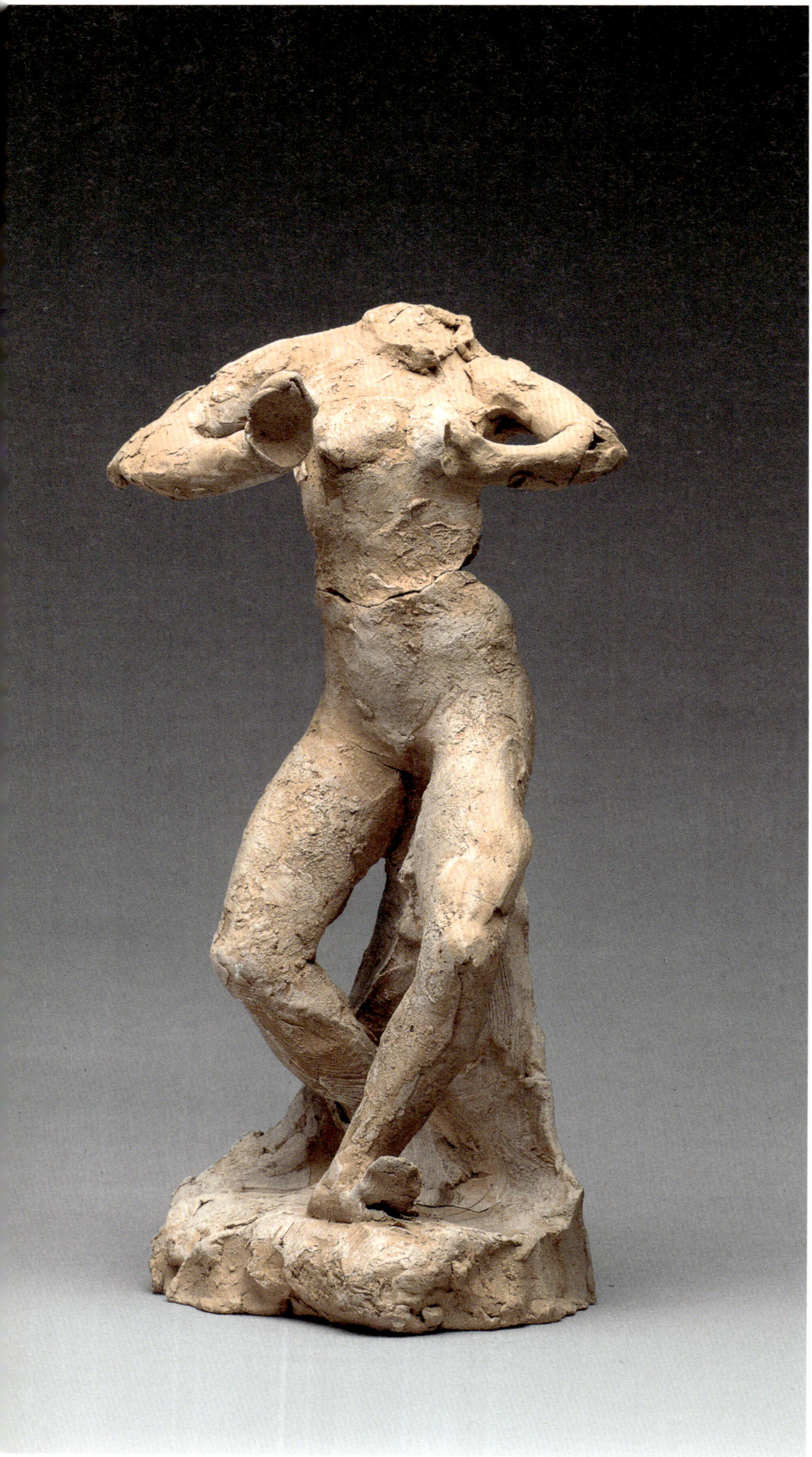

13

of the body are visible, which creates a very different impression from his ethereal drawings of Cambodians. The figure's movement in this pose separates the torso from the hips, either by a twist of the waist or by an isolated movement of the ribcage. The absence of a head, which is not unusual for Rodin in these late years, appears intentional here since the clay was cleanly sliced off whilst still fresh.[5] It seems that in the late drawings of dancers Rodin was interested in the expression of movement as an abstract idea, an essence not tied to a narrative, in which facial expressivity rarely if ever played a role. Even many of his drawings of Cambodians have simple ovoids for heads (cat.4 and 5, with and without hair).

More surprising is that Rodin has paid very little attention to modelling the hands, focusing only on their position in relation to the body. Why this should be is not clear; however, one might advance the supposition that the model – whoever she was – did not have the extraordinary faculty of hyperextension of the hands and fingers of Cambodian or Javanese dancers, which Rodin admired so fervently, and which he often sketched with attention (cat.14). The figure's nudity could further support this supposition.[6] The most famous Asian-style dance was performed by the French ballet star Cléo de Mérode at the 1900 Exhibition. Despite garnering much positive press attention, she did not, however, succeed in convincing the public they were watching an authentic spectacle: "It is not at all Cambodian but it is delicious", as one commentator at the time said.[7] KE & AG

5 Our thanks to Agnès Cascio for this observation.
6 See Paris 2006, pp.72–73.
7 Cited in Décoret-Ahiha 2004, p.226. See Alexandre Falguière's life-size sculpture after Cléo de Mérode, *La danseuse*, 1896 (plaster, Musée d'Orsay).

14 & 15

Four studies of hands, 1906 or after

Pencil and gouache on wove paper, 307 x 203 mm
Musée Rodin, Paris, D.4505

UNKNOWN MOULD-MAKER

Cast of a right arm (of a Javanese dancer?), one of a pair, c.1900

Plaster, 10.9 x 34.1 x 17 cm
Musée Rodin, Paris, S.5168

Among the things that most fascinated Rodin about the South-East Asian dancers he sketched was their faculty for hyperextension in the wrists and hands. The cast of a right arm (cat.15), one of a pair owned by Rodin and now in the collections of the Musée Rodin (see also fig.44), shows an arm in such a position. It was probably made after a life cast – that is, a cast taken directly on the arm of a living model, in this case probably a young adolescent girl.

The recent discovery of the moulds for this pair of arms, in the Musée Rodin, strongly suggests they were cast in his studio by one of the many skilled mould-makers and casters he employed.[1] The fact that the moulds are inscribed *danseuses javanaises* supports the idea that they were the likely original models.

The existence of an identical pair of arms (and a third arm in another position) in the collections of the École National des Beaux-Arts (ENSBA) in Paris sheds some light on the question of their making, even if it does not explain everything.[2] Comparing both pairs of arms together confirms that the pair in the Musée Rodin is the same as that in the ENSBA, the difference being the presence of an extra network of seam lines on the casts owned by Rodin.[3]

These contain two networks of seams, first a set of soft seam lines, corresponding to the seam lines on the ENSBA casts, and secondly a set of lines that correspond to the piece moulds in the Musée Rodin. The two arms in the ENSBA's collection therefore pre-date Rodin's, and they too were made from piece moulds, but different ones. Further, the Musée Rodin moulds appear not to have been made from the ENSBA arms, but from an identical ('sister') pair, whose lines are still visible on the inside surface of the negative piece mould. This makes Rodin's casts properly speaking casts of life casts rather than actual life casts.

The individual plaster casts of hands, arms, legs and feet that Rodin had his technicians make for him over the years – there are dozens of drawers of these sculptural fragments of body parts, which he called his '*abattis*', in the Musée Rodin – were cast from his own work for him to assemble together into new compositions. This arm evidently had another function, perhaps for study. Rodin did not integrate life-cast elements in his work other than, occasionally, real objects (e.g. using a life cast of an egg for his group of paired *Mouvement A* figures; see fig.43, p.72). That he apparently went to the trouble of having moulds and plasters made of these life casts may seem surprising given what we know of his attitude towards the technique of life casting. Rodin was still haunted by the accusation, made very early on his career, that he had reverted to life casting in making his life-size sculpture *The Age of Bronze*.[4] In this case, the excitement and curiosity engendered by the arrival of the Javanese in Paris perhaps trumped any bad feeling he might have had about life casting. Considering the ahistorical view that Rodin and others had of these cultures

1 The arms were first published in Paris 2006, with the suggestion that Rodin may have had them cast directly from the model, p.71.

2 Paris 2001, p.114, for an illustration of the cast of the right hand (comparable to S.5168, cat.15), which was described as an example of a woman or child with hyperextension of the fingers. It was reproduced again in Paris 2008, p.276, fig.147, where it was re-identified as the right hand of a Balinese dancer.

3 This was made possible by François Blanchetière and Philippe Comar. We are grateful to them and to Dominique Brisset for their forensic investigation of the moulds and casts.

4 See M.J. Hare, 'Autobiographical notes by Rodin in a letter to Gaston Schéfer, 1883', in *Revue d'art canadien*, vol. 17, no. 2, 1990, pp.158–62. Thanks to François Blanchetière for this reference and for sharing his own transcription of Rodin's autobiographical note of 1883. See also Rodin's mention of the episode to Dujardin-Beaumetz in 1913: Rodin 2008, pp.157–58.

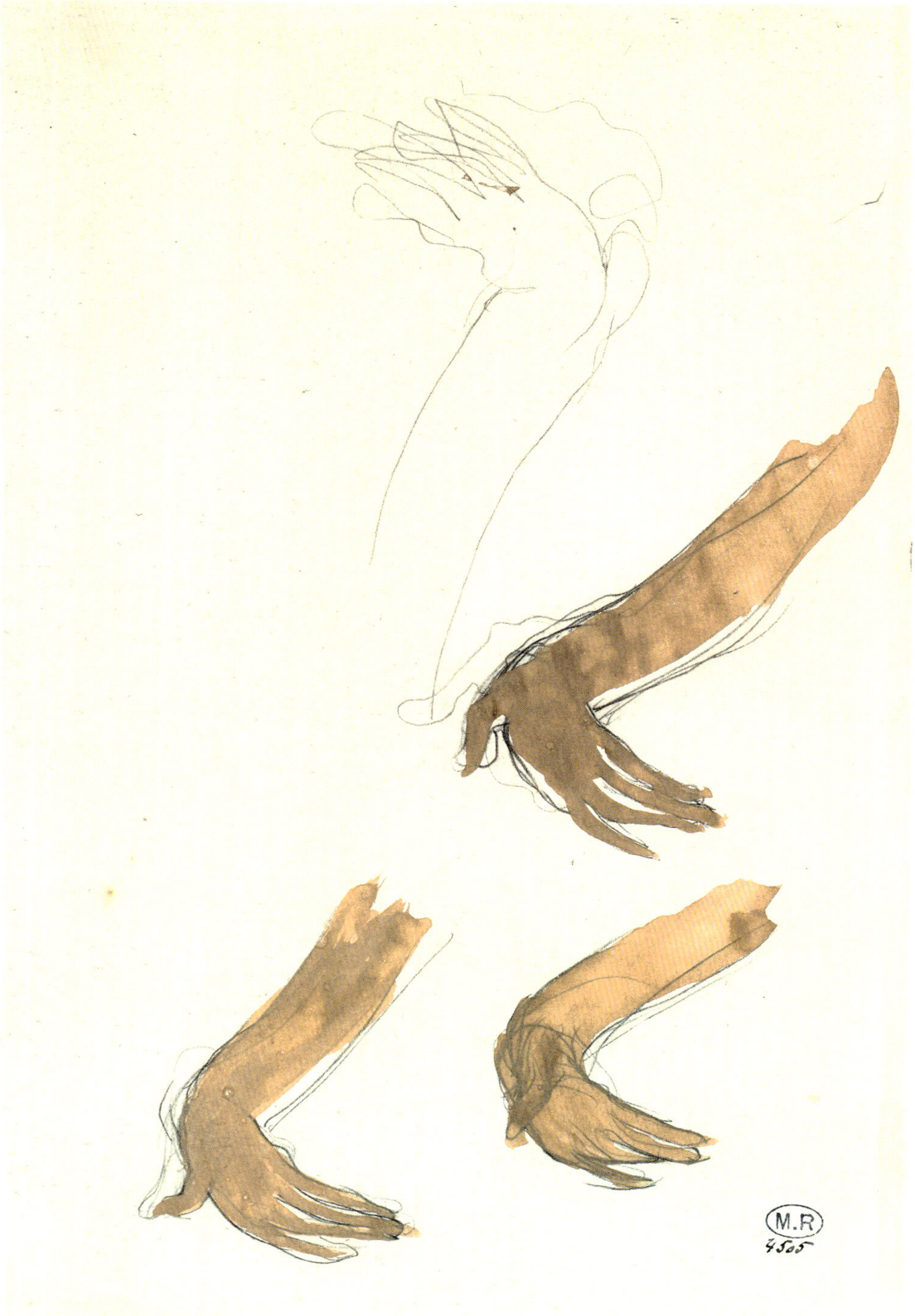
M.R
4505

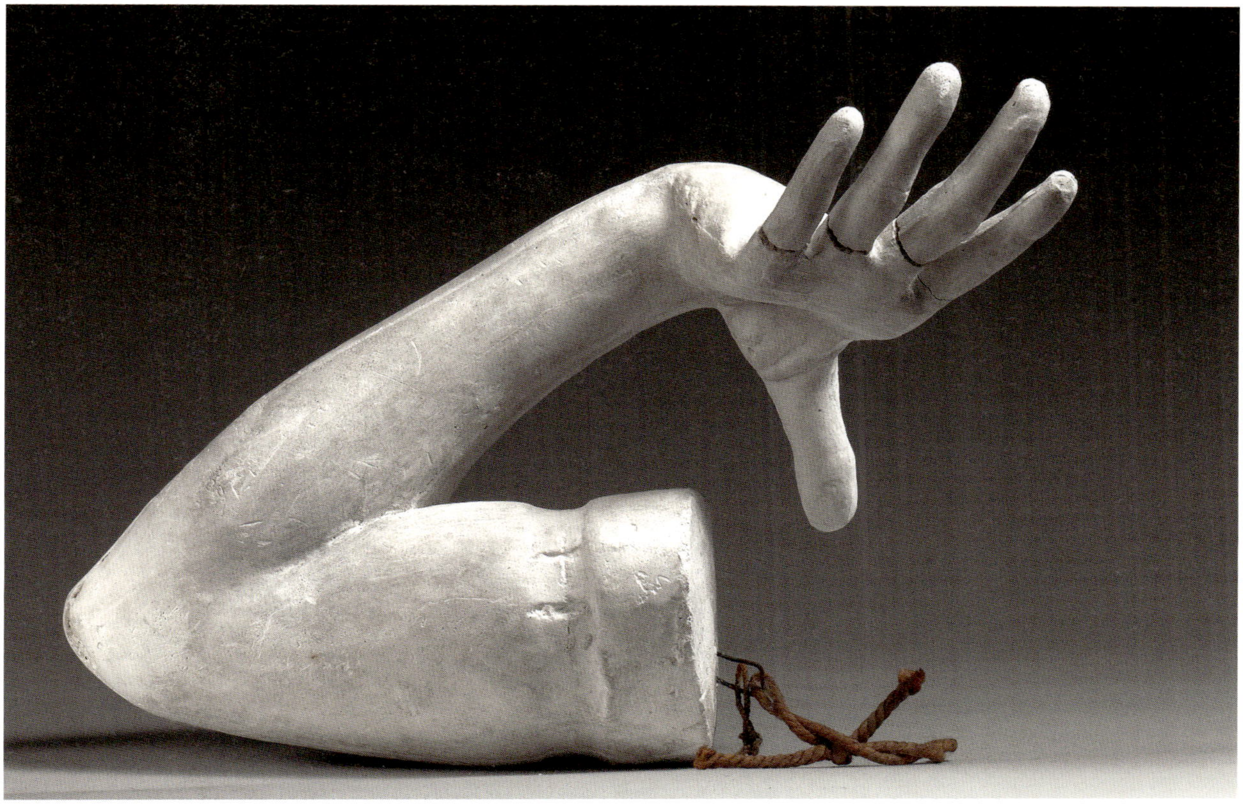

15

(see cat.11), perhaps for Rodin the casts had an aura of ancient sculpture.

The sheet with hand studies (D.4505, cat.14) shows the same flexed left hand four times. Rodin initially sketched their outlines in pencil and then reinforced these with darker lines in an effort to resolve the position of the thumb. By adding an opaque layer of gouache, Rodin obscured the detail of the pencil lines, simplifying the form to emphasise the gesture. The close similarity of these hands to the plaster cast (notably the left arm) and the focus of the sheet on the problem of resolving the thumb position could suggest that this drawing was sketched from the cast rather than in front of the model. KE & AG

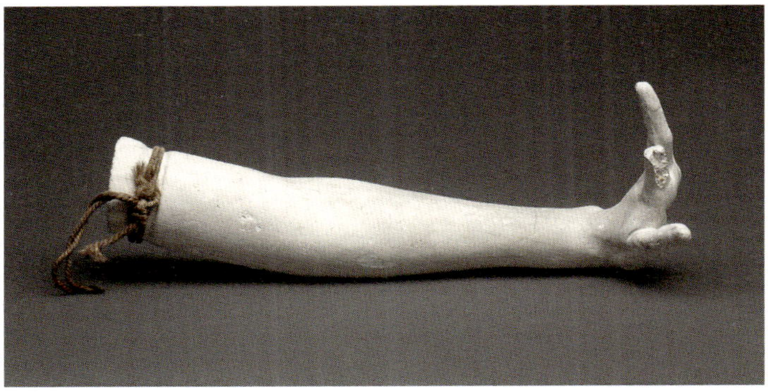

FIG.44
Unknown mould-maker
Cast of a left arm (of a Javanese dancer?), c.1900
Plaster, 37.2 x 10.5 x 14.5 cm
Musée Rodin, Paris, S.6336

16–18

VICTOR GOLOUBEV (?)

Shiva Nataraja, Chola bronze from Tiruvalangadu, South India, Chennai Government Museum (formerly Madras Museum), two details, before 1911

Gelatin silver prints, 230 x 288 mm
Musée Rodin, Paris, PH.16474 and PH.16475

VICTOR GOLOUBEV (?)

Plate illustrating *Shiva Nataraja, Chola bronze from Velankanni, South India, Chennai Government Museum (formerly Madras Museum)*, from Ananda Coomaraswamy, Victor Goloubev, E.B. Havell and Auguste Rodin, *Ars Asiatica: III – Sculptures çivaïtes de l'Inde*, Brussels (Van Oest), 1921

352 x 270 mm (closed)
Musée Rodin, Paris

In February 1911 the Russian-born aristocrat and archaeologist Victor Goloubev (1878–1945) wrote to Rodin from Calcutta telling him he would soon receive a "small series of photographs" that he was sure would please him.[1] The photographs, which may have been taken by Goloubev,[2] are of two eleventh-century Chola bronzes from Southern India representing Dancing Shiva (*Shiva Nataraja*), from Tiruvalangadu (cat.16 and 17) and Velankanni (cat.18). Count Kessler recorded in his journal entry of 1 July 1911, after a visit to Rodin, that he "spoke with admiration of Indian sculpture", and was studying the photographs Goloubev had sent him.[3]

Goloubev, who had become friends with the sculptor several years earlier while his wife was sitting for her portrait, asked him to write a text in response to these photographs, which he wanted to publish in a new journal called *Ars Asiatica*. Rodin wrote his piece in the form of a prose poem, to which he gave the title 'La danse de Çiva'. Although it was ready by 1913, publication was interrupted by the War and it only appeared in print posthumously, in the third edition of *Ars Asiatica* edited in collaboration with E.B. Havell and Ananda K. Coomaraswamy, in 1921, which included plates illustrating some of the same photographs (cat.18).

At the time Rodin wrote his piece, there was a strong prejudice against Indian sculpture, even in artistically advanced circles.[4] Coomaraswamy, who visited Rodin in 1913 (with an introduction from Rodin's friend the English painter William Rothenstein), was the foremost figure in a new wave of scholars promoting Indian sculpture by focusing on its aesthetic qualities. He was particularly interested in multi-limbed figure sculpture, and had already used photographs of both these bronzes in publications. By emphasising the timeless aspect of Indian sculpture, and by using the language of modernity, movement and dance to do so, Coomaraswamy broadened his appeal beyond scholars to artists.[5]

Although Rodin's interpretation of the bronzes was subjective, passages in his text dovetail with Coomaraswamy's essentialist approach. Notably, Rodin insisted on the geometry of the figures, the relationships between limbs, and of course the modelling. Rodin was already sensitive to Asian sculpture before receiving Goloubev's photographs, having acquired, for example, four modern casts of a monumental Buddha from a temple on the island of Java, which had been displayed at Paris's Great Exhibition in 1900, placing them in prominent locations in the garden and outside his home in Meudon.[6]

1 Letters in the V. Goloubev correspondence file, in the archives of the Musée Rodin.
2 A. Locke, 'The Dance of Shiva. Auguste Rodin', in exh. cat. *Chola: Sacred Bronzes of Southern India*, Royal Academy of Arts, London, 2006, p.146.
3 "*Er sprach mit Bewunderung auch von der indischen Plastik von Golubeffs Photographieen*": Kessler 2004, 1 July 1911.
4 See Turner 2010, p.258.
5 Turner 2010, p.252.
6 B. Garnier, 'Vivante immobilité, une collection de gestes antiques', in Légeret 2014, pp.133–50.

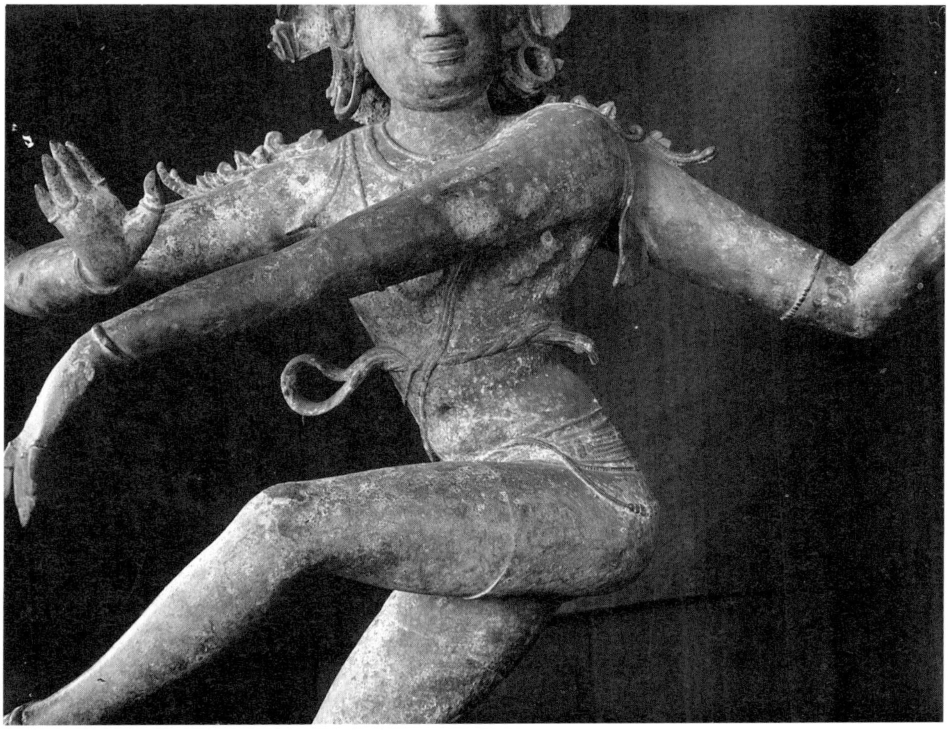

16

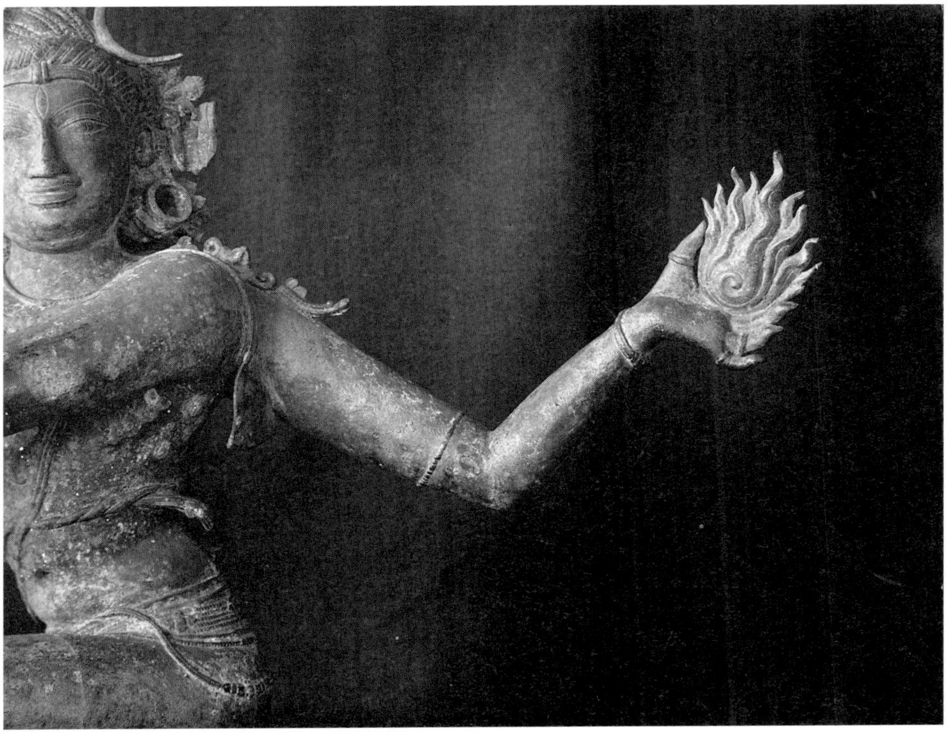

17

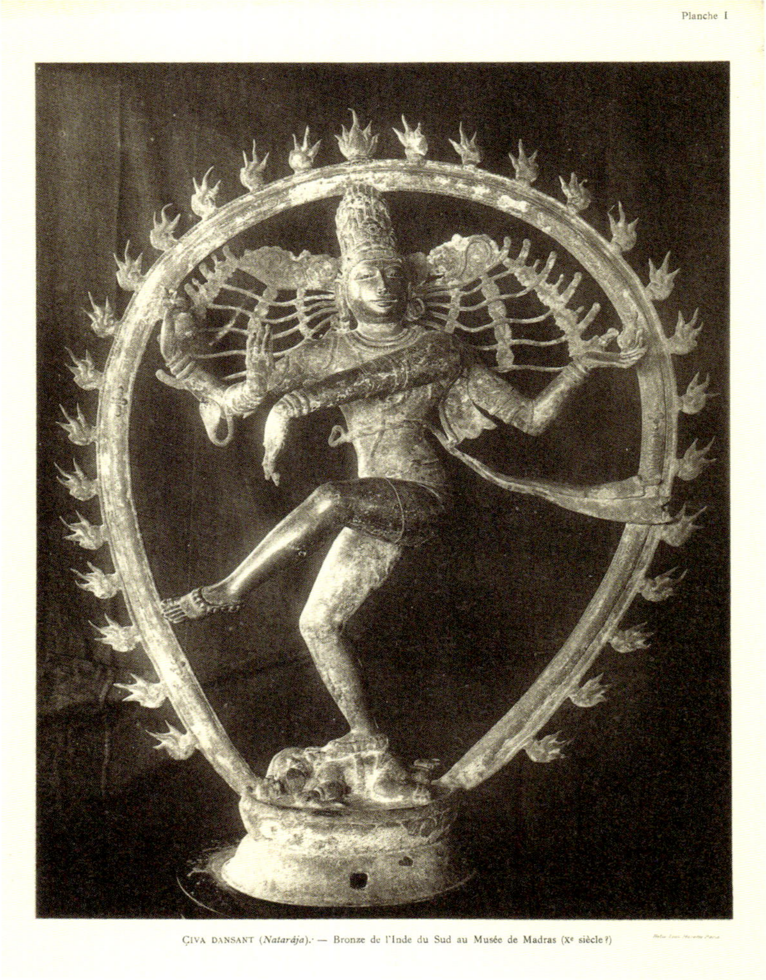

18

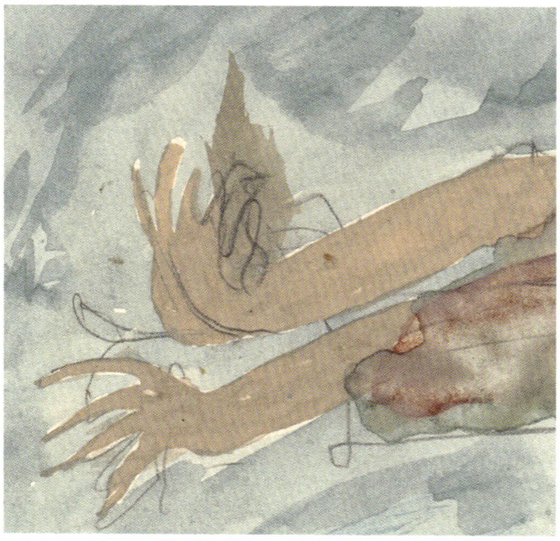

Detail of D.4468, cat.5

In 1914 he acquired several Indian wooden sculptures.

'La danse de Çiva' is written in a style that progresses across each figure and dwells on profiles, matching the views of the two bronzes offered by the photographs. In this it reveals Rodin's deep knowledge of anatomy and the human body in motion. "Like something divinely ordered, there is no hint of revolt in this form: everything is in its place. We understand the rotation of the arm even when it is motionless by looking at the shoulder blade, the way it protrudes, the ribcage, the admirable way the ribs are attached, fixed by scalloped edgings to maintain the shoulder blade and its action in place. And the flank that continues this torso, constrained here, gripped there, then widening out to articulate the two thighs, two connectors, two levers, perfectly angled, delicate legs that disport themselves on the ground".[7]

In the hand of the upper left arm of the *Dancing Shiva* bronze is a flame, which, together with the right foot stamping on the demon below, symbolises the god's destruction of ignorance and illusion. At some point, Rodin painted a flame on to the right hand of his watercolour of a Cambodian dancer in profile (cat.5; see detail). This is comparable to his addition of a leafy crown or a winged statuette to the hands of his Cambodians, so as to transform them into 'victories', except that here the shape strongly resembles a flame. Could this relate to a remark Rodin once made about dance, that "gestures when repeated create flames"?[7] While it is unlikely Rodin was responding to the meaning of the gesture, he would have known it, presumably, as an attribute of Shiva. AG

7 Translated in London 2006 (as above), pp.146–49. For the full text in French see Rodin 2008, pp.87–94.
8 "*Les gestes en se répétant font des flammes*": Coquiot 1917, p.85.

19–21

JEAN LIMET

Isadora Duncan dancing at a party in honour of Rodin at Vélizy, 30 June 1903

Aristotype print, 183 x 165 mm
Musée Rodin, Paris, PH.00889

STEPHANIE LUDWIG (Veritas Studio, Munich)

Ruth St. Denis in The Yogi, 1908

Gelatin silver print, 215 x 165 mm
Musée Rodin, Paris, PH.01715

Upper body with arms outstretched (Ruth St. Denis), c.1907

Pencil on wove paper, 201 x 310 mm
Musée Rodin, Paris, D.5694

22–24

Standing female nude holding her leg up in front of her (Hanako), c.1907

Pencil on wove paper, 310 x 200 mm
Musée Rodin, Paris, D.1134

Female nude walking forward (Hanako), c.1907

Pencil on wove paper, 309 x 200 mm
Musée Rodin, Paris, D.1148

Le Nu académique. Publication de documents photographiques à l'usage des artistes, 1 November 1905

252 x 194 mm (closed)
Musée Rodin, Paris

Rodin's daily sessions of life drawing with the model were necessary fuel for the creation of a new kind of work based on close observation in the studio: "I like drawing because it's a process that captures movements more quickly than sculpture",[1] he once said. His secretaries' diaries (dating from 1907 to 1913) show a steady stream of modelling appointments, and discrete spurts of productivity during which Rodin seems to have seen more than one model a day.[2] This sustained activity explains the huge output of drawings from this period. If one considers only the Musée Rodin's collection, there are about 5000 drawings dating from the late years, of which the overwhelming majority represent female nudes.

Although Rodin did not want his models to pose as they would in an academic studio, when he happened upon a pose he liked the model would have been asked to repeat it. Many models, such as Carmen Damedoz and Alda Moreno (cat.24) and probably countless others whose identities are even more poorly known, were dancers or performers of some kind as well as artists' models. Avant-garde dancers, whose careers were not yet all

1 P. Gsell, 'Rodin raconté par lui-même', *La Revue*, 1 May 1906, pp.99–100.
2 Archives of the Musée Rodin.

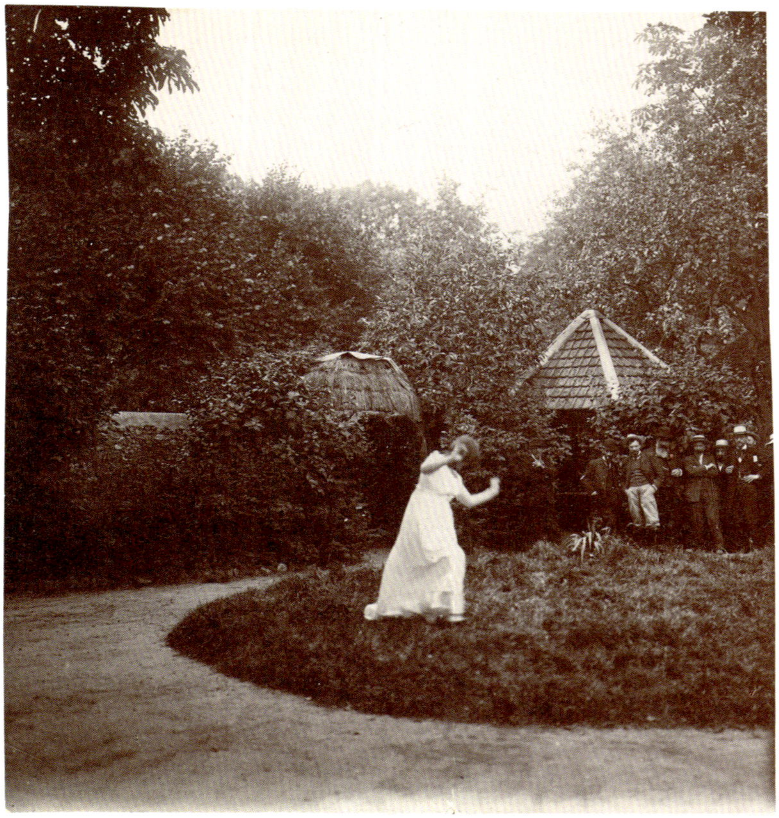

19

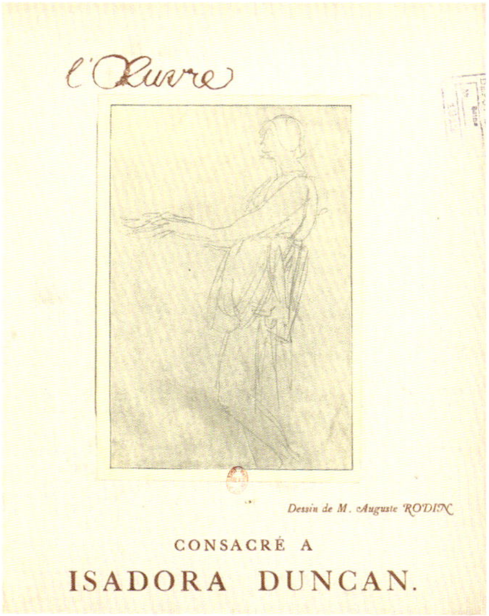

FIG.45
L'Œuvre, dedicated to Isadora Duncan, 1911, illustrated with a drawing of the dancer by Rodin
Bibliothèque nationale de France, Paris

that established, also posed for Rodin in order to enhance their artistic credentials. His large studio spaces also hosted experimental performances, for example the so-called 'slumbering dances' of a woman known only as 'Magdeleine', who performed in a trance with a pianist to an audience in Rodin's studio in May 1903.[3]

Rodin's friendship with the avant-garde music-hall star Loïe Fuller (cat.1) was helpful in this respect as she used her connections in the world of the theatre to introduce him to some of the innovative female dancers and performers of the era. Among the performers who came to pose in Rodin's studio were the two other major figures in the history of modern dance, fellow Americans Isadora Duncan (1877–1927) and Ruth St. Denis (1879–1968); the Japanese actress and performer Ohta Hisa, better known as Hanako (1868–1945), for whom Fuller acted as an interpreter during sessions; and the young French-Indian dancer known as Dourga L'Hindoue, who performed a revue number in the '*danse hindoue*' style at the Folies-Bergère before dancing in *Lakmé* at the Opéra Comique. Fuller herself may have modelled for Rodin during one of her many visits to Meudon, although no drawings of her have been securely identified.[4]

DUNCAN

On 30 June 1903, Rodin's friends organised a celebratory banquet in the woods at Vélizy near his home in Meudon on the occasion of his nomination to the title of Commandeur de la Légion d'Honneur. The sculptors Antoine Bourdelle, Jean Baffier and Lucien Schnegg all gave toasts to the older sculptor, and Isadora Duncan was invited to dance outdoors. In a photograph by Jean Limet (cat.19), who replaced Eugène Druet as Rodin's most trusted photographic collaborator, Duncan is caught mid movement, barefoot and wearing a typically flowing, Greek-inspired dress, as a group of male

3 E. Berr, 'Magdeleine chez Rodin', *Le Figaro*, 27 November 1903, p.2. She took her 'magnetic sleep' performances to Germany, where reviewers mentioned the Rodin connection. See the press cuttings in the Models files, under 'Madeleine', in the archives of the Musée Rodin.

4 But see Juliet Bellow's essay in this volume for a proposed identification of a drawing, and a discussion of the influence of Fuller, St. Denis and Duncan on Rodin.

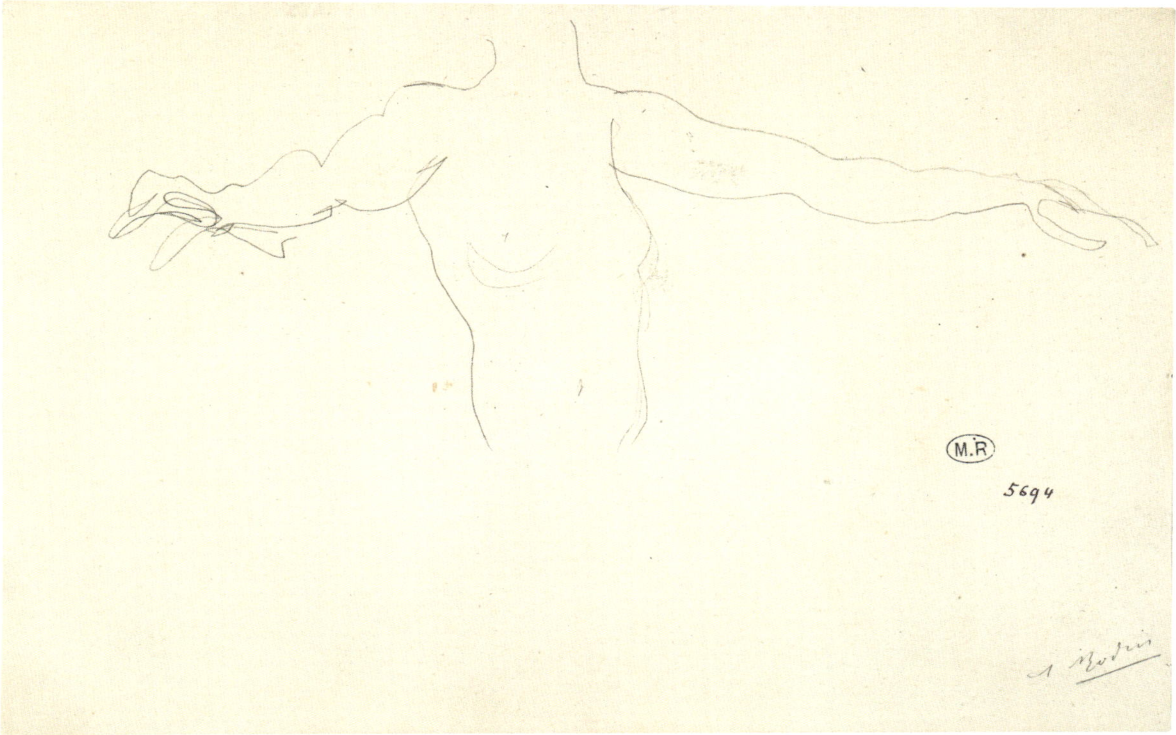

21

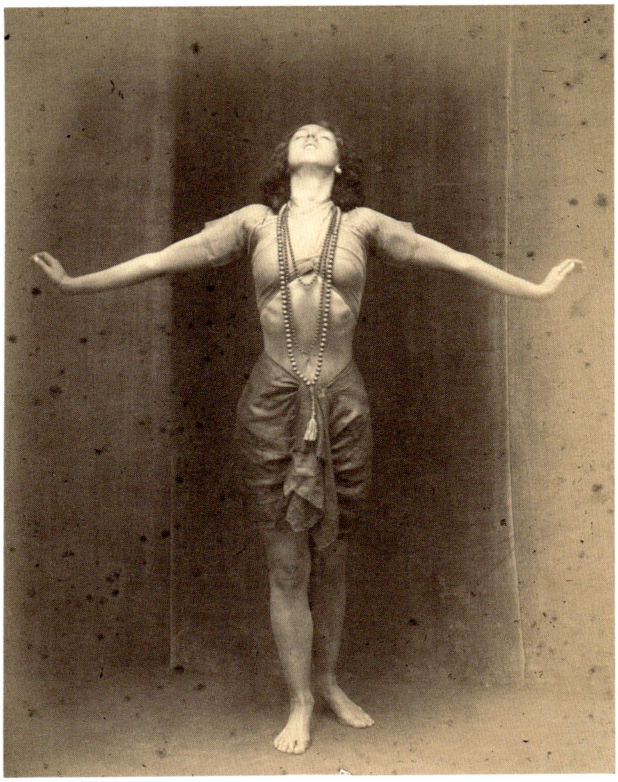

20

guests watch nearby with interest and perhaps wonder. Rodin would later make a small number of sketches of Duncan, which were published in the special issue of *L'Œuvre* dedicated to her in 1911 (fig.45). While Rodin admired Duncan's courage in breaking with the conventions of her time, his drawings of her appear quite static and, in comparison with his drawings after the moving figure (D.2363, cat.3) or his cantilevered and inverted figures (D.4418, cat.27; D.474, cat.32; or D.2296, cat.39), much less adventurous formally.

ST. DENIS

The comparison between the photograph Ruth St. Denis gave Rodin (cat.20), showing her in a pose from her solo choreography *The Yogi*, which she performed in 1908 (arms stretched out, hands broken at the wrists and chest and throat orientated towards the sky), and the drawing (D.5694, cat.21), part of a group of eight pencil sketches (D.5691–98) of a bare-breasted female figure in a similar wrapped skirt, suggests that St. Denis was indeed the model for these. She is believed to have modelled for Rodin on one or

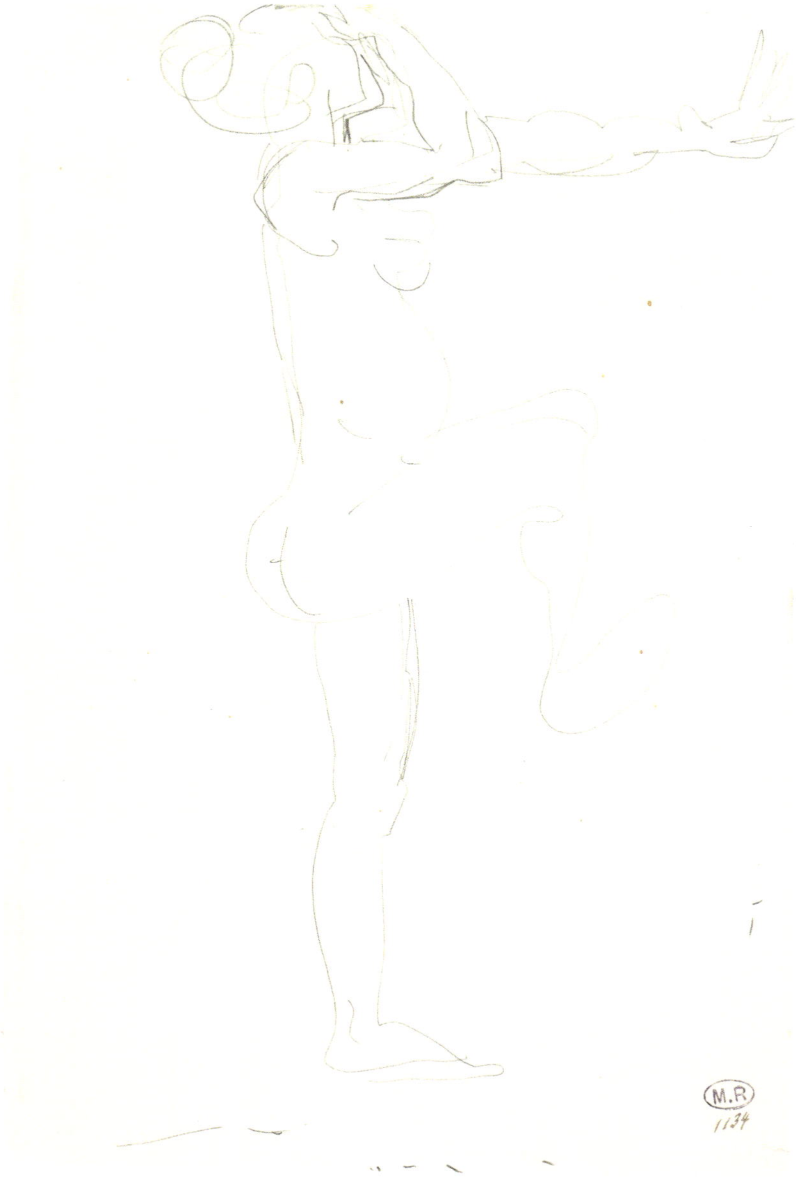

22

two occasions in late 1907,[5] and these drawings strongly suggest that she was dancing rather than simply posing in his studio. In each she is seen from a slightly different angle; taken as a group they show a set of flowing movements emphasising the arms, chest and back. Whilst in the photographic image she is captured in an emphatically ecstatic posture, Rodin's drawing interprets the gesture more subtly and with a sense of soft extension in the arms. Rodin's focus in this group is quite narrowly on the upper body, using the paper in a landscape orientation to extend the arms laterally.

HANAKO

At roughly the same date, Rodin seems to have made a group of about 20 nude movement studies in pencil of the Japanese actress Hanako, whom he had seen in a performance of a play called *Jingoro Hidari* (*La poupée de Tokyo*; Tokyo doll).[6] The two sketches of a nude, one lifting her leg (D.1134, cat.22) and one walking forward (D.1148, cat.23) belong to this group, which may be related to Rodin's intention of making a full-length sculpture of Hanako. More frequent, however, were the sessions in which she posed for a variety of masks and busts, reflecting Rodin's fascination with her performances in these westernised adaptations of traditional Kabuki that Fuller, her agent, wrote for her (under the pseudonym 'Loi-Fu'), and in particular with the scenes in which she enacted Japanese sacrificial suicide, or *hara-kiri*.

Rodin's method of sketching whilst observing the model intently is evident in these drawings, with his shorthand notation of extremities such as toes and fingers. Yet for all their apparent imperfections, such as distortions and repetitions (the figure in the nude walking forward, cat.23, has three breasts) or lack of space at the top of a sheet (the pencil line of her head is carried on over

5 Mentioned in December 1907 in Rodin's secretary's diary for that year, in the archives of the Musée Rodin.
6 F. Blanchetière, 'Un jeu de regards: Rodin et Hanako', in Paris 2007. pp.125–33.

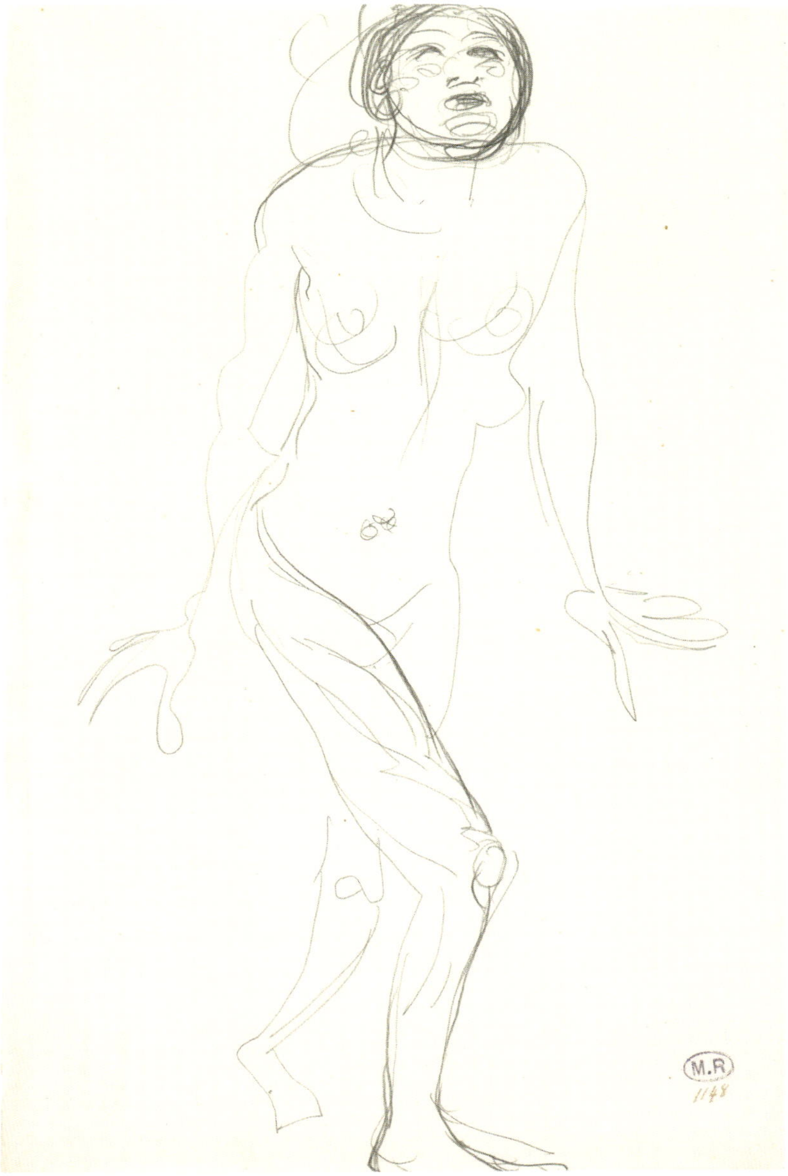

23

the edge), many of these kinds of quick drawings are nonetheless often precisely placed on the page. For example, Rodin frequently used the bottom edge of the sheet as a baseline on which to position a standing foot, such as in the nude walking forward (cat.23; see also cat.39), or used the orientation of the paper to emphasise a pose, as with the sketches of St. Denis (cat.21).

In the drawing of a figure walking forward with her right leg (cat.23), a number of small details give the drawing its theatricality, including the additional lines reinforcing the right leg, head and right shoulder, the upward-looking face and the oversized hands. The standing nude (cat.22) shows an athletic figure in a solid and strongly vertical position, making a very definitive hand gesture and not moving from her stance. Rodin liked to say of Hanako's ability to hold poses: "She is so strong that she can stay as long as she wants on one leg while raising the other before her at a right angle. Standing in this way, she looks as if she were rooted to the ground like a tree."[7]

MORENO

Rodin's last significant model, the acrobatic dancer Alda Moreno (d. before 1963), seems to have embodied his feminine ideal of strength. He met her through the sculptor Jules Desbois (1840–1935), who worked as Rodin's marble carver during these years, and whose model and companion she was. Moreno seems to have begun posing for Rodin in around 1903, then disappeared from view around 1905, and only reappeared again in late 1910, at which point she resumed modelling sessions at his studio until about 1913. This photograph of her (cat.24) was published in the November 1905 issue of *Le Nu académique*, one of the new genres of erotic 'artistic' magazines,[8] which Rodin seems to have purchased in late 1905 on the recommendation of a friend, Edmond Bigand-Kaire (1847–1924),

7 Rodin 1911/1984, p.51, and in P. Gsell and A. Rodin, 'La beauté de la femme', 1910, in Rodin 2011, pp.137–43, at p.141.
8 For similar titles, all published by Amédée Vignola, see Ellen McBreen, *Matisse's Sculpture: the Pinup and the Primitive*, New Haven and London (Yale University Press), 2014, pp.3ff., and Paris 2008, figs.157ff.

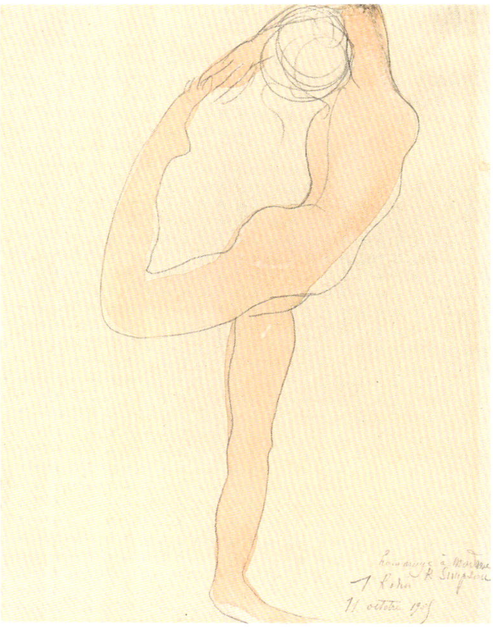

FIG.46
Auguste Rodin
Dancing figure, 1905
Pencil with watercolour on paper, 326 x 250 mm
National Gallery of Art, Washington, D.C., Gift of Mrs John W. Simpson, 1942

an eccentric captain in the merchant navy, collector and friend of artists such as Odilon Redon and Gustave Moreau. Bigand-Kaire seems also to have been a friend of both Desbois and Moreno (known in Rodin's circle as '*le petit modèle*'). He was trying to find her for Rodin and, unable to trace her, he informed him of the existence of these photographs of her, and gave Rodin the address so he could purchase the magazine himself. Rodin must have bought the magazine as an aide-mémoire, since it seems unlikely he would have sketched from the photograph, for not only was that not in his practice but among the group of over a dozen drawings of this pose is one in the National Gallery in Washington, D.C., which is dated 11 October 1905 (fig.46).

The photograph shows Moreno in the acrobatic pose that Rodin must have seen in his studio, for it provided him with the inspiration to make a number of drawings and the sculpted figure known as *Mouvement de danse* A between about 1903 and about 1911.[9] In the photograph Moreno is holding her right foot in her right hand, whilst her left arm is held out in front of her, coyly covering her breasts. She is pressing together her middle finger and her thumb, with her little finger crooked. While the gesture could suggest that Moreno was referencing a bastardised version of an Indian *mudra* (hand gesture) as made popular in the music-hall and by dancers like Mata Hari from about 1905, equally it could simply be a finishing touch to a teasing pose. Her supporting leg is strongly activated, involving both rotation and the pulling up of the muscles from the firmly planted foot. Her head is tilted back and slightly turned to gaze and smile suggestively at the camera. The most striking thing about this photograph is the model's unusually flexible spine, which allows her torso to simultaneously arc forwards and upwards.

This pose may be a variation of that illustrated in an early nineteenth-century engraving of acrobats' poses from the Franconi circus and a version of it is shown on a postcard published by the Moulin Rouge in about 1920 (see figs.12 & 13, p.30). The English writer Arthur Symons, "scholar in music halls"[10] and a friend of Rodin's, discussed this and similar poses in an article on music-hall acrobatics, such as the more advanced posture known as '*la jambe derrière la tête*', or 'leg behind the head', in which the held leg is straight up behind the head.[11] The photograph on the facing page shows Moreno on a trapeze cord, possibly evoking her profession as an acrobat (fig.11, p.29). AG

9 On Moreno's role in the development of the *Mouvements de danse* see Alexandra Gerstein's essay in this volume.
10 William Butler Yeats, cited in Pritchard 2003, p.36.
11 Symons 1917, p.317.

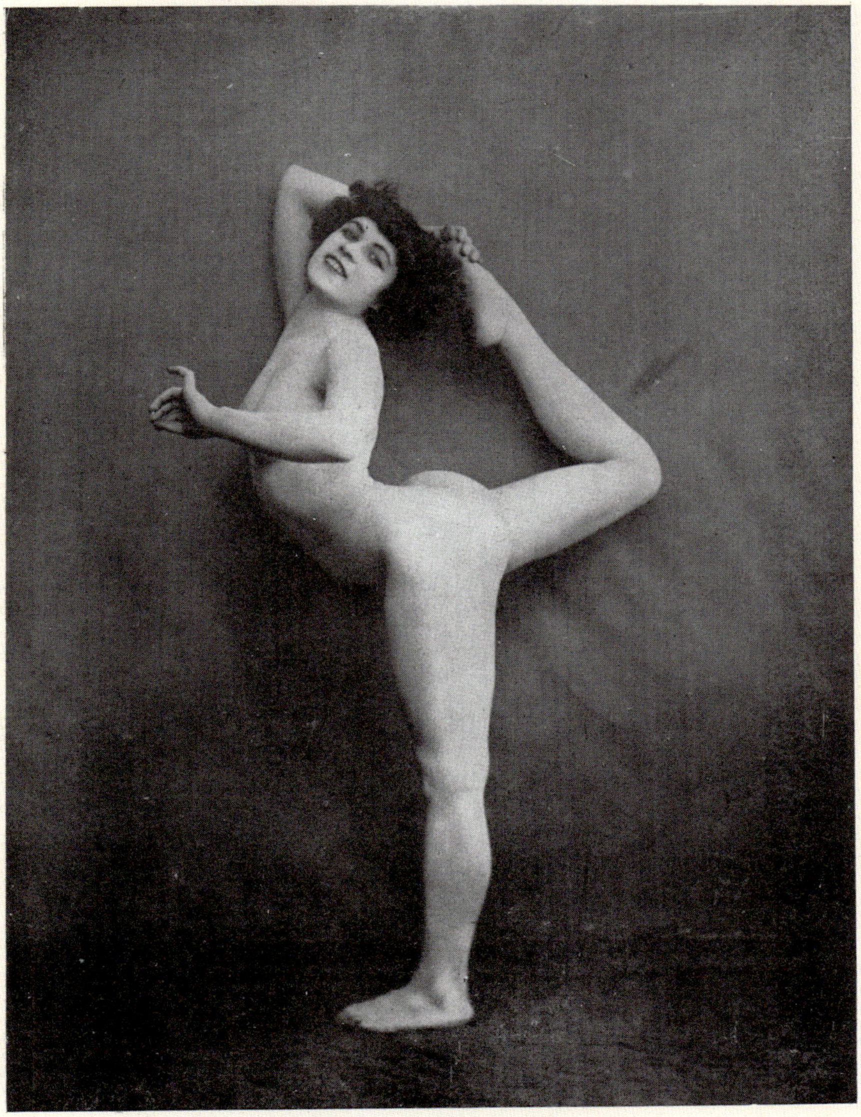

25

Female nude in profile holding her leg behind her head (Alda Moreno?), called vent or fleur du ciel or flambeau, c.1903–05

Pencil with stumping on wove paper, 310 x 202 mm
Inscribed: *vent / la fleur du ciel / pur flambeau* (wind / flower of the sky / pure torch)
Musée Rodin, Paris, D.2829

Female nude in profile holding her leg behind her head (D.2829, cat.25) was presumably drawn from life as it seems to capture the many adjustments the model would have had to make to maintain her balance in this pose. It is a slightly more advanced stage to that represented in another drawing of a nude figure in profile holding her leg behind her head (D.1746, cat.30). There is good reason to identify the model of this drawing as Alda Moreno, who came to pose for Rodin in 1903, and whose physique as seen in the photograph published in *Le Nu académique* of 1905 (cat.24) is close in so many details, such as the slight curve of the abdomen, athletic legs and muscular buttocks. As an acrobat, Moreno would have entered this pose with ease, as illustrated in the photograph, and she would probably have made only minor adjustments, mostly in her upper body, which is indeed where the greatest number of the drawing's lines are concentrated. Rodin captured every movement of the model as she refined and settled into her pose, and then added stumping and pencil shading to create depth and shadow notably around the outside of the figure and raised leg.

Moreno's standing leg, however, was drawn with just a few lines, and Rodin did not revisit it beyond amplifying the shape of the leg to make it appear both broader and stronger. This suggests that while she may have been settling her upper body her standing leg was quite stable and well established by this moment in the posture. By making the leg broader he gave a more solid anchoring for the upper body. The abdomen and bent leg were repositioned by pulling the leg upwards, resulting in an almost 45° angle with the standing leg, which acts as a plumb line, whilst her weight above the void is cantilevered more squarely.

In reworking this drawing Rodin explored themes of strength, lightness, stability and cantilevering, and of formal unity between the limbs, developing these further in his subsequent drawings of the pose by tweaking the positions of the lifted leg and upper body, and again in the terracotta and plaster versions of *Mouvement A* (cat.47 and 48), which may be considered the near-culmination of his research into the pose. Whilst the physical effort of maintaining the pose and the various tensions of the pose itself are still palpable in this drawing, all effort and tension are progressively obliterated in subsequent drawings and sculpture. Two details in particular, already present in this drawing, show how closely Rodin understood and captured the essence of Moreno's pose, with its oppositional forces pulling upwards and downwards.

The first detail is the foot, which is in the position Rodin often favoured for his standing figures, in which the paper edge is used as a base – but here the heel hovers just above the edge so that the foot is not flat but raised slightly. This contrasts with a number of other drawings in which the foot in profile sits flat on the edge of the sheet (e.g. cat.23 or 39). Here the foot is cut off by the edge of the sheet, presumably because Rodin ran out of space. Thereafter in the subsequent iterations of the pose (cat.26 and 27), he retained this motif of the cut-off foot, which imparts lightness and airiness to the pose. This ability to incorporate motifs found by chance during the creative process, and to set up situations in the studio that promoted such accidental discoveries was an important factor of Rodin's late work.

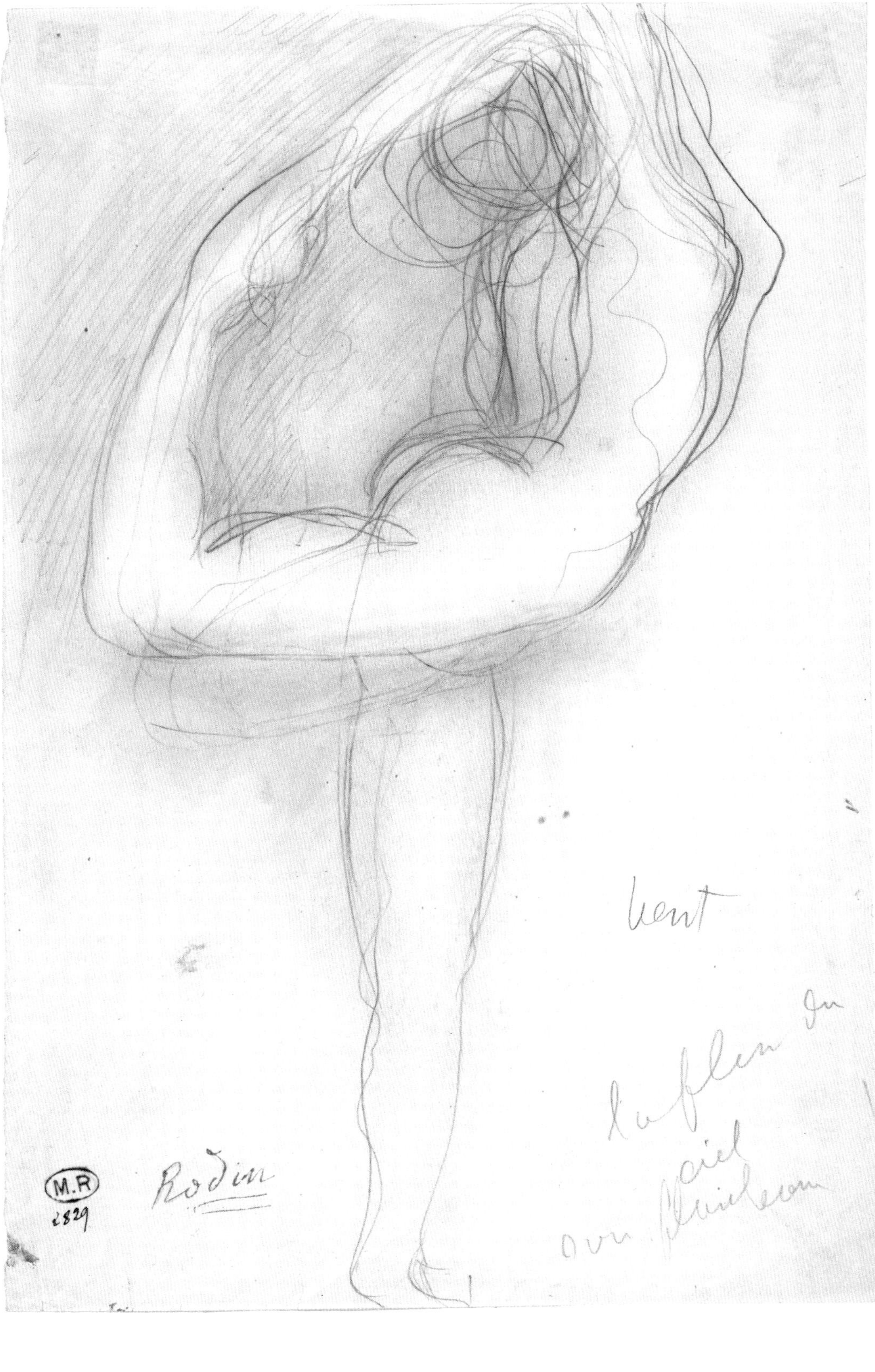
vent
la fleur du
ciel
M.R
Rodin

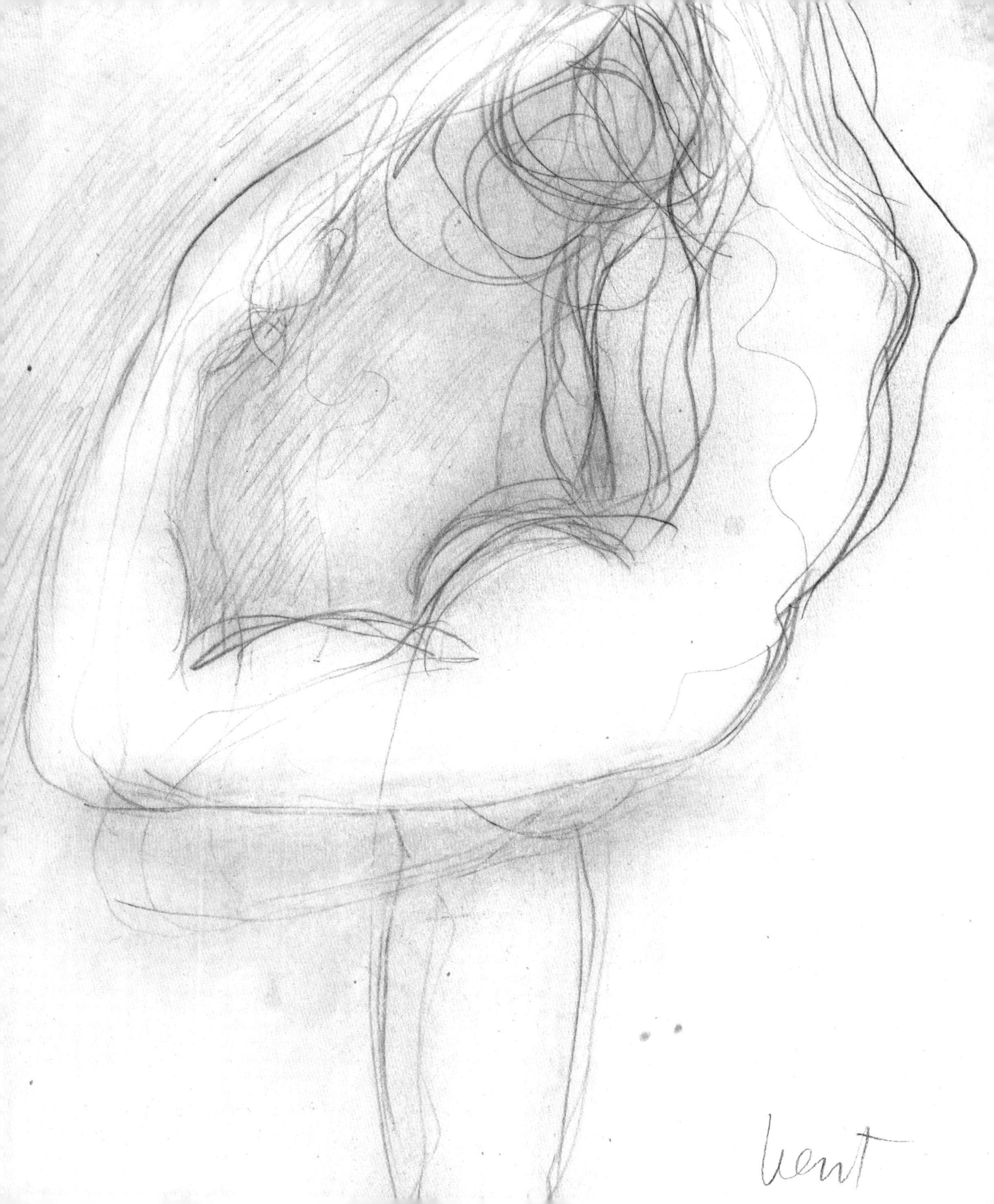

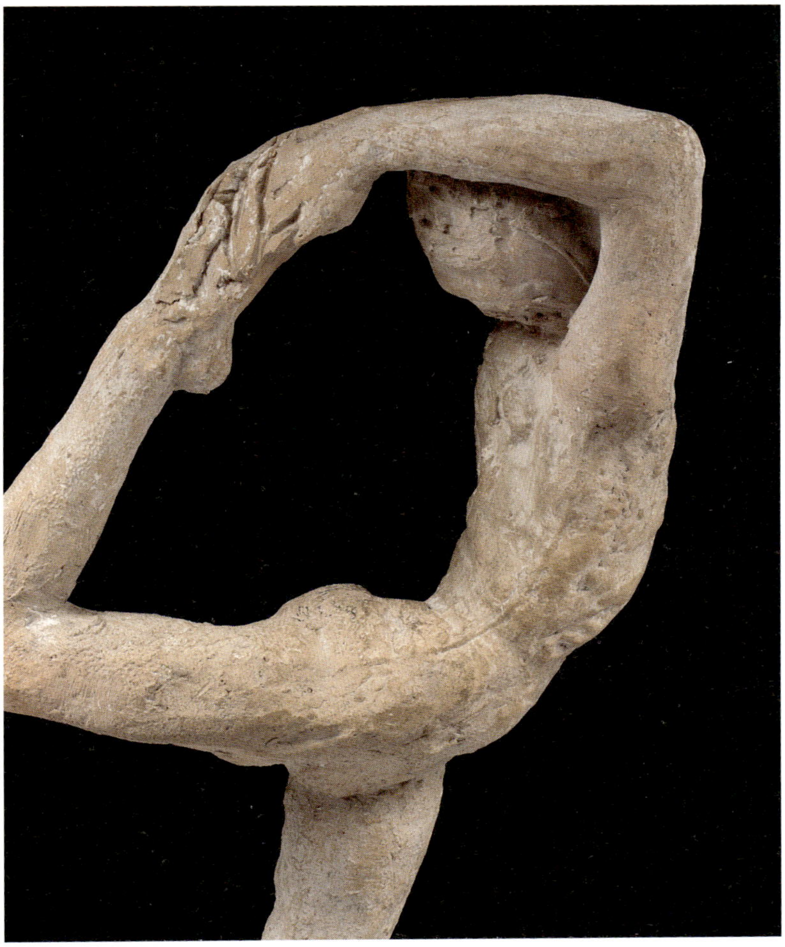

Detail of *Mouvement A*, cat.47

The second detail is the motif of the hand holding the foot. In all subsequent drawings of this pose and in the terracotta *Mouvement A*, Rodin sought to link them together into a single, seamless form (see detail). This is announced in this drawing, in which the transition between the two limbs is smoothed through stumping and shading. A similar desire to simplify is also seen in Rodin's progressive removal of the line in the figure's back indicating the presence of her left arm.

This drawing's inscription is typical of Rodin's evocations of nature and the elements in his drawings of female nudes. The 'torch' (*flambeau*) could be a reference to an idea he articulated in connection with his thoughts on 'the beauty of woman': "Yes, Victor Hugo understood it well! What we adore in the human body, even more than its beautiful shape, is the interior flame that makes it transparent."[1] Perhaps the most pertinent, in particular in terms of the direction Rodin would take later in relation to the idea of aviation, is the reference to the 'flower of the sky'. Wind and sky are found in a number of pencil drawings of a figure in similar poses, for example D.1043, which is inscribed *ardeur du ciel* (fervour of the sky).[2] AG

1 Rodin 1911/1984, p.52.
2 These references echo Mallarmé's descriptions of female dancers, which he likened to a "*glaive, coupe, fleur*": Mallarmé, cited in Starobinski 1971, pp.64–65. See also a similar inscription on D.4418, cat.27.

Detail of D.2829, cat.25

26–29

Female nude in profile holding her leg behind her head (Alda Moreno?), c.1903–05

Pencil with stumping on wove paper, 312 x 201 mm
Musée Rodin, Paris, D.2826

Female nude in profile holding her leg behind her head (Alda Moreno?), c.1903–05

Pencil, gouache and watercolour on wove paper, 327 x 246 mm
Inscribed: *comme un pur cristal comme un vase à champagne / fleur / volupté*
(like a pure crystal like a glass of champage / flower / bliss)
Musée Rodin, Paris, D.4418

Female nude holding her leg behind her head, seen from behind (Alda Moreno?), called Mouvement de danse, c.1903–05

Pencil with stumping on wove paper, 312 x 200 mm
Musée Rodin, Paris, D.2838

Dancer holding her leg behind her head, seen from behind (Alda Moreno?), c.1903–05

Pencil, gouache and watercolour on wove paper, 327 x 251 mm
Musée Rodin, Paris, D.4421

The sculptor Antoine Bourdelle (1861–1929), Rodin's assistant from 1893 to 1908, captured in a few words the master's fascination with and determination to explore certain poses in his drawings – "those that you rework a hundred times in contemplation, because they are essential attitudes of the human spirit and they offer harmonious and geometric juxtapositions, in line with the great movements of the cosmos".[1]

Many of Rodin's contemporaries described how he would draw a model from life, casually drop his many sketches to the floor, select one that satisfied him, and make a tracing from it. Bourdelle explained that Rodin would copy his drawings by tracing at a window, placing a drawing underneath a clean sheet of paper.[2] It is worth asking whether Rodin deliberately used lightweight paper, which would have appeared translucent in strong sunlight, thus enabling him to see the pencil lines underneath. He could make adjustments to the pose by simply shifting the bottom sheet from which he was tracing, an accurate and quick way of developing his ideas. Rodin could retain the contours of the figure that he was happy with

1 Bourdelle 1908, p.171: "*... ceux que vous reprenez cent fois dans le recueillement, parce qu'ils sont des attitudes essentielles de l'élan humain et qu'ils offrent des juxtapositions harmonieuses, géométriques, en parallèle avec les grands mouvements cosmiques*".

2 As described in Geissbuhler 1963, p.29. Another (indirect) reference to tracing at the window was made by the widow of one of Rodin's secretaries, René Cheruy, cited in K. Varnedoe, 'Rodin as a Draftsman – A Chronological Perspective' in Elsen and Varnedoe 1971, p.120, footnote 146. K. Varnedoe, 'Rodin's Drawings', in Washington 1981, pp.153–89, termed the drawings produced by this method 'second-generation' images (p.179).

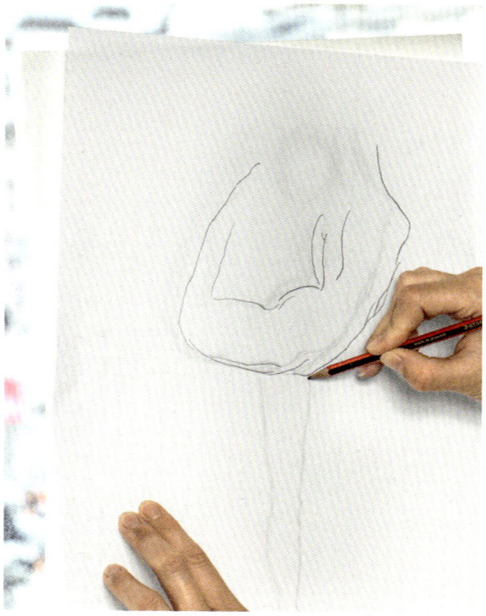

FIG.47
Example of tracing at the window, shifting the top sheet of paper to adjust details

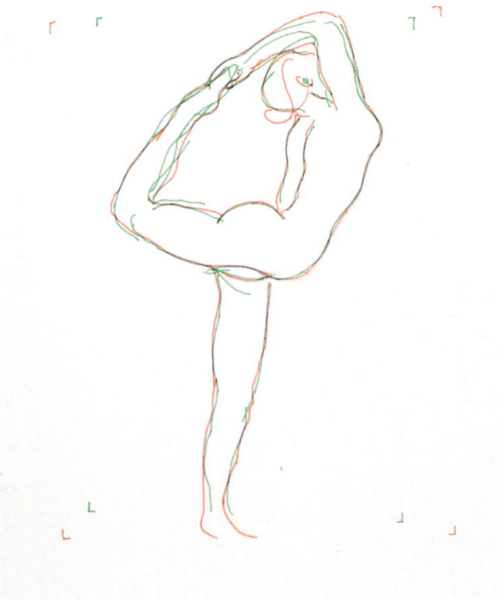

FIG.48
Overlaid tracings on clear polyester after drawings D.4418 (cat.27) and D.2843

and make minor alterations to parts of the pose that he felt needed to be resolved (fig.47). As has often been noted in the literature, this echoed Rodin's studio practice, in which he exploited the processes of sculpture, such as casting, enlarging or transferring to marble, in order to reproduce, alter and invent new compositions.

To investigate whether the process of tracing had indeed been used for the group of drawings in the Musée Rodin's collection, depicting a female nude in profile holding her leg behind her head, we made our own tracings of the main contour lines of several of these drawings (fig.48).[3] Comparing them with the life drawing of the same subject (D.2829, cat.25), and overlaying our tracings on to each other, confirmed that the scale of the figures in these drawings is almost identical and that the contour lines of breast, abdomen and standing leg are very close, with only subtle changes between them. It is interesting to note that there is no evidence of any media offset on the versos of these drawings, which one could expect to find when tracing with any pressure, especially if the traced line follows the line underneath exactly.

The pencil drawings in this group appear to be stages in the process of simplifying the pose, while the gouache and watercolour drawing of a nude figure in profile holding her leg behind her head (D.4418, cat.27), with its single contour lines and no traces of reworking, further simplifies the motif. Rodin's use of an opaque white gouache and dilute flesh-coloured wash accentuates the silhouette of the figure and emphasises the shape of the enclosed space within the raised leg and arm.[4] This interplay between solid forms and surrounding space is developed much further in the sculpture of this pose (see *Mouvement A*, cat.47 & 48), and has been linked to the influence of the photographer Edward Steichen on Rodin at this time.

Rodin's process of simplification is also evident in comparing the two drawings of a female nude holding her leg behind her head, seen from behind (D.2838, cat.28, and D.4421, cat.29). This view shows the model lifting her right leg, placing the genitalia in the centre of the drawing. The left arm is in the same position Moreno took for the photograph in *Le Nu académique* (cat.24).

While it is obvious in these views that the figure uses only her right arm to lift her right leg, in the profile views (cat.26 & 27) the position of the left arm is elided and the precise nature of the posture is somewhat ambiguous. Here, the strongest lines are those describing the contour of the buttocks, genitalia and both legs, with preliminary lines in the standing leg showing that Rodin adjusted it by slightly broadening its shape, perhaps to anchor its stance ever more firmly. It is striking that the upper body is represented in a very upright position, appearing in the same plane as the legs. Rodin captured Moreno's ability to hyperextend her back, which has led to a flattening of the perspective and a suppression of naturalistic detail in the gouache drawing, with the lifted leg now appearing as though placed at the side of the figure's head and the small gap between back and right leg closed up completely. AG & KE

3 Tracings from the original drawings were made of D.2826 (cat.26) and D.4418 (cat.27) and of two drawings not in the exhibition, D.2843 and D.5188, using a commercial tracing paper and pencil with no pressure applied. These pencil tracings were later transferred on to clear polyester with black waterproof pen to give better clarity when the polyester sheets were overlaid on to each other for comparison. We are extremely grateful to Sophie Biass-Fabiani for allowing us to work in this way.

4 A watercolour in the National Gallery of Art, Washington, D.C., *Dancing figure* of 1905 (fig.46, p.106), has a somewhat different shape, and the flesh tone, which contains white and is slightly opaque, is different, but it is otherwise similar to this group of drawings. We are grateful to Kim Schenck for sharing her observations on the layering of the media.

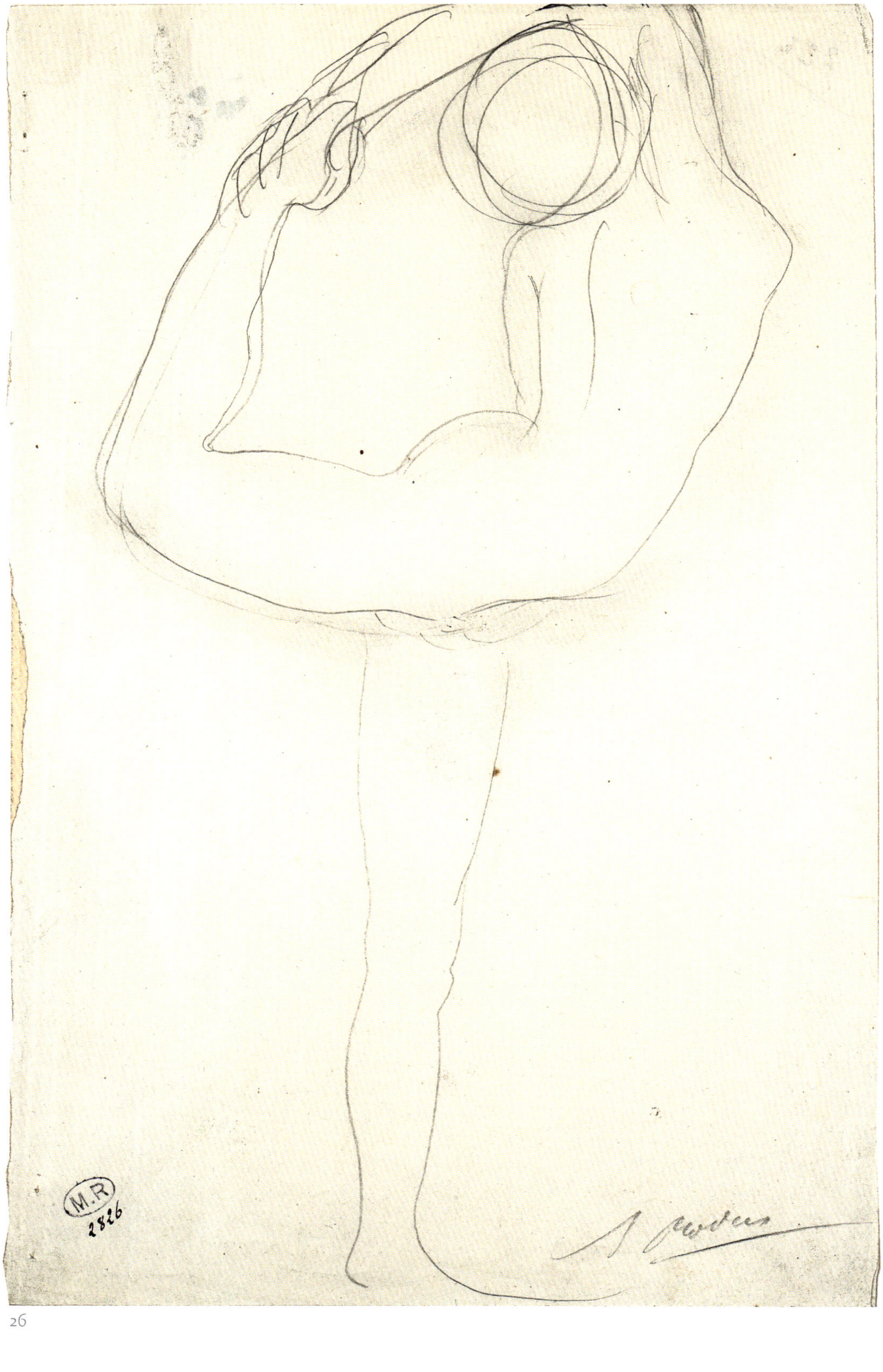
M.R
2826

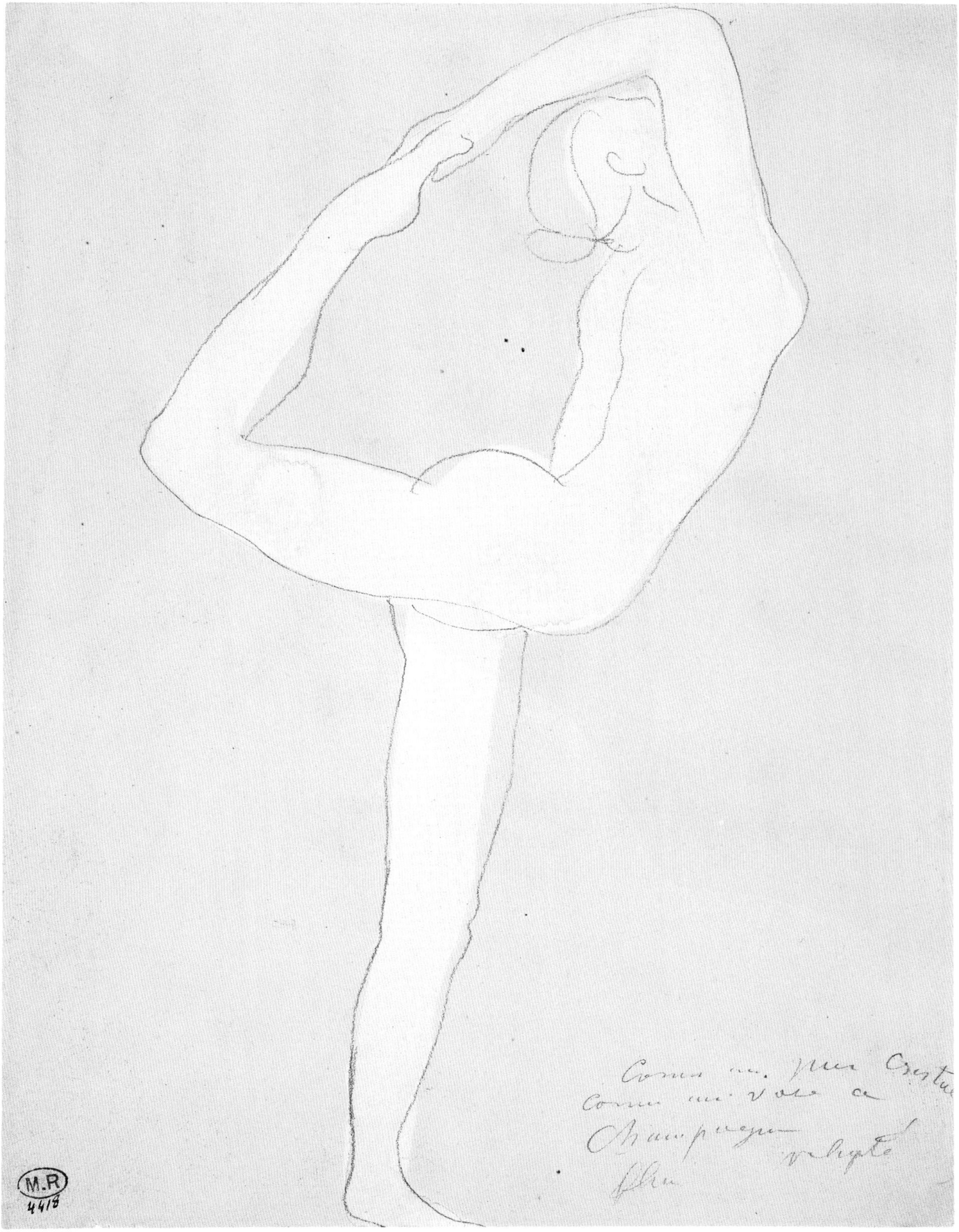

27

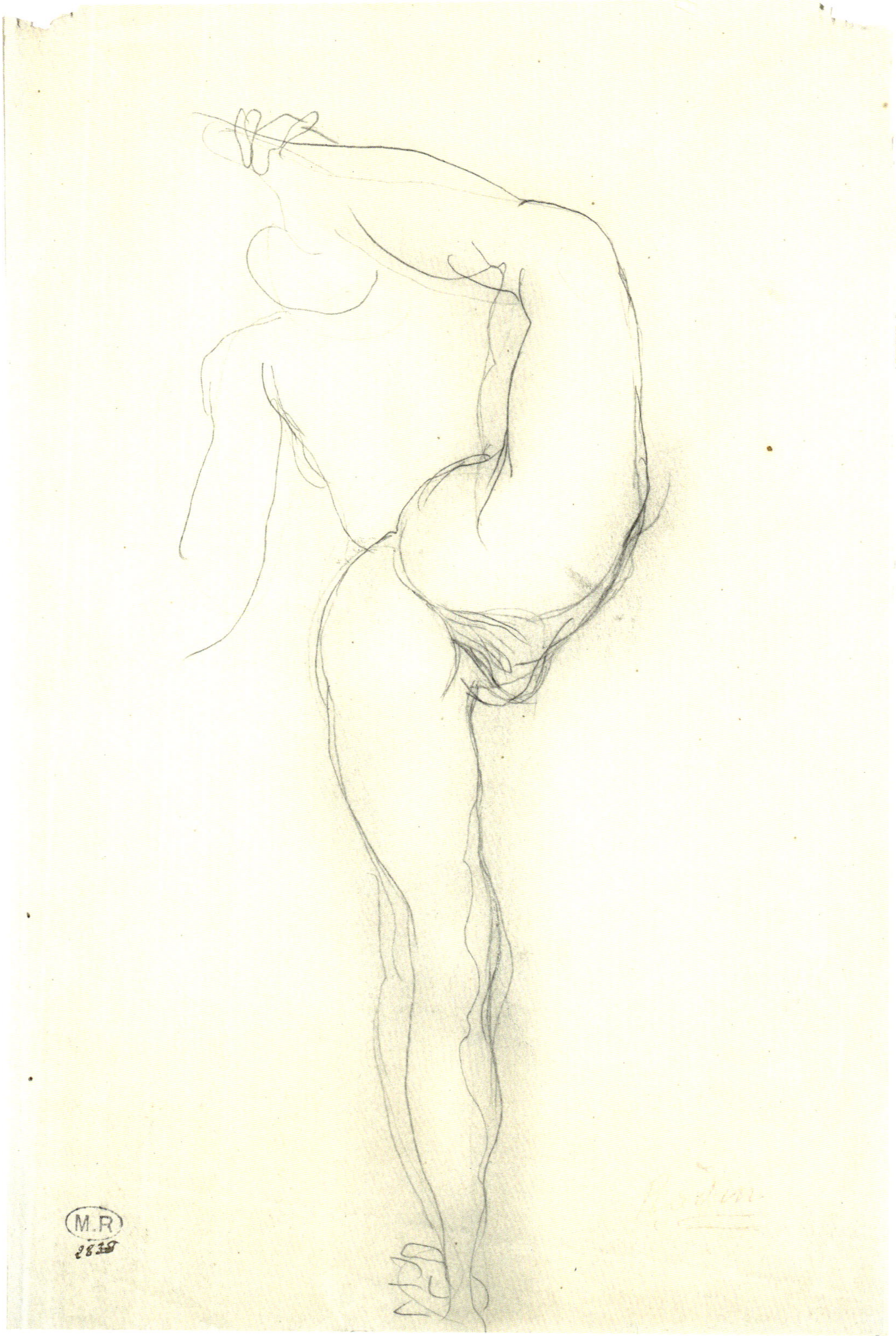
M.R

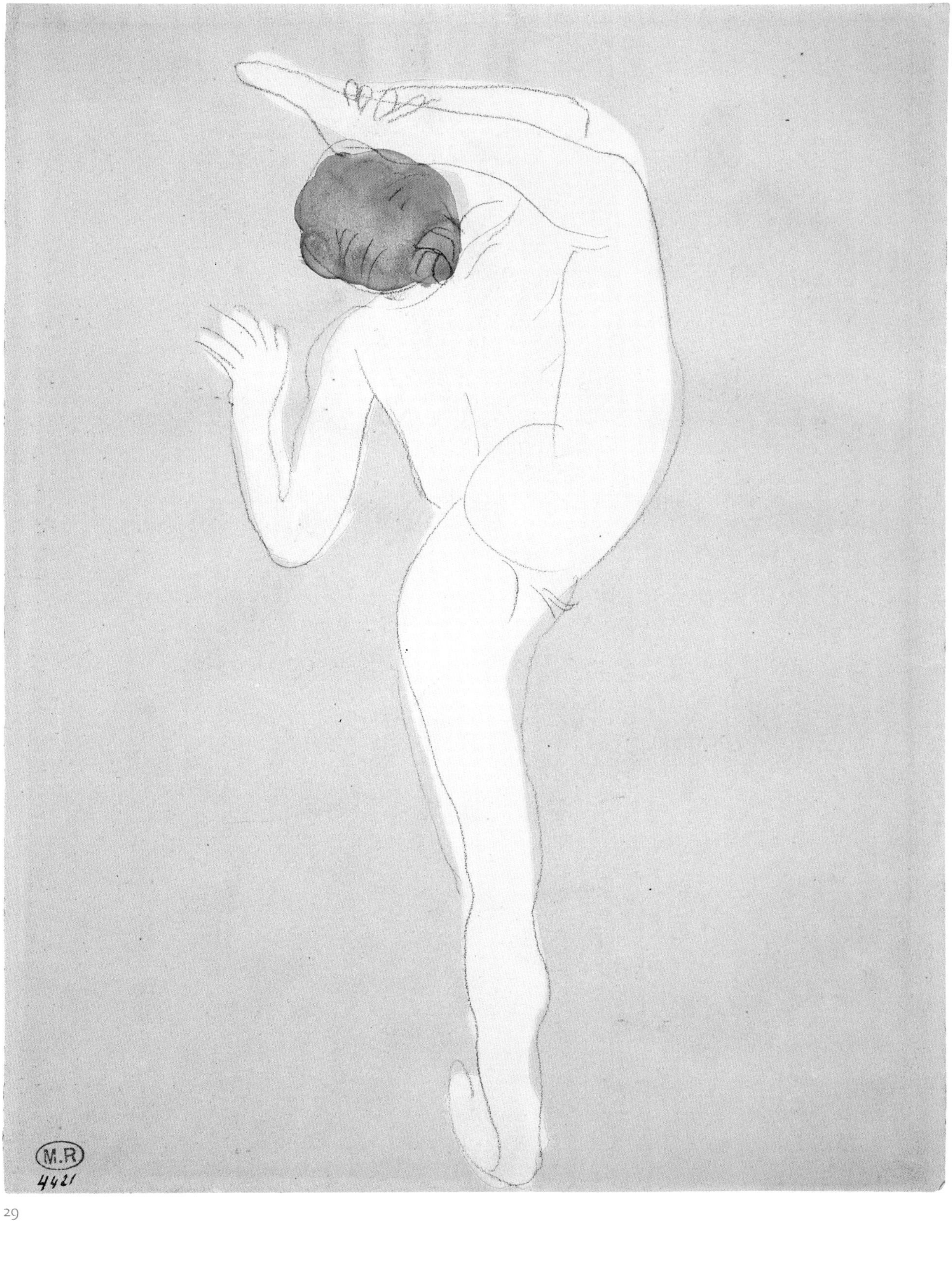
M.R
4421

30

Female nude in profile holding her leg behind her head (Alda Moreno?), c.1903–05

Pencil on wove paper, 312 x 202 mm
Musée Rodin, Paris, D.1746

FIG.49
Auguste Rodin
Female nude in profile holding her leg behind her head (Alda Moreno?), c.1903–05
Pencil on tracing paper, with blue ink smudges, 516 x 367 mm
Musée Rodin, Paris, D.6295

FIG.50
Auguste Rodin
Female nude in profile holding her leg behind her head (Alda Moreno?), called Mouvement de danse, c.1903–05
Pencil and watercolour on laid paper, 623 x 481 mm
Musée Rodin, Paris, D.5739

In this pencil sketch of a female nude in profile, holding her leg behind her head the perspective appears very close, and level with the torso and hips, with the genitals drawn as if seen from below. The body is tipped forward and the supporting leg is bent; this suggests that it was observed while the model was moving forward to get into position. Similar moments are captured in another two drawings in the Musée Rodin, of a figure with the same V-shaped back (D.1043 and D.1744), the inscription *respiration* on the latter perhaps echoing the idea of the figure's flowing sequence of motion.

This sketch (D.1746, cat.30) appears to have been the starting point for a suite of drawings where the same pose has been reproduced and ultimately simplified.[1] To copy the drawing initially Rodin placed a larger sheet of translucent tracing paper on to the pencil sketch and traced directly from it. He then made a second tracing from it with minor alterations and refinements (D.6295, fig. 49), and it is this drawing that seems to have been used to make the three watercolours in which Rodin moved away from a sketch that naturalistically captures a fleeting moment in the studio towards a more etiolated and stylised figure, whose diminutive scale is silhouetted against the cream background of the sheet.[2] The sense of a solid form floating in an open space is further reinforced by Rodin's use of a warm terracotta wash (D.5739, fig.50).

AG & KE

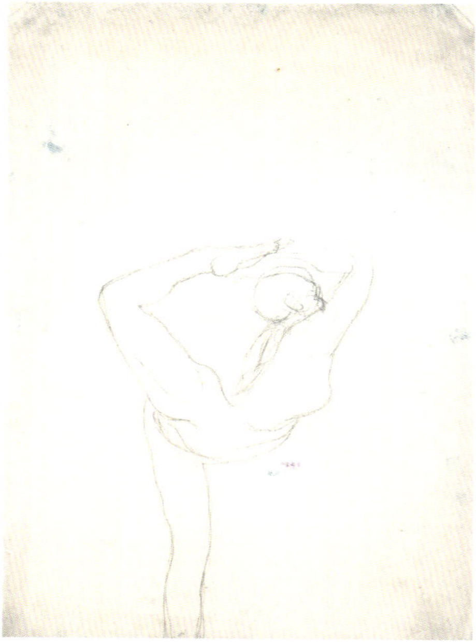

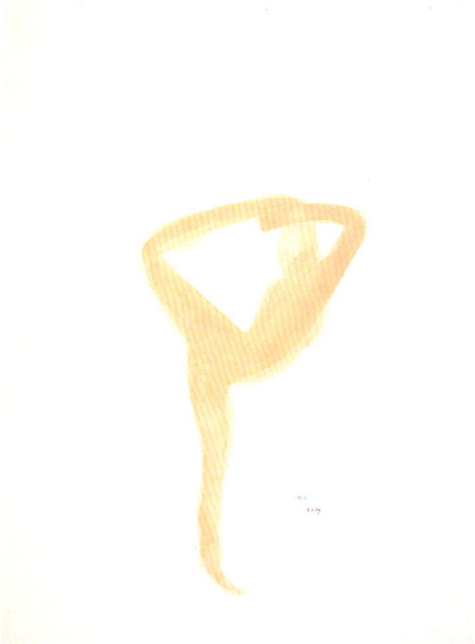

1 In this study we have compared the following drawings: D.1744, D.6295, D.6296, D.5739, D.5740 and D.5742, and made tracings of D.1746 and D.6296. A further drawing from this group (D.5511) shows the figure twice.
2 The three watercolours are D.5739, D.5740 and D.5742.

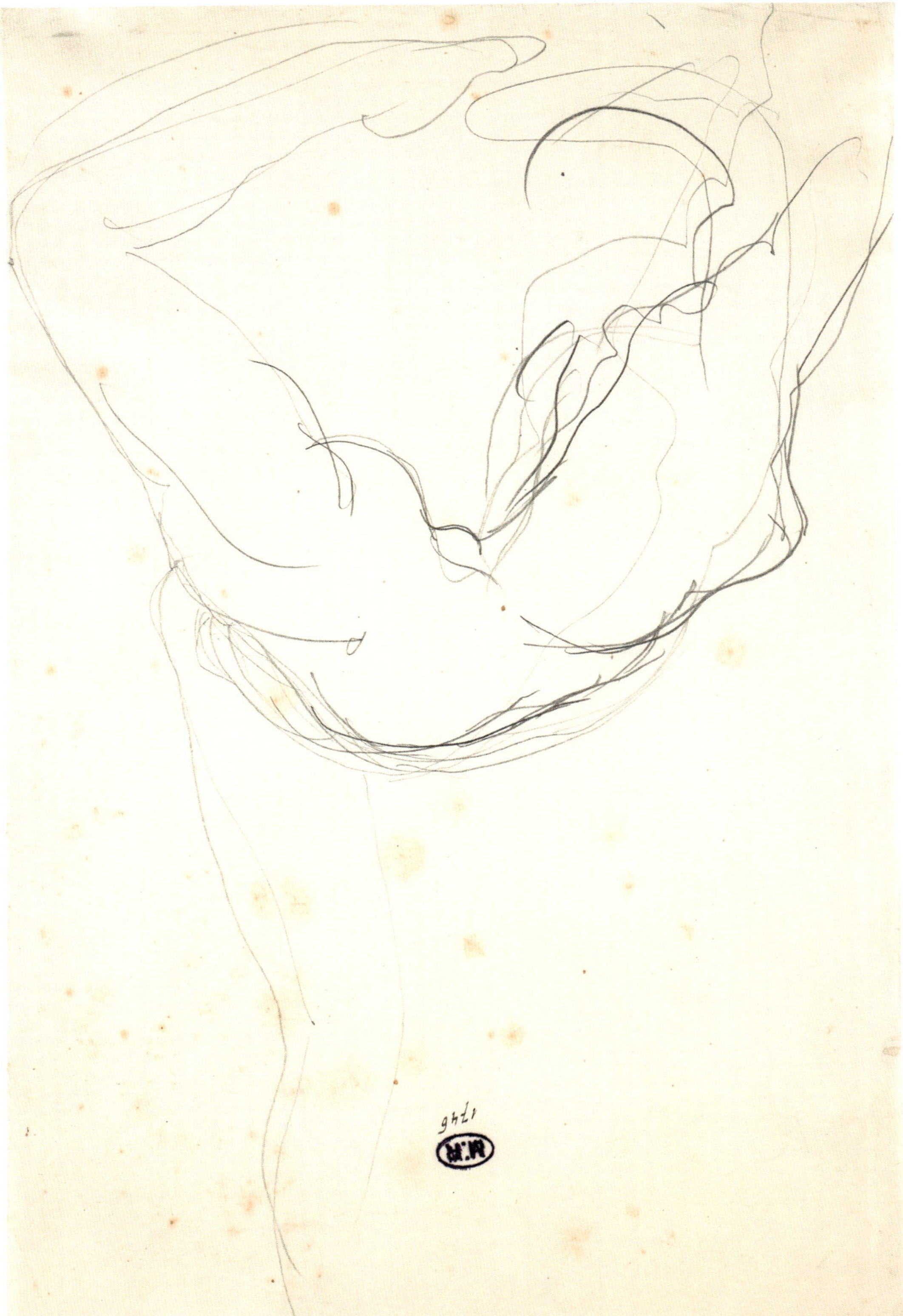

31

Male nude with outstretched arms, c.1900

Pencil and watercolour on wove paper, 245 x 319 mm
Musée Rodin, Paris, D.5090

Male nude with outstretched arms is an assured and precise drawing, whose steady and even pressure of the pencil, unbroken lines and absence of alterations raise the question whether it might have been drawn through the process of tracing. A pencil and stump drawing of the same subject, in a private collection (fig.51), is remarkably similar in scale and in many of its details: it was decided to compare the two drawings through the means of tracing, to help provide a further example of Rodin's process of duplication.[1] A tracing was made of the main contour lines of the figure for comparison (fig.52). When superimposed on to *Male nude with outstretched arms* (D.5090, cat.31), the tracing aligned exactly, as shown in fig.52, confirming that there was a close relationship between the two drawings, and the likelihood that Rodin used a tracing process to reproduce the outline. It is interesting to note that there were no modifications to any parts of the figure.

Rodin established the position of the figure by annotating *bas* (bottom) on the pencil and stumped drawing, which could suggest that the original position was the other way round, with the model originally sketched lying down on a table or other surface with his head hanging over the edge. If Rodin reversed the orientation of his drawing (which is characteristic of his late years), then in doing so he transformed what would have looked like a prone and lifeless figure into a dynamic figure lunging forward into space, his muscular physique caught in a moment of suspension, a reversal of Rodin's figures falling backwards in *The Gates of Hell*. The use of a flesh-coloured tint enhances the volume and solidity of the form, which was described by a contemporary as giving Rodin's drawings the appearance of antique terracotta figures.[2] AG & KE

1 We are grateful to the owner of the drawing for allowing the tracing to be taken and to Hannah Foster at Bonham's for kindly facilitating our study.
2 Charles Quentin, *The Art Journal*, no.187, 1902, p.216, cited in Paris 2011, p.147.

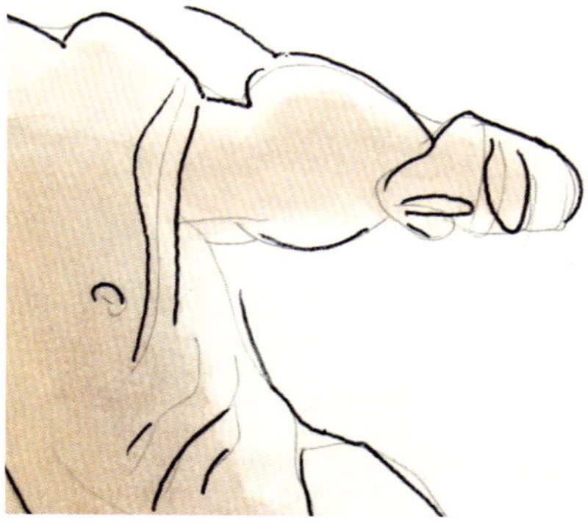

FIG.52
Detail showing our tracing of fig.51 overlaid on to D.5090, cat.31

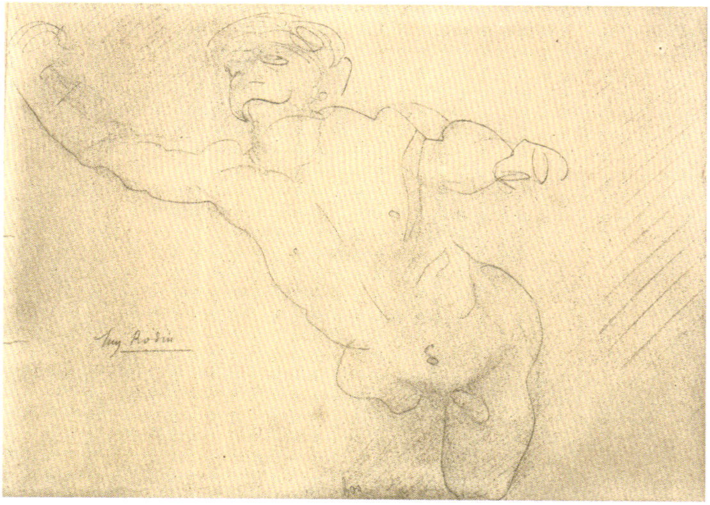

FIG.51
Auguste Rodin
Male nude with outstretched arms, c.1900
Pencil on paper, 228 x 317 mm
Private collection

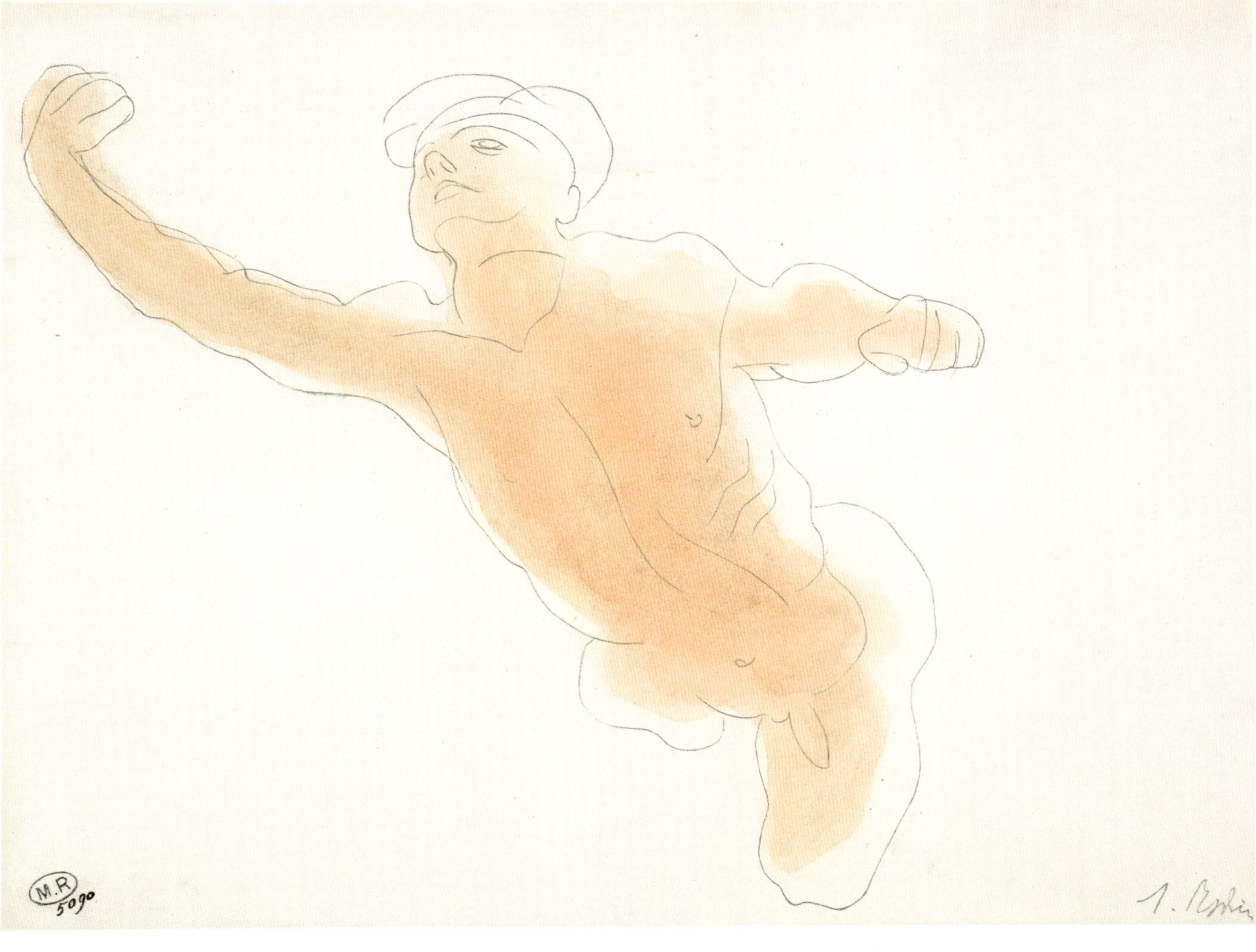

32–34

Male nude seen from below, lunging backwards, c.1900

Pencil on wove paper, 257 x 363 mm
Musée Rodin, Paris, D.474

Male nude in a bridge position, c.1900

Pencil on wove paper, 322 x 213 mm
Musée Rodin, Paris, D.1310

Legs of a male nude in a bridge position, seen from below, c.1900

Pencil with stumping and watercolour on wove paper, 325 x 251 mm
Musée Rodin, Paris, D.3949

Rodin's late oeuvre is striking for being overwhelmingly dominated by representations of women. There are sketches of male nudes, however, like these, focusing tightly and often from several perspectives, on a single figure in an acrobatic position (D.474, cat.32, for example, seems to be the underside view of D.5090, cat.31). Male models appear in Rodin's register of models, like his female models, often identified with one or two words about their physique, such as "bearded" or "muscly". Rodin liked to sketch muscular models, like the American Samuel S. White (on whom he based *L'Athlète américain*).[1] A lithograph of a man in a bridge pose, similar to D.1310 (cat.33), was published in 1902 as an illustration to the novel *Les Supplices du jardin* by Rodin's friend Octave Mirbeau. In the drawing (cat.33), the model must have been observed in a transitional position, perhaps as he was coming out of the pose. This is suggested by the asymmetry of the torso, with more weight resting on the right elbow than on the left. The abstract watercolour (D.3949, cat.34) seems to have been initially drawn from the life model. Pencil and stumping still visible in the centre of the drawing shows the outline of a man in an acrobatic bridge position seen from the front (the opposite view of D.1310, cat.33). This perspective, with the genitals at the top and the legs hanging down parallel to the picture plane, is similar to that of a series of pencil sketches in the Musée Rodin, in some of which the model's wheeled modelling stool is shown.[2] Rodin's famous method of modelling 'profiles', whereby he studied a model from all angles and perspectives, turning the model on his stool and turning himself around the figure, is discernible in these sketches.[3] In this drawing, Rodin changed the orientation of the legs with a few stronger pencil lines, covered nearly the entire sheet with a pink-red wash and applied deep tones of blue watercolour over the outer edges, transforming it from a sketch of a model in the studio into an abstract image vaguely resembling an architectural structure, perhaps a bridge in reference to the pose. AG

1 Paris 1990, p.16, and, on White, pp.41, 57.
2 For example, D.2302 and D.2304, without the stool; D.993 and D.2305, with the stool.
3 On sketching from a variety of angles, see Rodin to Dujardin-Beaumetz in Rodin 2008, pp.100–01.

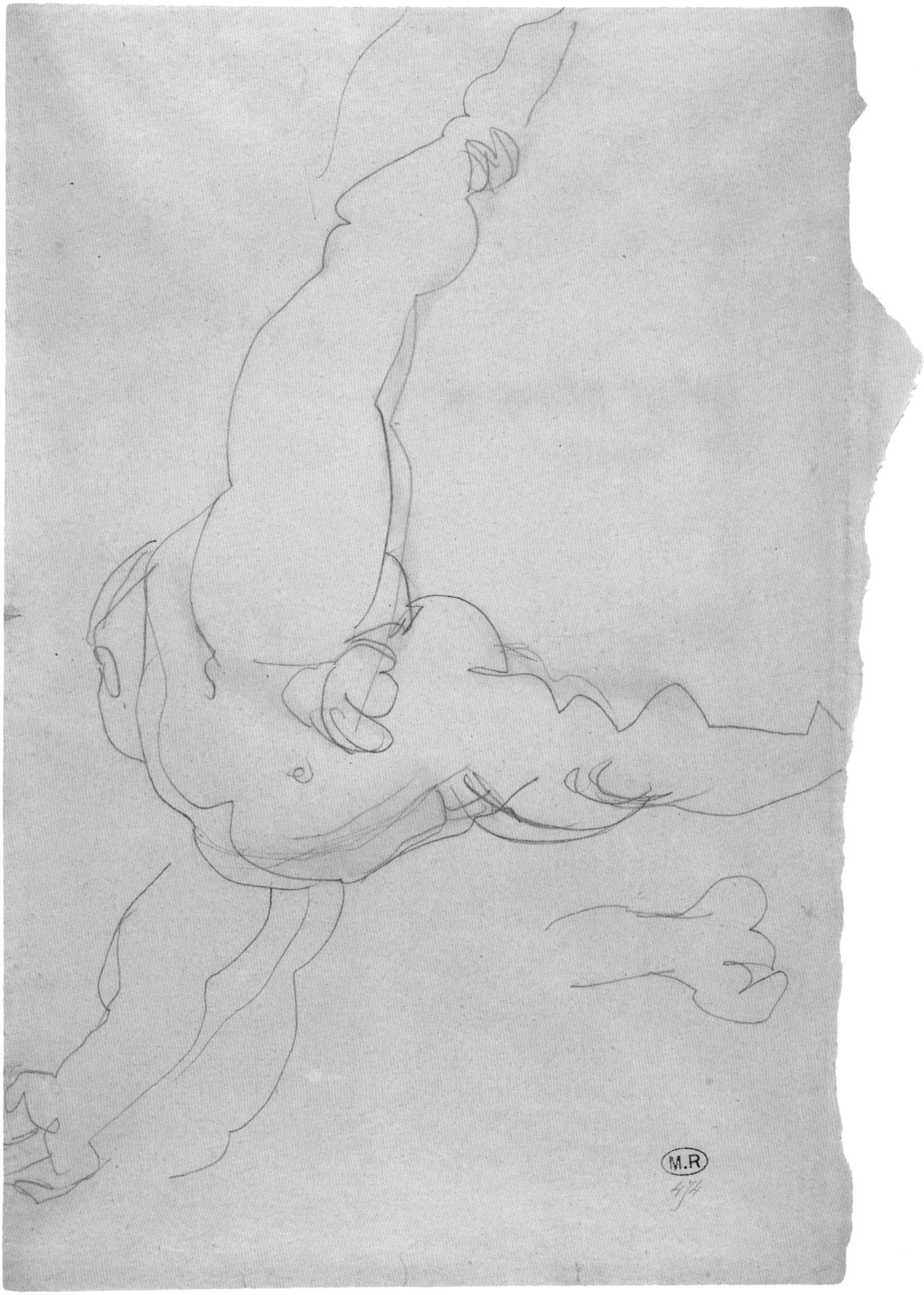

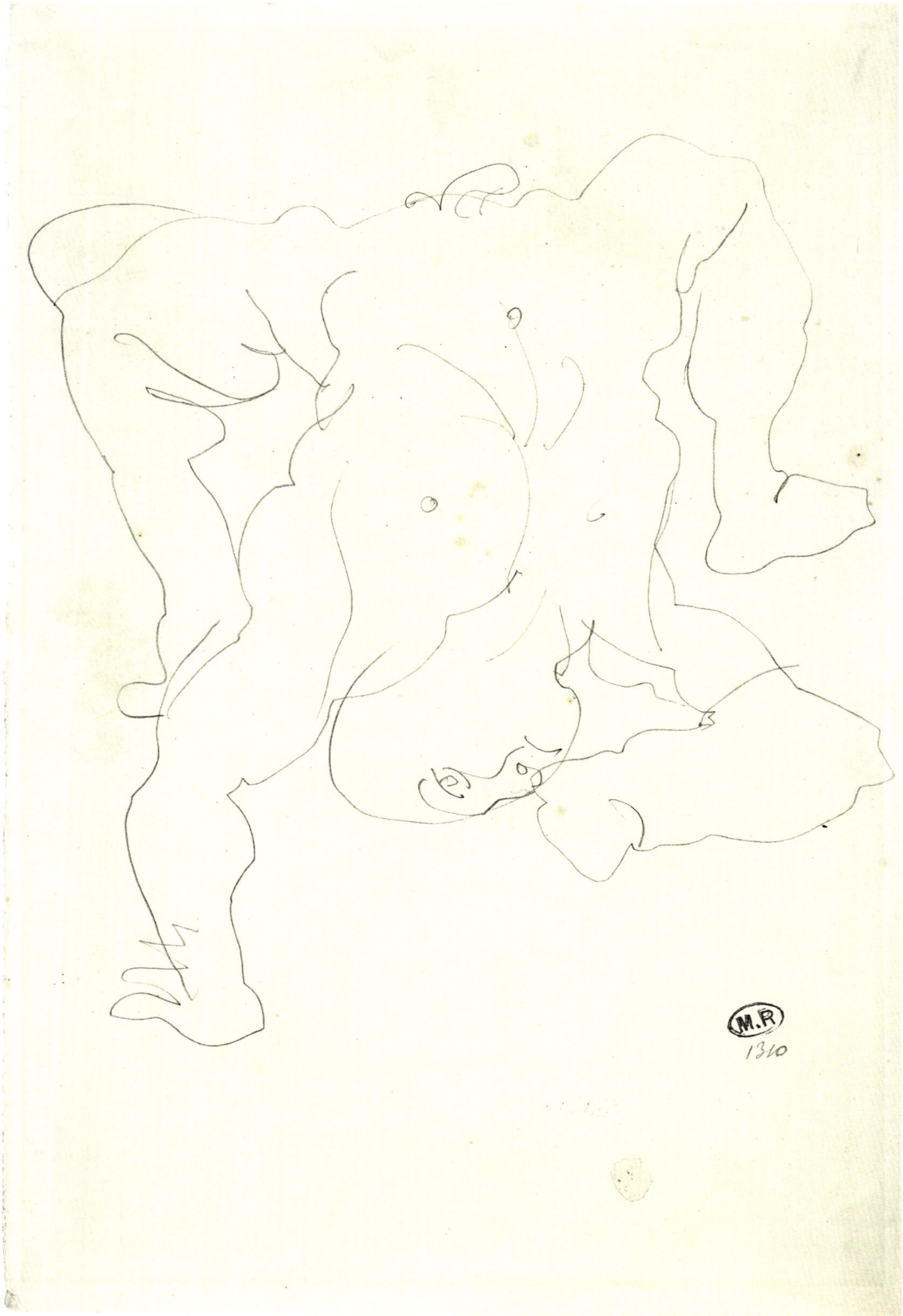
M.R
1310

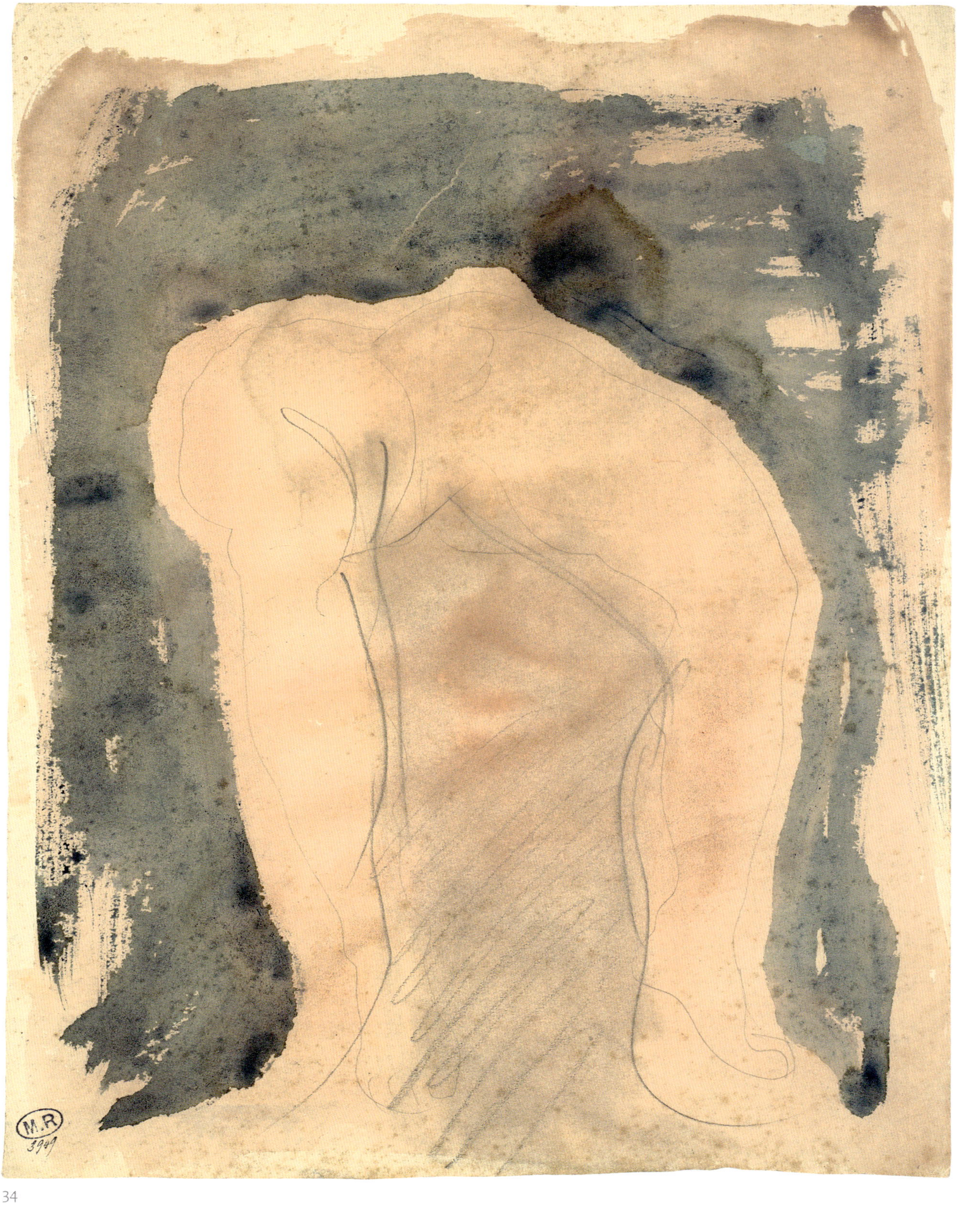
M.R
3949

35 & 36

Cut-out of a female nude with long hair, bending backwards, after 1896

Pencil and watercolour on wove paper, 275 x 214 mm
Musée Rodin, Paris, D.5222

Cut-out of a female nude, after 1896

Pencil and watercolour on wove paper, 201 x 300 mm
Musée Rodin, Paris, D.5235

These two drawings show figures who appear to be flying since we do not know what their bodies are resting on. Both forms are highly simplified and exaggerated to the limits of reality, tending towards geometrical forms – squares and circles. The line of the bust has three undulations signifying the breasts, ribs and belly.

The woman leaning backwards (D.5222, cat.35) is clearly standing, but Rodin has not bothered to draw her feet, cutting off the legs at the ankles. The paper's cut edge is visible at the ankle where the drawing stops. The fact that we cannot see the feet accentuates the sense that the woman is bursting upwards. The body's abstract nature is manifest in its perfection of form and near-90° angles – the back is horizontal. The head is barely painted at all, but strongly indicated by the thick, vertical mass of hair and accompanying mass of the arms, which makes the most suspended part of the body also the most substantial and colourful, drawing the viewer's attention. The difficulty in reaching this position is in relaxing the body in order to bend over backwards as far as possible. The extreme position and greenish skin colour transform the body into an object or, more precisely, an architectural form. This is a characteristic aspect of the paper cut-outs, which are the culmination of a process of reworking and simplification.

Rodin reworked this cut-out figure in another cut-out, placing it in an oblique position and without as much hair, which makes that drawing lighter overall (D.5234). In another drawing exploring a similar position (D.5221), the model is kneeling rather than standing as she leans over backwards, so she is able to support herself by putting her hands behind her knees or possibly on her ankles. This position can be held for longer, although the horizontal back forms a right angle with the back of the thighs. In this series Rodin's portrayal of the female body is almost architectural, equating a static form with a dynamic dance pose, which he clearly did not regard as contradictory, since he gave the title *architecture* to one of the dance drawings that is very similar to *Mouvement D* (D.1817; fig.61, p.166).

The second drawing, a cut-out of a nude (D.5235, cat.36), is harder to relate to reality. The figure is lying down, the feet touching the actual edge of the paper, but it is hard to understand the nature of the space on which they rest. The body is supported by the left arm, as shown by the bent hand. The position looks relaxed, as though it can be held without effort. The right foot rests on the left foot, the right arm is gently folded over the head. The body curves in a circular arc. A pencil drawing from life of this figure (D.759) does not give any additional information on the figure's pose or surroundings. We could hypothesise that the figure is sliding off a bed on which she has been lying. A fairly similar curve is found in another paper cut-out that could be the completion of this movement in progress – the standing woman leans against another figure (D.5205, fig.53). The androgyny of the body in these drawings serves to heighten the strangeness of the pose[1] – Rodin is clearly seeking to undo the laws of gravity.[2]

1 This type of figure is also similar to another, recognisable by its implausibility, which Rodin frequently used in different compositions (figure in a couple D.5705–06–07 and figure alone D.4619, 1370, 1240). The fluidity of the pose is perhaps only apparent, since one of the drawings is entitled *torture* (D.4619).

2 The Museum of Modern art, New York, has a watercolour of this figure (inv. 254.1976) which has inscriptions on three different sides of the sheet: *l'ange rebelle précipité sur la terre / enfer; enfer devant l'effroy* (sic) */ trapèze*. The last is a reference to an acrobatic pose.

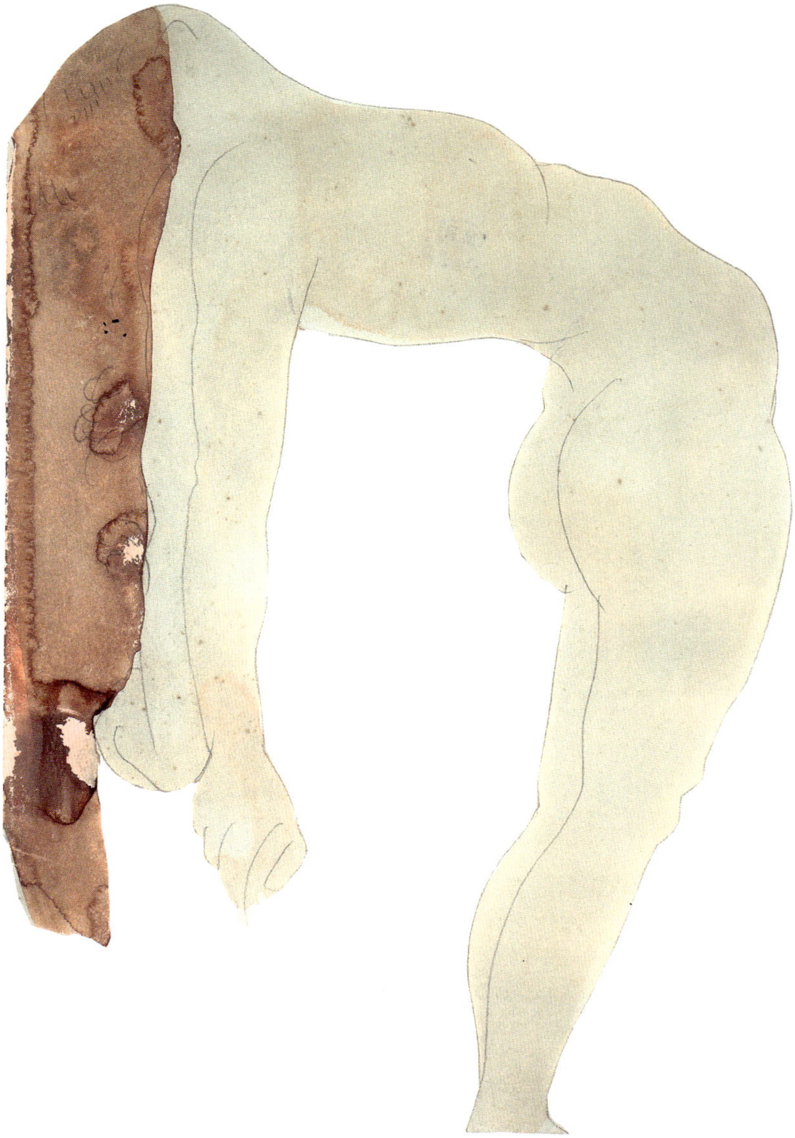

35

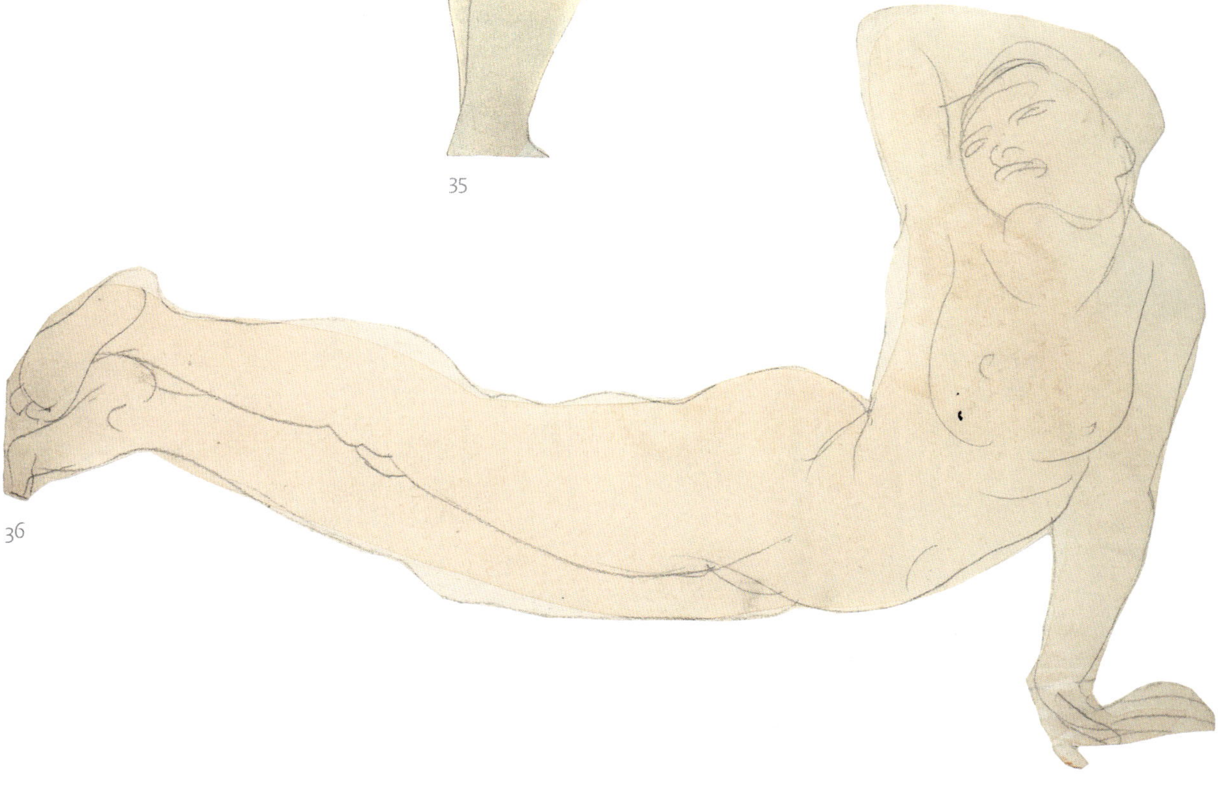

36

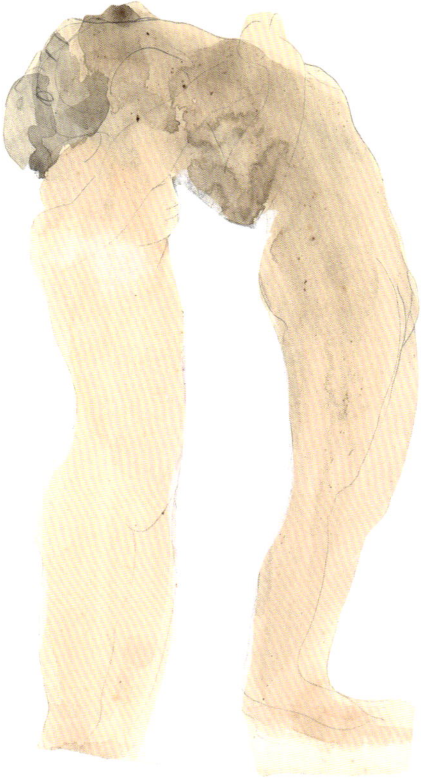

FIG.53
Auguste Rodin
Cut-out of a female nude bending backwards, leaning on the shoulders of a kneeling female nude, after 1896
Pencil and watercolour on wove paper, 320 x 158 mm
Musée Rodin, Paris, D.5205

This paper cut-out is similar to another showing two figures cut from a single paper sheet (D.5254). One woman supports the other, who can then relax her body in a way that would be impossible if she had to move by herself. The orientation for viewing these two women is different from the cut-out of a nude (cat.36), since they are standing rather than lying down.

Another paper cut-out (D.5207), in which the body is leaning backwards towards the right, also shows a fluid and relaxed curve. The detail of the bent wrist is not present, but the angle formed by the back and buttocks is very similar and reflects a body with an unusual flexibility, to which Rodin was particularly drawn in this period. His capacity to reinterpret his figures in other orientations than that of reality shows his interest in figures floating in an undefined space that counters gravity. The word 'floating' seems particularly appropriate to Rodin's research: one of the inscriptions of this series is *laisse flotter* (allow to float; D.1621). The drawing on which it appears shows a woman doing a roll, forwards or backwards – a spherical figure being the best suited for rendering it impossible to determine the orientation for viewing.

Rodin's aim is to show figures seemingly isolated from the background. To this end he uses bright, plain colour, on either the figures themselves or the background, as though to turn the figure into a negative. He did this using watercolour or even stumping. The idea of paper cut-outs, which he has used here, was destined for great things in the twentieth century and corresponds in drawing to his practice of assemblage in sculpture.[3] Here he shows himself to be a forerunner in relation to the practices developed by Picasso and Matisse and then by the Surrealists. SBF

3 On the paper cut-outs see Nadine Lehni in Paris 2011, p.50, and exh. cat. *Matisse Rodin*, Musée Rodin, Paris, and Musée Matisse, Nice, Paris, 2009.

37 & 38

Female nude with a raised leg (Alda Moreno), called Offrande à Vénus, c.1910–13

Pencil with stumping on wove paper, 362 x 231 mm
Inscribed on two edges: *offrande a venus* [sic] and *rampant / sur les nuages / stèle* (offering to Venus and crawling / on the clouds / stele)
Musée Rodin, Paris, D.1837

Female nude stretching, reoriented vertically, called Rapidité du trait, c.1910?

Pencil on wove paper, 210 x 310 mm
Inscribed: *rapidité du trait* (quickness of line)
Musée Rodin, Paris, D.2853

Female nude with a raised leg (D.1837, cat.37), inscribed 'offering to Venus' (*offrande a venus* [sic]), shows a woman bent forward with her legs in the standing splits position. The many lines that define the legs, arms and back indicate that this is a drawing done quickly from life. The fact that the right leg is slightly bent and the left leg was differently arranged before its final position was chosen may suggest that the model was standing, but in many other drawings the pose appears on the floor. The sense of offering is conveyed by the fact that the body is completely open, as are the genitals. Rodin was interested in capturing the bust and limbs; the head is barely detailed, the hair is absent and the hands and feet are off the edges of the paper. Another drawing in the same series is also entitled 'offering to Venus' (*Offrande à Vénus*; D.5965). Here the model is seen from the front, rolling on to her back holding her legs over her head. Common to both drawings are the open genitals, fully visible and clearly drawn. A second inscription, *sirène* (siren, mermaid) suggests that to Rodin the position of a woman bent over evoked the ruin of all men.

Rodin liked to name and rename his drawings and began adding inscriptions in the period of the so-called 'black' drawings of the 1880s. Written beneath the image, often some time later, these inscriptions make it easier to understand the drawings and indicate which way up they should be viewed, which is not always the same as their orientation when drawn.[1] In Rodin's last period, to which these drawings belong, he would sometimes reinterpret a drawing and change its meaning, as he did with his sculpture by placing one or more plaster figures together in a group.[2] The drawing D.5965 can be read more than one way up, as demonstrated by the orientation of the second inscription. Rodin's friend Louis Gillet (1876–1943) reproduced this figure on a smaller scale in a series of three drawings (D.2297–98–99; see fig.7, p.20) serving as an aide-mémoire for the positions Rodin had drawn (originals preserved in the Musée Rodin). The title 'Offering to Venus' given to the figure in its appearance here enables the model to be identified as Alda Moreno, since another drawing in this group, D.2298, mentions her name: *Mlle Moreno / espagnole / une des premières / qui aient dansé / nue / une amie d'Esnée* (Mlle Moreno / Spanish / one of the first / to have danced / nude / a friend of Esnée's). It offered Rodin an opportunity for the simultaneous exploration of his two favourite themes, dance and the female nude in motion.

In the new vision he offers here (cat.37), the woman is on the ground, *rampant sur les nuages* (crawling on the clouds). The substance on which she rests is hard to describe or to identify – a few

1 "The christening of drawings was an entertainment in Meudon, when he had coffee with friends in an arbour shaded by a bushy sophora. He would hand his guests his drawings one by one, saying, 'What shall we call this?' But he seldom accepted other people's suggestions": Gsell 1920, p.21; and later, "He would look at the figures in his drawings any way up .... For him there was no right or wrong way up", p.22. A similar account is given by Marcelle Tirel, *Rodin intime ou l'envers de la gloire*, Paris, 1925, p.91.

2 See Sophie Biass-Fabiani, 'Quand Rodin écrit sur ses œuvres', in Montreal 2015, pp.114–23.

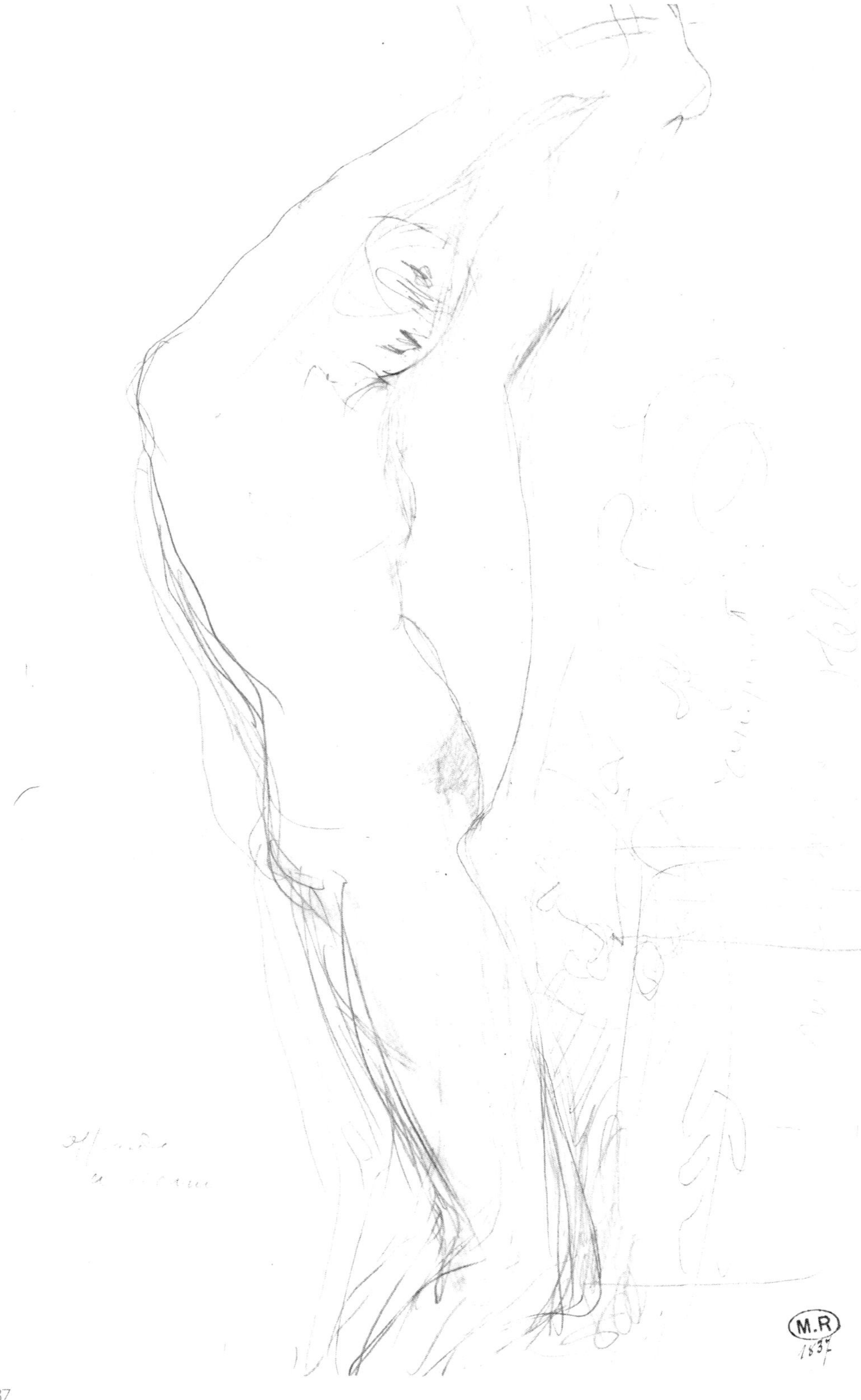

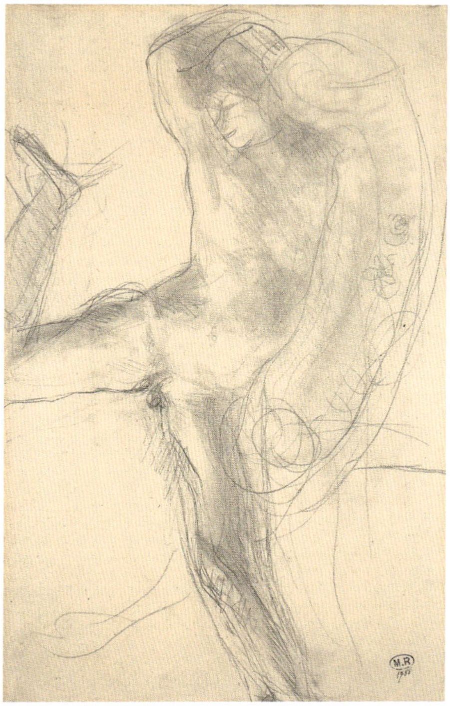

FIG.54
Auguste Rodin
Female nude standing on her left leg (Alda Moreno), c.1910–13
Pencil with stumping on laid paper, 382 x 237 mm
Musée Rodin, Paris, D.1788

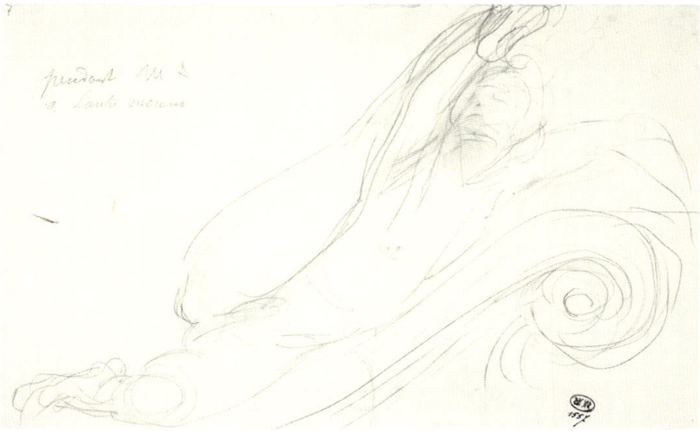

FIG.55
Auguste Rodin
Female nude reclining, called Pendant Michel-Ange or Alda Moreno, c.1910–13
Pencil with stumping on wove paper, 231 x 362 mm
Musée Rodin, Paris, D.1557

straight lines form a rigid architecture, countered by two curling lines emphasising the genitals and the fold of the knee. A few small signs can be interpreted as floral motifs on fabric, while the word *stèle* gives an ancient connotation to the whole. Rodin often reproduced the motif that might be the arm of a divan or an indication of a swinging movement with a scroll at either end (D.1788, fig.54). In another drawing showing Moreno (D.1557, fig.55), a scroll serving as an armrest evokes the plinth supporting the figures on the tomb of Lorenzo de' Medici, which Rodin had copied in his youth while travelling in Italy, notably the representations of *Night* and *Day*.[3] We know that these were figures he particularly admired. He seems to have been happy with the result – in a play on words he has *MA* – Michelangelo – mirrored by AM, Alda Moreno (in the inscription *pendant M.A. / à L'autre Moreno* (M.A. pendant / to the other Moreno).[4]

The undefined substance over which the woman crawls in D.1837 (cat.37) reappears in another drawing in which the clouds serve as a background accessory (D.4408). Here too dance is present, since this is a tripod pose, like that of the sculpted figure *Mouvement C* (cat.54). Two options for viewing and interpretation are offered by the titles of that drawing: *lever du soleil* (sunrise) on one side shows the figure rising into the sky, while *sortant du nuage* (coming out of the cloud) has it descending.

Another drawing (D.2583, cat.38) shows a woman apparently captured in motion, trying to take flight: her legs are spread wide and her bust is not yet against her front leg, just as her arms are reaching forward to her leg but do not touch it. The feeling that the drawing shows a moment seized from a movement in action is heightened by the fact that only the outlines have been drawn, apart from a few folds in the waist and buttocks. The head is represented by a vague, incomplete circle. The hands and feet are not detailed. We can also view the figure vertically as a woman preparing for a handstand. Either way, the

3 See D.5117, 5118 and 5119; on Michelangelo's importance for Rodin, see *Rodin et l'Italie*, Rome (De Luca), 2001.
4 A comparison with the model's muscular physique and Michelangelo's sculptures might also have been suggested by the fact that Alda Moreno lived in rue Michel-Ange in Paris.

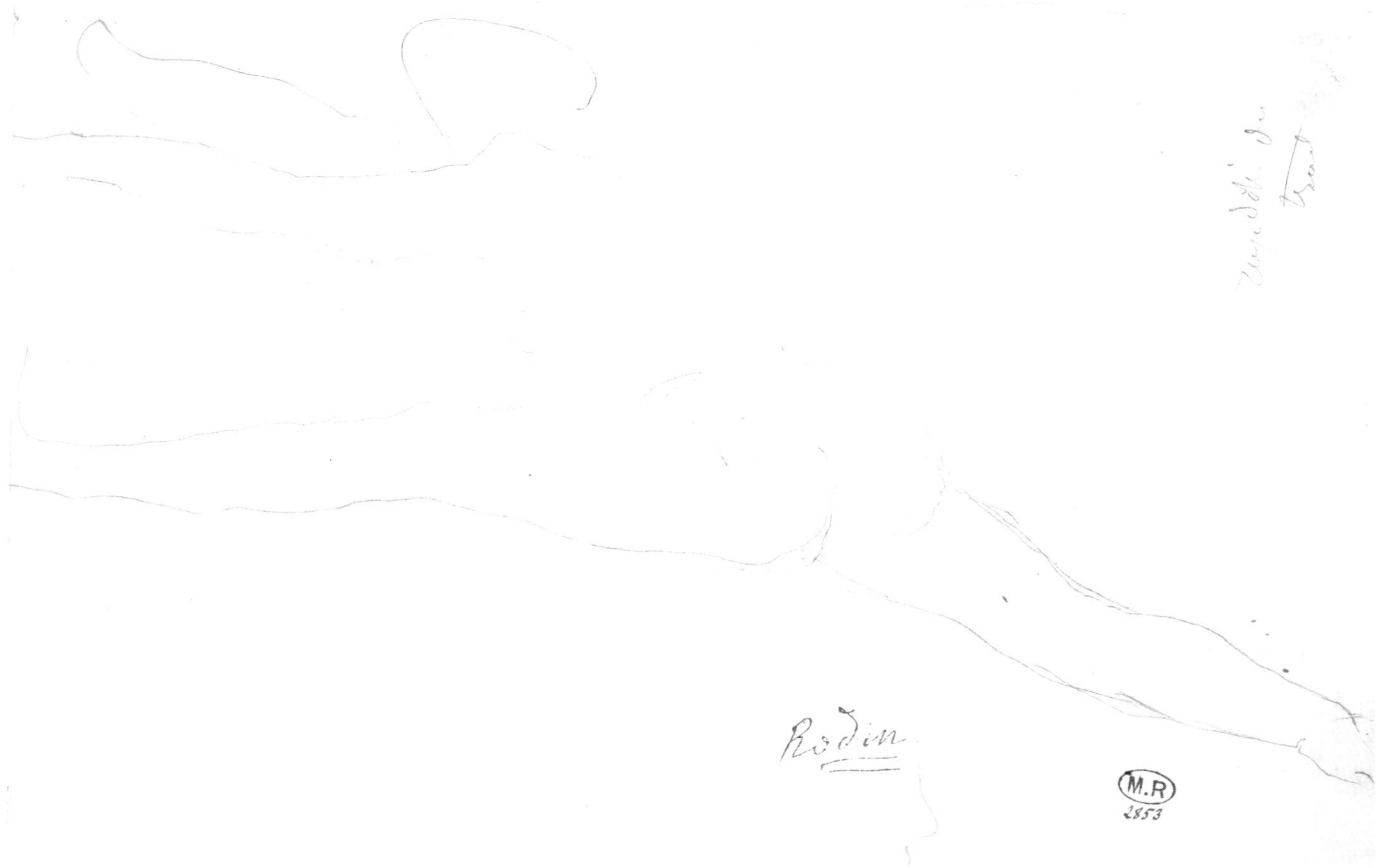

38

orientation for reading the inscription is different from that in which the drawing was made. We read *rapidité du trait* (rapidity of line), which is a note of the state of mind in which the drawing was made. The position is close to the sculpted figure of *Mouvement C* (cat.54) or, more distantly, *Mouvement G* (cat.59). Rodin did not use specific preparatory drawings in working on his sculptures but, as here, he made studies of similar poses from life. A variant on this fleeting position – legs wide apart, arms stretched forward to spring into a handstand – appears in another drawing (D.1650) with the inscription *éclair* (lightning) reading vertically, unlike the real movement.[5]

In another example showing a model in the splits position (D.4022), Rodin has transformed the figure: the arms are moving asymmetrically, while a broom drawn in pencil along the leg stretching back reinforces the inscription *balai petite sorcière* (broom little witch). We have suddenly left the motif of the dancer behind, but the movement is still fast and the floating or flying movement of the figure is clearly affirmed, as though caught in a snapshot. The same pose is used for another watercolour (D.4413), showing a woman emerging from a blue wash, which in Rodin's work usually represents water. SBF

5 This drawing can be compared to another showing the same position with no inscription (D.1648).

39–41

Female nude in a tripod position, c.1900?

Pencil with stumping on wove paper, 308 x 197 mm
Musée Rodin, Paris, D.2296

Cut-out of a female nude in a tripod position, c.1900

Pencil and watercolour on wove paper, 321 x 184 mm
Musée Rodin, Paris, D.5202

Female nude in a tripod position, reoriented vertically and sideways, called La fleur, c.1900?

Pencil with stumping, watercolour and gouache on wove paper, 326 x 251 mm
Inscribed on two sides: *la fleur* and *bas* (the flower / bottom)
Musée Rodin, Paris, D.4914

Female nude in a tripod position (D.2296, cat.39) captures a figure with her hands widely spaced and firmly planted on the ground, her supporting right leg both straight and active, whilst her raised left leg is reaching dynamically away and upwards. There is an opposition in this pose between the anchor of the tripod and the gravitational pull of the raised leg, which takes it in an arc. The drawing has the characteristics seen in many of Rodin's life drawings, where he has quickly noted details, such as the right thumb, indicating that the hand was splayed palm face down on the ground, or the crook of the left hipbone.

The pose in these three drawings recurs with very little variation in a group of about a dozen drawings (see, for example, fig.56), which seem so close to each other in their general structure as well as their details that Rodin could have traced them. The group includes the pencil drawing (cat.39), which appears drawn from life; a series of gouache and watercolour drawings, such as *Female nude in a tripod position, reoriented vertically and sideways, called La fleur* (D.4914, cat.41); and two cut-outs, including *Cut-out of a female nude in a tripod position* (D.5202, cat.40), which were first drawn in pencil, painted in gouache and then cut out following the pencil contours of the figures.[1]

To see whether in fact Rodin used a tracing process to develop this group of drawings, we

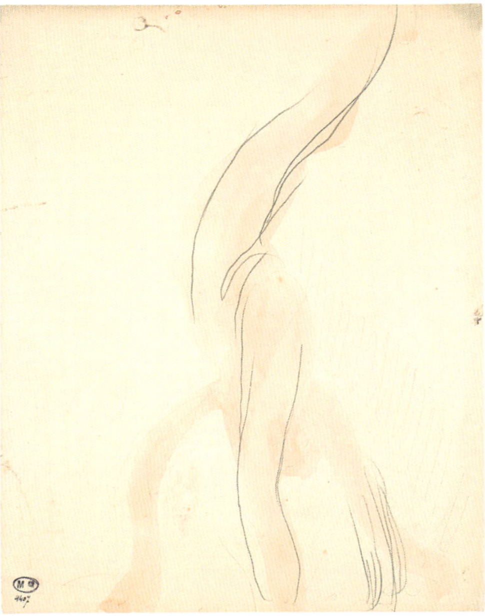

FIG.56
Auguste Rodin
Female nude in a tripod position, c.1900
Pencil and watercolour on laid paper, 328 x 251 mm
Musée Rodin, Paris, D.4407

1 Comparison drawings of this pose at the Musée Rodin are: D.2295; D.4419; D.4420; D.4403; D.4404; D.4407; D.4408; D.4409; and the cut-out D.5229. See Junod 1992, p.38, footnote 49, for a list of these and further drawings of the pose seen from various perspectives. See Varnedoe in Washington 1981, pp.180 and 185–86 for a discussion of reorientation in relation to the tripod pose and the cut-outs.

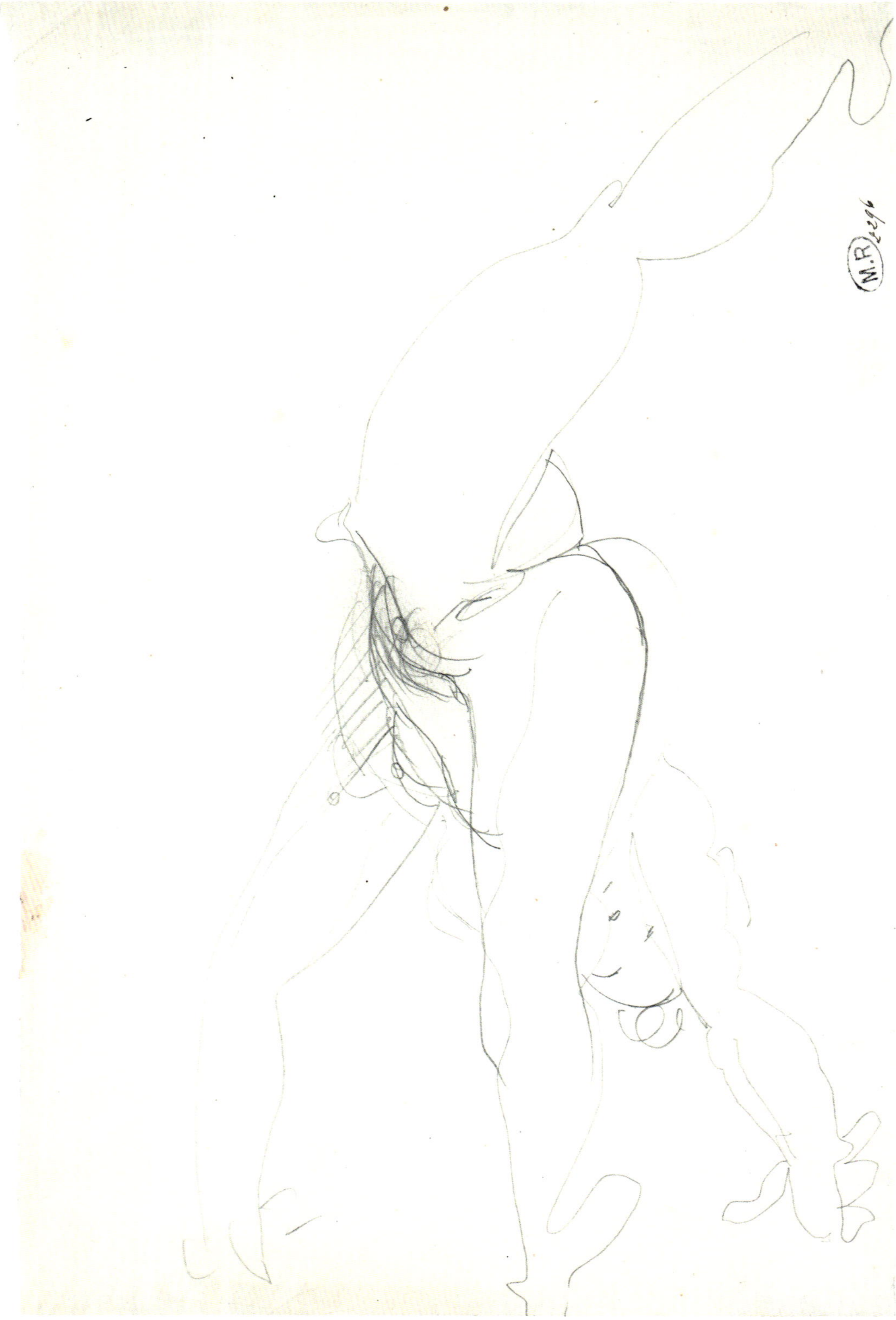

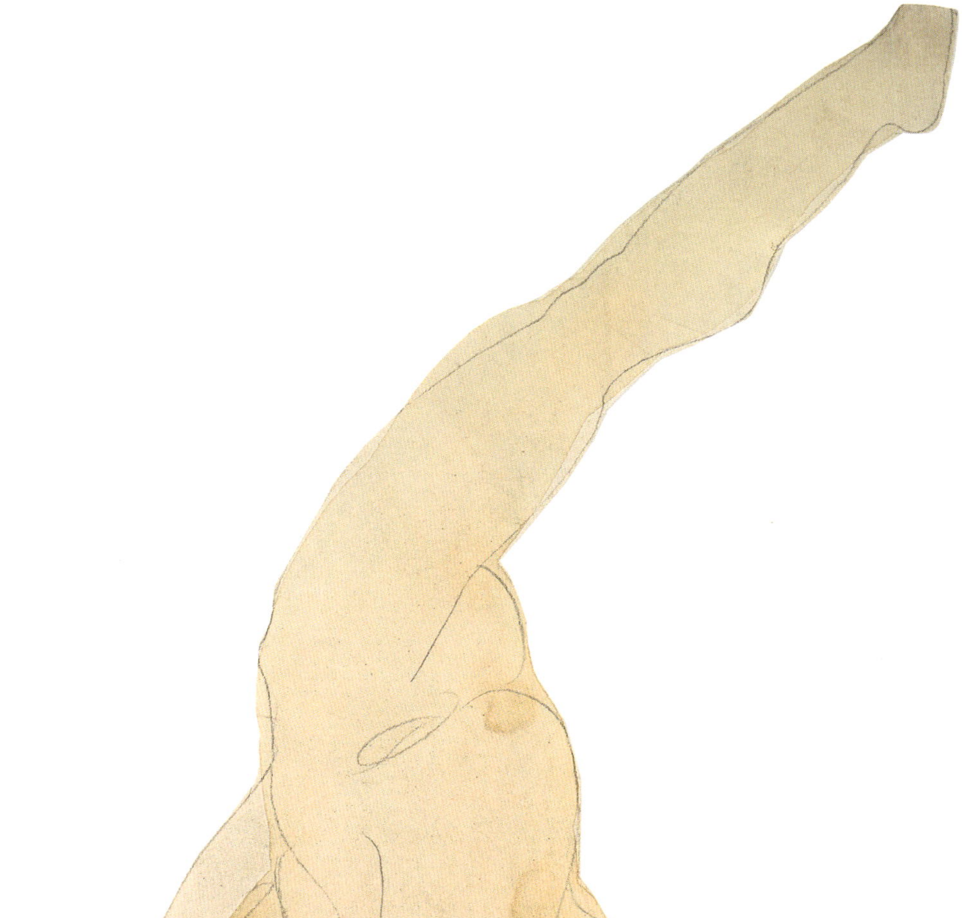

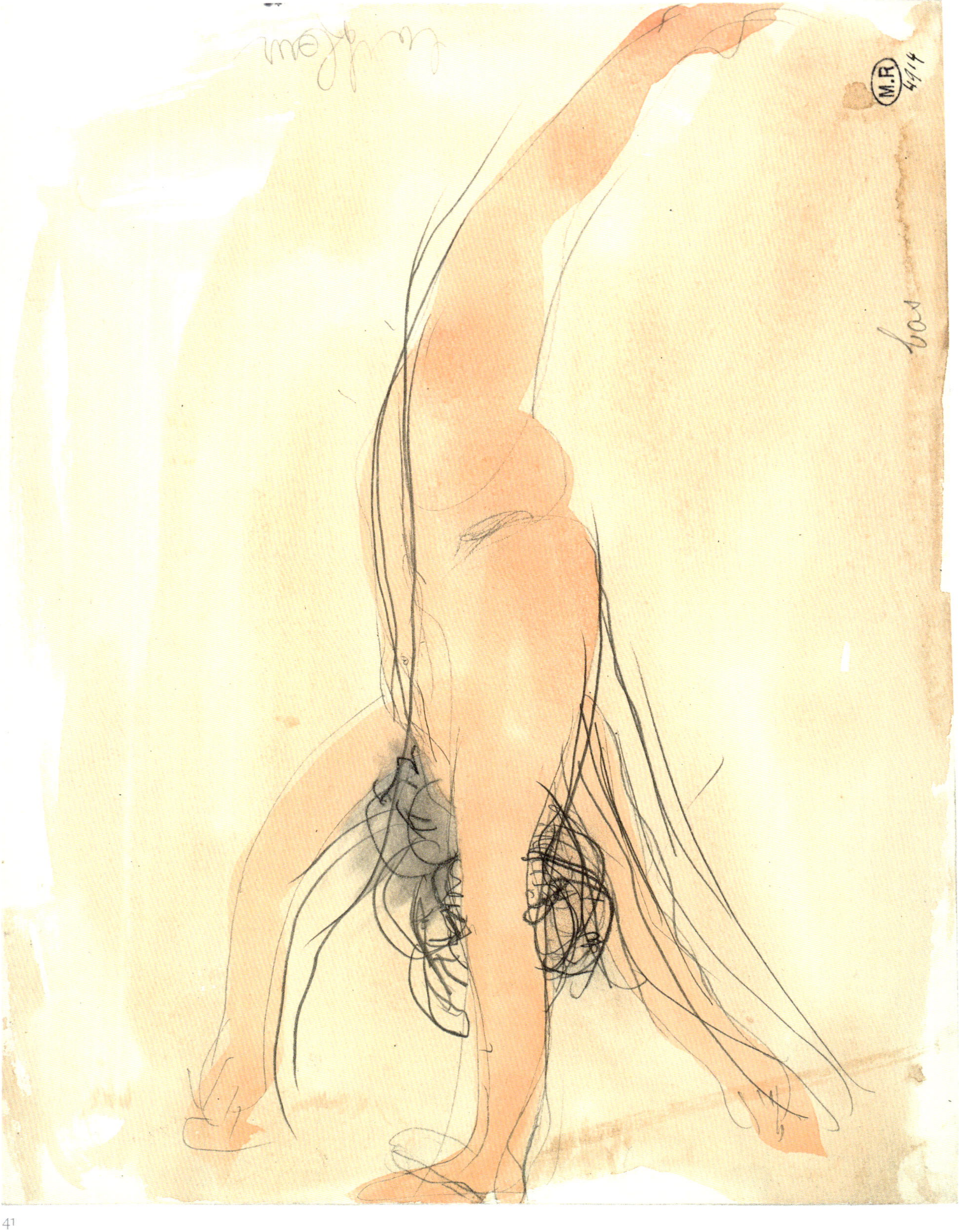

41

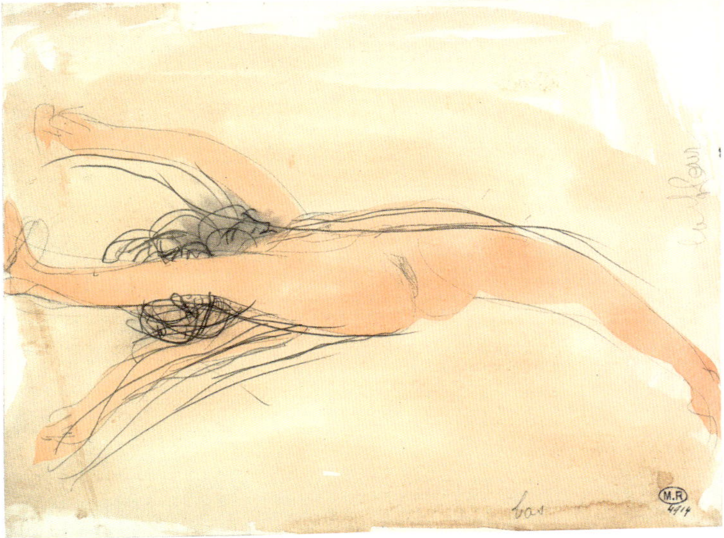

D.4914, cat. 41 reoriented

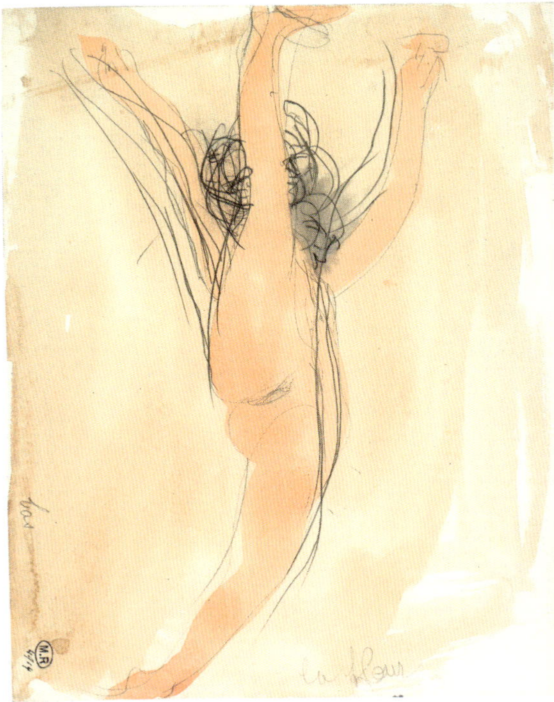

D.4914, cat. 41 reoriented

ourselves traced a selection for comparison.[2] It was observed that the scale of the figures is virtually identical in all the drawings and that the position of the buttocks remains constant, with small changes to the arms and legs. It is therefore likely that Rodin evolved his motif through the kind of 'dynamic' tracing, possibly at a window, already observed in relation to the group of drawings derived from *Female nude in profile holding her leg behind her head* (cat.25, 26 & 27).

In the series of drawings of tripod poses, Rodin seems to have been preoccupied with creating a compact and symmetrical form (fig.56 barely has any indication of a head), with the limbs simply pivoting outwards from it. This may explain the difficulty he had in many of the drawings in positioning the head, which did not fit neatly into the geometry of the form, and the presence in some drawings, such as *Female nude in a tripod position* (cat.41), of additional lines just outside the arms and legs that seem to echo and reinforce their downward or upward movements.

Rodin often turned his drawings round, inscribing various ideas or simply the word '*bas*' (bottom) on the sheet, as in cat.41, thus suggesting two or three orientations for the same work. With his series of cut-outs, he created two-dimensional paper sculptures that were freed from the constraints of the page and could be moved around independently. *Cut-out of a female nude in a tripod position*, dated *c.*1900 (cat.40), is so close to Rodin's terracotta figure known as *Mouvement C* of 1911 (cat.54), that it is worth asking whether, when he started working on the *Mouvements de danse* around 1911, he would have turned to look at it again, for its simplicity of form and versatility as an expression of grounding, uplift and extension are all present in the sculpture. AG & KE

2 D.4419, D.4404, and the cut-outs D.5202 (cat.40) and D.5229.

42–46

Assemblage of two figures, called Alpha and Beta, c.1911?

Plaster, 34 x 30 x 11.5 cm
Musée Rodin, Paris, S.3671

Piece moulds used in making the Mouvements de danse, c.1911?

Mould of the torso of *Alpha*: 22 x 18 x 24 cm; standing leg: 13 x 28 x 17 cm; right arm and leg: 15,5 x 36 x 23 cm
Musée Rodin, M.681 bis
Mould of the torso and right thigh of *Beta*: 16 x 36 x 21.5 cm; left standing leg: 11.5 x 27.5 x 15 cm;
right arm: 12.5 x 21.5 x 14.5 cm; left arm: 11 x 22 x 15 cm; mould of the *Head of the Slavic Woman* : 15 x 15 x 16 cm
Musée Rodin, M.681

Leg, 1911

Terracotta, 9.7 x 4.3 x 2.5 cm
Musée Rodin, Paris, S.6705

Torso and leg, 1911

Terracotta, 12.5 x 9.5 x 5.5 cm
Musée Rodin, Paris, S.6416

Figure in a crawling movement from the Mouvements de danse series, 1911

Terracotta, 36.8 x 14.6 x 5.9 cm
Musée Rodin, Paris, S.6362

By early to mid 1911, Rodin had modelled two small figures in clay, one a standing figure with an accentuated arch in her back, holding her foot behind her head with one hand (now called *Alpha*), and the other lunging forward, upper body straight and more or less parallel to the floor (now called *Beta*). These were probably made quickly in the studio in front of the model, presumably Alda Moreno, who we believe was the model for the drawings of the standing posture, probably completed or resolved by 1905 (see cat.25–30) and probably for other postures too. Neither of the two figures had heads, and the standing figure had only one arm, making it in profile appear close to the drawings of the pose.

At some point, Rodin asked one of his mould-makers to cast the two figures in plaster, a more durable material than clay, which also allowed him the possibility of making further casts. The clay figures had to be cut up for the fabrication of moulds: three moulds for the standing figure, *Alpha* (cat.43, 1–3: one for the torso, one for the standing leg, and one for the raised arm and leg) and five moulds for the lunging figure, *Beta* (cat.43, 4–8: one for torso and right thigh, one for the right lower leg, one for the standing leg, one for the right arm and one for the left arm). Once all the body parts had been cast in plaster, they were assembled in the precise position of Rodin's original figures, thanks to the presence of registration marks incised on to the body parts.[1]

Next, Rodin decided to bring the two figures together into one composition, which he did with some very crudely applied plaster slip. This could have been done at almost any time after the initial casting in plaster, months or even years later. The lack of care in finessing the join strongly suggests it was Rodin, rather than one of his skilled craftsmen, who assembled the figures, perhaps to judge quickly the effect of a grouped composition.

1 For a detailed discussion of the making of the *Mouvements de danse*, see the technical essay by Blanchetière, Cascio and Lévy in this volume.

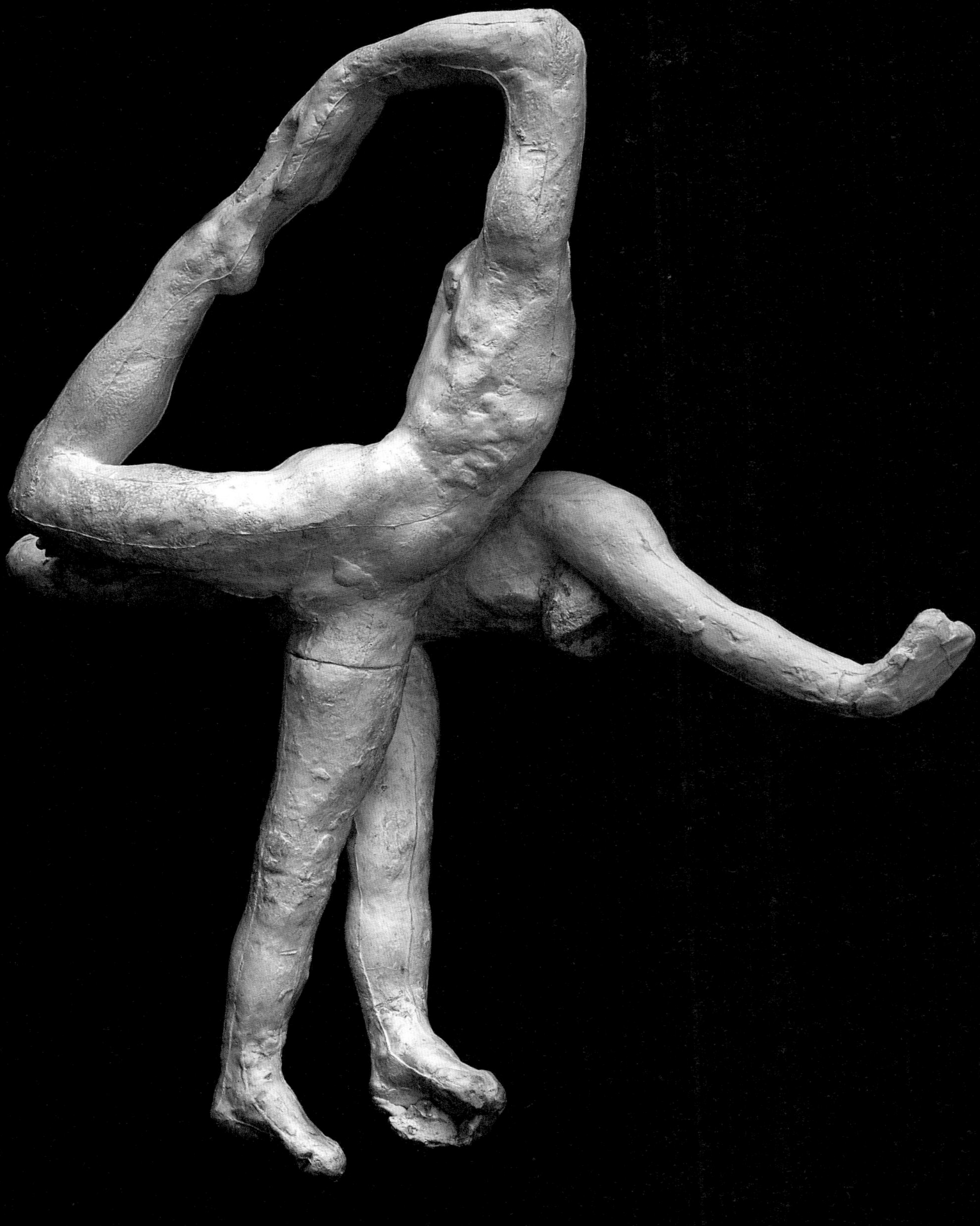

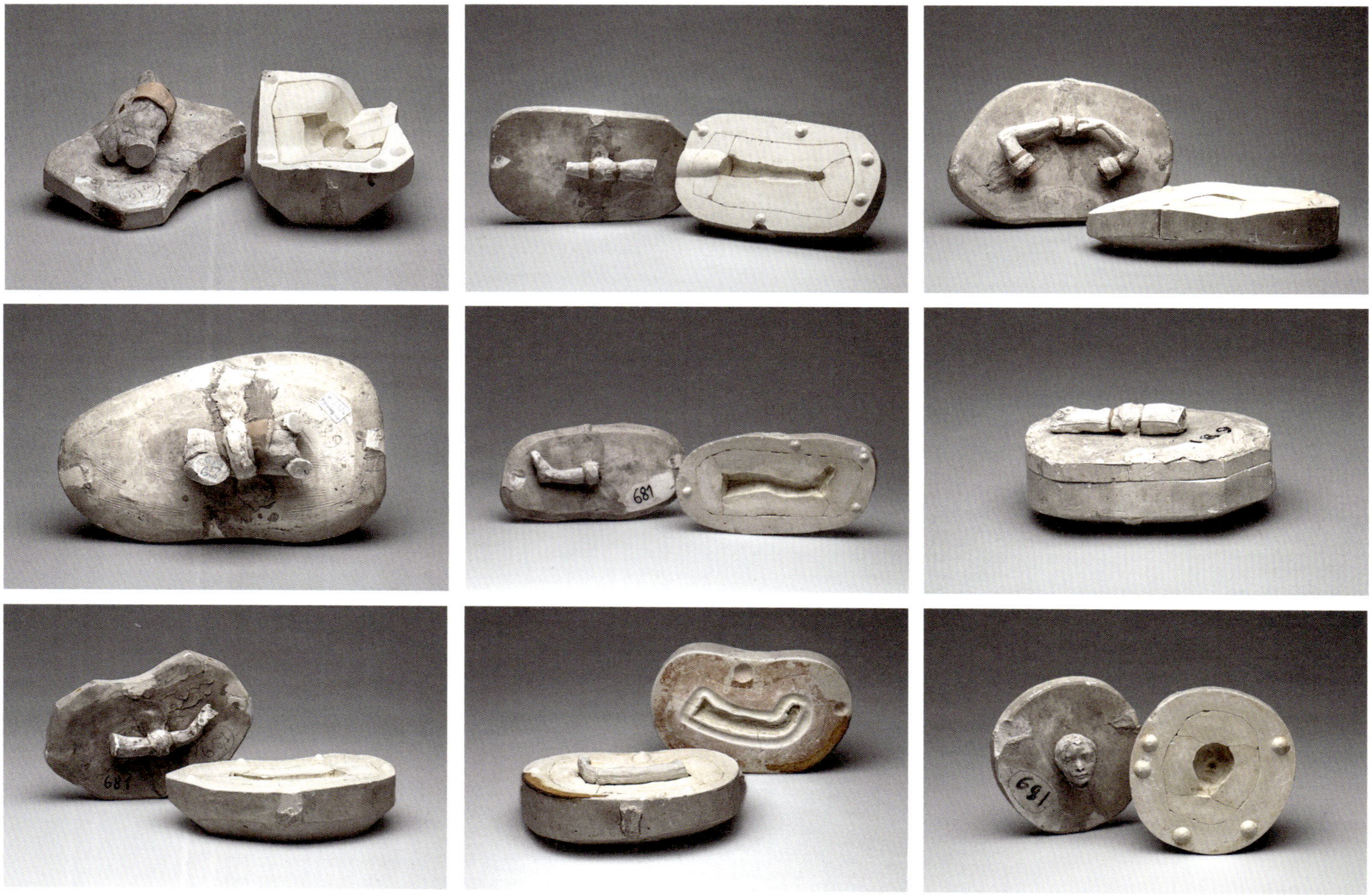

43

Moulds, with plaster casts attached to the lid for identification purposes

LEFT TO RIGHT: 1. mould of the torso of *Alpha*; 2. mould of the standing leg of *Alpha*; 3. mould of the right arm and leg of *Alpha*; 4. mould of the torso and right thigh of *Beta*; 5. mould of the right lower leg of *Beta*; 6. mould of the left standing leg of *Beta*; 7. mould of the right arm of *Beta*; 8. mould of the left arm of *Beta*; 9. mould of the *Head of the Slavic Woman*

In some aspects the group recalls Henri-Joseph's Rutxhiel's marble group *Zephyr and Psyche* in the Louvre (fig.57). Not only is there a hint of a formal resemblance in the pairing of the two poses but it is worth speculating that the iconography might have resonated with Rodin's interest at the time in the story of Psyche and in the idea of the wind as personified by Zephyr. A number of late drawings of female nudes refer in their inscriptions to the wind (see cat.25) and other elemental forces.

At some point, Rodin seems to have stuck a head on to the lunging figure, which has since fallen off, but its existence is suggested by the substantial lump of plaster slip around the neck, which would have served to secure it to the body (see the reconstruction, fig.59, p.154). This kind of experimentation with assembling body parts (called '*abattis*') was in line with Rodin's studio practice, but was pushed a little further here. Rodin had his mould-maker re-use the moulds that had served to cast the figures in plaster as press-moulds for clay body parts. The lower right leg of the lunging figure *Beta* (S.6705, cat.44) is a rare survival of an unattached *abattis* from this series, and the torso and bent leg (S.6416, cat.45) is the only known example of a fragmentary piece from the series. Rodin must have instructed his mould-maker not to assemble the parts since he wished to construct figures out of them. Among the strangest is the figure without a head that seems to be in a crawling position (S.6362, cat.46). Unsurprisingly, it was not cast in bronze along with the rest of the series.

Although no documentation survives concerning the *Mouvements de danse*, it seems highly plausible that a letter Rodin wrote to his trusted mould-maker Eugène Guioché on 17 March 1911 refers to this project. In this letter, Rodin specifically mentioned that Guioché was press-moulding a series of small figures (in fact, he would have been press-moulding *abattis*, not figures, but the instruction is presumably given with the brevity that would have come from frequent communication) and asked him to select a head of a suitable size from his stock of *abattis*: "My dear Guioché, Could you please make me about ten heads, no matter which, to go with the figurines you are press-moulding".[2]

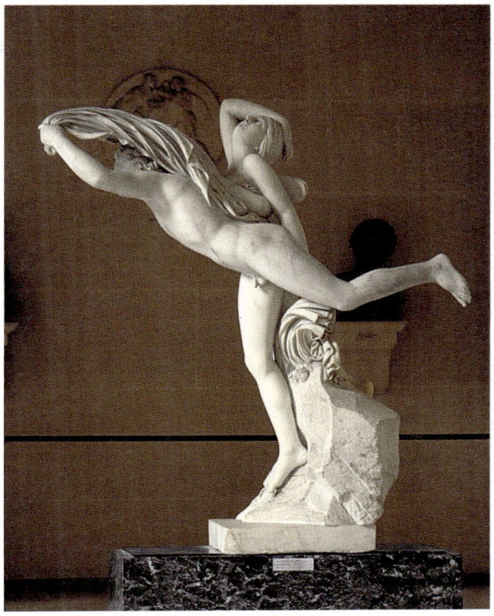

FIG.57
Henri-Joseph Rutxhiel
Zephyr and Psyche, 1814
Marble, 162 x 141 cm
Musée du Louvre, Paris

Guioché selected the head known as *Tête de la femme slave (Head of the Slavic Woman)* developed twenty years earlier. This kind of delegation of aspects of the creative process that would have an aesthetic impact on the finished work had become quite habitual for Rodin in the late years, and, while it seems to reflect a lack of interest in some of the detail, it has been recently and convincingly interpreted as a form of close collaboration with his assistants, since the

2 "*Mon cher Guioché, Pourriez-vous me faire, je vous prie, une dizaine de têtes, n'importe lesquelles qui aillent avec les figurines que vous estampez*". See Alexandra Gerstein's essay for a proposed chronology of the *Mouvements de danse*.

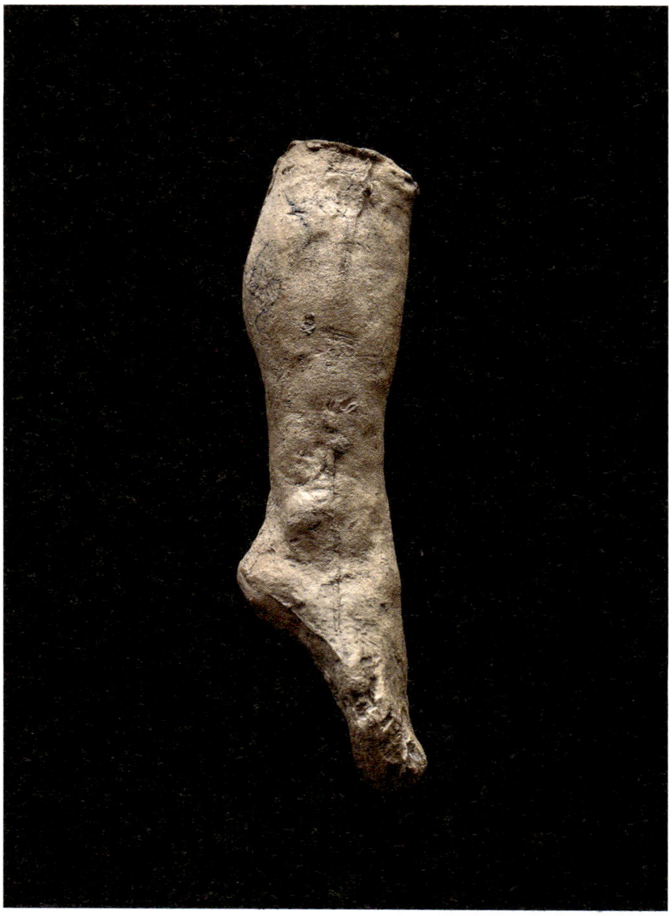

44

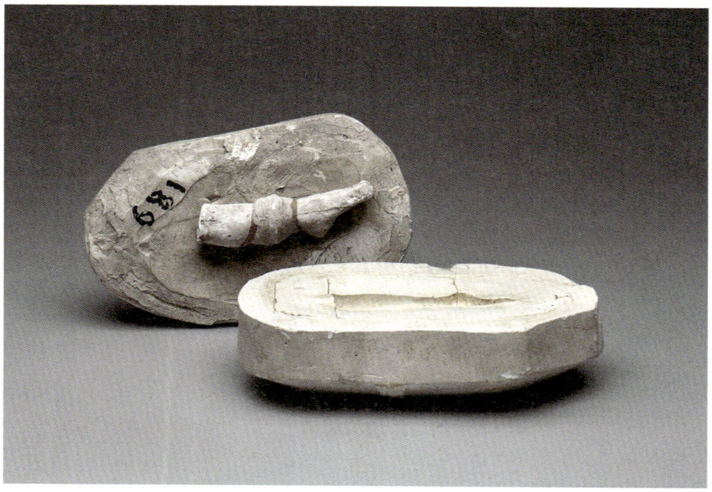

Detail of cat.43, Mould of the lower right leg of *Beta*

appearance of Rodin's sculpture at this time was more and more the result of the interface with studio practices such as casting, enlarging and transferring to marble.[3] Guioché could either have re-used an existing mould to press-mould ten new clay heads (and perhaps to cast a plaster head of *Beta* at the same time) or else made a new mould from an existing clay or plaster head. That level of technical minutiae is lost but much of the rest can be reconstructed thanks to the vast archival documentation and collection of moulds of the Musée Rodin. We know, for certain, that, from this kit of nine moulds, Rodin would have had at his disposal quite a large number of clay body parts and heads to play with, which could have been made for him in several campaigns or all at once. We know that, from these, he created the series of a dozen figures that were given the title of *Mouvements de danse* and cast in bronze posthumously. If, as seems likely, he made the series in one campaign (rather than having several groups of parts press-moulded at various intervals), then it probably did not take longer than a couple of weeks to construct and alter them, considering that the clay would otherwise have begun to lose its malleability. It seems very few people saw the series, and the only person to have written about them at all is Count Kessler, who described them as "unfinished" works, which expresses well their lack of 'finish' and their experimental character.[4]

3 See for example, Blanchetière 2013.
4 For a discussion of Count Kessler's visits to Rodin, see the essay by Antoinette Le Normand-Romain in this volume.

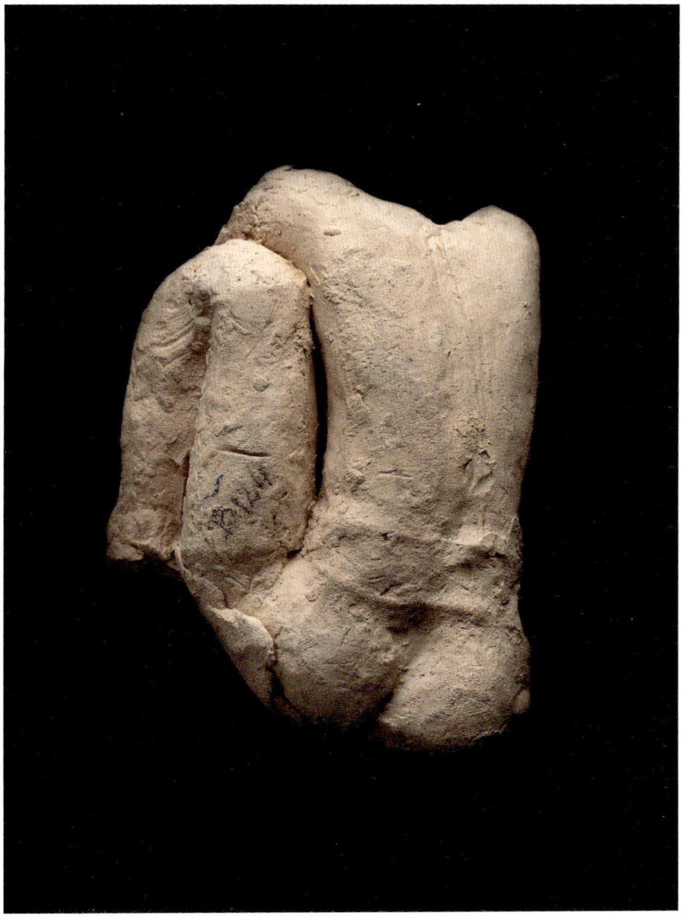
45

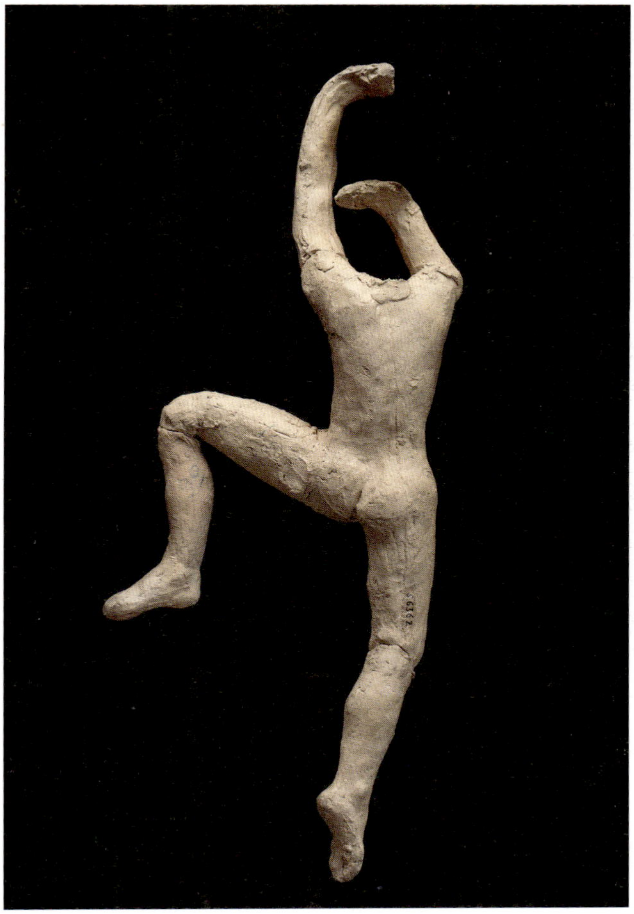
46

47–50

Mouvement A, 1911

Terracotta, 29.2 x 14.8 x 7.9 cm
Musée Rodin, Paris, S.5492

Mouvement A, 1911 or after

Plaster slip over plaster, 31 x 13.8 x 8.3 cm
Musée Rodin, Paris, S.3303

Assemblage of two Mouvement A figures, or Pas de deux A, 1911 or after

Plaster, 32 x 17 x 13.6 cm
Musée Rodin, Paris, S.357

Mouvement A, enlargement, 1956 (original plaster, 1911 or after)

Bronze, cast by Georges Rudier (no.3), 70.5 x 30.2 x 21.9 cm
The Samuel Courtauld Trust, The Courtauld Gallery, London, S.2006.LB.3

As the technical study for this exhibition has demonstrated (see Blanchetière, Cascio and Lévy, pp.61–76), all of the figures in the series of the *Mouvements de danse* were assembled using the limbs and torsos of the 'original' plaster casts *Alpha* and *Beta* (cat.42). Only *Mouvements* A and E derive from the body parts of *Alpha* (see diagram, pp.66–67); all the others derive from *Beta*. Comparing *Mouvement A* (cat.47 and 48) with the various drawings of a nude figure in profile holding her leg behind her head (cat.25–27, 30), the most notable differences are that *Mouvement A* has acquired a left arm and that the head, which was just nestled in the crook of the neck, has become an active and expressive part of the sculpture. Obviously these are not so much differences as they are developments of an idea expressed in graphic terms into an idea expressed sculpturally. In *Mouvement A* Rodin amplified the idea of formal unity in the pose and imparted a more sensual character to it, for example with the detail of the head touching the top of the left arm. Rodin flattened the junction of hand and foot by scraping the clay flat while it was not yet dry. The idea of circular motion, inherent in the pose itself, with its twists and diagonal tensions, is reinforced by the position of the arms reaching up and back, and the upward motion is further enhanced by the addition of the neck stretching back. On paper, Rodin had explored the pose in various orientations (fig.58), of which the horizontal position resembles an acrobatic limbering exercise on the floor.[1]

Rodin was evidently pleased with the form in sculpture since he subsequently had it cast in plaster (cat.48), made an assemblage of two *Mouvement A* figures (cat.49), made two further assemblages, this time attaching a pair of wings to each of the figures, and had the single figure enlarged to a little more than twice its initial size (cat.50). The foot in *Mouvement A* (cat.48) rests very lightly on the ground, with the heel slightly lifted – a detail already present in the life drawing of a nude figure in profile holding her leg behind her head (cat.25) and seen in all subsequent developments from it (cat.26–27). This adds to the idea of upward movement, and imparts lightness to the figure, in contrast to the effort required to maintain the pose. The assemblage of two *Mouvement A* figures (cat.49) is interesting: Rodin

1 I would like to thank Viola Bruni, a former acrobat with the Accademia dell'arte circense, for this insight.

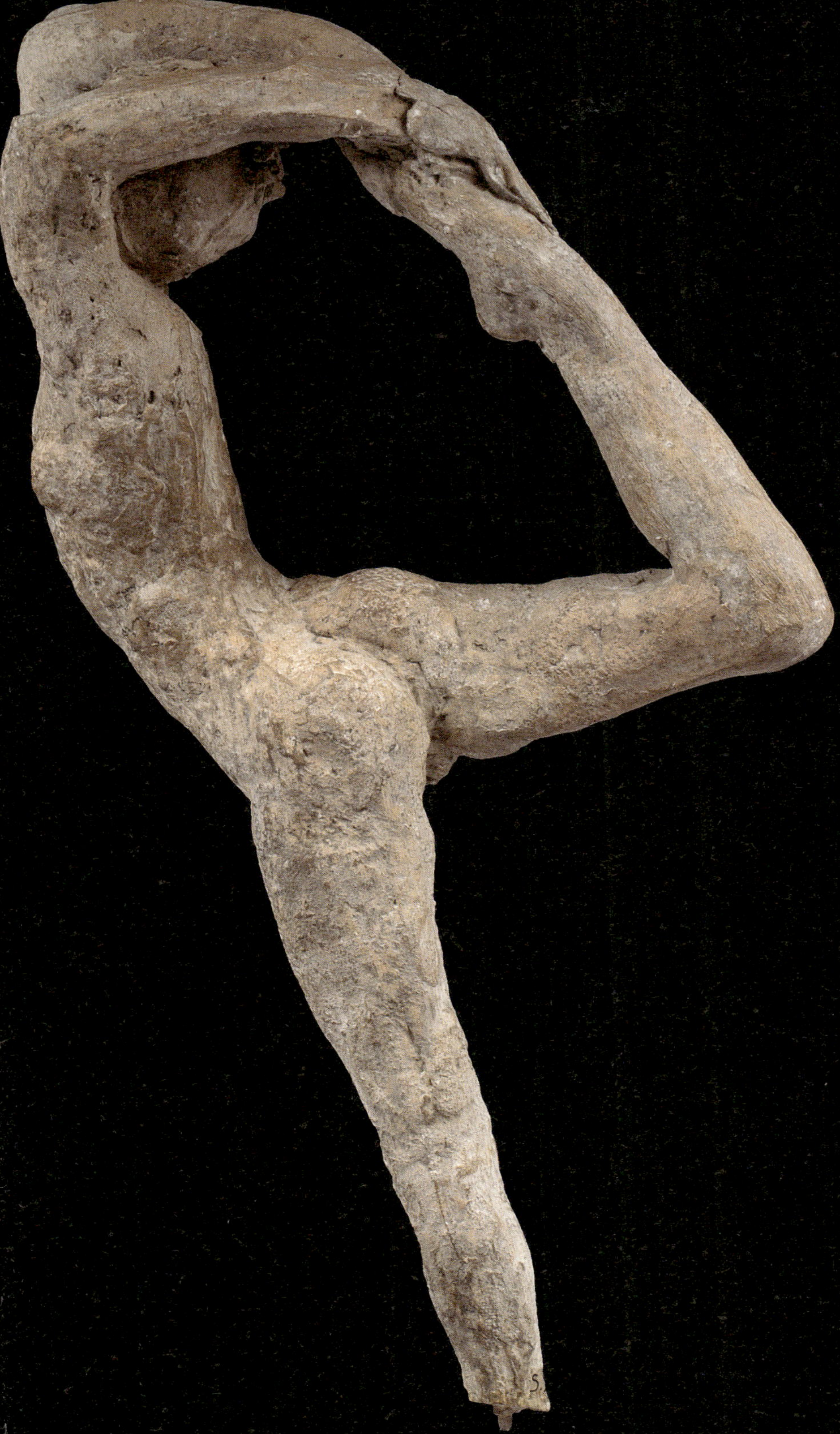

47

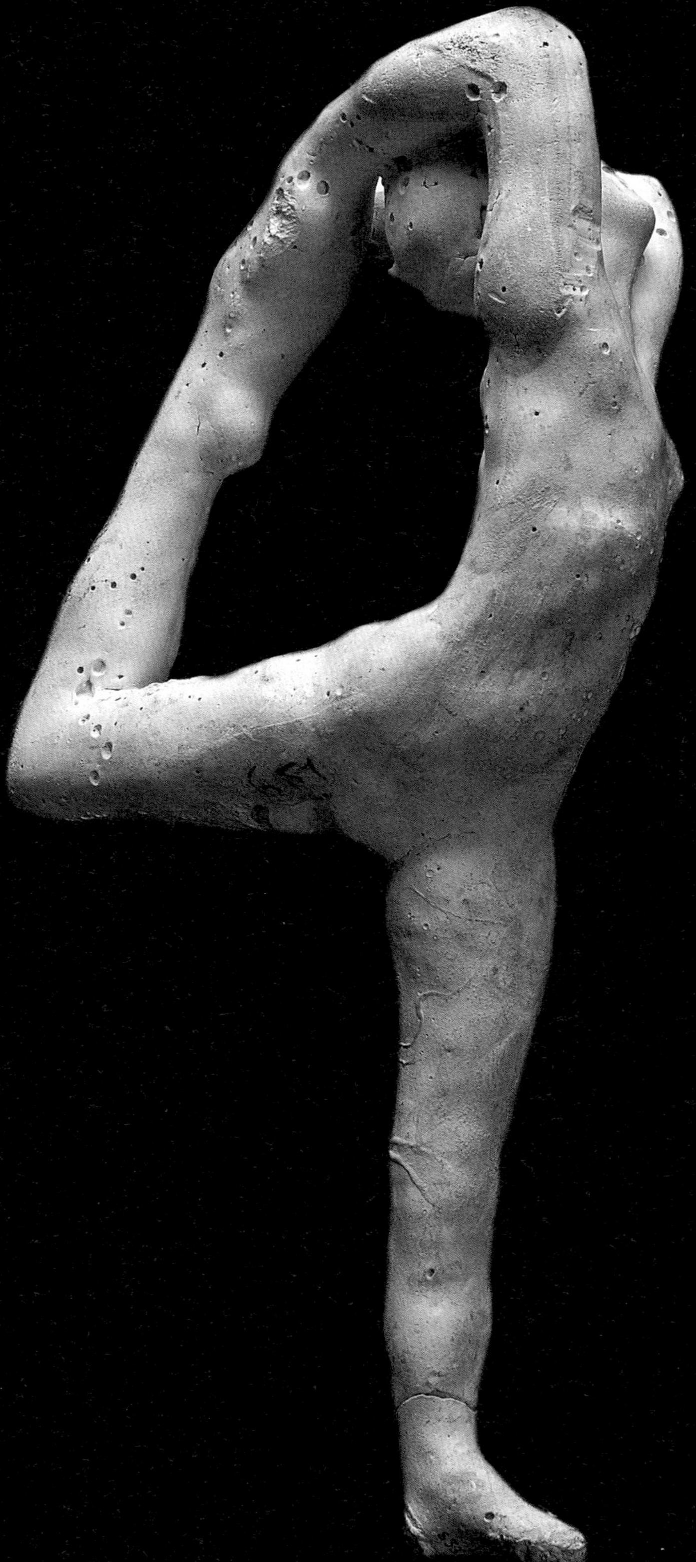

has canted one figure ever so slightly forward and the other figure ever so slightly backward, almost as if they had slipped. In the two assemblages of *Mouvement A* figures with wings on a column (one of which is on an egg), the impossible lightness of the stance makes sense because the figures are apparently preparing to fly: one is tipped forward, her toes barely touching the top of the column or egg, and the other is already airborne (fig.19, p.36 and fig.43, p.72). This group seems to have been connected to a monument to aviators Rodin was planning in these years.[2] The writer Michel Georges-Michel, in his recollection of a visit to Rodin's studio of about 1913, referred in response to seeing this figure to a statue of *Diana* resting softly on her toes by Jean-Antoine Houdon, a sculptor admired by Rodin.[3]

Rodin had *Mouvement A* enlarged by more than two times its height, perhaps to test out the effect of the work at an increased scale. This was posthumously cast in bronze (cat.50) for the Musée Rodin by Georges Rudier in 1956, and

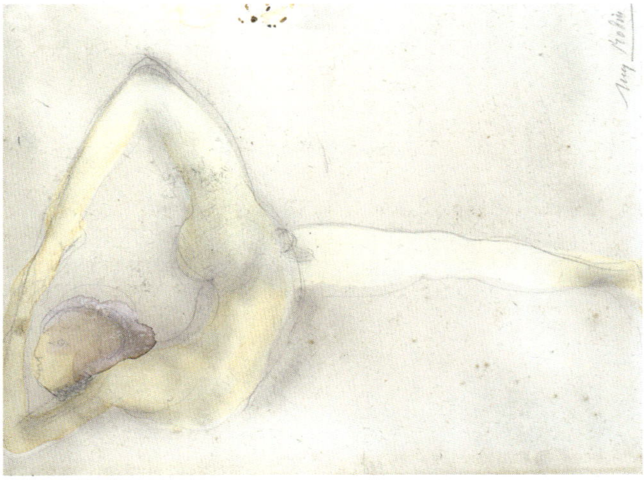

FIG.58
Auguste Rodin
Female nude holding her leg behind her head (with the addition of a small penis and beard), reoriented according to the inscription *bas* (bottom), c.1900-05
Pencil and watercolour on paper, 326 x 250 mm
Private collection

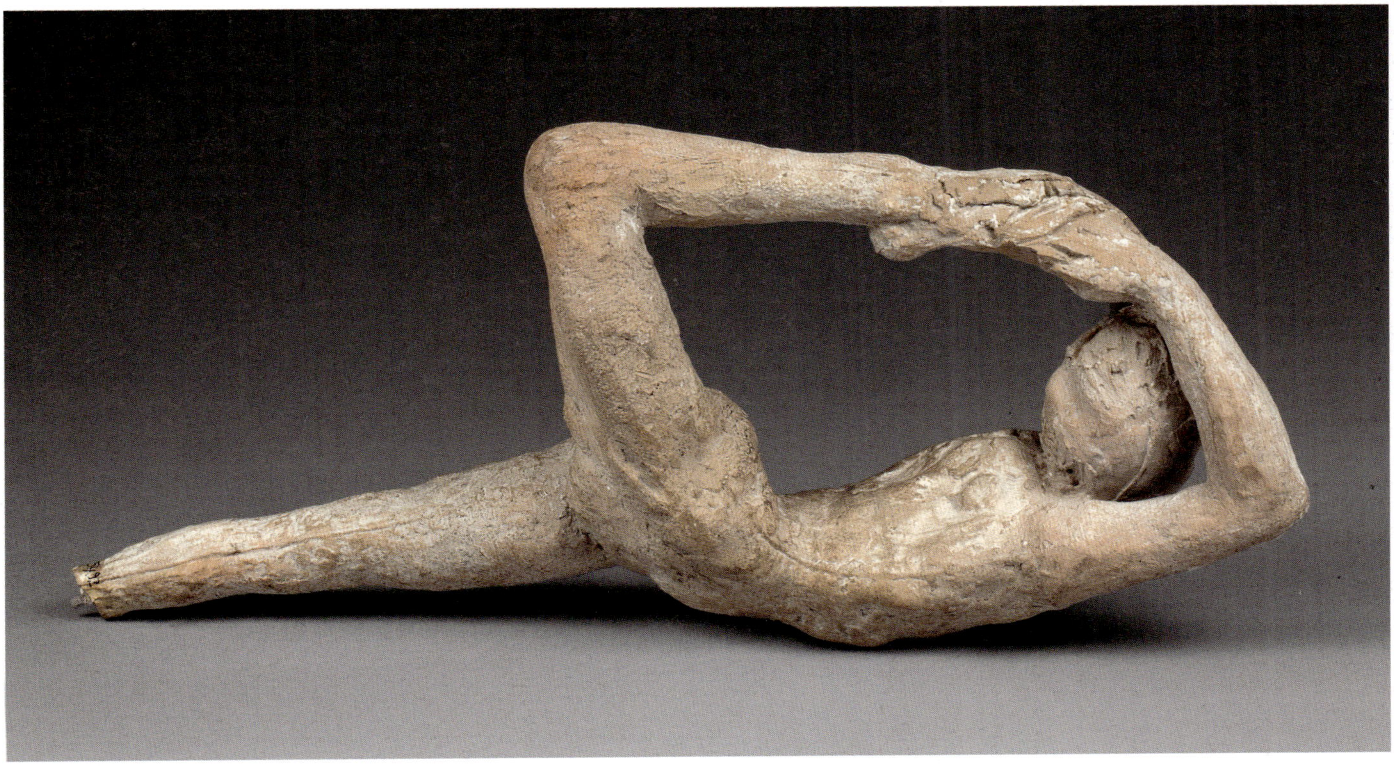

47

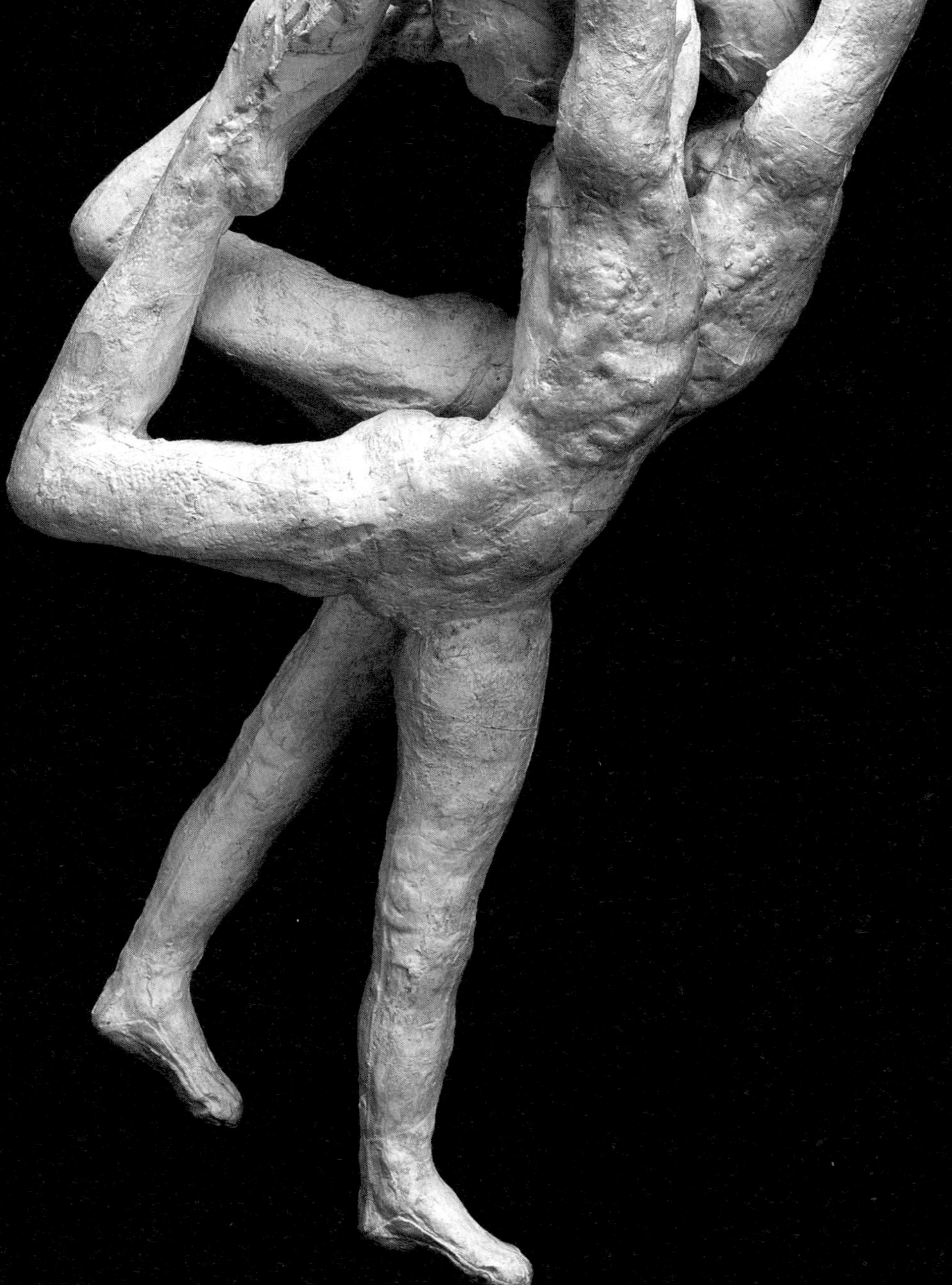

bought by the London gallery Roland, Browse & Delbanco in August of that year. This gallery became the Musée Rodin's unofficial agent in Britain following an exhibition it held of Rodin's bronzes in 1953, in which they mostly showed small bronzes, including "the first five of the series of *Danseuses*". Over the years the gallery bought about fifty *Mouvements de danse*, and sold them very quickly. This figure was marketed in England as *Grande Danseuse A*. The present bronze was bequeathed to the Courtauld's collection by the dealer Lillian Browse, for whom it was apparently bought by an acquaintance who understood how much she "coveted" it, in her words. The considerable correspondence between the Musée Rodin and the gallery, concerning, among other things, prices, waiting times, transport and the quality of the bronzes, gives an idea of the commercial side of the Musée Rodin under its director Cécile Goldscheider.[4]

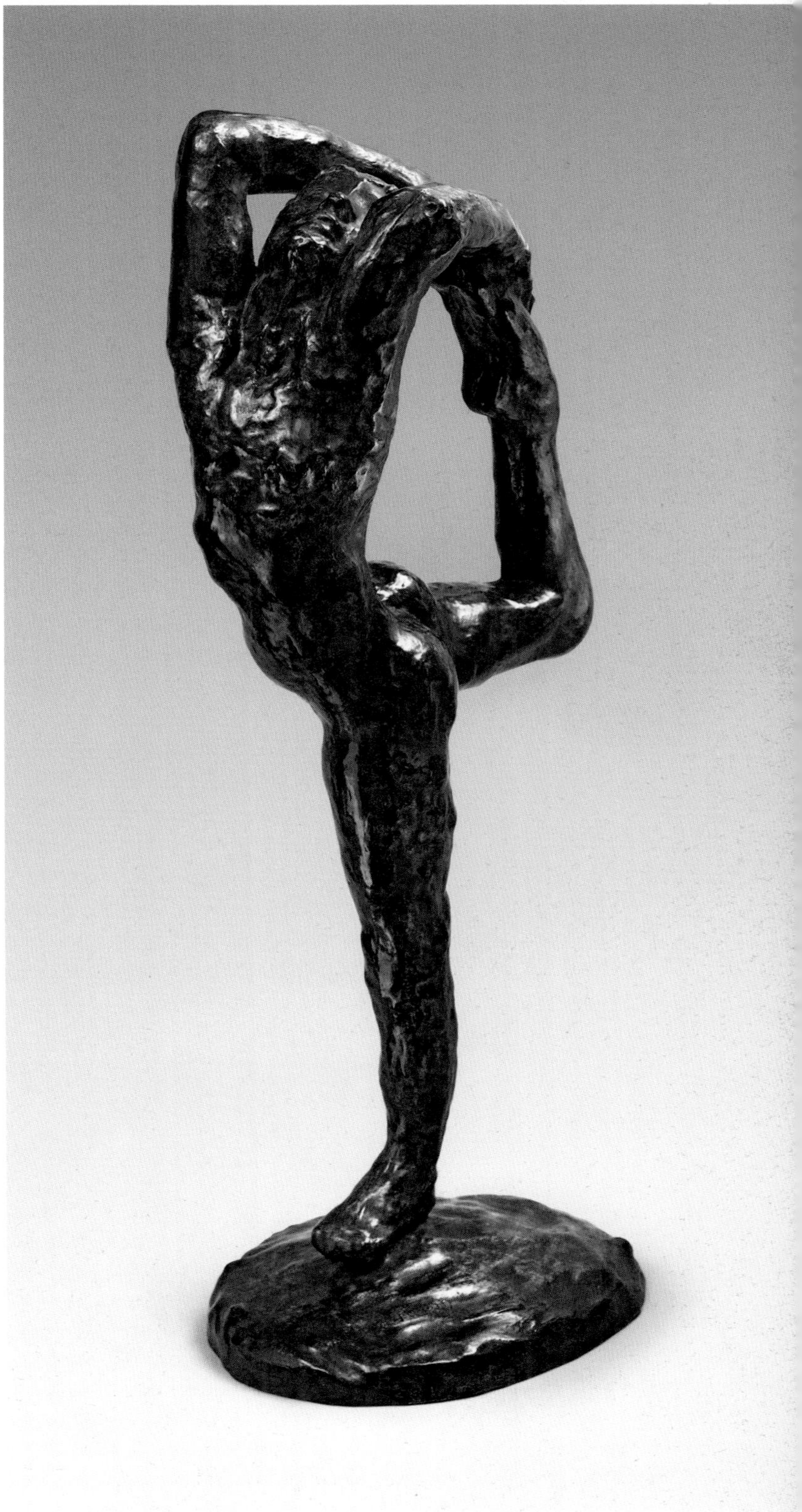

50

2 Georges-Michel 1942, p.261–70. See Blanchetière, Cascio and Lévy in this volume, pp.72–73. Rodin's discussion of the 'French' type of female beauty, as exemplified by Houdon's *Diana*, seems an appropriate comparison with this figure. See Rodin, 'La beauté de la femme', 1910, in Rodin 2008, pp.140–41.

3 See Blanchetière, Cascio and Lévy in this volume, p.72.

4 Archives of the Musée Rodin. See Browse 1999, pp.162–66. This is one of four Rodin bronzes bequeathed by Lillian Browse to The Courtauld Gallery, the others being *Nijinsky* (cat.80), *Scream* and the assemblage *Pas-de-deux B*.

51–53

Mouvement E, 1911

Terracotta, 37.5 x 26 x 12.2 cm
Musée Rodin, Paris, S.225

Mouvement E, 1911 or after

Plaster, 31.2 x 15.5 x 7.5 cm
Musée Rodin, Paris, S.3286

Standing nude in a three-quarter profile holding her right foot behind her with her right hand (Alda Moreno), called Aviation, c.1910–13

Pencil on wove paper, 361 x 231 mm
Inscribed: *souveraine d'équilibre / emblème de puissance / aviation* (sovereign balance / emblem of power / aviation)
Musée Rodin, Paris, D.1629

Rodin had *Mouvement E* (cat.51 & 52) cast in plaster, which suggests that he considered it a successful enough composition on which he wanted to continue working (doing the same for A, B and G). Although the sculpture preserves some of the upward motion of *Mouvement A*, notably in the front arm curving skywards and in the position of the supporting foot, which is not flat but slightly hovering, the general impression is of stability rather than ascent. Unlike the pose that inspired *Mouvement A*, which involves tension pulling the body upwards to maintain balance, this pose itself is more balanced. Rodin's sculpture reflects this stability, which it further reinforces through strong horizontal and vertical axes. The differences between the two sculptures are all the more striking considering that both figures were built up around casts of an identical torso. This demonstrates how Rodin conceptualised the human body in terms of architectural harmony, with the overall aspect of a work determined by the relationship of properly proportioned parts rather than by the parts themselves. Rodin was thus able to repurpose body parts that were conceived originally for a different function (here, the torso was twisting and pulling upwards in the more challenging pose of *Alpha*), and make them work in a new context. As he was working with malleable clay, he could also pull and bend it at will. Details, such as placing the figure's gaze straight ahead rather than skywards, or the elongated right arm reaching far back to take hold of the lifted leg, which creates a very definite rectangular shape between the limbs, contribute towards the impression of stability. A final flourish of the work is the lifted arm extending upwards, with the hand appearing to hold an indeterminate object in a triumphant gesture, perhaps of victory.

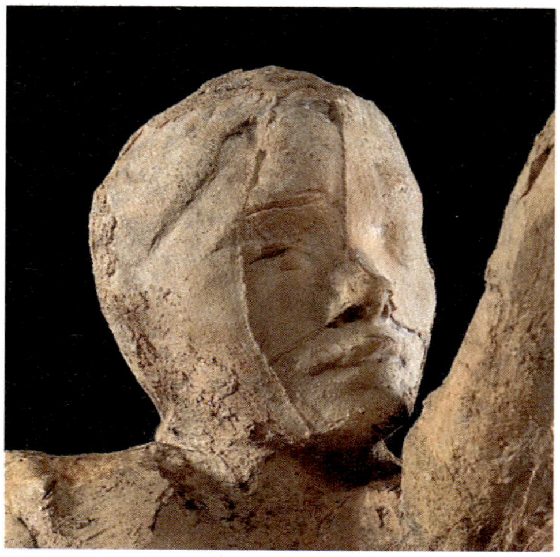

Detail of S.225, cat. 51

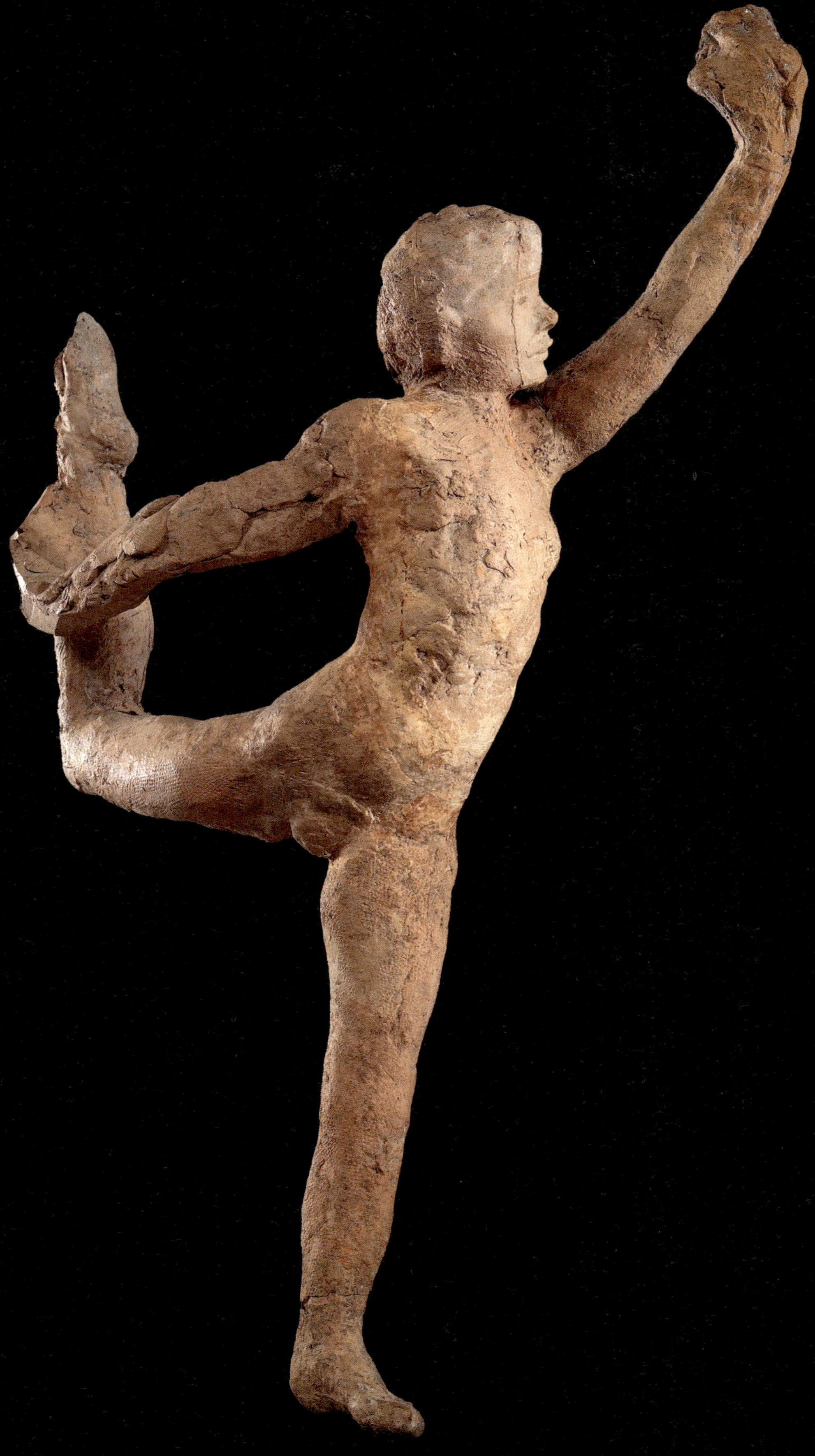

51

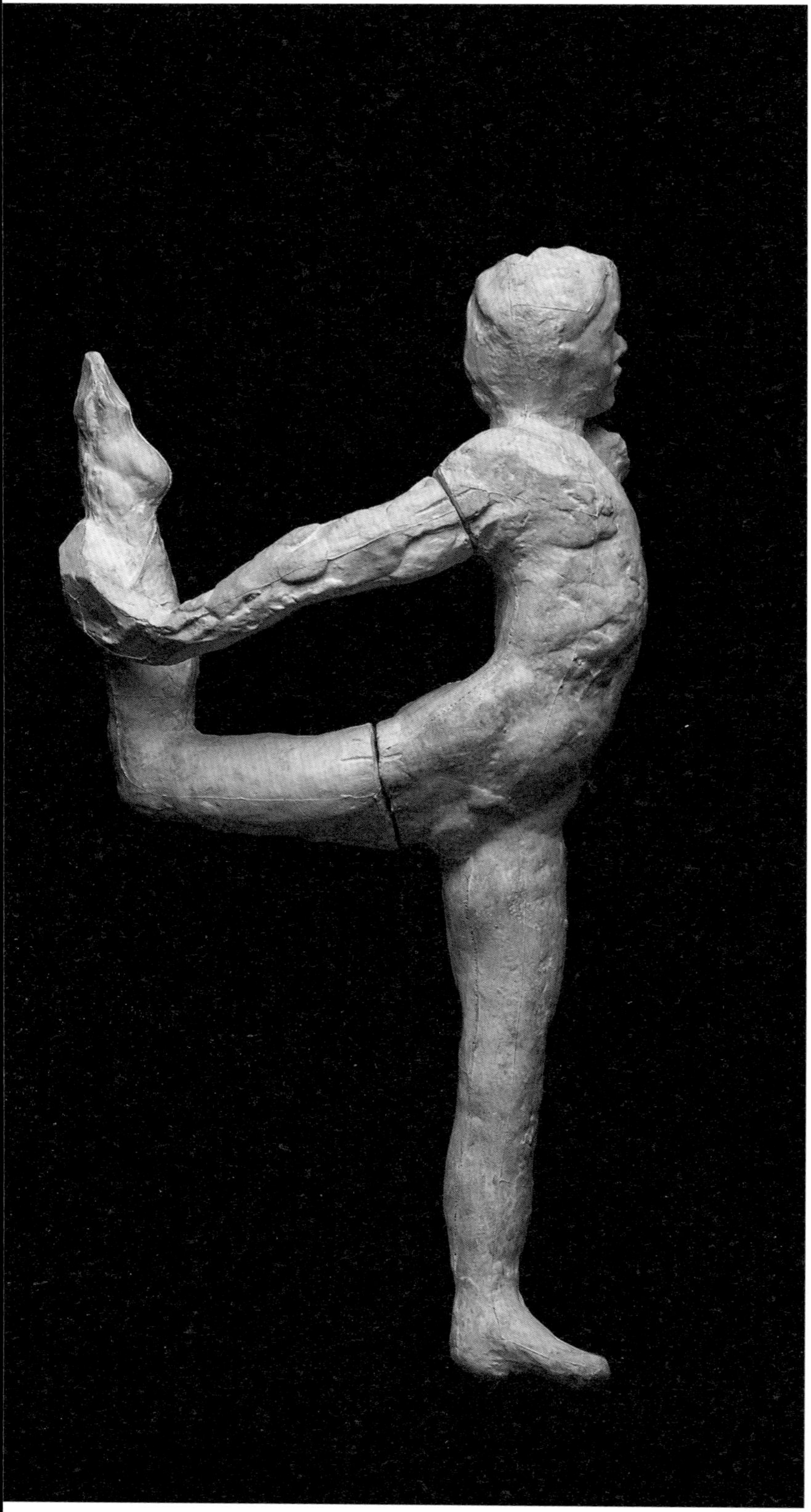

52

A simple pencil drawing of a standing nude in a three-quarter profile holding her foot behind her with her right hand (D.1629, cat.53) offers a side view of the same pose with only minor differences, notably in the way the arm reaching for the raised leg wraps around the ankle, which in the drawing produces a squarer shape between the limbs. This drawing expresses the idea of stability explicitly in its inscription, which translates as 'sovereign balance / emblem of power / aviation'. It is interesting that in these small figure studies Rodin seems to be exploring both the idea of stability and the idea of a dynamic upward current associated with flight and aviation. The inscription could be viewed in the context of a letter of early 1911 in the archives of the Musée Rodin in which a pilot explains the role of stability in aerodynamics, as opposed to speed and motion.[1] AG

1 André Dumoulin to Rodin, 2 January 1911, Dumoulin correspondence file, archives of the Musée Rodin.

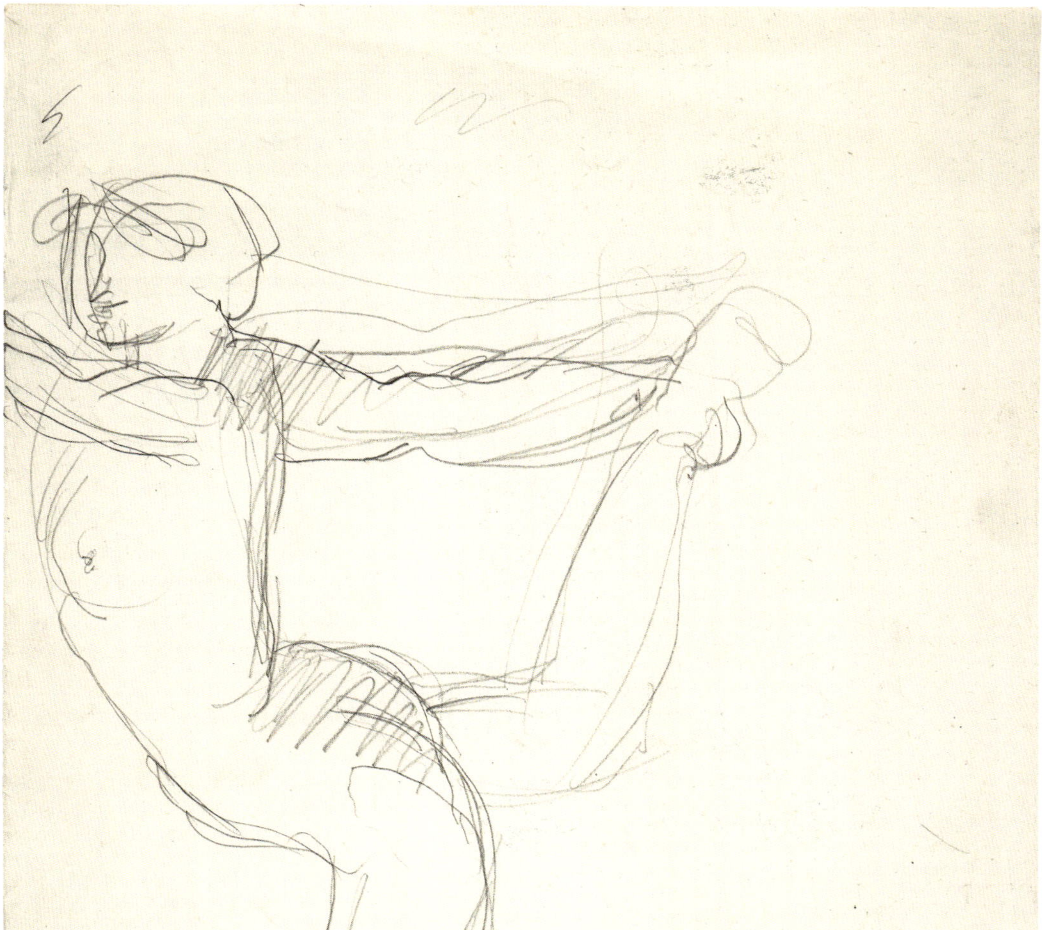

53

54–55

Mouvement C, 1911

Terracotta, 34.3 x 18.1 x 11.8 cm
Musée Rodin, Paris, S.5830

Female nude stretching, c.1900

Pencil with stumping, watercolour and gouache on wove paper, 327 x 252 mm
Inscribed: *bas* (bottom)
Musée Rodin, Paris, D.4414

Mouvement C (cat.54), along with *Mouvement G* (cat.59), is the most versatile of the figures in the series. Rodin developed the pose in a group of drawings dating to around 1900–05, showing a figure in a tripod position (see cat.39–41), and he may have seen the lunging pose of *Beta* (see cat.42 and fig.59, reconstructed) as a preparatory move into this posture. Although the figure appears to be most stable in the tripod position, two further orientations of *Mouvement C* are equally plausible: standing up and kicking with the motion of a music-hall dancer (analogous to D.4914, cat.41, oriented upwards), or on its back, in a dynamic stretching position with arms in the air.

The watercolour and gouache drawing of a nude stretching (D.4414, cat.55), with one hand on the ground and the other pulling her upper body towards her leg, shares with *Mouvement C* a sense of variability in orientation. It was, apparently, initially sketched as a floor-based posture, and another drawing (D.4254) shows what the pose must have looked like before Rodin moved the arm position from hugging the lower left leg (still visible in cat.55) to quickly and crudely placing it in a position on the ground. AG

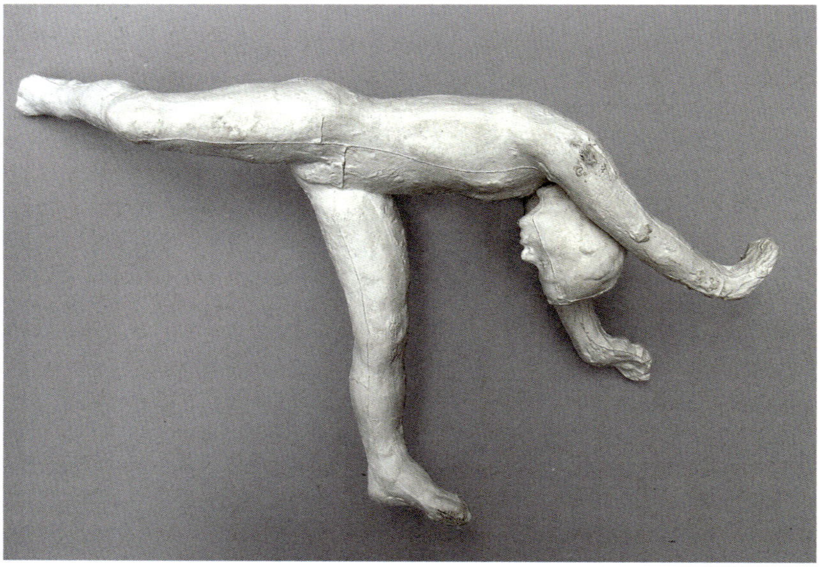

FIG.59
Modern cast and proposed reconstruction of *Beta*, 2016

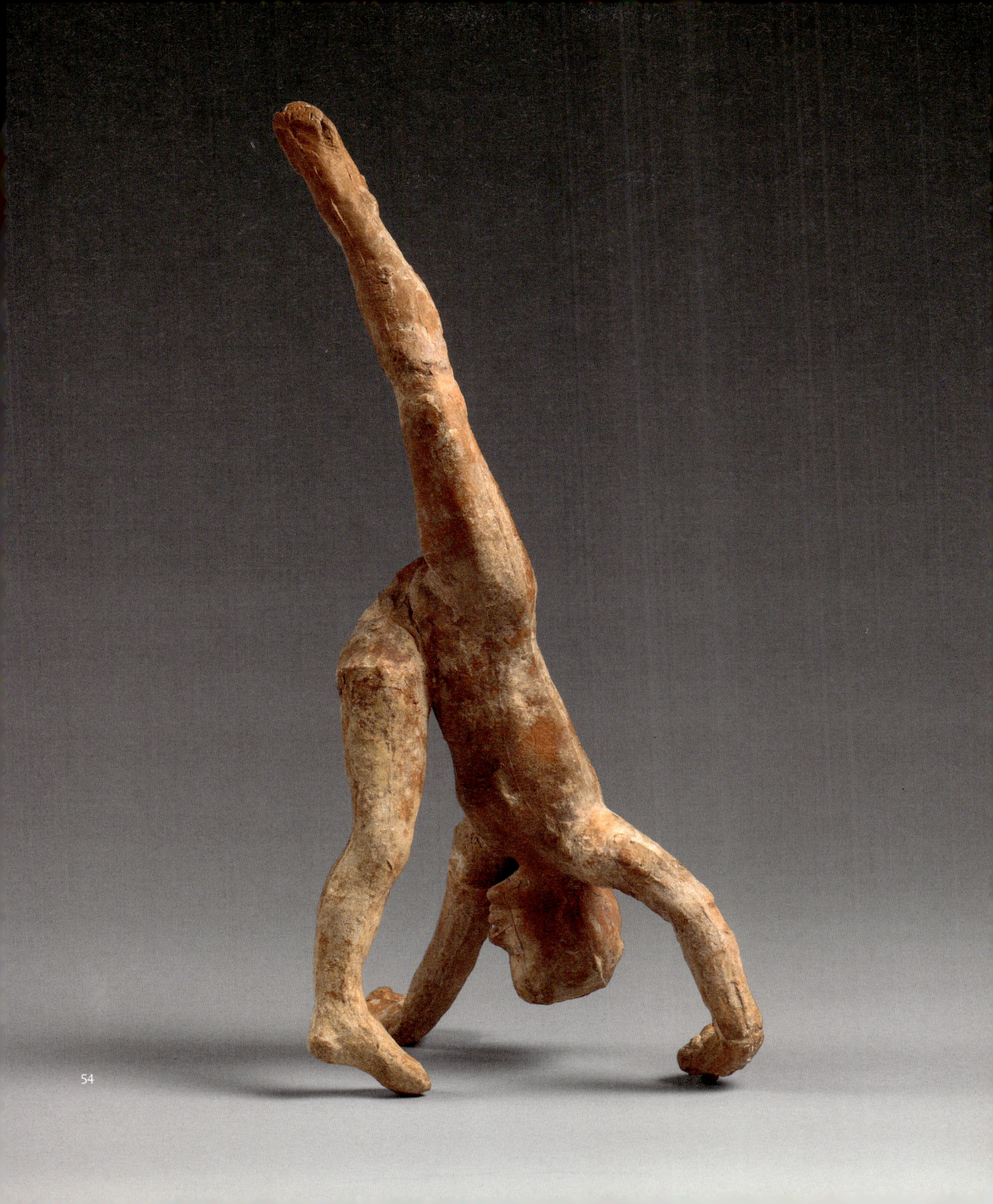

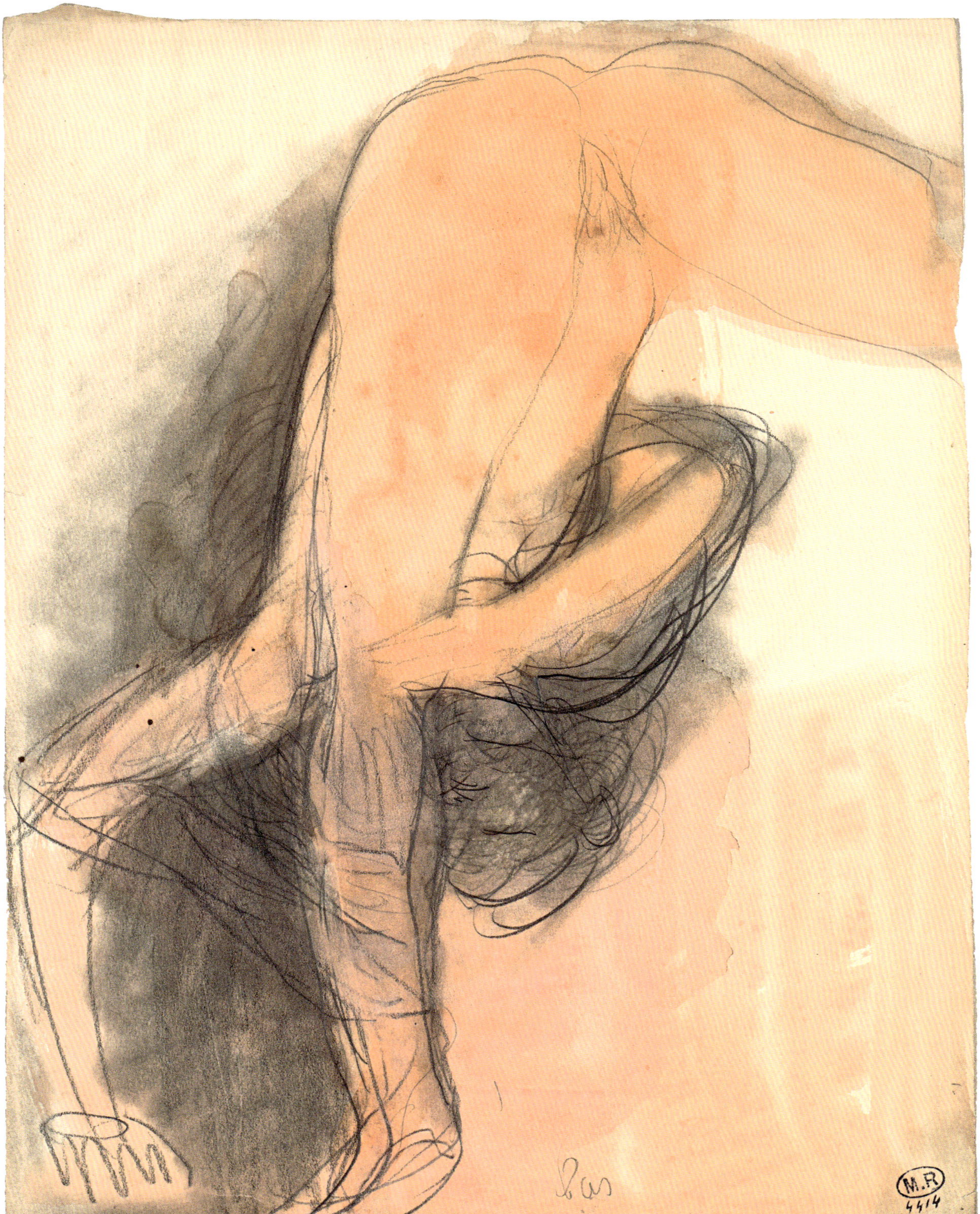
M.R
4414

56–58

Female nude pulling her leg over her shoulder, after 1909

Pencil with stumping on laid paper, 382 x 233 mm
Musée Rodin, Paris, D.1804

Mouvement B, 1911

Terracotta, 33 x 13 x 11.8 cm
Musée Rodin, Paris, S.3796

Mouvement B, 1911 or after

Plaster, 33.6 x 12.2 x 10.5 cm
Musée Rodin, Paris, S.3669

Mouvement B (cat.57 and 58) may represent a paused transitional move into an acrobatic levering of the upraised leg behind the torso.[1] As such it fits in with what Rodin told Paul Gsell about movement in *L'Art*, the collection of interviews published in 1911: "movement is the transition from one attitude to another", and, further, the artist "makes visible the passage of one pose into the other".[2] In *Mouvement B*, the right hand and left foot pull against each other, and the left hand slips through to create the tension necessary to maintain such a posture. A comparable intertwining of limbs is found in the drawing of a figure appearing to pull her leg over her shoulder and through her arm, possibly observed when the model was stretching on the floor (D.1804, cat.56). *Mouvement B* also operates as a floor-based stretch, which suits the version without a head, B+ (cat.61), particularly well.

The left leg of *Mouvement B* is twisted in a physically impossible rotation: the hip and upper thigh come out at a slight twist from the torso, where the hip joint would be, but then the leg below the knee twists again in another direction. This results in an aesthetically pleasing curved line, which expresses the essence of the pose, and echoes Rodin's statement that "Always, always, I have copied nature in its naivety, and it is by exaggerating movement that I sometimes obtain a flexibility that approaches the truth".[3] *Mouvement B* is the only figure of the series that Rodin had translated into marble (see fig.42, p.71). AG

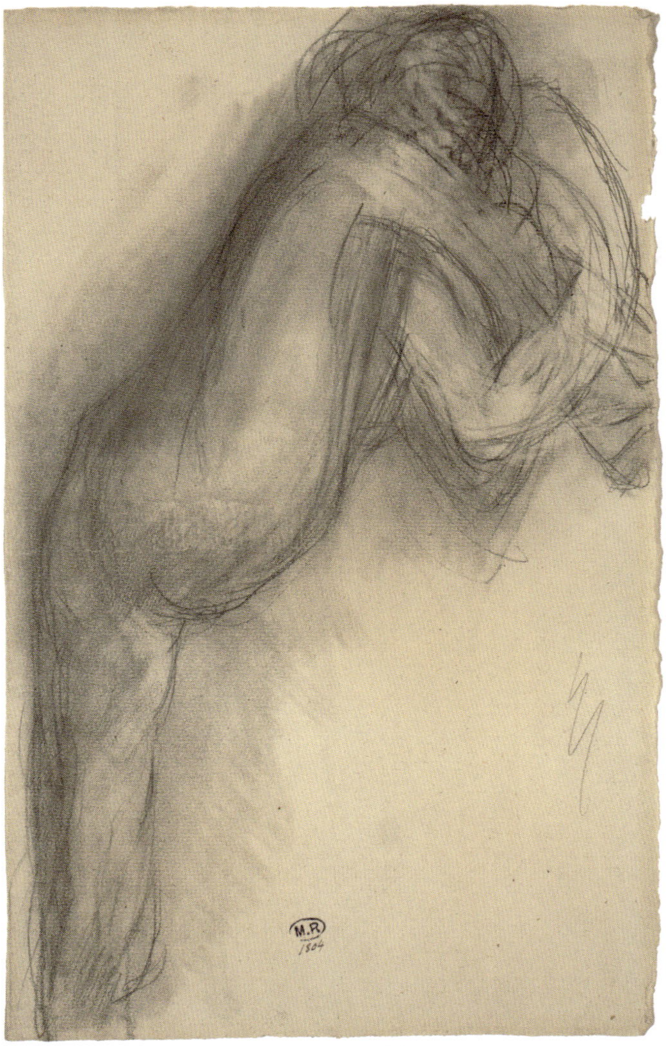

56

1 I am grateful to Viola Bruni for this insight.
2 Rodin 1911/1984, pp.28 and 29.
3 "*Toujours, toujours, j'ai copié la nature dans sa naïveté, et c'est en exagérant le mouvement que j'obtiens parfois une souplesse qui se rapproche du vrai*": from 'Rodin par lui-même', in *Je sais tout*, March 1910, in Rodin 2008, pp.53–58, at p.55.

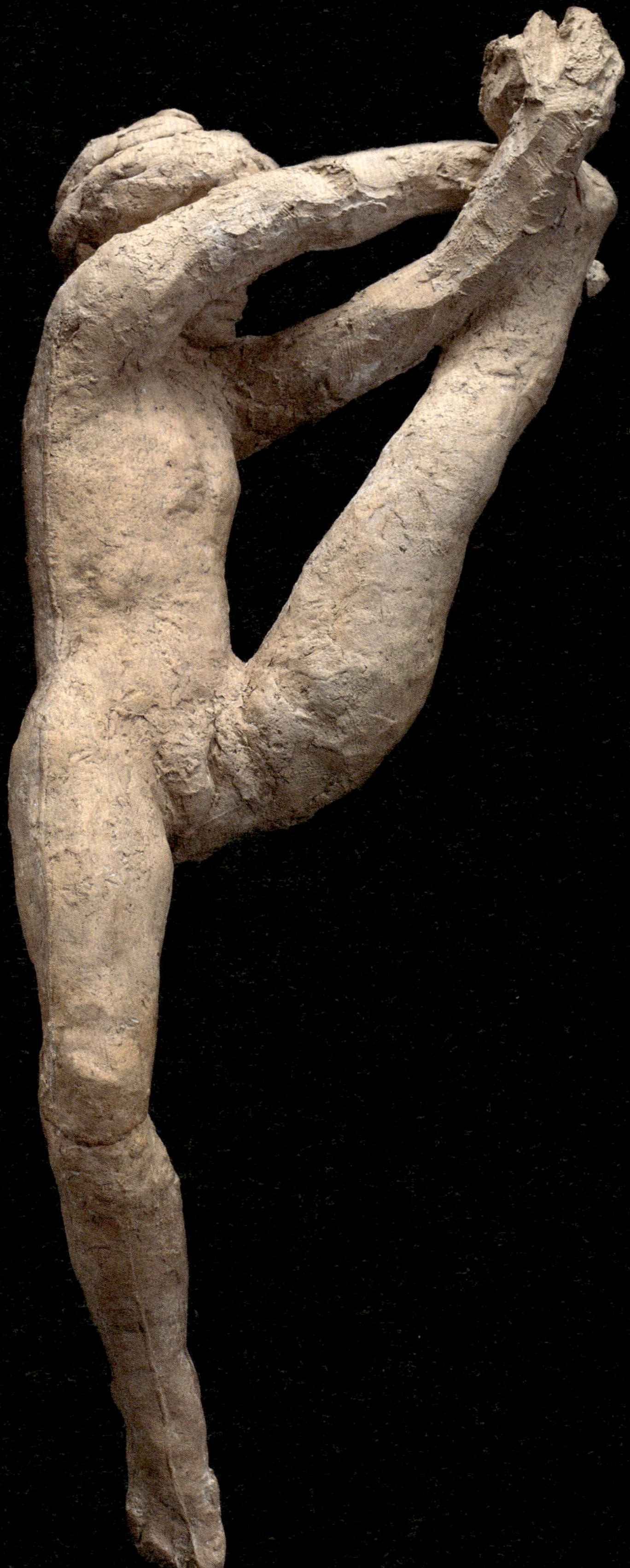

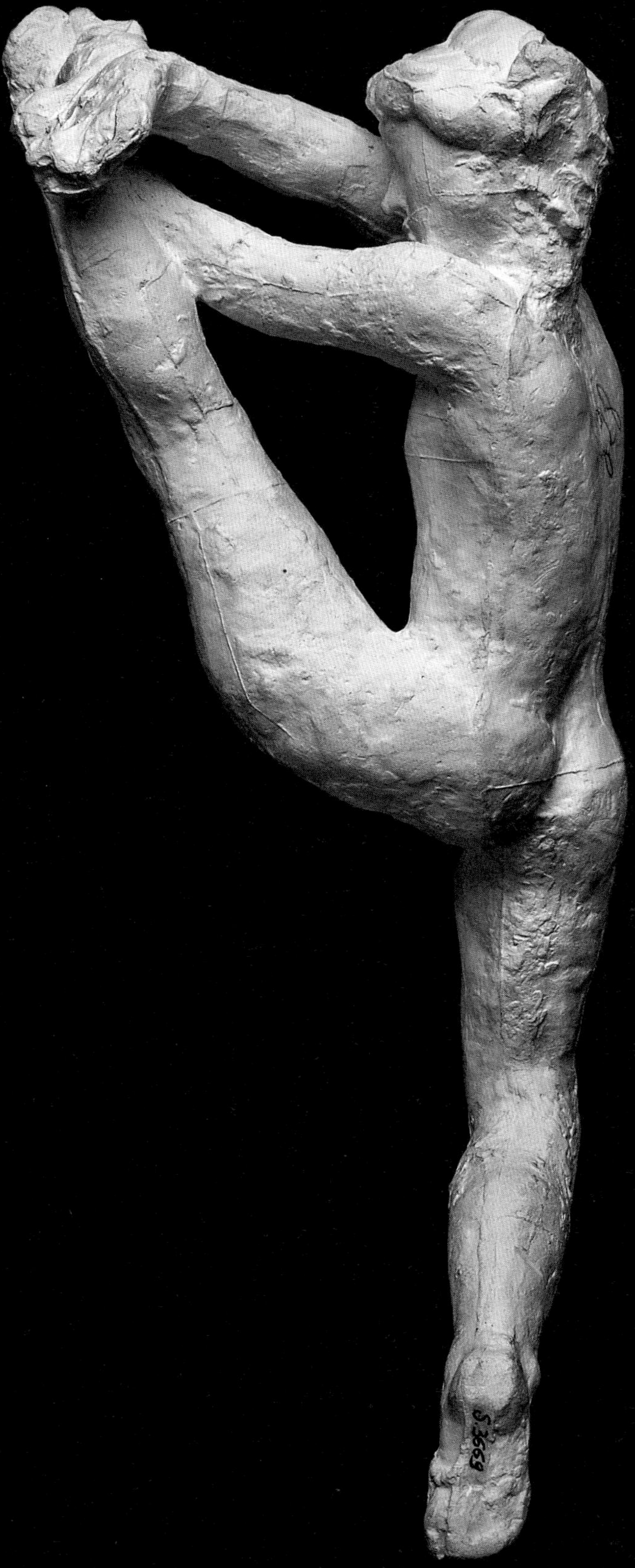

59–62

Mouvement G, 1911 or after

Plaster slip over plaster, 32.5 x 11.5 x 8.5 cm
Musée Rodin, Paris, S.1051

Mouvement H, 1911

Terracotta, 27 x 11.8 x 9 cm
Musée Rodin, Paris, S.118

Mouvement B+, 1911

Terracotta, 34.6 x 9.4 x 8.9 cm
Musée Rodin, Paris, S.5491

Female nude standing on her left leg and stretching forward, or in a headstand, after 1909

Pencil with stumping on laid paper, 383 x 298 mm
Musée Rodin, Paris, D.1812

In these poses, the figures stretch deeply, always with an active left leg and a slightly bent right leg. Various orientations are possible: as all three sculptures rest comfortably on the horizontal, representing floor-based stretches, they can also be turned around. Orientating *Mouvement H* (cat.60) so it is upside down brings it close to the pencil sketch of a figure stretching (D.1812, cat.62), which could have been drawn with the model either in a headstand position or else leaning against a wall, as shown here. The drawing is somewhat difficult to read because there was a fold in the sheet, just where the head and arm abruptly end, which has since been flattened out. Rodin would probably not have noticed the fold and simply used it as the edge of the sheet. It is worth noting that another drawing in this series, which shows the model in a similar position either on the floor or, as seems more plausible in this case, in a standing stretch against a wall, is inscribed *Mlle A.*, presumably for Alda Moreno (D.1834). When *Mouvement G* (cat.59) is inverted it shares similar qualities of extension in the legs with the tripod position of

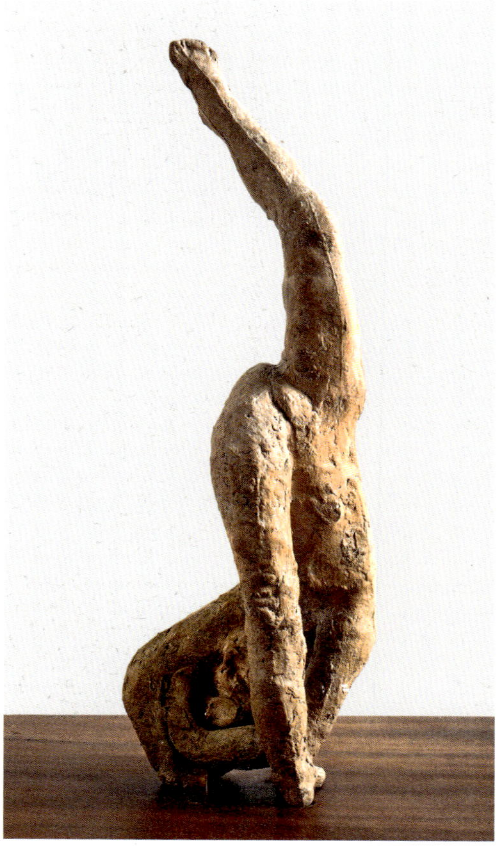

FIG.60
Auguste Rodin
Mouvement G, 1911
Terracotta, *c.*32 x 11.5 x 8.5 cm
Galeria Nazionale d'Arte Moderna e Contemporeana, Rome

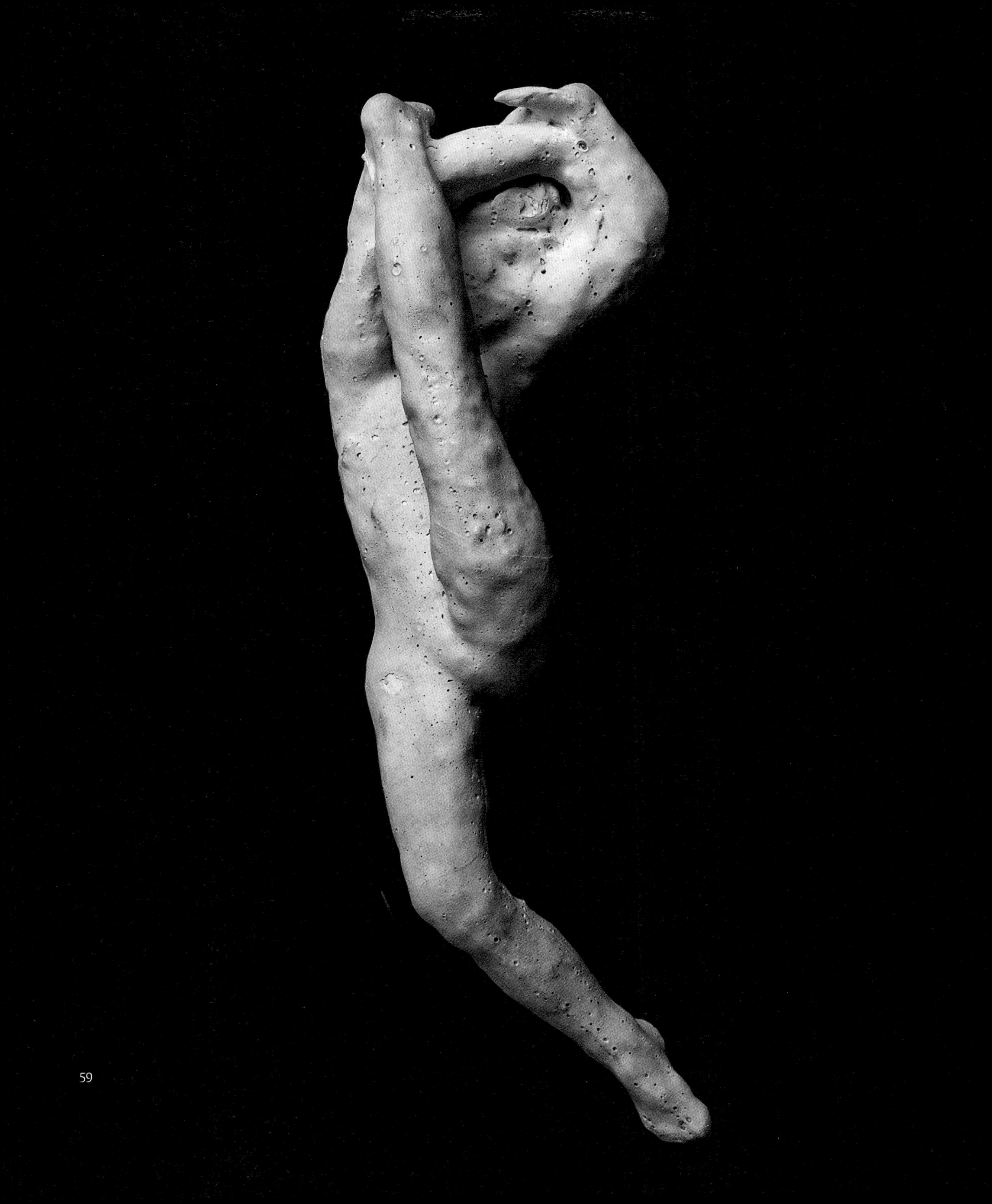

Mouvement C (cat.54). However, the hands and arms of *Mouvement G* are closer together, giving it a quality of movement that is more like a headstand preparation. The way the arms cradle the head creates a support for the sculpture, which makes it stand almost unaided in an inverted vertical position, perhaps confirming this as the optimum one. *Mouvement G* was one of the four figures in the series that Rodin carried on to the further stage of casting in plaster (the others are A, B and E). Rodin covered the work in a plaster slip, which both subdues any detail by 'enveloping' the forms in a smooth and even texture (comparable to his use of stumping in his drawings of the 1910s), and exploits the accidental nature of the process (dipping the work into a vat of slip) to arrive at a surface that moves away from representation towards abstraction.

Mouvement G is the only terracotta figure in the series of the *Mouvements de danse* with which Rodin is known to have parted (fig.60).[1] Its provenance in the collection of the widow of Count Enrico di San Martino e Valperga (1863–1947), a prominent Roman senator and cultural impresario who, along with influential modernist art critics such as Vittorio Pica and Ugo Ojetti, championed Rodin's work in Italy, makes it worth asking how and when he could have acquired it.[2] Although they met in 1902, the real connection was undoubtedly made around 1911 when San Martino organised the Rome Biennale, in which he made sure Rodin was well represented. In 1913, he organised the exhibition of the Secessionists in Rome, in which he managed to secure an entire room for Rodin's work. San Martino's letters to Rodin show that he was particularly keen that the sculptor send his

1 There is another figure, one of the two versions of *Mouvement I* (cat.65), but the circumstances are far less clear in that case.

2 Bequeathed by San Martino's widow to the Galeria Nazionale d'Arte Moderna. I would like to thank Stefania Frezzotti for first alerting me to the significance of the provenance of this work, which unfortunately could not be lent to the exhibition.

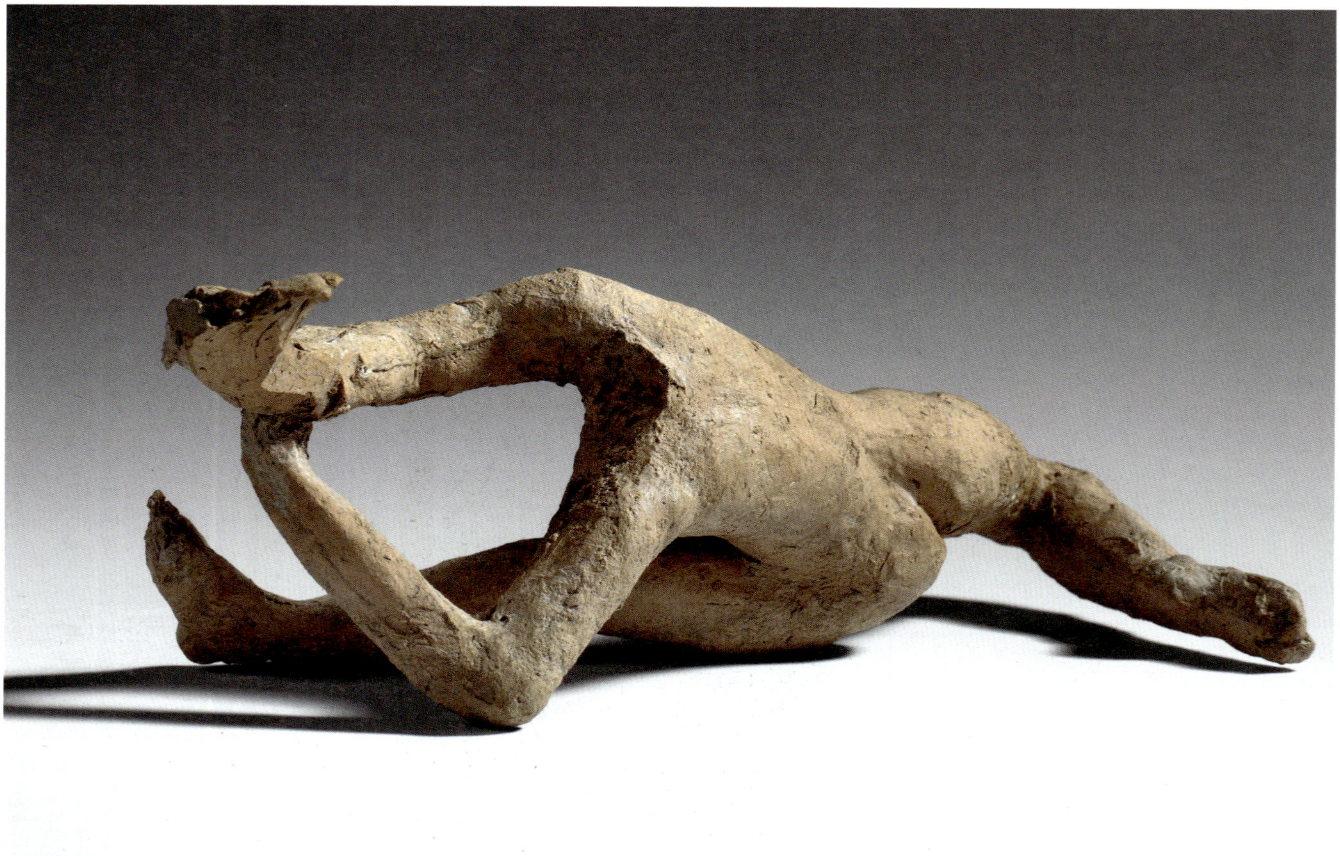

60

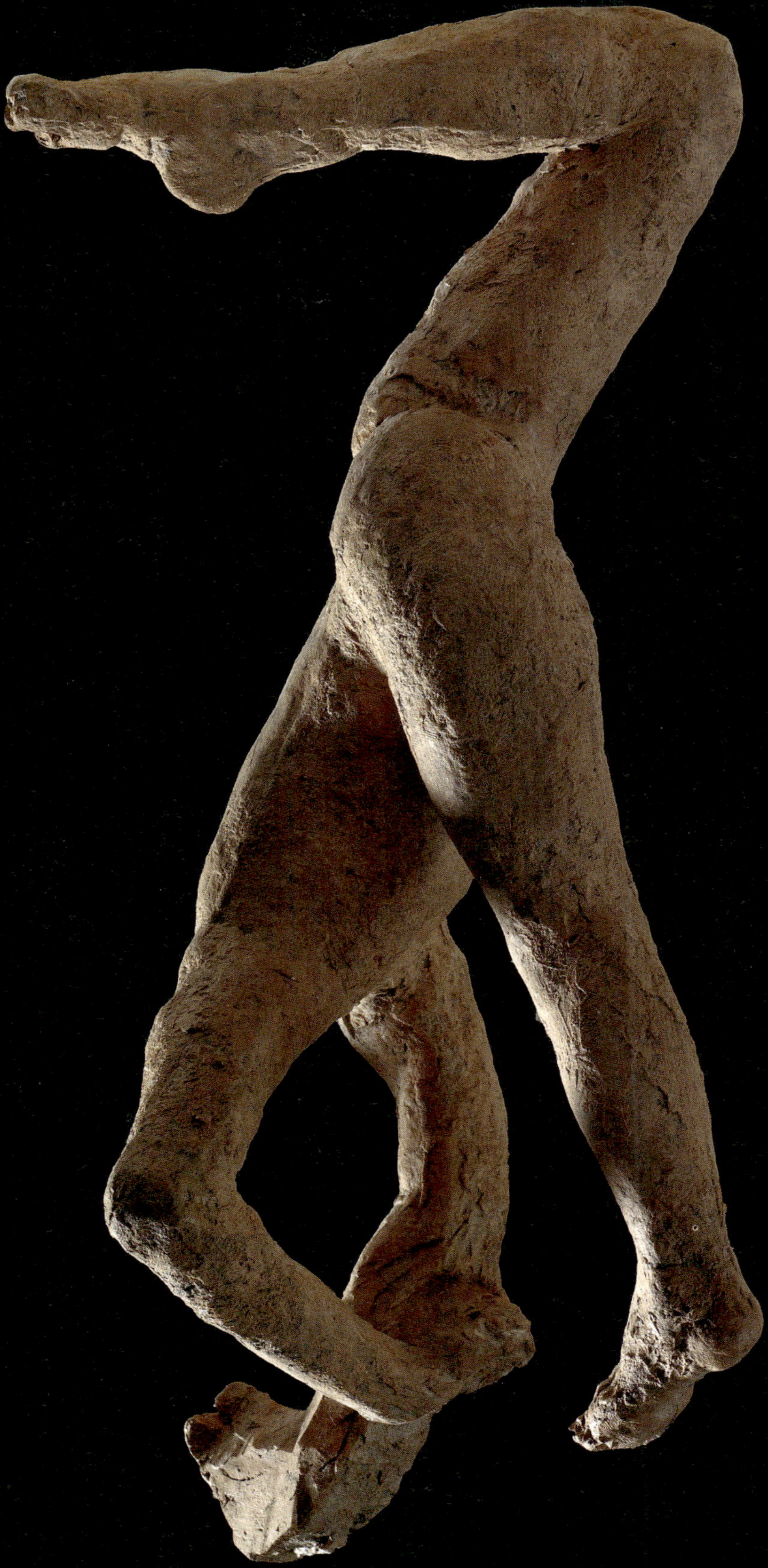

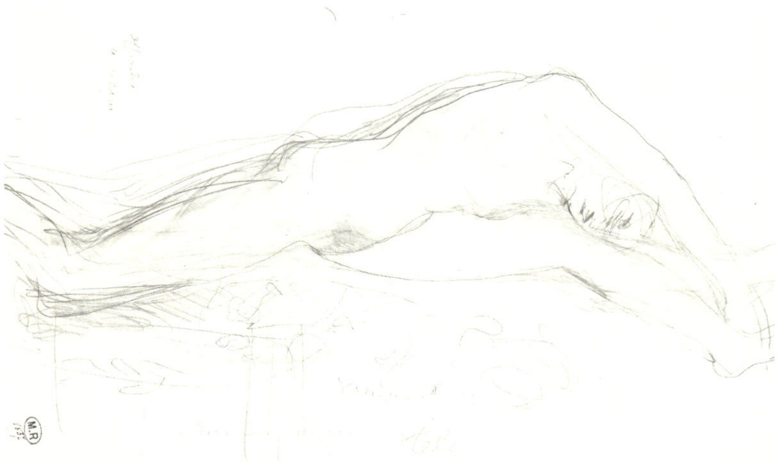

D.1837 (cat.37) reoriented

newest sculpture, and that he wanted to show a varied typology, including small works.

The *Mouvements de danse* were never discussed in this correspondence. However, it is reasonable to suggest that Rodin offered the terracotta figure to San Martino as a thank-you present, perhaps in about 1913, for having included him in two major exhibitions in Rome. San Martino seems to have visited Rodin several times in Paris or Meudon during these years. A note dated 24 December 1912 informs the sculptor that he is looking forward to visiting the studio to see the works he has promised to show him; and a note in early January 1913 confirms a visit to Meudon.[3] The significance of Rodin's selection of such an

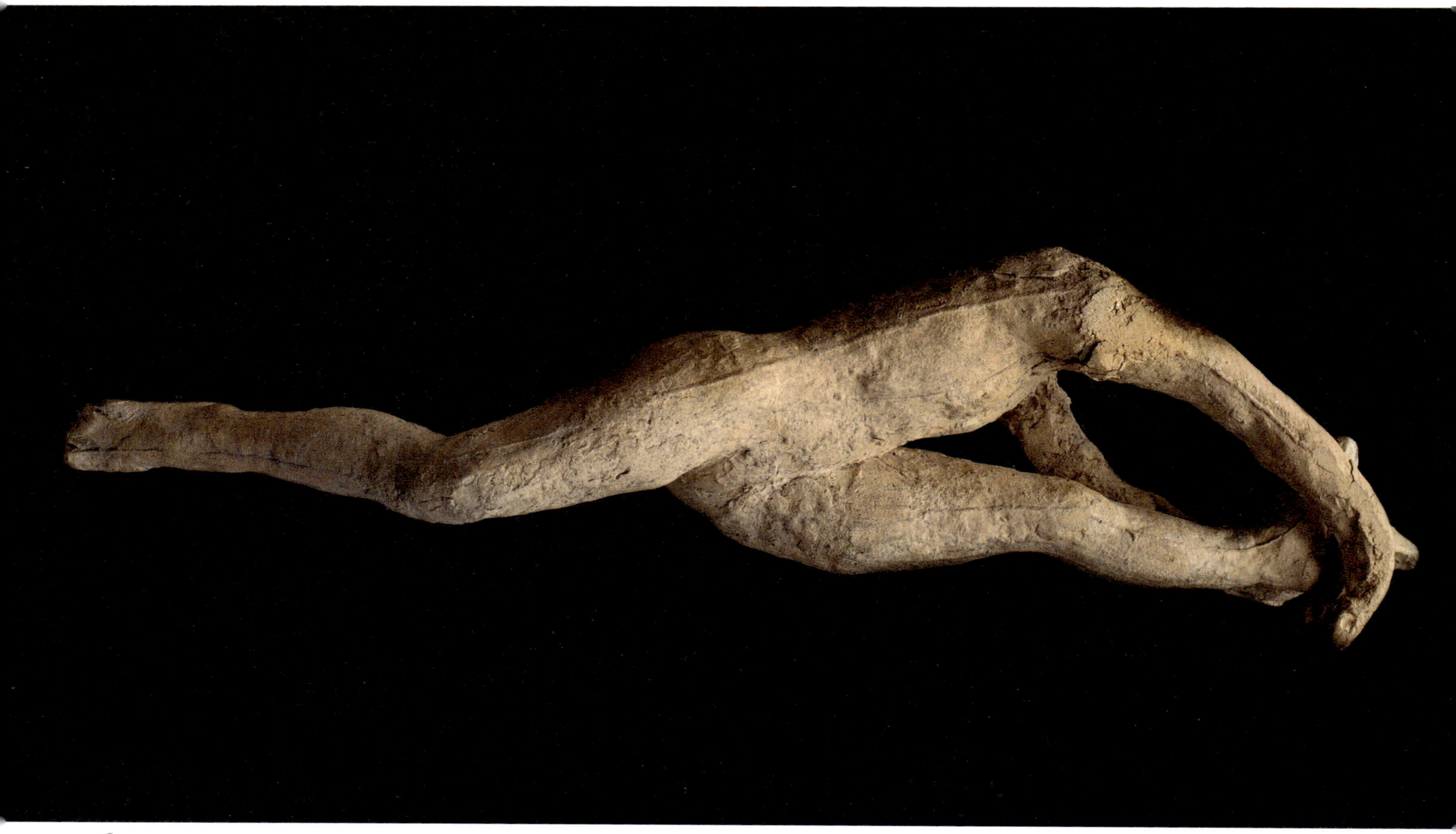

61

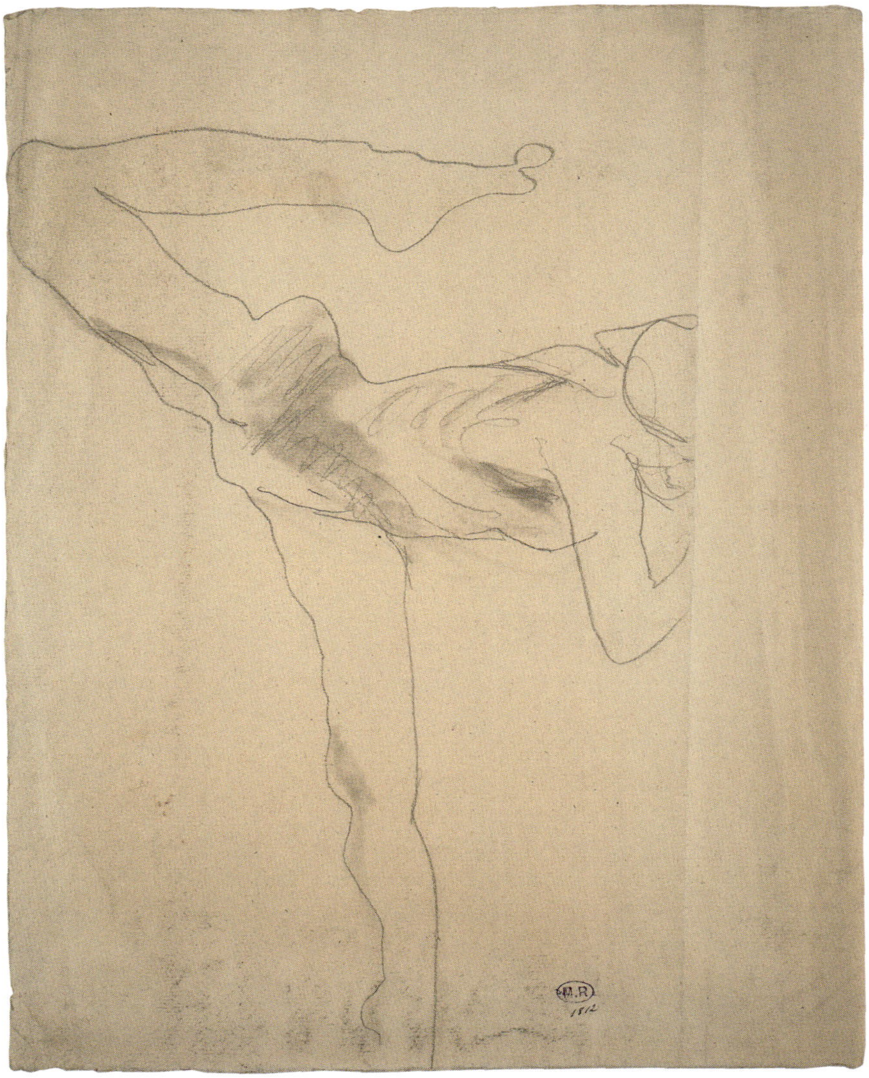

62

intimate and apparently experimental work as a gift shows quite clearly that he knew San Martino was capable of appreciating it. As the journals of Count Kessler demonstrate, Rodin showed the works to only a few people, apparently worried they would be badly received. This gift, as that must be what it was, is particularly significant in the context of the Italian reception of Rodin as a modern artist, and is comparable to the presents he made of his drawings to the critics Pica and Ojetti in these years.[4] AG

3 Enrico di San Martino e Valperga file, in the archives of the Musée Rodin.

4 I would like to thank Barbara Musetti for this comparison, and for her suggestion of the date of 1913 for the gift to San Martino. On the reception of Rodin in Italy, see Musetti 2008.

63–65

Mouvement D, 1911

Terracotta, 33.5 x 10.4 x 9.5 cm
Musée Rodin, Paris, S.5493

Mouvement I, 1911

Terracotta, 23.5 x 12.5 x 8 cm
Musée Rodin, Paris, S.1052

Mouvement I+, 1911

Terracotta, 26 x 17 x 9.8 cm
Musée Rodin, Paris, S.6662

In these poses, the figure gathers her knee to her chest, with a slight twist of the torso, in a stretch, which can, again, be orientated in various positions, each time lending a slightly different quality to the movement represented. *Mouvement D* (cat.63) could be placed on its side, echoing a drawing of the pose which Rodin seems to have turned around to inscribe *architecture* twice, along its length, above and below the figure (fig.61). The sculpted figure of *Mouvement D* appears to be contained and delicate, in contrast to the other figures in the series, which are both more open and more active. The tenderness of the pose is reinforced by the head nestling in the right shoulder. When turned on the side, the figure's tilted head and slightly asymmetrical chignon acts as a pillow. The hands, which seem to be placed to emphasise their hyperextended wrists, are the most detailed of the series, with incised lines indicating the fingers, as is particularly noticeable from below or if turned in the hand.

Mouvement I (cat.64 & 65) exists in two slightly different versions (I and I+).[1] The figure is again shown stretching with a slight twist of the upper body towards the bent knee, probably in a pose requiring the use of a block or step of a different height to lift the left leg on to. In one of these (cat.64), the head is slightly tilted, like *Mouvement D*, touching the upper part of the left arm. In the other (cat. 65), the figure is upright. The head is framed by the right arm forming an arc around it, its palm facing out and reinforcing a sense of the horizontal plane. The left arm is placed in front, resting on the bent right knee, and the shape of the hands echo each other. The wrists of all three figures are hyperextended in positions that recall Rodin's drawings of Cambodians, but the flowing lines of these are replaced here by an impression of angularity and decisiveness in the gestures. AG

1 *Mouvement I+* (S.6662, cat.65) was acquired by the Musée Rodin in 1995. It is said to have belonged to one of Rodin's mould-makers, Georges Depeper, who was a member of his studio in the last years of Rodin's life, and was working for him, and then for the museum, until 1919. It is not clear how the work might have ended up in his possession. See Le Normand-Romain 1996, p.62.

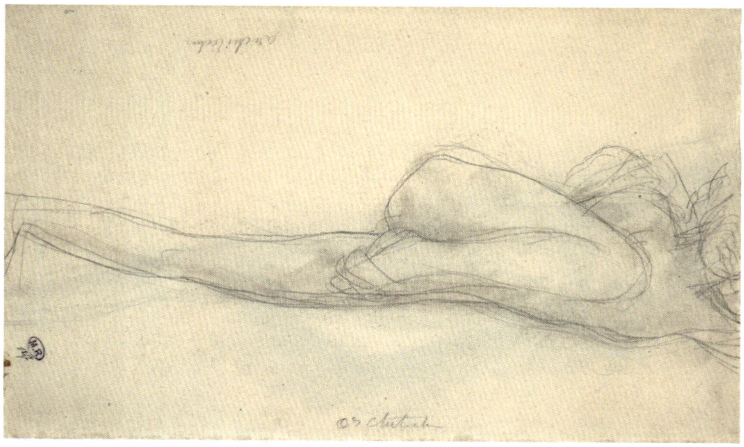

FIG.61
Auguste Rodin
Female nude, called Architecture (Alda Moreno?), c.1910–13
Pencil with stumping on laid paper, 384 x 237 mm
Musée Rodin, Paris. D.1817

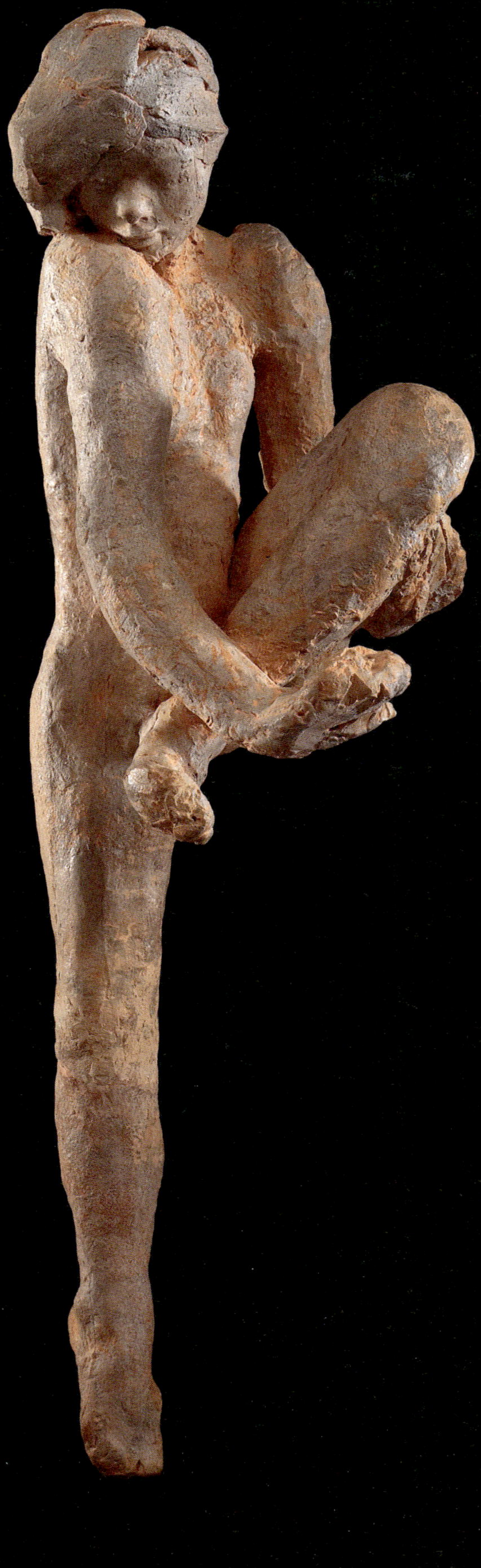

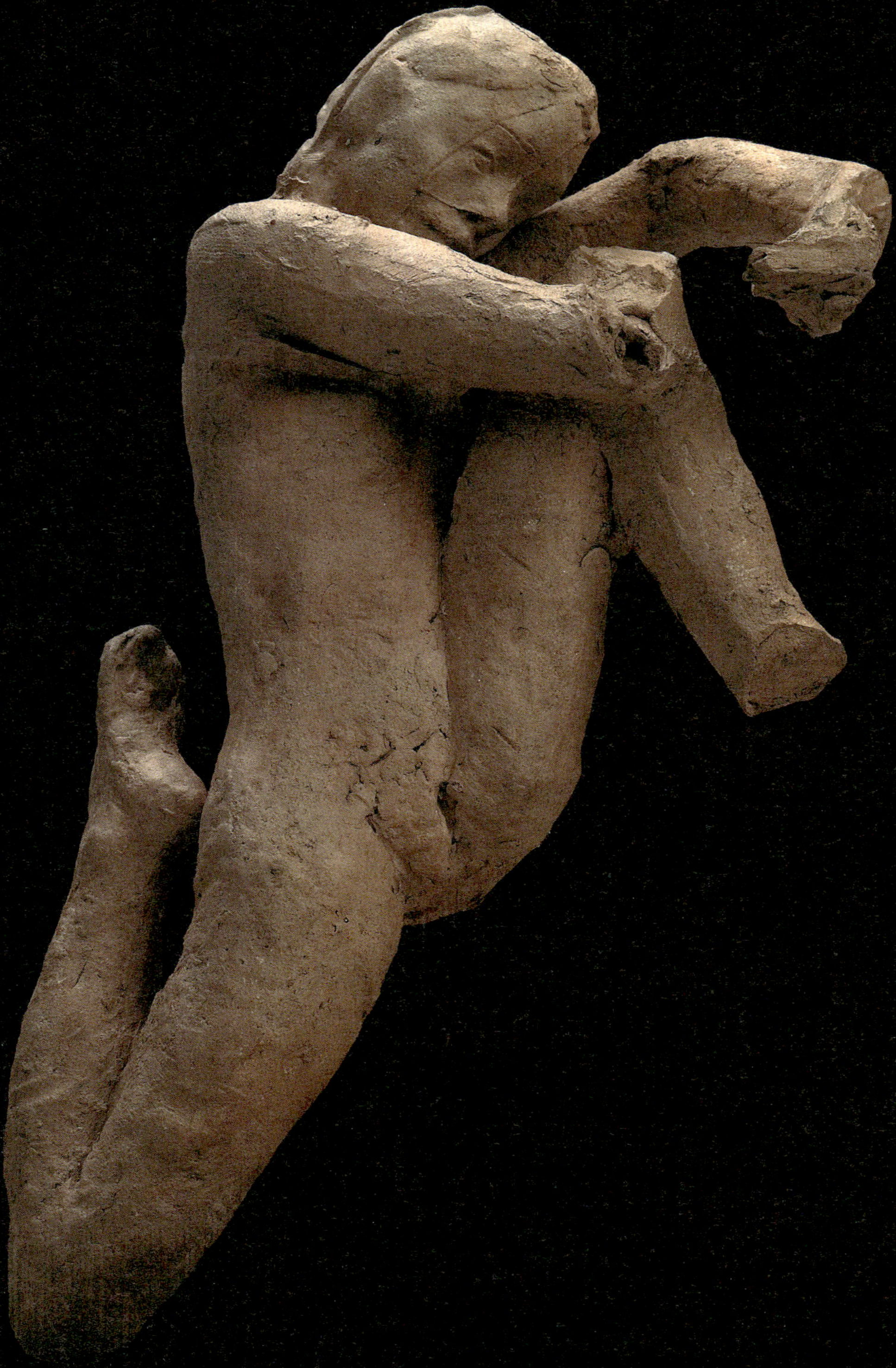

64

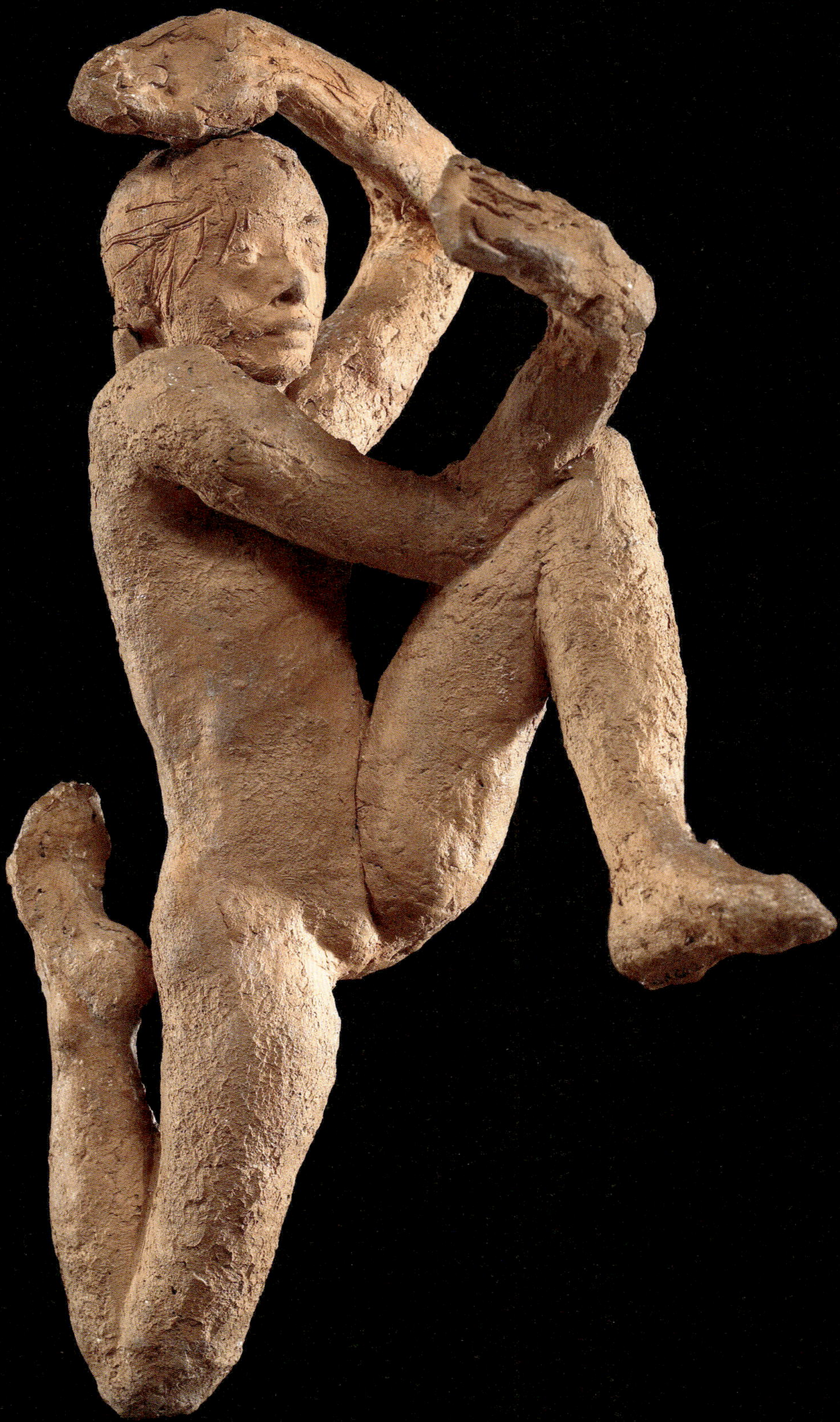

66–68

Huddled seated figure, from the *Mouvements de danse* series, 1911

Terracotta, 11.6 x 23 x 11.5 cm
Musée Rodin, Paris, S.3845

Seated figure folding forward and hugging her legs, called *La butte*, after 1909

Pencil with stumping on laid paper, 234 x 380 mm
Inscribed on the verso: *la butte* (the mound)
Musée Rodin, Paris, D.1775

Huddled seated figure, reoriented (Alda Moreno), c.1910–13

Pencil with stumping on laid paper, 235 x 383 mm
Inscribed: *bas* (bottom)
Musée Rodin, Paris, D.1859

A seated nude with an exaggeratedly curved back is shown folding over her legs in two drawings and in a terracotta figure, which is part of the *Mouvements de danse* group. The figure appears huddled to form a complete shape in the drawing showing the figure upside down (D.1859, cat.68) and in the terracotta figure (S.3845, cat.66). In the other drawing (D.1775, cat.67) the arms actively hug the legs; here the model may have been sitting on a surface with her hands grasping her knees so that the lower legs hang down at an angle.

These figures are part of a group of related drawings, mostly in pencil with stumping and so probably from after 1909, in the Musée Rodin's collection, in which Rodin explored variations on the form of the enclosed figure, bending and elongating limbs to obtain beautifully languid curves. There seems also to be a connection, certainly in the drawing showing the figure upside down (cat.68), to a number of watercolours of a similarly self-contained figure turned upside down and appearing to fall, such as a drawing in the collection of the Pierpont Morgan Library called *Lucifer* (1981.10), with its inscriptions referring to a fallen meteorite. In Rodin's sculpture the theme of crouching is familiar, but here the pose seems to express the extreme suppleness and flexibility of the model, one who was capable of wrapping her limbs around her body. The figure was, perhaps unsurprisingly given its challenging and limited viewpoints, never cast in bronze with the rest of the series. AG

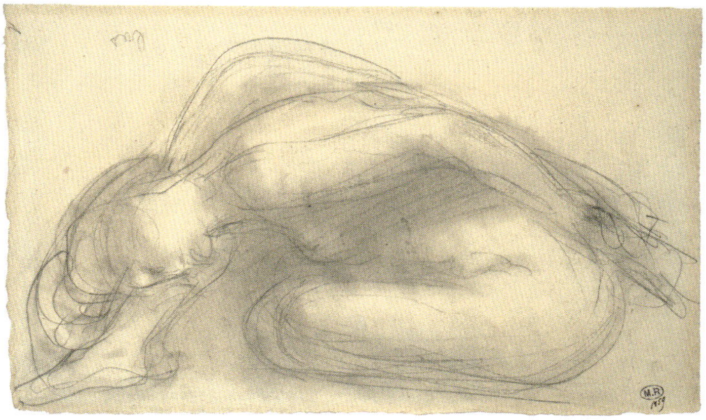

D.1859, cat.68, reoriented

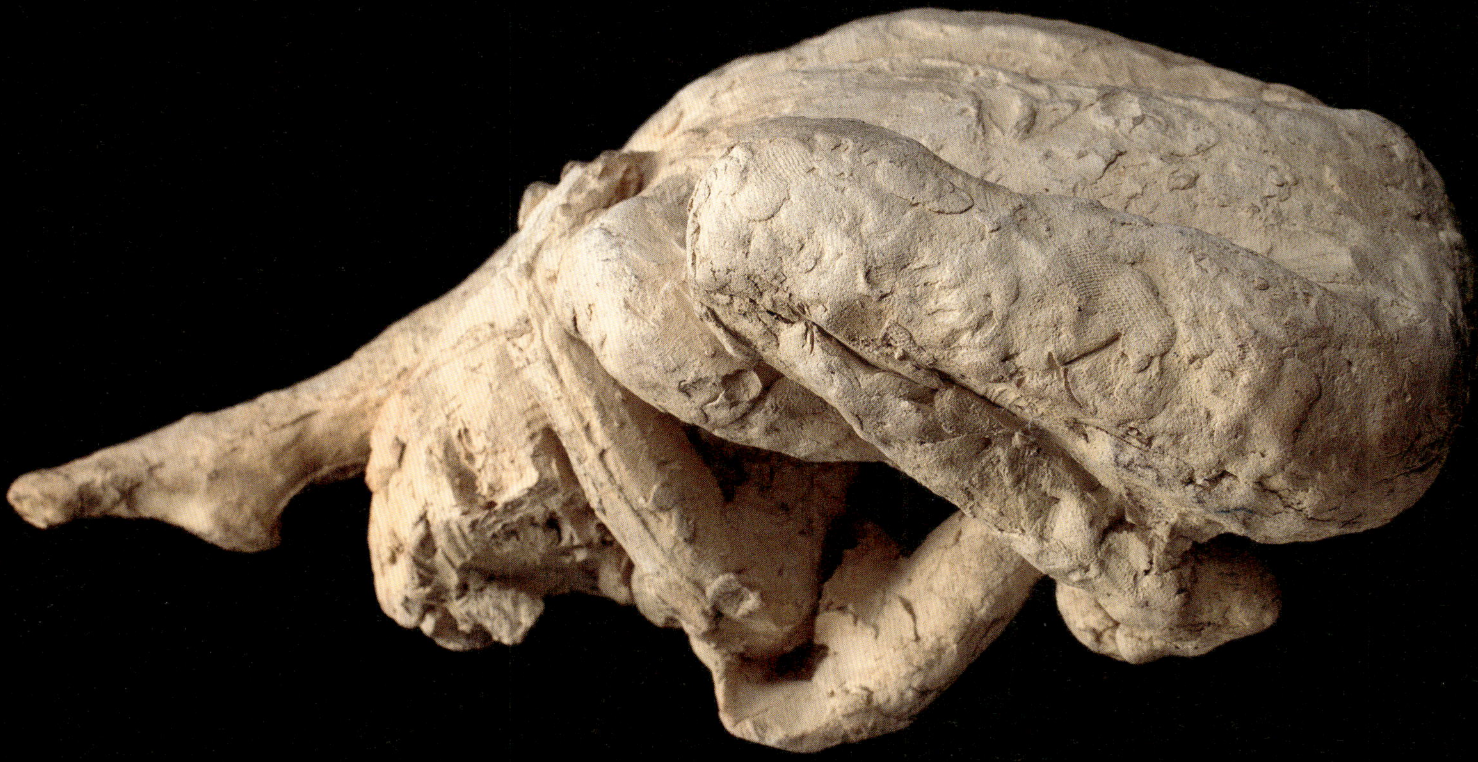

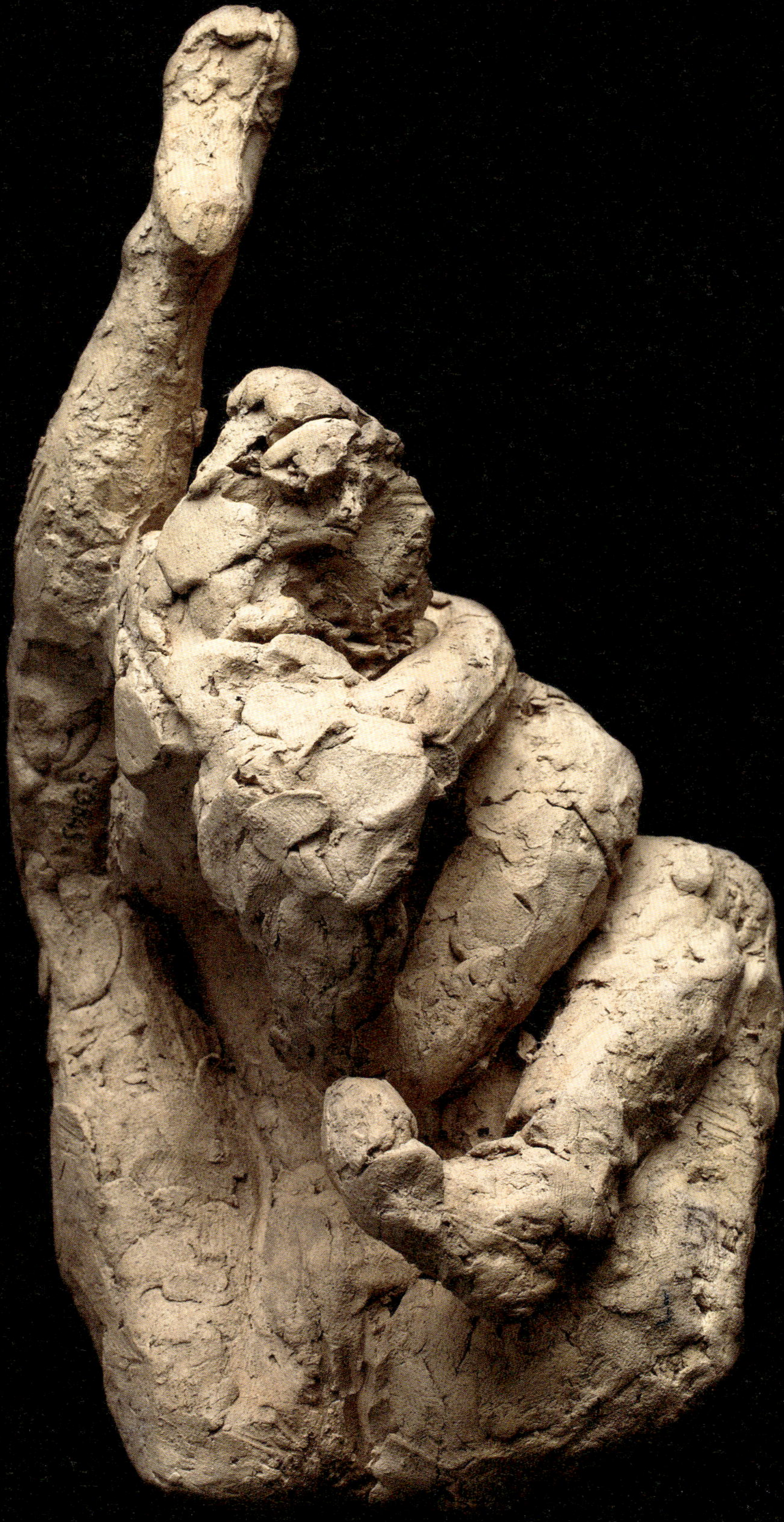

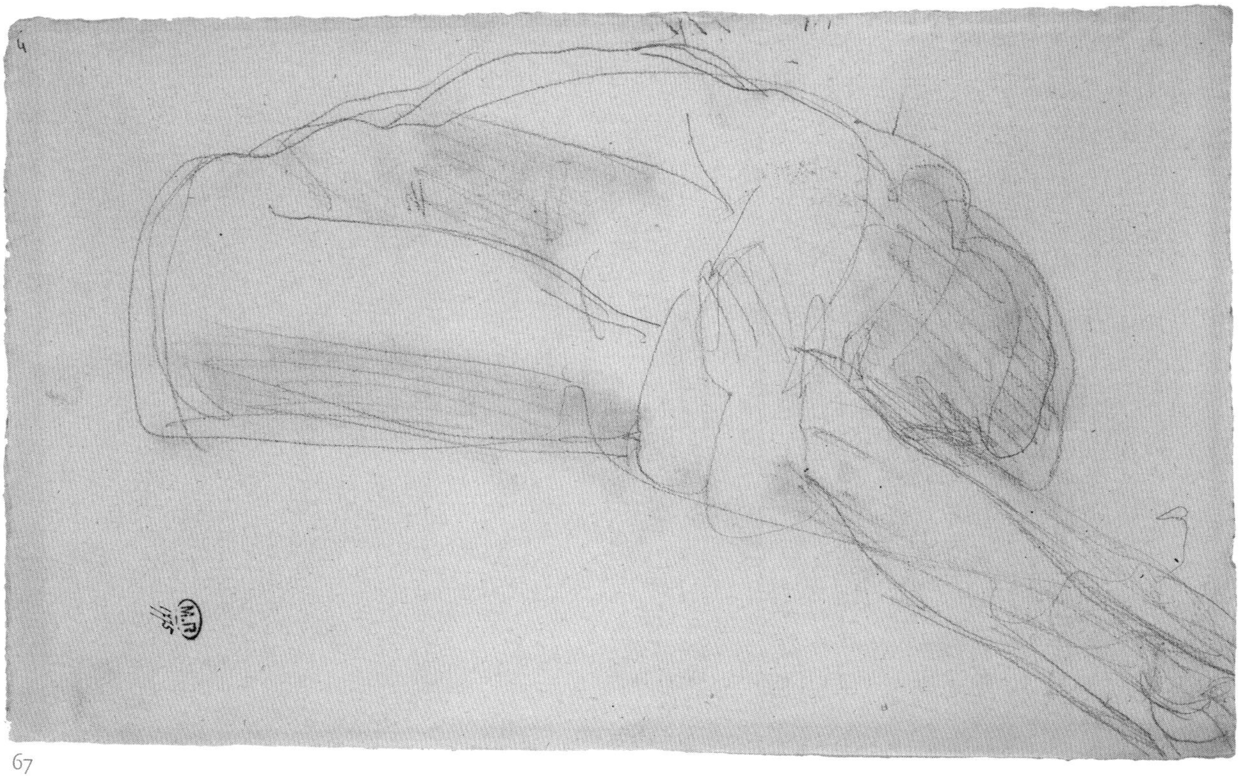
67

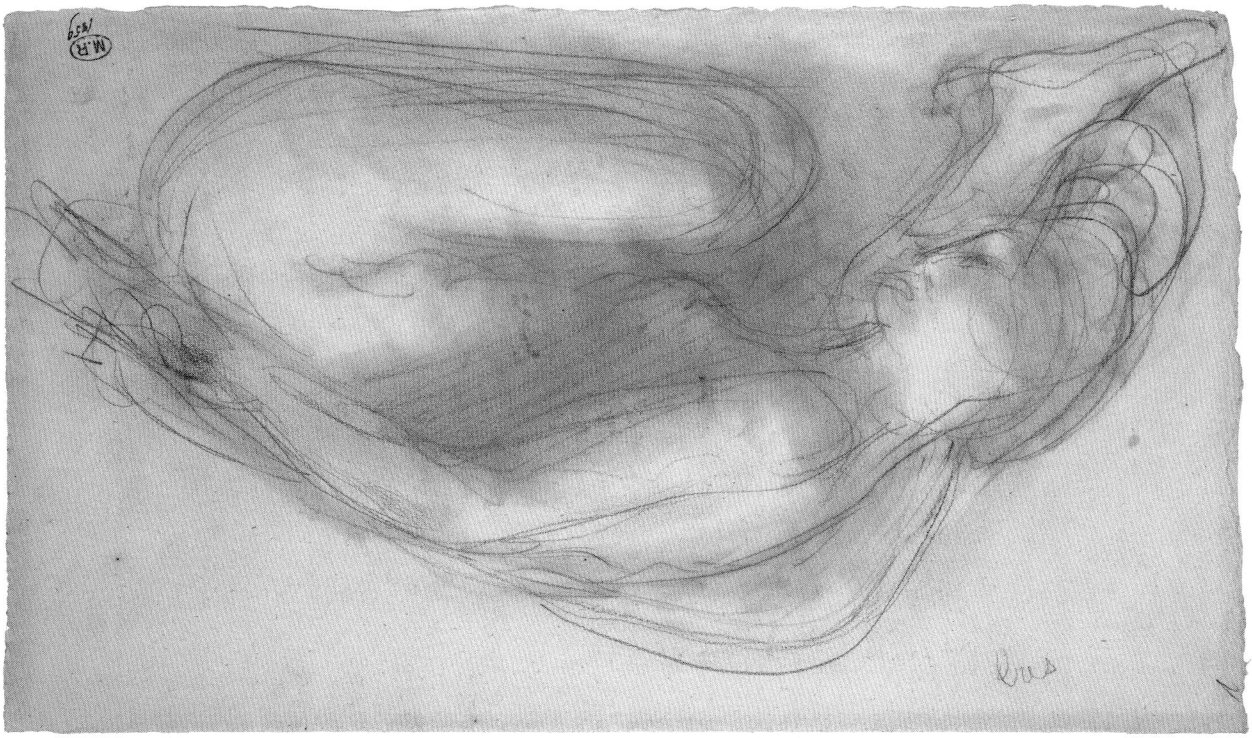
68

69–71

Crouching female nude seen from the back, shoulders draped, c.1900?

Pencil and watercolour on wove paper, 324 x 245 mm
Musée Rodin, Paris, D.5021

Crouching female nude seen from the back, pressing down on her hands, one leg bent, the other flexed, after 1909

Pencil with stumping on laid paper, 240 x 381 mm
Musée Rodin, Paris, D.1781

Crouching female nude in profile, c.1900?

Pencil and watercolour on laid paper, 235 x 384 mm
Musée Rodin, Paris, D.4919

The three drawings show figures seen from behind or in profile, rather than looking at the viewer. Their attention is focused on their bending movement. An inscription on another drawing of this type refers to concentration: the female figure is bending in two and above we can make out the word *concentre* (concentrates; D.1620). The crouching figures are all precariously balanced and would have been drawn quickly. This gives the figures an air of strangeness and fragility, even though Rodin's use of watercolour on two of the drawings gives them a finished aspect that emphasises their suspension of time.

Rodin's drawings often show crouching figures, seen from all angles – front, back and in profile – with hands on the ground or balancing on tiptoe. The motif also appeared very early in his sculptural work with the *Femme accroupie* (*Crouching Woman*) from *The Gates of Hell* and the woman held by a man in *Je suis belle* (*I am Beautiful*) and by a woman in the assemblage of two *Eve* sculptures (S.184). A woman in a curled up position (fig.62) shows that Rodin was not solely interested in dance movements where the legs are extended. This small sculpture seems to show what might be a flexible dancer in a resting pose. The pencil

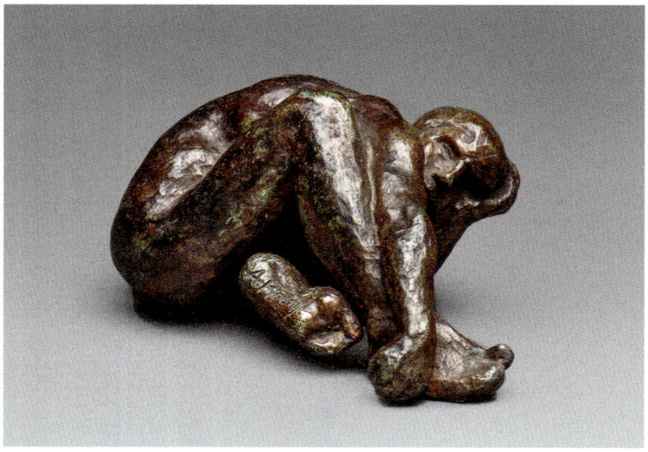

FIG.62
Auguste Rodin
Crouching Dancer, c.1895–1900
Bronze, 8.3 x 17.5 x 11.7 cm
Musée Rodin, Paris, S.635

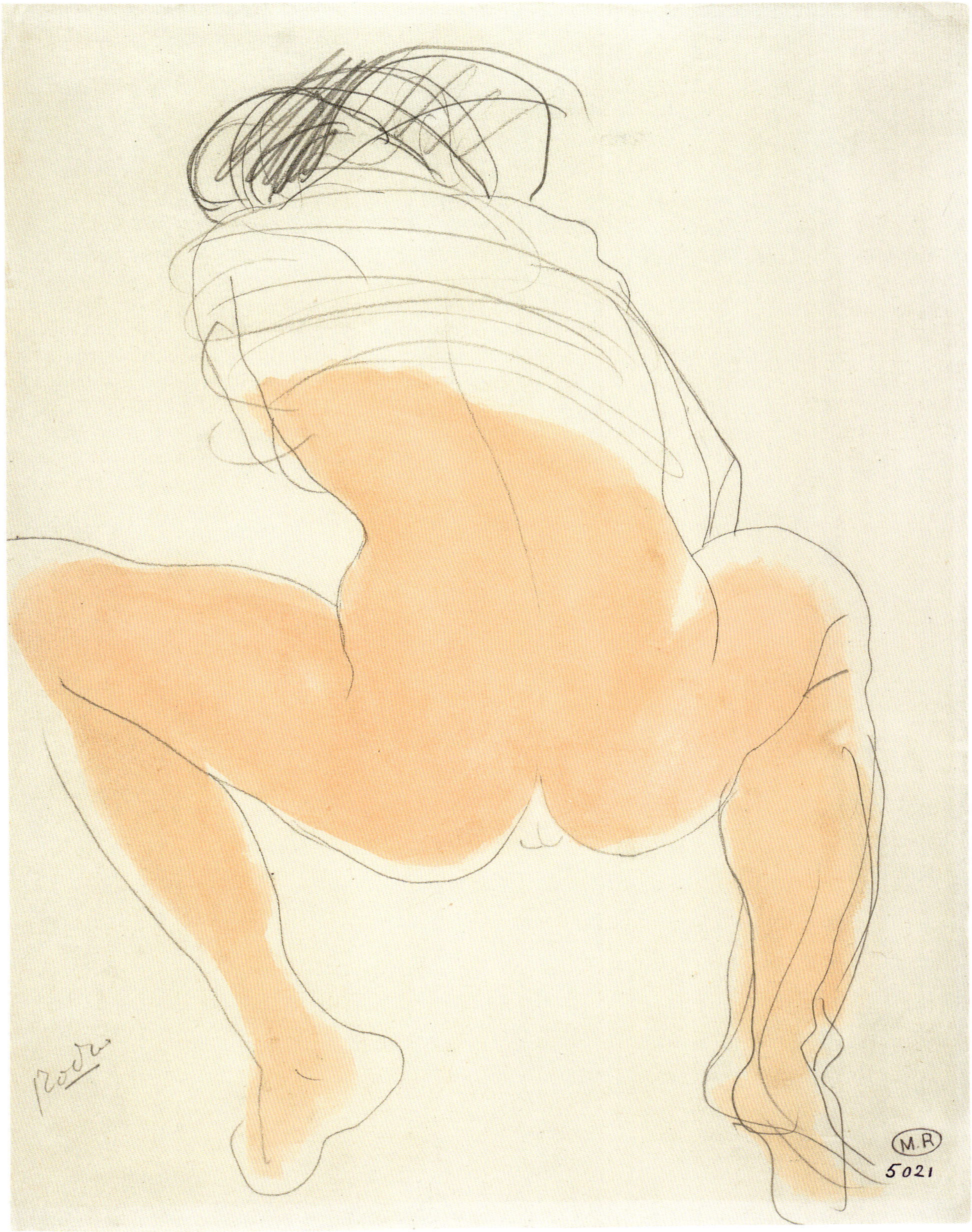
M.R
5021

drawing of a crouching woman from the back (D.1781, cat.70) shows the model raising her right leg. This is clearly a drawing made from life, while looking at the model, since the lower part of the extended leg is very thin. The figure's position recalls that of the sculpture *Iris* seen from behind (1891–93) and of *Mouvement F* (cat.72). The double outline of the back suggests that the model was raising her hand in preparation for standing up and that Rodin redrew the back to adjust to that movement. The few traces of stumping give the figure a degree of solidity. The drawing of a crouching woman seen in profile, her arms reaching forwards (D.4919, cat.71), suggests a balancing effort. The figure's placement in the top half of the paper reinforces the sense that the position is precarious. The more assured, simplified nature of the drawing indicates that Rodin had already made several drawings of the same composition, of which examples are held in the Musée Rodin.[1] He also used a drawing on tracing paper (D.1646) with pencil shading to act as a transfer to reproduce the composition. This figure was an object of particular interest for him.

1 These are D.1559, D.4920–23 and D.1684.

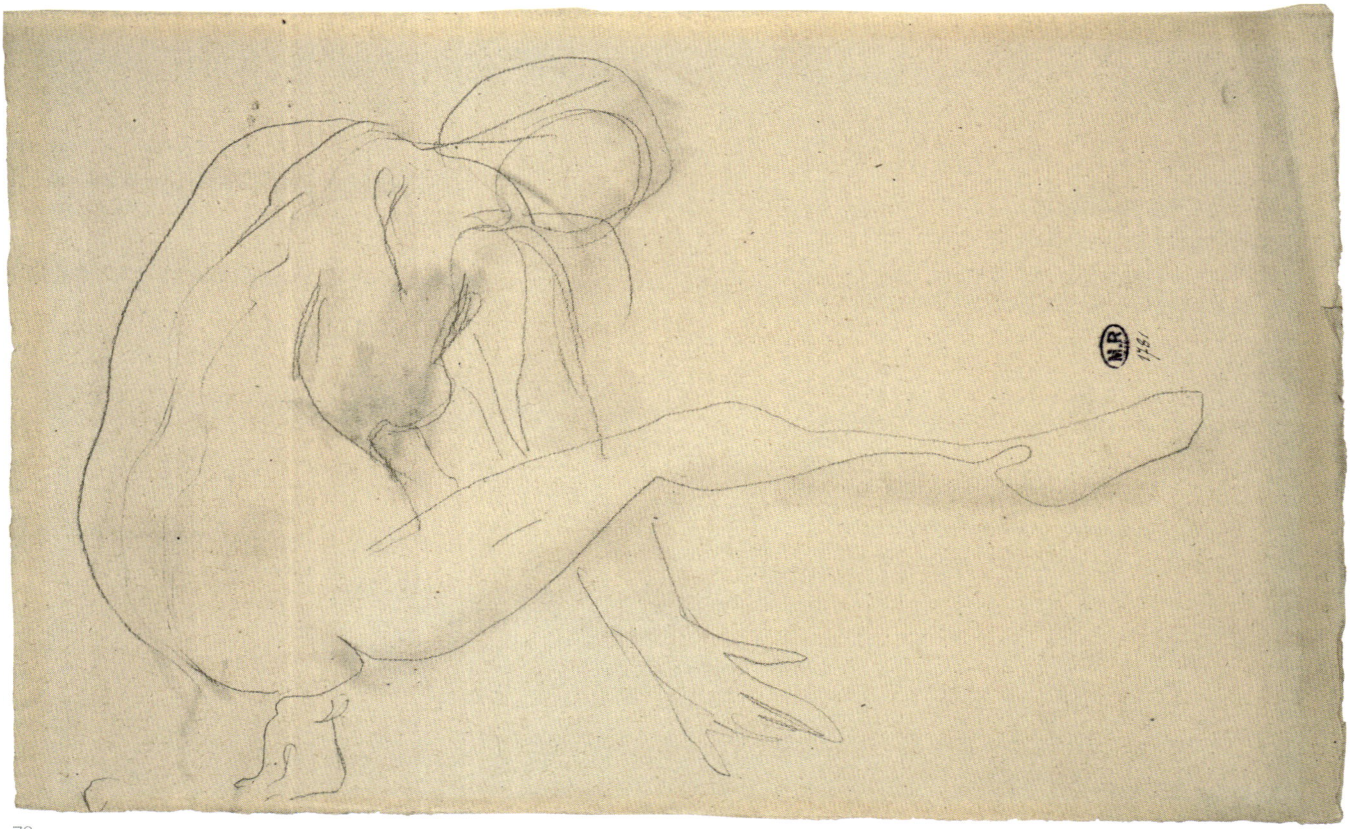

70

The drawing of a crouching nude from the back (D.5021, cat.69) shows a figure (with emphasised genitals that could indicate a vulva, since the series based on this model clearly defines her as female) with legs open, in the process of undressing. The difference between clothing and skin is marked by the use of watercolour, which covers only the naked skin and leaves the rest of the drawing uncoloured, notably the top of the figure's back, which is covered by clothing. Rodin's habit was never to allow the initial line drawing to constrain the watercolour. The unpredictable result adds to the tension and dynamism of the work. One drawing (D.4068) shows the same figure in a slightly less crouched posture, since underneath the model is a horizontal line that is difficult to interpret but could be some kind of stool or bench of which the outline no longer appears in this version. Two drawings in pencil only (D.486 and D.880) show the same figure, but more grounded and with the muscular effort more tangible. SBF

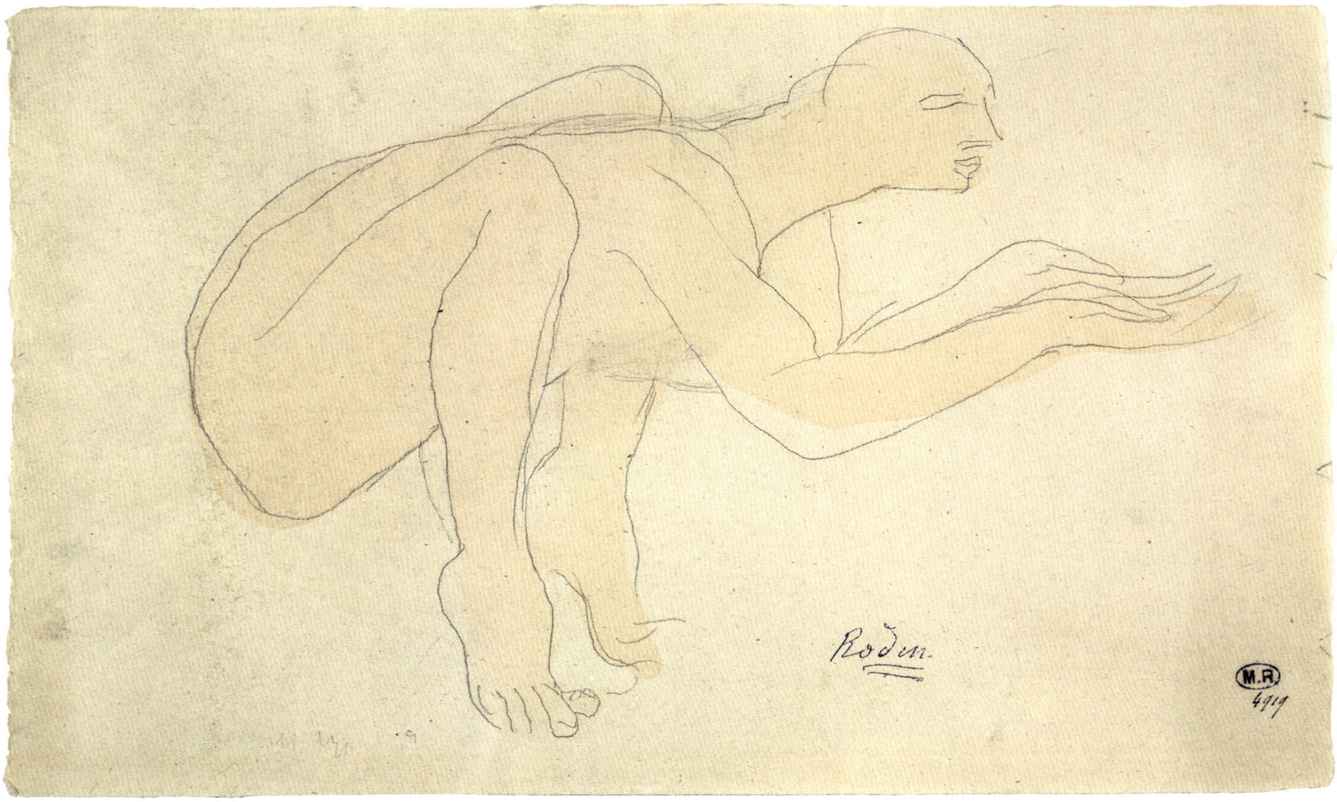

71

72

Mouvement F, 1911

Terracotta, 26.5 x 29 x 14.7 cm
Musée Rodin, Paris, S.5831

Mouvement F (cat.72) shows a body in motion, executing a dynamic warrior-like leap in the air. This figure can really only be seen in one orientation, and is not related to limbering or stretching or preparing a pose. The right arm curves over the head in a similar way to *Mouvement I+* (cat.65) but the impression that position conveys in this sculpture is not the same, as here the right arm echoes the left arm's circular motion, jutting out unnaturally from the shoulder as if drawing a circle in space. The legs, on the other hand, have a solid strength, which makes the lower body particularly energetic.

In its compression of two different, and even contradictory, movements in the upper and lower body, *Mouvement F* is a synthesis of upward motion rather than the true representation of a jump in the air, and in this resonates with Rodin's conception of movement in art, as expressed to Paul Gsell in 1911, in which he explained why photographers only "freeze" time, whereas the artist understands the totality of movement, and, by compressing the unfolding drama of the various stages of movement into one image or one form, is capable of representing its true essence. Not only must the action be represented as a summary of its past moments but also as an announcement of the moments to come, as Rodin further explained in his interviews with Henri Dujardin-Beaumetz in 1913: "To express a movement in all its character and truth, it is important that it be at once the result of the successive moments that have preceded the moment that one has fixed, and that it announces the sensation of those that will follow".[1] AG

1 *"Pour exprimer un mouvement dans tout son caractère et sa vérité, il importe qu'il soit à la fois le résultat des mouvements successifs qui ont précédé le moment où on a fixé, et qu'il donne par avance la sensation de ceux qui vont suivre"*: Rodin 2008, p.113.

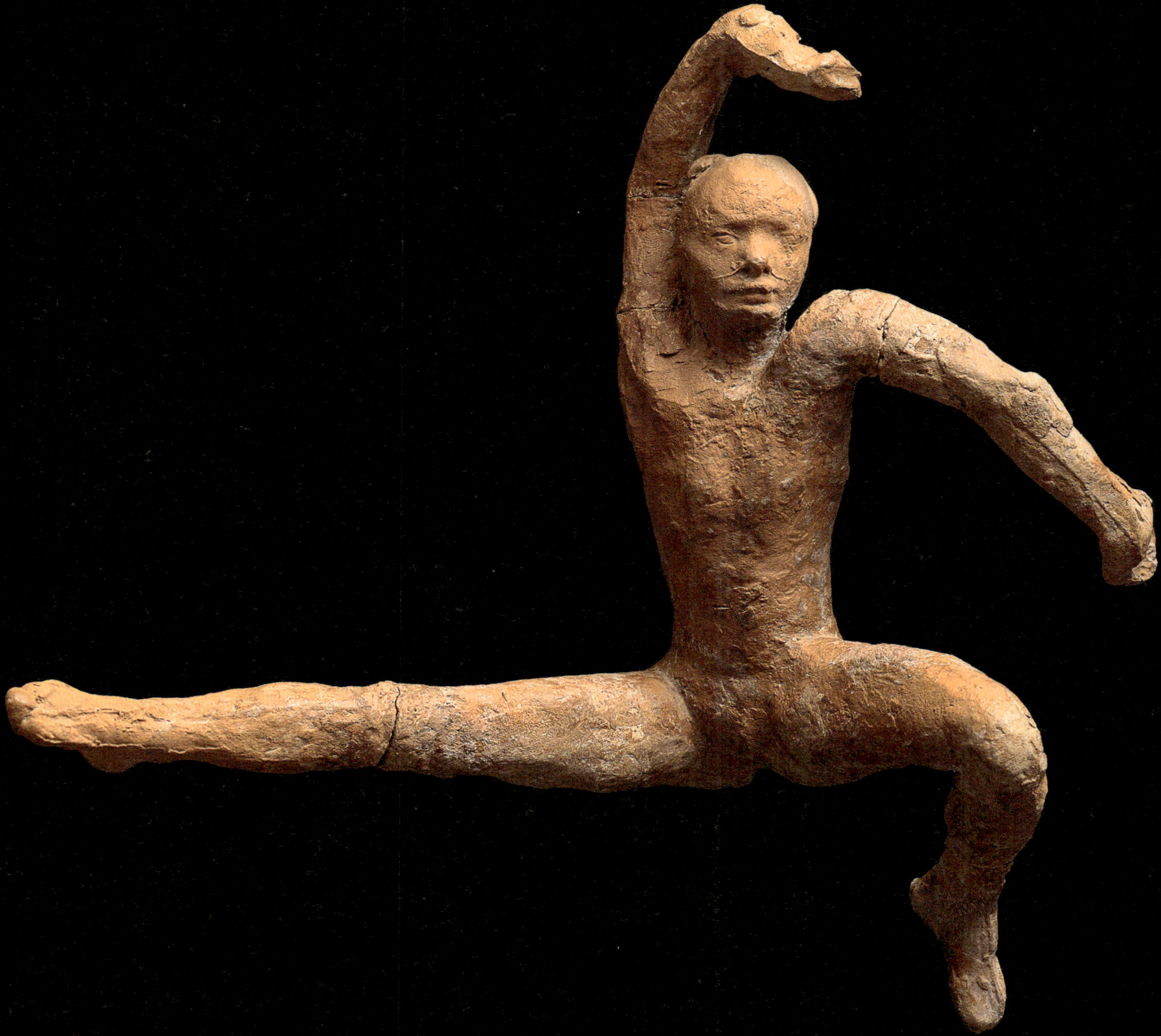

73–75

Female nude in the splits position, after 1909

Pencil with stumping on laid paper, 240 x 383 mm
Musée Rodin, Paris, D.1796

Female nude, leaning forward with her hands on the ground and her lower body lifted, after 1909

Pencil with stumping on wove paper, 197 x 305 mm
Musée Rodin, Paris, D.1784

Female nude leaning forward on her hands, one knee bent, after 1909

Pencil with stumping on wove paper, 228 x 352 mm
Musée Rodin, Paris, D.7181

The second half of the nineteenth century had seen a revival of interest in acrobatics, to which the figures' movements in these three drawings seem closer than they are to dance. All seem to have been drawn from the same model, Alda Moreno, recognisable by her contortionist's flexibility, which was of particular interest to Rodin in these late years. Rodin chose to capture her supple, athletic body in motion, since the positions he drew are transitional and would have been difficult to maintain. One of the poses is not realistic in the orientation from which the drawing (D.1859, cat.68) is viewed, since the woman is in fact upside down on her back.

Rodin has arranged each of the present three drawings in the same way on the paper. As usual only the body is drawn; no other element is either depicted or suggested. When the body is shown in negative rather than positive form – in other words the space around it is slightly darkened – this is not a representation of a shadow cast on an element, it is simply the air that draws the shape of the body, which seems to be standing out against a coloured background. In these stumped drawings Rodin often surrounds the body with a slight halo, so that it seems to arise out of an undefined space.[1]

The bodies – or their centre of gravity at least – are placed high on the paper. The lower half of the paper beneath the figure doing the splits (D.1796, cat.73) is left empty, creating an impression of someone leaping high over the ground. The body of the woman whose bust is over her knee seems not to be touching the ground, but climbing on something high, so that the foot closest to the ground is already in the air (D.7181, cat.74). The body is irregularly arranged on the paper, almost wedged top left, while there is a little space around the left foot bottom right. The female nude crouching and resting on both forearms (D.1784, cat.74) seems to be preparing to do a headstand, so her feet, which are above her hands, have already left the ground without having yet reached a position of balance. This is the most grounded position in these three drawings but, paradoxically, the base formed by the hands is not clearly portrayed. One hand is rapidly and largely symbolically suggested in a few lines, the fingers rapidly drawn and a little too large, with no real concern for realism.

The most detailed, carefully drawn part is the fold of the abdomen. In these 'flying' figures the head and face are rather strangely represented: the head of the lying figure is suggested by a sphere with no anatomical detail; that of the bent figure is turned towards the artist but there is no detail to the hair, line of the nose or eyes; the nose and eyes of the figure doing the splits are suggested

1 On the pencil with stump drawings: "When he was approaching seventy, Rodin continued to use pencil and stopped modelling with the brush. He continued to stump outlines with his finger (*Vers sa soixante-dixième année, Rodin continuant à se servir du crayon, cessa de modeler avec le pinceau. Il continua d'estomper avec le doigt les traits du contour*)": Gsell 1920, p.23. See Paris 2011, p.231.

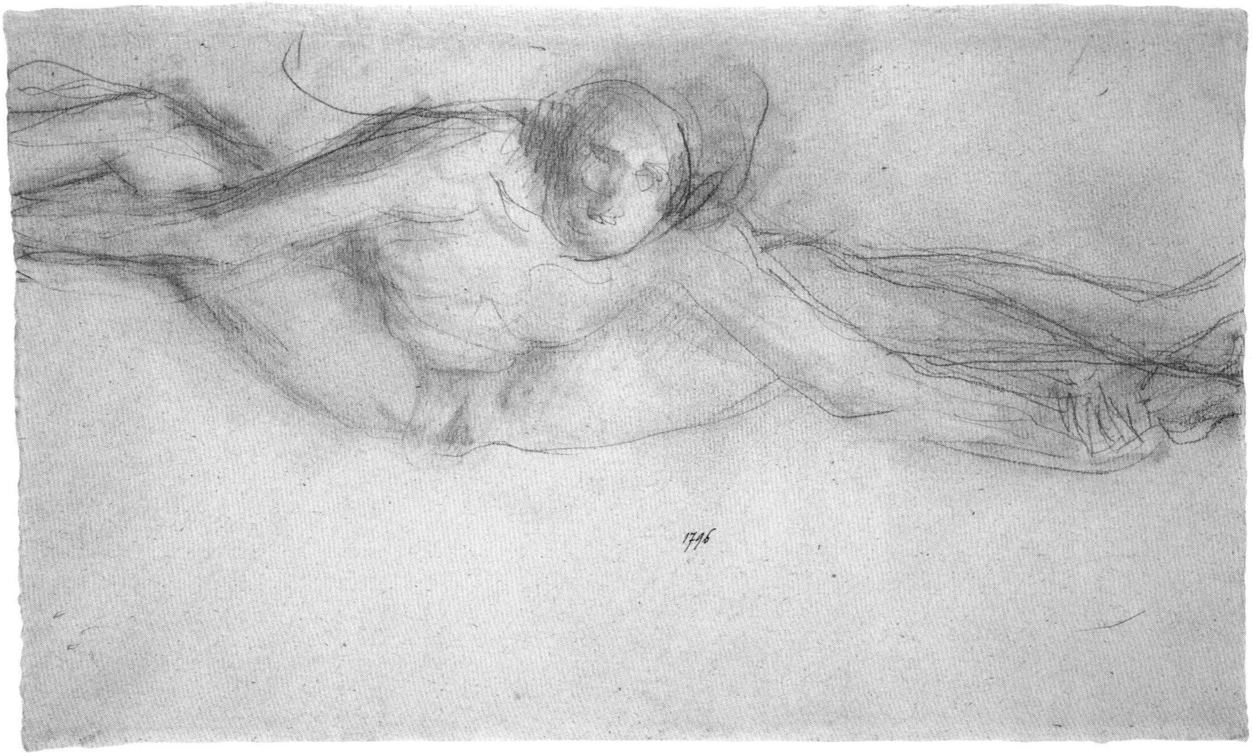

73

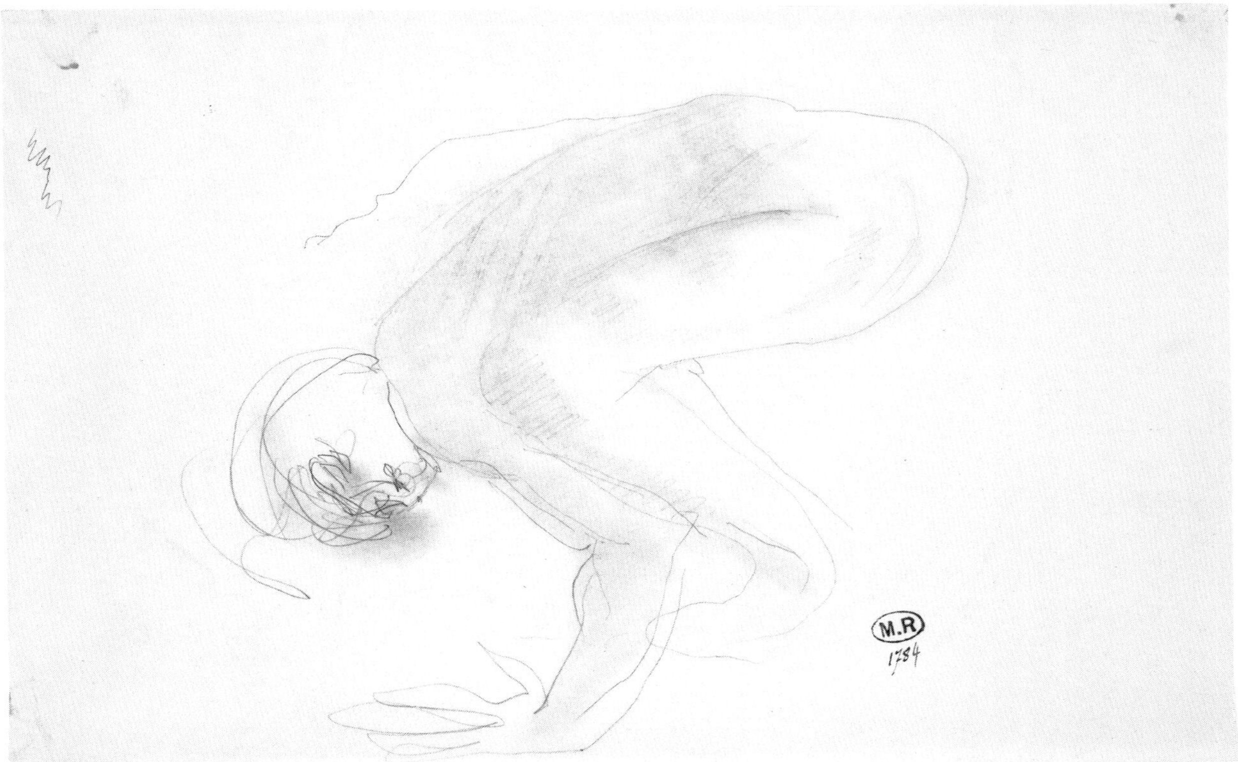

74

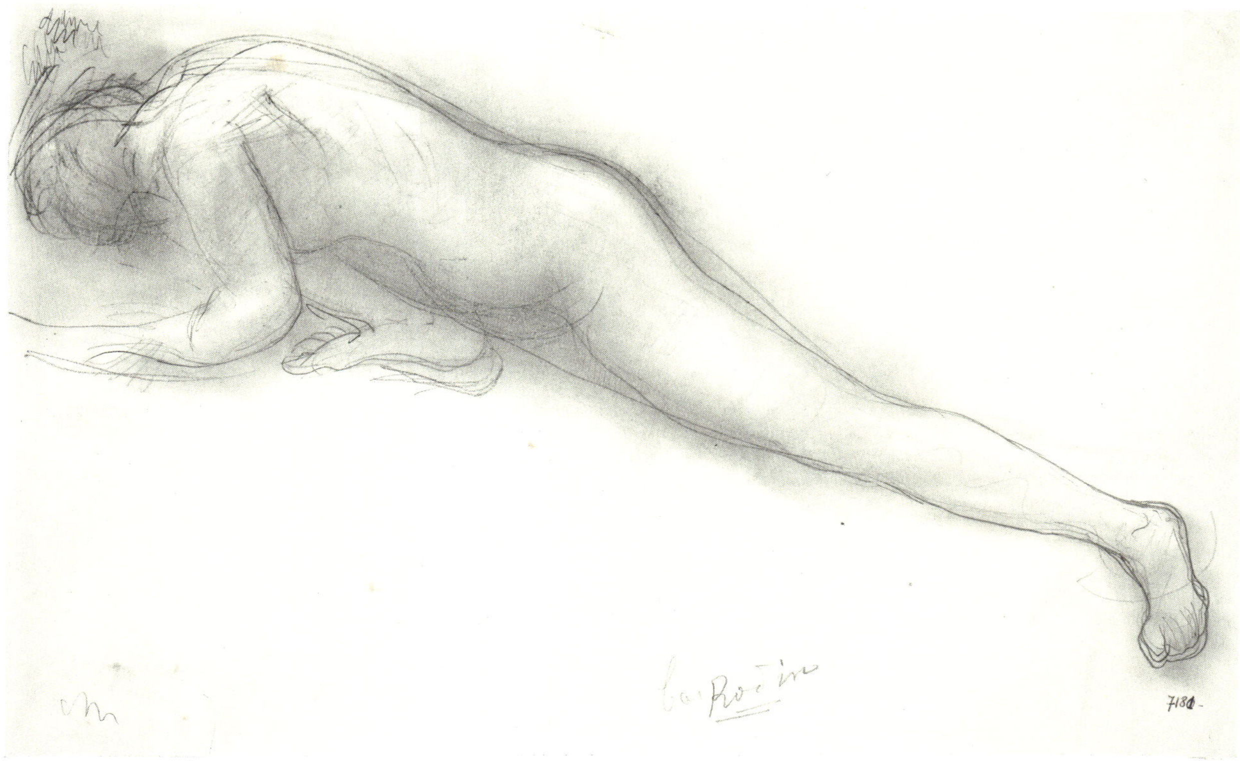

75

by a shadow created largely by stumping.
The portrayals of these three suspended bodies, paused in motion, are more synthetic than individualised. This is reinforced by the use of stumping.

One figure (D.7181, cat.75) is similar to the sculpture *La Terre* (Earth). This much earlier work dating from 1883 shows a woman lying on her front without arms or legs, but the plaster (fig.63) is more static and rectilinear; the buttocks do not protrude from the line that goes from the back to the legs. In the drawing Rodin has introduced a real sense of movement. This was not his aim in the sculpture, which is rooted in the earth. SBF

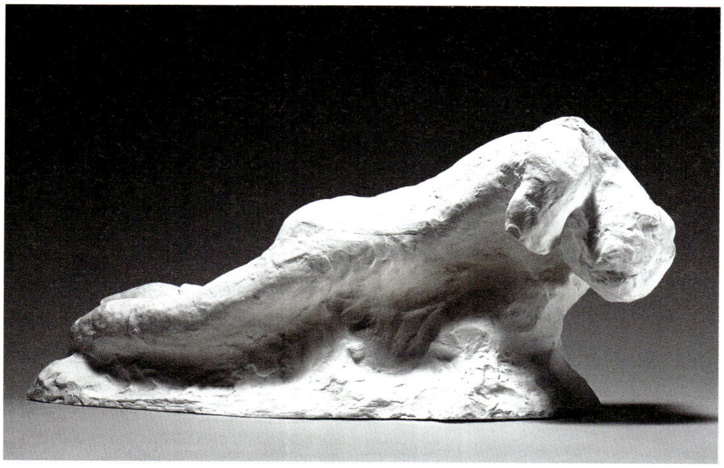

FIG.63
Auguste Rodin
La Terre, 1883
Plaster, 20 x 49 x 18 cm
Musée Rodin, Paris, S.856

76–80

Upper body of a male nude (Nijinsky), 1912

Pencil on laid paper, 317 x 238 mm
Musée Rodin, Paris, D.2333

Standing male nude with right arm bent and raised towards the face (Nijinsky), 1912

Pencil on laid paper, 321 x 235 mm
Musée Rodin, Paris, D.2331

Drawing of a male nude (Nijinsky?), on the base of an assemblage with a variant of the sculpture Le Jour, 1912?

Pencil on plaster, 20.5 x 19 x 7.6 cm
Inscribed in pencil: *vierge / cierge /* Iris / *faune* (virgin / church candle / Iris / faun)
Musée Rodin, Paris, S.2783

Nijinsky, cast in 1957 or later (original model, 1912)

Plaster, 17.5 x 10 x 6 cm
Musée Rodin, Paris, S.890

Nijinsky, cast in 1958 (original model, 1912)

Bronze, cast by Georges Rudier (no.6), 17.7 x 9 x 5.2 cm
The Samuel Courtauld Trust, The Courtauld Gallery, London, S.2006.LB.5

L'Après-midi d'un faune, choreographed and performed by Vaslav Nijinksy (1890–1950), was shown to a private audience at the Théâtre du Châtelet the day before its world premiere on 29 May 1912. The ballet featured gestures that were deliberately awkward, had very little dancing in the conventional sense, and ended in a scene of heightened sexuality. There was a commotion when the performance ended, with traditionalists booing loudly, but Rodin and others were won over by Nijinksy's interpretation of a lustful faun. Rodin had already attended the Ballet Russes from the time of their first season in Paris in 1909. His companion at both the rehearsal and the premiere was Count Harry Kessler, who had had the idea of involving Rodin so that he could make "a public statement of support", Nijinsky and Diaghilev fearing that the production might well be unfavourably received.[1] His plan worked; at the end of the rehearsal, Rodin went on stage and agreed to be presented to Nijinsky. On the journey home, he apparently turned to Kessler and told him: "The man who has conceived this is a genius. Now, Nijinsky captivates me. I would be happy to show him my works."[2]

Rodin then made a much more significant 'public statement' in the form of an article praising Nijinsky in the newspaper *Le Matin*. In the article, which was drafted for him by the art critic Roger Marx, Nijinsky is described as having "physical perfection, harmony of proportions and the extraordinary ability to bend his body to the

1 Kessler 2004, 23 May 1912, cited in Berger 2003, p. 48, note 18. The most complete discussion of this encounter is in Berger 2003 (but some of the dates are divergent from other sources and it was written without knowledge of the existence of drawings of Nijinsky: see below, note 6.) See also Paris 1989 and 2000, p.99. On Rodin and Nijinsky see Bellow 2002–03 and her essay in the present volume, especially pp.53–54.

2 *"L'homme qui a conçu ça, est un génie. Maintenant, Nijinski me tient. Je serais heureux de lui montrer mes œuvres"*: Kessler 2004, 27 May 1912.

interpretation of the most varied feelings".[3] On the same day an article by the editor of *Le Figaro* savaged the production and in particular Nijinsky, who was accused of indecency. A second article in *Le Figaro* then attacked Rodin, criticising the French state for allowing him free reign in the beautiful eighteenth-century Hôtel Biron (now the Musée Rodin) in exchange for the promise of the gift of his works after his death. This was part of a general context of criticism of Rodin's art as obscene by certain parts of the press.

It was in these circumstances that Nijinsky visited Rodin's studio with Kessler and Diaghilev. Kessler's diaries are the most reliable and complete source of information on the visit to the Hôtel Biron, which by this date Rodin used not only for entertaining but also as a studio, as much as his large, purpose-built studio in Meudon. Kessler, among the few people to have seen the *Mouvements de danse*, reported "Nijinsky could hardly contain his wonderment over these little figures".[4] After lunch Diaghilev and Kessler left Nijinsky on his own for the modelling session; towards the end of the day Diaghilev returned, apparently finding sculptor and dancer asleep, the latter dressed only in a thin shawl. The episode,

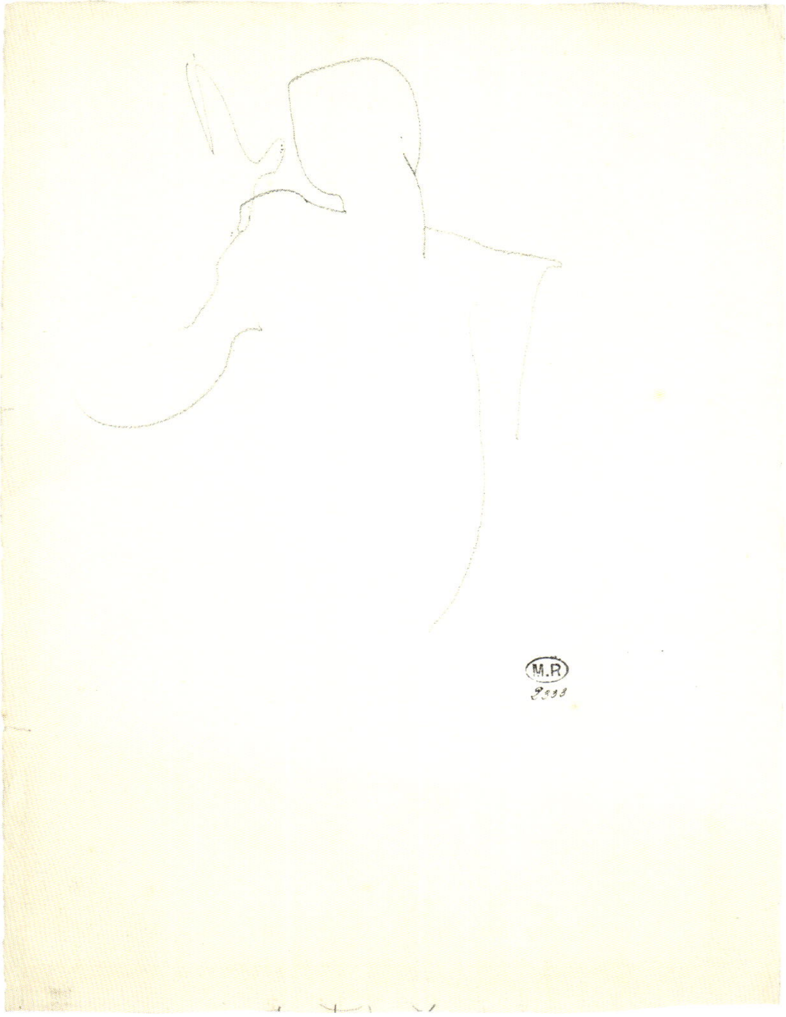

76

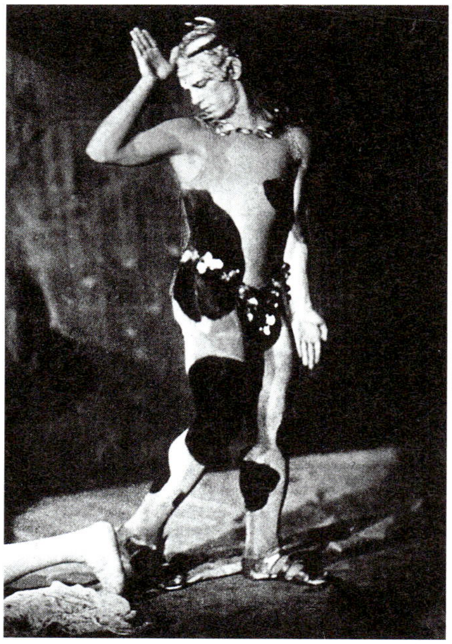

FIG.64
Vaslav Nijinsky in *L'Après midi d'un faune*, photographed by Karl Struss, New York City, 1916 (detail)
Harvard Library, Cambridge, Mass., Howard D. Rothschild Collection

3 "*Nijinsky a pour avantage distinctif la perfection physique, l'harmonie des proportions et l'extraordinaire pouvoir d'assouplir son corps à l'interpretation des sentiments les plus divers*": Rodin, 'La rénovation de la danse', *Le Matin*, 30 May 1912, in Rodin 2011, pp.143–46, p.145.

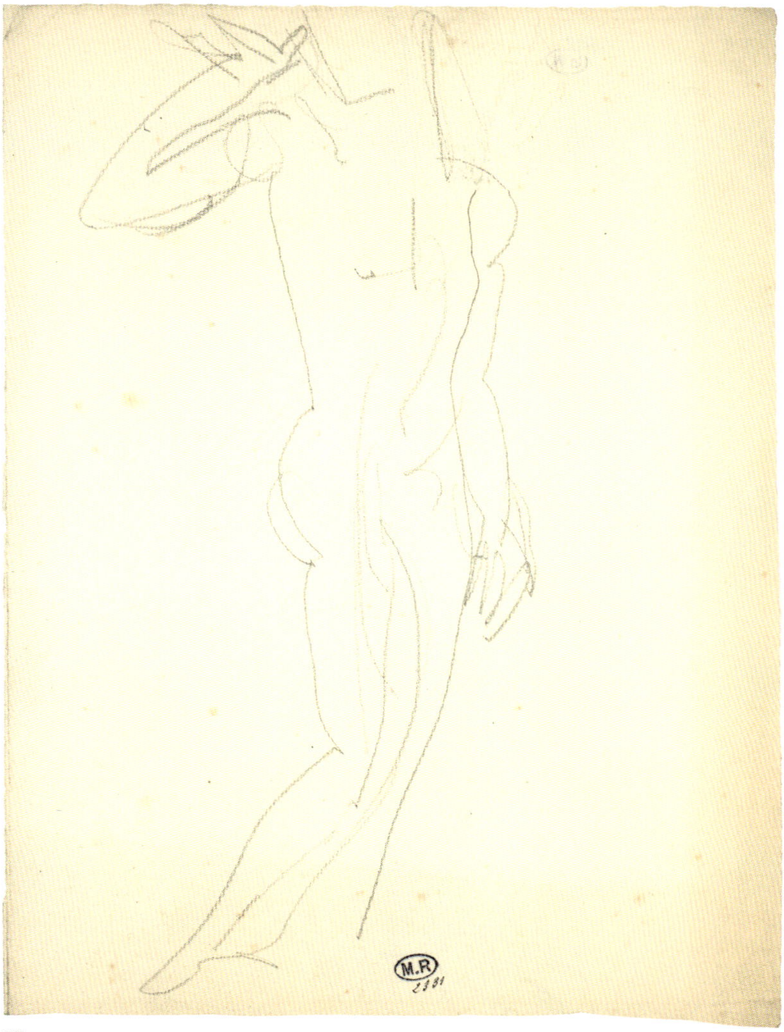

77

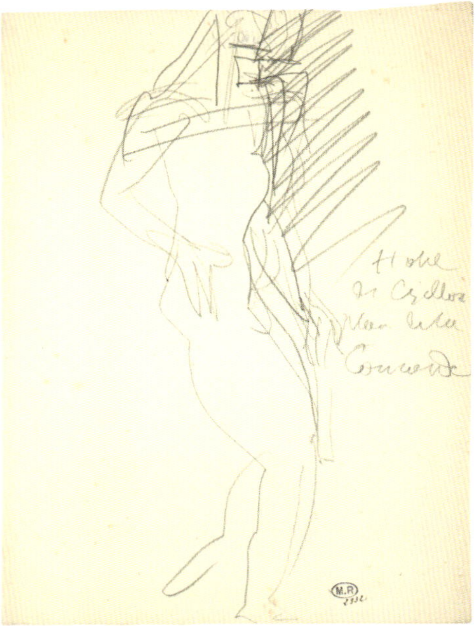

FIG.65
Auguste Rodin
Standing male nude, partially crossed out (Nijinsky), 1912, verso of D.2331, cat.77
Musée Rodin, Paris, D.2332

whether true or not, was reported in the press as yet another example of the debauched goings-on at the Hôtel Biron under Rodin. It seems likely that this was the only visit Nijinsky made to Rodin's studio.[5]

Until the 1950s, there was no sculptural evidence of this famous encounter, and it is even more recently that a couple of slight pencil drawings have been identified as probably representing Nijinsky.[6] The two drawings in this exhibition are in fact two halves of the same sheet (the left half D.2333, cat.76, and the right D.2331, cat.77).[7] On the verso of the more developed of these (cat.77), Rodin sketched a male nude in profile with lines that suggest difficulty in rendering the angularity of position of the arm, head and shoulders (fig.65). On the recto the body is drawn in strong and confident lines, free of hesitation. Both sides capture specific moments in the choreography of *L'Après-midi d'un faune* (see fig.64), and the recto a pose Aristide Maillol also

4 "*Nijinsky konnte sich vor Bewunderung über die kleinen Figuren kaum fassen*": Kessler 2004, 2 June 1912.
5 Although contemporary sources mention subsequent visits to Rodin, Berger 2003, p.46, rejects this.
6 D.2331 and its verso (D.2332) were identified in print for the first time in Bellow 2002–03. Coincidentally the dance historian Philippe de Lustrac had already also proposed this identification to the curators of the Musée Rodin.
7 I am grateful to Kate Edmondson for making this identification.

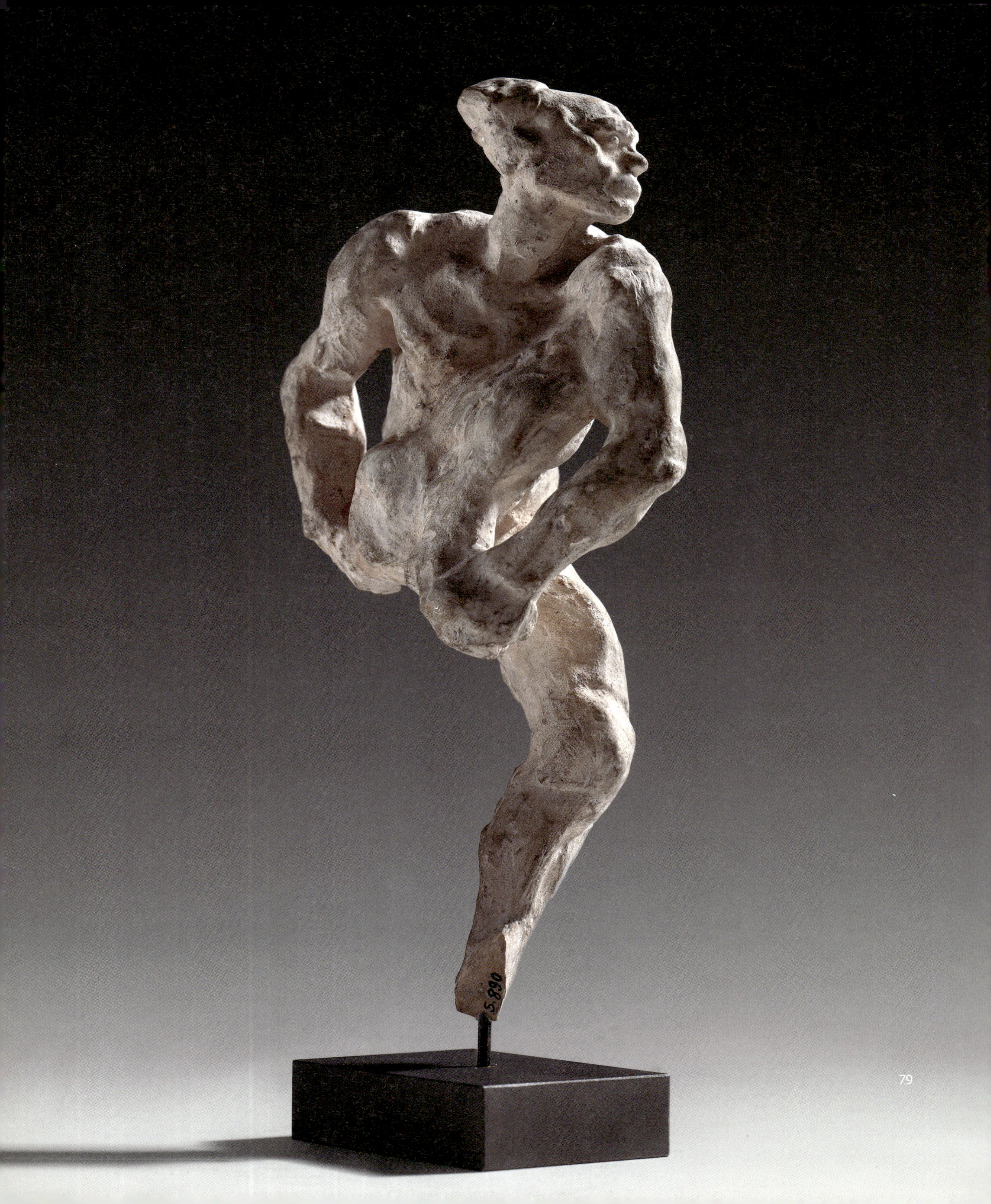
S.890

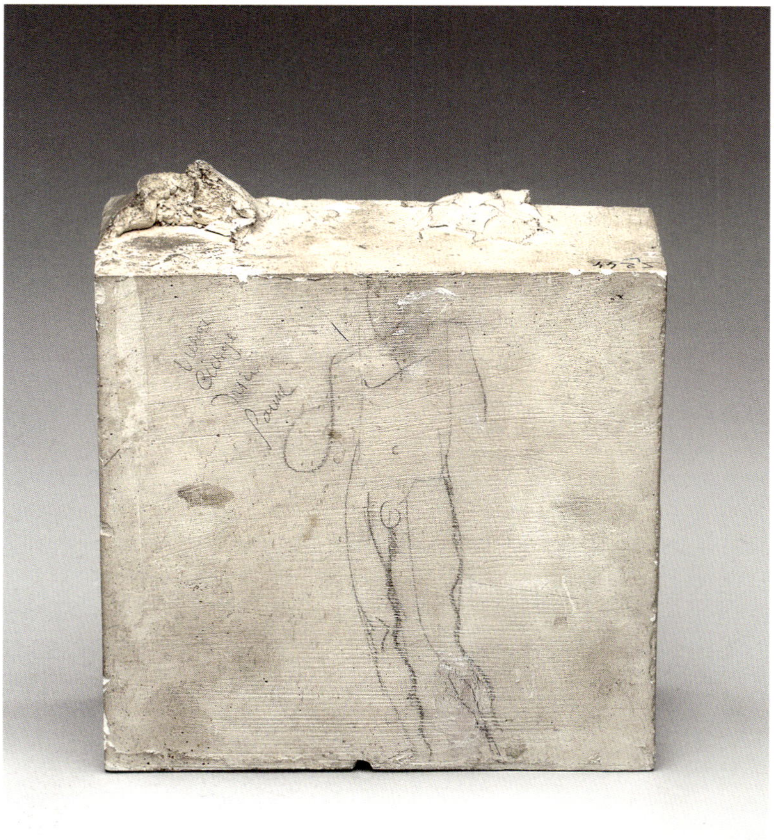

78

sketched during a modelling session with Nijinsky (also arranged by Kessler), corresponding well with Rodin's observations (through Marx) in 'La rénovation de la danse': "His look observes, his arms straighten, his hand opens in the distance, his fingers tightened one against the other, his head turns with a lust which is deliberately awkward and yet which one would think was natural".[8]

A journalist visiting Nijinsky in his *loge* in 1913 wrote of seeing on display "*quelques courbes de Rodin*" (a few curves by Rodin),[9] which could correspond to the type of drawing shown in the sketch of an upper body and head (D.2333, cat.76). Although made up of only a few lines, they are enough to identify the movements of Nijinsky's faun – the exaggerated curve in the neck emphasising the turned head, and the characteristic raised and open right hand. Its elliptical style recalls the drawing of Ruth St. Denis (cat.21), which also focuses on capturing a characteristic gesture in a few succinct lines.

The figure in another pencil drawing, this time on a plaster block (S.2783, cat.78), may be identified as belonging to this group of sketches after Nijinsky. The block was the base of an assemblage comprising a standing female, a variant of his sculpture *Le Jour* (*Day*), of twenty years earlier, which has since come unattached but whose fixing point is still visible. Nothing more is known about this work, but the reference to a *faune* in the inscription further suggests a possible connection with Nijinsky.[10] The assemblage itself is not as curious as it might seem since Rodin sometimes wrote on his plasters.[11] It encapsulates the experimental quality of Rodin's late studio practice, the magpie approach to materials and the meshing of drawing and sculpture in one work.

In the early 1950s a mould in the reserves of the Musée Rodin was identified as for a figure

8 "*… son regard épie, ses bras se tendent, sa main s'ouvre au large, les doigts l'un contre l'autre serrés, sa tête se détourne avec une convoitise d'une maladresse volue et qu'on croirait naturelle*": Rodin 1912, in Rodin 2011, p.145.

9 20 May 1913, in *Gil Blas*.

10 It seems from a trace of plaster slip at the top of the block that there was an additional figure in the assemblage, but it has not (yet) been found. This block has only recently been identified in the collection and I am grateful to colleagues at the Musée Rodin for suggesting its inclusion in the exhibition.

11 See S. Biass-Fabiani, 'Quand Rodin écrit sur les œuvres', in Montreal 2015, pp.114–24.

12 It had been inventoried simply as *Figure d'homme*, no.642 in the original museum inventories. I am grateful to François Blanchetière for this information. The dramatic reference in Browse 1987, p.807, to the discovery in 1957 of a mould "in two halves" (i.e. top and bottom) seems to have led to the belief that it was a sculpture rather than a mould that was discovered in the 1950s. For example, see exh. cat. *Danser sa vie*, Centre Pompidou, Paris, 2011, p.58, note 1. Logically this means that neither of the two plasters of Nijinsky in the Musée Rodin are lifetime casts, but that both were made in or after 1957.

of Nijinsky.[12] A plaster cast from it was made in 1957 and the following year the museum began casting an edition of twelve bronzes (plus one for the museum), which sold out almost immediately. By late 1958, Roland, Browse & Delbanco, the London gallery acting as unofficial agent for the sale of posthumous bronzes by Rodin, had purchased four bronze figures of Nijinsky from the museum's formidable director, Cécile Goldscheider, having attempted at first to buy the whole series. Lillian Browse, one of the three directors and herself a former ballerina so personally very interested in the subject of dance, had seen the plaster in Paris the year before, and after several letters over the summer of 1958 in which she asked for (and finally received) a photograph of the bronze, wrote to ask whether it was possible for the gallery to buy "the whole series of twelve". "If it is possible for you, we would like to make a firm purchase of the whole series of twelve. We already have a few clients who are impatiently awaiting the little bronze; also Roland and I would like to buy it for our personal collections."[13] Goldscheider responded several days later on 6 October, suggesting they could buy up to three: "Your enthusiasm for the little Study after Nijinsky encourages me in my choice of small unknown works by Rodin. There can be no question of ceding the whole series of twelve casts .... The work has not been shown to any gallery, we have simply reserved the first casts for museums."[14] On 8 October Browse wrote back to ask that, after the initial three, could the museum reserve them *"autant d'épreuves que possible"* (as many casts as possible), as, with only three, their clients would suffer because they would be "*égoistes*" (selfish), which seems to imply that Roland and she were indeed each planning to buy a Nijinsky, leaving only one for sale in the gallery. On 20 October 1958 the gallery placed an order for four Nijinsky bronzes, which were delivered on 12 December 1958. A document in the Musée Rodin's archives lists the four as sold at the gallery's spring exhibition in April 1959. Lillian Browse evidently bought one for herself, which she left to the Courtauld as part of the bequest of works from her collection.[15]

In this work, the torsion in the pose is comparable to the gathering motion of *Mouvement I*, but that is where the comparison ends, since *Nijinsky* was obviously modelled of a piece, and has an integrity and a compactness which are absent in the *Mouvements de danse*.[16] The play of tightly interlocking negative spaces that reveal themselves as the sculpture is turned, perhaps on a base or in the hand, reinforces the dramatic logic of the tiny work, for with each quarter turn a new profile is revealed, which is sympathetic if not equal to the way in which Nijinsky's choreography famously created a series of images in profile. AG

13 *"Si cela vous est possible, nous voudrions prendre, achat ferme, toute la série de douze. Nous avons déjà quelques clients qui attendant avec impatience ce petit bronze; aussi Roland et moi voulons l'acheter pour nos collections particuliers [sic]"*: letter of 1 October 1958. The correspondence with Roland, Browse & Delbanco is in the Musée Rodin archives.

14 *"Votre enthousiasme pour la petite Étude d'après Nijinski m'encourage dans le choix de petites pièces de Rodin inconnues. Il ne peut être question de vous céder la série complète de douze épreuves .... L'œuvre n'a été montré à aucune galerie, nous avons simplement réservé les premières épreuves pour des musées."*

15 Browse 1987, p. 808.

16 The sculptor Georg Kolbe sketched Nijinsky in a similar pose when he came to a modelling session in his studio in late 1912, illustrated in Berger 2003, p. 48.

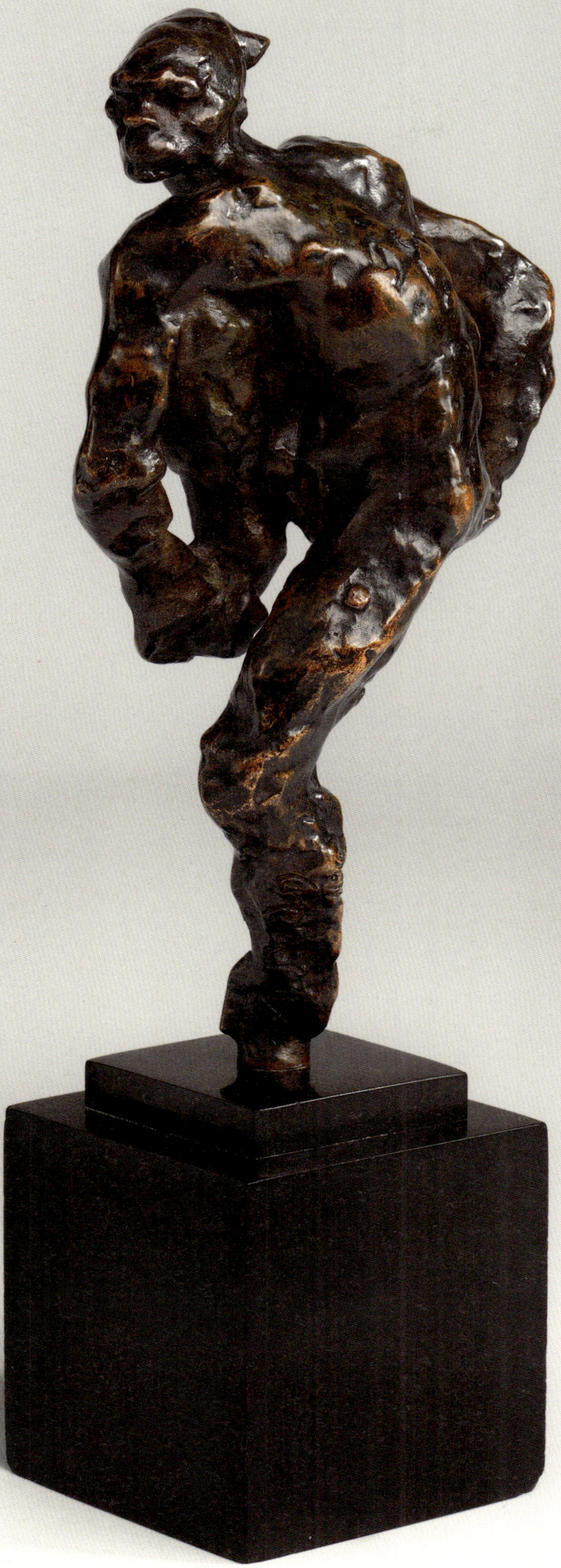

BIBLIOGRAPHY

AMIEL 1931
Denys Amiel, *Les spectacles à travers les âges*, Paris (Éditions du Cygne), 1931

BEAUSIRE 1988
Alain Beausire, *Quand Rodin Exposait*, Paris (Musée Rodin), 1988

BELLOW 2002–03
Juliet Bellow, 'Reforming the Dance: Auguste Rodin's *Nijinsky* and Vaslav Nijinski's *L'Aprés-Midi d'un Faune*', *Cantor Arts Center Journal*, vol.3, 2002–03, pp.172–85

BERGER 2002
Ursel Berger, 'Three Sculptors and a Dancer: Nijinsky's Relations with Maillol, Rodin and Kolbe', *Apollo*, vol.156, no.490, November 2002, pp.42–48

BLANCHETIÈRE 2013
François Blanchetière, 'Larger Figures, Simpler Forms', in exh. cat. *Moore Rodin*, ed. A. Feldman, The Henry Moore Foundation, Herts, and Compton Verney, Warwickshire, 2013, pp.118–25

BLANCHETIÈRE 2014
François Blanchetière, 'Hasards de l'atelier', in exh. cat. *Rodin. L'accident. L'aléatoire*, Musée d'Art et d'Histoire, Geneva, 2014, pp.124–29

BLANCHETIÈRE 2016
François Blanchetière, 'Mouler, tirer, modifier, mouler à nouveau. Rodin et le moulage', *Situ. Revue des Patrimoines*, vol.28, 2016, https://insitu.revues.org/12743

BOURDELLE 1908
Antoine Bourdelle, 'Les dessins du sculpteur Rodin', *La Grande Revue*, année 12, no.1, 10 January 1908

BROWSE 1987
Lillian Browse, 'False castings of Rodin bronzes', *The Burlington Magazine*, vol.129, no.1017, December 1987, pp.807–08

BROWSE 1999
Lillian Browse, *Duchess of Cork Street, The Autobiography of an Art Dealer*, London, 1999

BUTLER 1993
Judith Butler, *Rodin: The Shape of Genius*, New Haven (Yale UP), 1993

CLADEL 1903
Judith Cladel, 'Auguste Rodin pris sur la vie', *La Plume*, Paris, 1903

CLÉMENT-JANIN 1903
Noël Clément-Janin, 'Les Dessins de Rodin', in *Les Maîtres Artistes*, no.8, 15 October 1903, pp.285–87

COQUIOT 1917
Gustave Coquiot, *Rodin a l'Hôtel de Biron et à Meudon*, Paris (Ollendorff), 1917

CORRESPONDANCE DE RODIN
Alain Beausire and Florence Cadouot, edd., *Correspondance de Rodin, 1860–1917*, 4 vols., Paris (Musée Rodin), 1985–92

DÉCORET-AHIHA 2004
Anne Décoret-Ahiha, *Les Danses exotiques en France 1880–1940*, Paris (Centre national de la danse), 2004

DE MÉNIL 1905
Félicien de Ménil, *Histoire de la danse à travers les âges*, Paris (A. Picard et Kaan), 1905

DUMONT 2011
Agathe Dumont, 'Interprètes au travail: danseurs et acrobats, de l'indiscipline à la désobéissance', *memento* (HorsLesMurs – Centre national de ressources des arts de la rue et des arts du cirque), no.3, October 2011, pp.2–9

DUCREY 1996
Guy Ducrey, *Corps et graphies. Poétique de la danse et de la danseuse à la fin du XIXe siècle*, Paris (Champion), 1996

ELSEN AND VARNEDOE 1971
Albert Elsen and Kirk Varnedoe, with Victoria Thorson and Elisabeth Chase Geissbuhler, *The Drawings of Rodin*, New York (Praeger), 1971

GAUDET 2014
Guillaume Gaudet, *La Réception critique des monuments français d'Auguste Rodin*, Rennes (Presses universitaires de Rennes), 2014

GEISSBUHLER 1963
Rodin: Later Drawings, with Interpretations by Antoine Bourdelle, trans. Elisabeth Chase Geissbuhler, London (Peter Owen), 1963

GEORGES-MICHEL 1942
Michel Georges-Michel, 'Rodin', in *Peintres et sculpteurs que j'ai connus*, 1900–1942, New York (Brentano), 1942, pp.261–70

GSELL 1920
Paul Gsell, *Douze Aquarelles d'Auguste Rodin*, Geneva and Paris (Éditions Georg), 1920

GUTSCHE-MILLER 2015
Sarah Gutsche-Miller, *Parisian Music-Hall Ballet, 1871–1913*, Rochester (URP), 2015

GÜSE 1985
Ernst-Gerhard Güse, *Auguste Rodin. Drawings and Watercolours*, London (Thames & Hudson), 1985

JÄRVINEN 2009
Hanna Järvinen, 'Dancing without Space: On Nijinsky's *L'Après-midi d'un faune* (1912)', *Dance Research*, vol.27, no.1, April 2009, pp.28–64

JUDRIN 1984–92
Claudie Judrin, *Inventaire des dessins*, 6 vols., Paris (Musée Rodin), 1984–92

JUNOD 1992
Philippe Junod, 'Rodin et les métamorphoses d'Icare', *La Revue de l'Art*, no.96, 1992, pp.31–39

HAXELL 2000
Nicola A. Haxell, 'Ces dames du cirque', *Modern Language Notes*, vol.115, no.4, September 2000, pp.783–800

KESSLER 2004
Harry Graf Kessler, *Das Tagebuch*, ed. Jörg Schuster, Stuttgart (Cotta), vol.4, 2004 (1906–14)

LÉGERET 2014
Katia Légeret, ed., *Rodin et la danse de Çiva*, Saint-Denis (Presses Universitaires de Vincennes), 2014,

LE NORMAND-ROMAIN 1996
Antoinette Le Normand-Romain, 'Un nouveau Mouvement de danse de Rodin (1840–1917)', *La Revue du Louvre et des musées de France*, no.4, 1996, pp.59–62

LE NORMAND-ROMAIN 2007
Antoinette Le Normand-Romain, *The Bronzes of Rodin*, Paris (Musée Rodin and RMN), 2007

LONDON 1987
Catherine Lampert, *Rodin: Sculpture and Drawings*, London (Arts Council of Great Britain), 1987

LONDON 2006
Catherine Lampert and Antoinette Le Normand-Romain, exh. cat. *Rodin*, Royal Academy of Arts, London, 2006

LUDOVICI 1926
Anthony M. Ludovici, *Personal Reminiscences of Auguste Rodin*, London (John Murray), 1926

LUSTRAC 2004
Philippe de Lustrac, 'Nijinski et ses sources : la chronophotographie, l'art assyrien et l'aviation', *Ligeia*, nos.49–52, January–June 2004, pp.5–27

MARTIGNY 1994
Claudie Judrin, ed., exh. cat. *Rodin: Dessins et aquarelles des collections suisses et du Musée Rodin*, Fondation Pierre Gianadda, Martigny, 1994

MARTIGUES 1992
Sophie Biass-Fabiani, ed., exh. cat. *À notre ami Bigand, Rodin, Redon et Moreau*, Musée Ziem, Martigues, 1992

MONTREAL 2015
Nathalie Bondil and Sophie Biass-Fabiani, edd., exh. cat. *Métamorphoses dans l'Atelier de Rodin* (English edn *Metamorphoses. In Rodin's Studio*), Museum of Fine Arts, Montreal, 2015

MUSETTI 2008
Barbara Musetti, *La Réception critique d'Auguste Rodin en Italie, de la fin du XIXe au début du XXe siècle*, Paris (Université de Paris IV – Panthéon-Sorbonne), 2008

NEW YORK 1963
Exh. cat. *Rodin*, Museum of Modern Art, New York, 1963

NEW YORK & OTHER CITIES 1963
Exh. cat. *Rodin (1840–1917). An Exhibition of Sculptures and Drawings*, Charles Slatkin Gallery, New York, etc., 1963–65

PARIS 1963
Cécile Goldscheider, exh. cat. *Rodin inconnu*, Musée du Louvre, Paris, 1962–63

PARIS 1979
Exh. cat. *Rodin et l'Extrême-Orient*, Musée Rodin, Paris, 1979

PARIS 1990
Hélène Pinet, exh. cat. *Rodin et ses modèles. Le portrait photographié*, Musée Rodin, Paris, 1990

PARIS 2000
Martine Kahane, exh. cat. *Nijinsky 1889–1950*, Musée d'Orsay, Paris, 2000

PARIS 2001
Édouard Papet, ed., exh. cat. *À Fleur de peau. Le moulage sur nature au XIXème siècle*, Musée d'Orsay, Paris, 2001

PARIS 2006
Dominique Viéville, ed., exh. cat. *Rodin and the Cambodian Dancers: His Final Passion*, Musée Rodin, Paris, 2006

PARIS 2007
François Blanchetière and Bénédicte Garnier, edd., exh. cat. *Rodin. Le rêve japonais*, Musée Rodin, Paris 2007

PARIS 2011
Dominique Viéville and Nadine Lehni, edd., exh. cat. *Rodin 300 Dessins. La Saisie du Modèle 1880–1917*, Musée Rodin, Paris, 2011

PEIGNIST 2009
Myriam Peignist, 'Histoire Anthropologique des Danses Acrobatiques', *Corps*, vol.2, no.7, 2009, pp.29–38

PINET 2006
Hélène Pinet, 'Comédie ou Lever de Rideau. Rodin et ses modèles', in Dominique Viéville, ed., exh. cat., *Figures d'Éros, dessins et aquarelles 1890–1917*, Musée Rodin, Paris, 2006, pp. 12–29

PRITCHARD 2003
Jane Pritchard, '"More Natural than Nature, More Artificial than Art": the Dance Criticism of Arthur Symons', *Dance Research: The Journal of the Society for Dance Research*, vol.21, no.2, 2003, pp.36–89

REYNOLDS AND MCCORMICK 2003
Nancy Reynolds and Malcolm McCormick, *No Fixed Points: Dance in the Twentieth Century*, New Haven (Yale UP), 2003

RILKE 1931
Rainer Maria Rilke, *Lettres à Rodin*, preface by Georges Grappe, Paris (Éditions Émile-Paul Frères), 1931

RODIN / GSELL 1911
Auguste Rodin, L'Art. *Entretiens réunis par Paul Gsell*, Paris (Bernard Grasset), 1911

RODIN 1911 / 1984
Auguste Rodin, Art: *Conversations with Paul Gsell* [1911], trans. Jacques de Caso and Patricia B. Sanders, Berkeley (University of California Press), 1984

RODIN 1914
Auguste Rodin, *Les Cathédrales de France*, with an introduction by Charles Morice, Paris (A. Colin), 1914

RODIN 2008
Augustin de Butler, ed., *Éclairs de pensée : écrits et entretiens sur l'art (Auguste Rodin: entretiens avec Henri Dujardin-Beaumetz)* [1913], Paris (Éditions du Sandre), 2008

RODIN 2011
J. Paul Morel, ed., *Faire avec ses mains ce que l'on voit. Textes, lettres et propos choisis*, Paris (Éditions Mille et une nuits), 2011

STAROBINSKI 1970
Jean Starobinski, *Portrait de l'artiste en saltimbanque*, Geneva (Albert Skira), 1970

STEINBERG 1972
Leo Steinberg, 'Rodin', in *Other Criteria: Confrontations with Twentieth-Century Art*, New York (Oxford UP), 1972, pp.322–403

STREHLY [1904]
George Strehly, *L'Acrobatie et les acrobates. Textes et dessins*, Paris (C. Delagrave), [1904]

SYMONS 1917
Arthur Symons, 'Dancers and Dancing', in *The Lotus Magazine*, vol.8, no.7, April 1917, pp.314–18

SYMONS 1929
Arthur Symons, 'Auguste Rodin', in *From Toulouse-Lautrec to Rodin with some Personal Impressions*, London (John Lane The Bodley Head), 1929

TIREL 1925
Marcelle Tirel, *The Last Years of Rodin*, trans. R. Francis, London (A.M. Philpot), 1925

TURNER 2010
Sarah Victoria Turner, 'The "Essential Quality of Things": E.B. Havell, Ananda Coomaraswamy, Indian Art and Sculpture in Britain, c. 1910–14', *Visual Culture in Britain*, vol.11, no.2, pp. 239–64

VAUXCELLES 1908
Louis Vauxcelles, 'Les Dessins de Rodin', in exh. cat. *Exposition de dessins d'Auguste Rodin*, Galerie Devambez, Paris, 1908

WAGNER 1993
Anne Wagner, 'Rodin's Reputation', in Lynn Hunt, ed., *Eroticism and the Body Politic*, Baltimore (Johns Hopkins University Press), 1993

WASHINGTON 1981
Albert Elsen, exh. cat. *Rodin Rediscovered*, National Gallery of Art, Washington, D.C., 1981

PHOTOGRAPHIC CREDITS

Cat.1–7, 11–12, 14, 16–23, 25–41, 53, 55–56, 62, 67–71, 73–77, figs.5, 7, 16, 17, 20, 22, 26, 49–50, 54–55, 61, 63, 65: © Musée Rodin (photo: Jean de Calan); cat.8–10, figs.3, 19: © Musée Rodin, Paris; cat.13, 24, 43–47, 54, 57–58, 61, 66, figs.11, 62: © Agence photographique du musée Rodin - Pauline Hisbacq; cat.15, 51, 60, 63–65, 79: © Musée Rodin (photo: Christian Baraja); cat.42, 48–49, 52, 59, 72, 78: © Agence photographique du musée Rodin - Jérôme Manoukian; cat.50, 80: © The Samuel Courtauld Trust, The Courtauld Gallery, London; fig.1: Image Conway Library, Courtauld Institute of Art, London; fig.2: © Tate, London 2016; fig.4: © Victoria and Albert Museum, London 2016; figs.6, 21 © Musée Rodin (photo: Herve Lewandowski); fig.9: B. Rousseau conservation départementale du patrimoine de Maine-et-Loire, musée Jules-Desbois Parçay-les-Pins; fig.10: Photo (C) RMN-Grand Palais (musée d'Orsay) / Daniel Arnaudet / Jean Schormans; fig.13: Collection Gérard Jouhet, Paris; fig.15: © Christie's Images / Bridgeman Images. © ADAGP, Paris and DACS, London 2016; figs.24, 45: © BNF; fig.25: Image The New York Public Library; fig.27: Photo © RMN-Grand Palais (musée d'Orsay) / Droits réservés; fig.46: Image courtesy National Gallery of Art, Washington; figs.51, 58: © Private Collection; fig.57: © Musée du Louvre, Dist. RMN-Grand Palais / Pierre Philibert; fig.60: Rome, National Gallery of Modern and Contemporary Art. By permission of Ministero dei Beni delle Attività Culturali e del Turismo. Photo: Antonio Idini; fig.64: Image Harvard Library, Howard D. Rothschild Collection.